SECURITIES ACCEPTABLE TO THE
LENDING BANKER

L. C. MATHER

B.Com. (London), F.C.I.S., *Fellow of the Institute of Bankers*

SECURITIES ACCEPTABLE TO THE LENDING BANKER

WATERLOW (LONDON) LIMITED

BY the same author

THE LENDING BANKER
Fourth (Revised) Edition 1972

BANKER AND CUSTOMER RELATIONSHIP
AND THE ACCOUNTS OF
PERSONAL CUSTOMERS
Fourth (Revised) Edition 1971

THE ACCOUNTS OF
LIMITED COMPANY CUSTOMERS
Third (Revised) Edition 1972

SECURITIES ACCEPTABLE TO
THE LENDING BANKER
Third (Revised Edition) 1973
©

WATERLOW (London) LIMITED
Holywell House, Worship Street
London EC2A 2EN
Printed in Great Britain by
Waterlow (Dunstable) Limited

CONTENTS

5

CONTENTS *(continued)*

PREFACE

Sound bank lending is based on the premise that the borrower will repay the indebtedness within a reasonable time from trading receipts and profits or from other known sources, but prudence demands that security should usually be taken as a form of insurance in case there may be any untoward, unexpected development which hinders this normal sequence and jeopardises the bank's position. The purpose of this book is to review the practical and legal aspects of the securities which are acceptable to the lending banker, and it is hoped that the contents will be of assistance to all those who are responsible for obtaining and perfecting security to safeguard the position of their bank.

This book has been produced in response to many requests from readers of THE BANKERS' MAGAZINE who found the original articles helpful in their daily work. It completes the series of four volumes covering the field of practical banking. Being unable to devote sufficient time to the task myself, I was fortunate to have the friendly support of my colleague, Mr. M. G. Wilcox, M.B.E., who has edited and collated the text for this reprint in book form. I am deeply indebted to him for the time taken in preparation of the manuscript, reading of the proofs, and the tedious task of preparing the Index and a Table of Cases. I pay just tribute to his patience and hard effort in preparing what should be a most helpful reference book for all practical bankers.

L.C.M.
Riverhead
Kent
May 1960

PREFACE TO SECOND EDITION

The importance of security to the lending banker continues unchanged and the demand from practical bankers for this volume has necessitated the preparation of a fresh edition. The contents have again been brought up-to-date by Mr. M. G. Wilcox, M.B.E., and I am indebted to him for the time and trouble he has devoted to this work.

L.C.M.
Seal
Kent
February 1966

PREFACE TO THIRD EDITION

Continuing demand for this volume and the many changes introduced since 1966 in the law and practice relating to bank securities have given rise to a fresh edition. The contents have been brought up-to-date by my colleague, Mr. C. W. Bransdon, to whom I am heavily indebted for his industry and enthusiasm.

L.C.M.
Seal
Kent
July 1972

TABLE OF CASES CITED
Figures in italics, following case reference, denotes text page

TABLE OF CASES CITED _(continued)_

TABLE OF CASES CITED (*continued*)

TABLE OF CASES CITED (*continued*)

TABLE OF ABBREVIATIONS
CONCERNED WITH CASE REFERENCES

A.C.	Appeal Cases	1891–current
Ad. & E.	Adolphus & Ellis	1834–1840
All E.R.	All England Reports	1936–current
App. Cas.	Appeal Cases	1875–1890
Atk.	Atkyns	1736–1755
B. & C.	Barnewall and Cresswell	1822–30
Beav.	Beavan	1838–66
Ch.	Chancery Division	1891–current
Ch. App.	Chancery Appeal Cases	1865–75
Ch. D.	Chancery Division	1875–90
Cl. & Fin.	Clark and Finnelly	1831–46
Com. Cas.	Commercial Cases	1896–1941
Cox, c.c.	Cox's Criminal Cases	1844–1941
E. & B.	Ellis & Blackburn	1851–1858
Eq.	Equity Cases	1865–75
Ex.	Exchequer Reports (Welsby, Hurlstone and Gordon)	1847–1856
Hare	Hare	1841–1853
K.B.	King's Bench	1901–52
L.J. Ch.	Law Journal Reports, Chancery	1831–1949
L.R.	Law Reports	1865–current
L.R.H.L.	House of Lords, English and Irish Appeals	1866–1875
L.T.	Law Times Reports	1859–1947
Lloyd's Rep.	Lloyd's List Reports	
Mer.	Merivale	1815–17
N.I.	Northern Ireland Law Reports	1925–current
Q.B.	Queen's Bench	1891–1900
Q.B.D.	Queen's Bench Division	1875–90
S.C.	Session Cases	1906–current
S.L.T.	Scots Law Times	1893–current
Sol. J.	Solicitors' Journal	1857–current
Taun.	Taunton	1808–1819
T.L.R.	Times Law Reports	1884–1952
Ves. Jnr.	Vesey Junior	1789–1816
W.L.R.	Weekly Law Reports	1953–current
W.N.	Weekly Notes (Reports)	1866–1952
W.R.	Weekly Reporter	1853–1906

Chapter I General Considerations—Various Types of Security

Although a banker does not lend against security, it is prudent wherever possible to obtain security as a form of insurance available in the background should some untoward and unexpected development occur to jeopardise the safety of the advance. Generally speaking it is only reasonable to expect the borrower to provide support in the form of security when this is sought and this is indeed one of the accepted basic principles of lending.

The ideal advance is one which is granted to a reliable customer for an approved purpose in which that customer has adequate experience, safe in the knowledge that the money will be used to advantage and repayment will be made within a reasonable period from trading receipts or known maturities due on or about given dates. Given these essentials, security is taken as an insurance in case of need and it must always be remembered that the test of any sound insurance is that it should be available, readily realisable and sufficient when required. Nothing is more disconcerting than to find that the security, taken as an insurance against the unexpected, is inadequate or cannot be realised when it is most needed. The care which has to be exercised to ensure that the various forms of security are at all times of adequate value with a watertight title to the bank is discussed fully from the practical and legal standpoint in this volume. At the outset there are some general considerations and definitions to be considered.

THE CANONS OF A GOOD BANKING SECURITY

The essential attributes of a sound banking security may be listed as follows, it being recognised that in practice a bank is often willing—perhaps as a matter of expediency—to accept security which does not meet all these requirements:—

1. The *value* of the security should be *readily ascertainable* and *reasonably stable* over the years, providing sufficient margin for depreciation. For obvious reasons, any security subject to frequent wide fluctuations in price is unsuitable unless there is a substantial margin between the original value and the maximum advance.

Under this heading, compare the ease with which the value of a quoted share, bought and sold daily on a stock exchange, can be determined, with the problem of assessing the value of a specialised factory or other industrial building. Think also of the relative stability of a good debenture stock compared with a speculative holding of ordinary shares in a mining company.

2. The security should be *readily realisable* in all conditions, with a *simple title* which preferably is transferable without undue cost or trouble.

A quoted share can be sold within hours in the market, but the sale of a house or other building is usually a matter for protracted negotiation. The cost of selling shares quoted on a stock exchange is definite and relatively small. The legal and agency expenses entailed in the sale of a property may be considerable. A life policy can be promptly surrendered practically without cost, whilst by contrast some time may have to be granted to a guarantor before he can meet his liability.

3. The bank should be able to obtain a *safe, unquestionable title*, without undue trouble or expense. The legal mortgage of shares is clearly achieved in a much more simple and cheaper manner than a legal mortgage of unregistered land, the title of which has to be examined and reported upon by the branch solicitor.

4. The bank should incur *no liability* to third parties arising out of its title to the security. For example, partly paid shares involve liability in the event of a call and leasehold property may occasion liability for dilapidations upon the expiry of the lease.

The advantages and disadvantages of typical securities will be reviewed under these headings as each security is discussed in the ensuing pages.

DIRECT SECURITY

The simplest definition of direct security is that taken from the Bankruptcy Act, 1914, being *any mortgage, charge, or lien on the assets of the borrower*. The value of such security has, of course, to be deducted from the amount of the debt when proving for dividend in the bankruptcy or liquidation of the borrower.

COLLATERAL SECURITY

There are three interpretations of collateral security, but it is prudent in banking practice to limit the meaning to the first of these three definitions.

1. To the practical banker collateral security is *any security deposited by a third party* to secure the indebtedness of the customer and it has the advantage that, in the event of the bankruptcy or liquidation of the borrower, the value of such security may be ignored in the proof for dividend against the failed estate. In other words, the bank can prove for the full amount of the advance (less the value of any direct security) and fall back upon the collateral security for any deficit. The relationship between the lending banker and the depositor of collateral security, including a guarantor, will be discussed fully later.

2. From the standpoint of the Inland Revenue a collateral security has meant a subsidiary or secondary security to the primary security for stamping purposes. With the passing of the Stamp Duty Finance Acts of 1970 and 1971 much of the duty formerly payable has been abolished and the present position is summarised at the end of this chapter, under the heading 'stamp duty'.

3. Lastly, the term 'collateral security' is loosely used outside banking circles to denote all forms of security which run side by side with the lender's right of action against the borrower for repayment of the debt. This interpretation of the term is best ignored by the practical banker.

GENERAL DEFINITIONS OF SECURITY

It is now appropriate briefly to define and distinguish between the various methods by which a banker may obtain security in both formal and informal manner:—

1. Mortgage

A mortgage may be defined as a conveyance of a legal or equitable interest in property by the borrower or third party, known as the mortgagor, to the lender, described as the mortgagee, as security for the payment of a debt.

A legal mortage of land is created by the mortgagor granting an interest in the land to the mortgagee for a term of years, subject always to the mortgagor's right of redemption whereby the interest in the land has to be reconveyed to the mortgagor upon repayment of the debt so secured. The mortgagor retains possession as well as the legal ownership of the land.

With a legal mortgage of other forms of security, such as stocks and shares and life policies, the title to the property is transferred to the mortgagee subject to the equity of redemption of the mortgagor. In this event, possession of the security and the title thereto passes to the mortgagee lender.

An equitable mortgage is created by the mere deposit of the certificates relating to stocks and shares, the title deeds or land certificate of property, or a life policy, as the case may be, with or without a memorandum of deposit as evidence of the intention of the parties. In general, a *legal mortgage* gives the lender rights against the property itself, whereas an *equitable mortgage* gives the lender no rights against the property without an order of the Court. These differences will be explored in detail later.

2. Pledge

The essence of pledge is possession and the term normally applies to the deposit of negotiable securities such as bills of exchange and bonds to bearer or quasi negotiable securities, such as bills of lading or other documents of title to goods. Goods themselves can be pledged to a bank as security by their deposit in an independent warehouse in the name of the bank. The pledgee of goods or property has the right to retain them as security for the debt and usually has the power, if need be, to sell the property pledged to recover the debt, any surplus proceeds being handed over to the pledgor. Written evidence of the pledge is not legally essential but normally desirable, as will be seen when detailed consideration is given to advances against produce in Chapters XXIX and XXX. In any event, it is a formal contract of security whereby the goods are deposited with the creditor or lender on condition that they will be redelivered to the depositor if the debt is repaid or can be sold if the borrower defaults.

3. Lien

A lien is the right of a person in possession of the securities or goods of another to retain them until the owner discharges his debt or other obligation to the possessor. *A particular lien* arises where goods can be retained only to cover a particular debt. For example, a carrier has a lien on the goods in his possession for payment of the freight of those goods. *A general lien* is a right to retain all or any goods in the possession of the lender or creditor to cover the general balance of monies due to him from the owner in respect of any transactions, which may be unconnected with the goods in question. In short, a particular lien is limited to one transaction, whereas a general lien covers all transactions between the parties concerned. The point is that lien arises in the usual course of business without any express contract between lender and borrower, or debtor and creditor. Unlike pledge, it is an informal form of security, and *usually gives the right only to retain possession, with no power of sale.* Many types of agents have a general lien over all goods and securities of their principals or clients which come into their possession in the normal course of business. For example, a stockbroker or solicitor has a lien on his clients' securities for amounts due by the client, and a wharfinger can retain goods until the storage dues have been paid.

A *banker's lien* is exceptional in that it includes a *power of sale* and is in effect an *implied pledge.* The rights and limitations of a banker's lien are dealt with in Chapter II.

4. *Set-off*

Money deposited with a bank becomes the property of the bank, subject to the obligation to repay to the depositor upon demand or within the agreed period of notice in the case of a deposit account. The relationship is that of debtor and creditor and it is, therefore, incorrect to say that a banker has a lien over money in a credit account of a borrower. The right to look upon any credit balances as security is a right of set-off which is examined in detail in Chapter XXXII.

5. *Hypothecation*

Security may be taken over goods or the proceeds of goods which are not in the possession of the lender. In the absence of possession, there can be no pledge, but the owner of the goods may undertake to give possession when called upon so to do. Such form of security is a hypothecation, defined by Hart as 'where property is charged with the amount of a debt, but neither ownership nor possession is passed to the creditor, it is said to be hypothecated'. This form of security is sometimes accepted where advances are made against goods and it is impossible to obtain a valid pledge. In practice, a letter of hypothecation is frequently confused with a letter of set-off. They are not the same thing and it is well to emphasise that a letter of hypothecation is a charge upon goods which are *not* in the possession of the bank, whereas a letter of set-off is an acknowledgment of the banker's right to set-off credit monies (which are in the possession of the bank) against any indebtedness of the depositor or of a stated third party.

6. *Guarantee*

A guarantee is a personal security of *secondary* liability whereby one person known as the guarantor promises to be liable for the debts of another person referred to as the principal debtor. It is a collateral security, being an engagement to be answerable either for the payment of a debt of, or for the performance of some act by, another party, who must be under a legal obligation to pay the debt or to perform the act. Reduced to its simplest terms a guarantee might read 'If X does not pay you, I will do so—signed Z'. The contract of guarantee must be evidenced in writing.

7. *Indemnity*

An indemnity is a personal security of *primary* liability which need not be in writing. It arises where one person shoulders direct personal responsibility for the liability or obligation of another. In the case of a simple guarantee the guarantor cannot be called upon to meet his liability until the principal debtor defaults, but anyone giving an indemnity is liable without need for any call upon the debtor. Reduced to its simplest terms a document or statement made in these words 'If you lend £100 to P, I will see that you are repaid' is an indemnity.

All these seven forms of security, personal and impersonal, direct and collateral, are taken by a bank in various ways and forms to-day and, having established the general principles, a detailed study can be made of all banking securities under appropriate headings. The responsibility of those in the securities' department of a branch bank is considerable and a wide knowledge of the technical and practical features relating to all types of security is essential. Each bank has its own printed forms of charge and method of record and counter-check, but the principles involved are universal and merit very close study in relation to the actual security forms and books used by the bank of the reader.

8. Stamp Duty

For many years it was a statutory requirement that forms of charge should attract stamp duty. The rates of duty varied according to the type of document and were amended from time to time by various Acts of Parliament. Most stamp duties were abolished by the Finance Acts of 1970 and 1971 and although it is no longer necessary to stamp most forms of charge the student banker is still obliged to have a basic understanding of stamping, if only to know how to deal with forms of legal charge dated prior to the 1st August, 1971.

Stamp duties were either 'fixed', that is where the duty was a fixed sum per document (e.g. agreements under hand, guarantees under hand, all stamped 6d), or ad valorem, that is, where the duty was based on the amount of the advance. Legal mortgages attracting ad valorem rates of stamp duty were divided into two categories; primary charges and secondary or collateral charges. Prior to the 1st August, 1971, where two or more legal mortgages were taken to secure the same debt, the first mortgage or primary document was stamped at the full rate of duty, whilst the remaining mortgages attracted a lower rate of duty as collateral documents. In addition, the secondary or collateral documents would have been impressed with a 'Duty Paid Stamp', thereby indicating that the full rate of duty had been paid on the primary document, and on release they would have been impressed with blue stamps up to the value of duty paid on the primary document. This was known as 'denoting' and attracted no extra fee. Equitable mortgages attracted a lower scale of duty under hand and the same scale of duty as for legal mortgages if under seal.

Where a legal charge dated prior to 1st August, 1971 is to be released, any secondary charges dated prior to 1st August, 1971 must be fully denoted before either the primary or the secondary charge(s) are released. To assist in determining whether a legal charge has been fully denoted, the following table gives the rates of stamp duties previously required.

17

B

AD VALOREM STAMPING—LEGAL MORTGAGES

Primary Charge

Prior to 1.8.47.—2/6d% of the highest amount advanced

1.8.47. to 31.7.63.—5/–%   ,,

1.8.63. to 31.7.70.—2/6d%   ,,

1.8.70. to 31.7.71.— (i) not exceeding £300:—

        5p for every £50 or part of £50 to the highest amount advanced.

    (ii) exceeding £300:—

        10p for every £100 or part of £100 of the highest amount advanced.

Secondary Charge

Prior to 1.8.70.—6d% maximum 10/–

1.8.70. to 31.7.71.—5p for every £200 or part of £200 of the highest amount advanced but not exceeding 50p.

It was a bank's normal practice to stamp a security to cover the highest amount advanced, unless a limiting clause appeared in the mortgage deed. Complications arose in the case of *In re Waterhouse's Policy* (1937) 1 Ch. 415, and although the case is now largely of historical interest, the problems it presented should be understood. Briefly, a customer of the Bank of Ireland mortgaged to the bank his £500, with profits, policy which was payable at age sixty, or previous death. The mortgage was stamped to cover £500, but the overdraft was at all times in excess of that figure. When the assured reached sixty years of age, the amount payable under the policy, including profits, was £963, and the debt to the bank was £619. The company signified its willingness to pay £963 to the bank provided it would certify that the maximum amount advanced under the mortgage had not exceeded £500. Being unable to give this certificate, the bank instead forwarded the authority of the customer for payment of the entire proceeds to the bank or, alternatively, indicated that they would be content to collect £500, the amount which the charge was stamped to cover, and the remainder could be paid direct to the assured. The assurance company declined to meet either request on the grounds that the mortgage was inadequately stamped and paid £963 into court, leaving the bank and the assured to take legal action. In the opinion of the company, by reason of Section 88 (2) of the Stamp Act, 1891, when the bank granted advances in excess of £500 the policy became security for the increased debt and should have been stamped additionally and, unless and until it was so stamped, it could not pay against the bank's discharge.

Farwell, J., held that the bank was entitled to claim £500, and the assured the balance of £463, together with any interest accrued. He was of the opinion that it was a perfectly good security for the amount covered by the stamp, but for no more. On the other hand, the Board of Inland Revenue was not prepared to accept this view, and in a letter to the Institute of Bankers, dated 17th July, 1937, stated that an unlimited security should be stamped up to cover the total sum advanced at any time. In view of the uncertainty which prevailed, generally speaking, banks followed the requirements of the Inland Revenue.

Part One: The Nature and Attributes of Security (continued)

Chapter II   Banker's Lien—an Informal Security

A *lien* may be defined as the right to retain the property of another until such time as the owner thereof has paid his debt due to the person in possession of the property subject to the lien. It is an informal security arising from the usual course of business between debtor and creditor and needs no documentary evidence or formal agreement to support it. A *particular lien* arises out of a particular transaction whereby goods can be retained to meet a debt resulting from the sale or delivery of those goods, whereas a *general lien* enables the creditor to retain any goods in his possession to cover the net amount outstanding due from the owner of them in respect of any transactions not necessarily relating to the goods actually held. Lien usually affords a right to retain the property only until the debt is paid. There is no power of sale.

In the normal course of business a bank handles securities and documents for customers and its general lien has been judicially recognised. In *Brandao* v. *Barnett* (1846) 12 Cl. & Fin. 787 Lord Campbell stated in the House of Lords that 'Bankers have a general lien on all securities deposited with them as bankers by a customer, unless there be an express contract, or circumstances that show an implied contract, inconsistent with lien'. The test, therefore, is whether the securities came into the hands of the banker in the ordinary course of business or whether they were handed to the bank for a special purpose inconsistent with lien, such as for safe custody. Some examples can be examined later, but it is prudent here to emphasise that the general lien does not extend to those securities which to the bank's knowledge do not belong to the customer who is indebted to the bank. On the other hand, if the bank is quite unaware that negotiable securities are not the property of the customer depositing them any right of lien over them can be upheld.

In the Brandao case a man named Burn, the London agent of the plaintiff, who was a Portuguese merchant, dealt with exchequer bills on behalf of his principal and kept his account with the defendant bankers. The exchequer bills were usually deposited in locked tin boxes held by the bank on behalf of its customer who retained the keys. On a certain date he extracted bills from the boxes and handed them to the bank to collect the interest due on them and to exchange them for other bills. The bank made the required exchange, but whilst the new bills remained in its possession the account of Burn became overdrawn and he failed, whereupon the bank claimed a lien on the bills which it so held. The plaintiff succeeded in the Court of Common Pleas, but the decision was reversed upon appeal and eventually restored in his favour by the House of Lords. Lord Campbell ignored the finding of the Lower Court that as the bills were the property of Brandao there could be no lien as against him and decided that there was an implied agreement inconsistent with lien. 'Now it seems to me, that in the present case there was an implied agreement on the part of the defendants, inconsistent with the right of lien which they claim. The bills . . . were not to remain in the possession of the defendants; and the defendants, in respect of them were employed merely to carry and hold until the deposit in the tin box could be conveniently accomplished'.

Taking the negative aspect first, it is clear that a bank cannot have any lien over items left with it for a specific purpose because there is then an express or implied contract inconsistent with lien. Thus articles deposited for safe custody are probably not subject to its general lien. Moreover, if securities are deposited for a particular loan or an advance never granted, the right of lien cannot be exercised. For example, it was decided in *Wylde* v. *Radford* (1864) 33 L.J. Ch. 51, that where a conveyance of two separate properties was deposited and a charge created on only one of them, the bank had no general lien over the remaining property. Again, in *In re Bowes, Earl of Strathmore* v. *Vane* (1886) 33 Ch. D. 586, where a £5,000 life policy was deposited with a memorandum evidencing that it was held by the bank as security up to £4,000, plus interest and other charges, it was decided that the bank could not claim more than £4,000 and charges within the limit set out in the form of mortgage. In the words of Mr. Justice North:—

'It is said that the bankers have a banker's lien; that Bowes was their customer, and handed over to them the policy as security, that they had it in their hands and were entitled to hold it, not only for the £4,000, interest and commission, for which they had a written agreement, but that in addition they had a further right as bankers to hold it in respect of the rest of his debt to them; or in other words they claim a right under the special contract in writing and also under an implied contract. It appears to me that this is inconsistent with the terms of the agreement, which is for a security for a sum not exceeding £4,000 principal and no more, with interest and commission, and that when the contract says so in so many words that the charge is for a sum not exceeding £4,000, the charge is limited to that amount . . . It has not been suggested that the sale was wrong in any way; and it may well be that bankers who have a power of selling securities deposited, when they have sold, and have clear money in their hands after satisfying the charge, may be entitled to say they will set off that money against further sums due to them; but that seems to me a totally different case from the present, where the security is of a wholly different nature, and the bank had no power of sale. It is quite true that, after a demand for payment had been made, the bank might have insisted on having a mortgage with a power of sale. No such demand was made or mortgage given, the bank never had a power to sell and convert the policy into money . . . It seems to me that the express terms of this deposit were that sums not exceeding £4,000 were to be paid out of the policy moneys, and it would be inconsistent with that, in the absence of any additional agreement, to allow the bank to hold the policy for something more.'

A similar decision was reached with regard to securities deposited to secure a specific loan in *Cuthbert* v. *Robarts, Lubbock & Co.* [1909] 2 Ch. 226, see also *Lucas* v. *Dorrien* (1817) 7 Taun. 278 and in *Symons* v. *Mulkerer* (1882) 46 L.T. 763 it was held that no lien could be exercised over securities handed to a bank for sale through a stockbroker. The negative test, therefore, is whether the securities were deposited with the bank for a special purpose and the most usual contract inconsistent with lien in daily practice is the acceptance of items for safe custody.

LEGAL CONTROVERSY

It is difficult to define exactly what securities are subject to the banker's lien and before attempting a practical solution, it is of interest to compare the opinions expressed by two of our leading authorities. To quote Paget's 'Law of Banking': 'The better view would seem to be that the lien only attaches to such securities as a banker ordinarily deals with for his customer, otherwise than for safe custody, when there is no question or contemplation of indebtedness on the part of the customer . . . collection is no doubt the primary idea of the banker's functions with regard to securities subject to lien'. On the other hand, Hart, 4th Ed. page 843, adopts a much wider view by defining banker's lien as 'the right of retaining things delivered into his possession as a banker, if and so long as the customer to whom they belong, or who had the power of disposing of them when so delivered, is indebted to the banker on the balance of the account between them, provided the circumstances in which the banker obtained possession do not imply that he has agreed that his right shall be excluded'. Basically, the lien extends to negotiable securities handled by the bank in the ordinary course of its business. As long ago as 1863, Kindersley, V.C. stated 'what is intended is such securities as promissory notes, bills of exchange, exchequer bills, coupons, bonds of foreign governments, etc., and the Courts have held that if such securities are deposited by a customer with his banker, and there is nothing to show the intention of such deposit one way or the other, the banker has, by custom, a lien thereon for the balance due from the customer'. (*Wylde* v. *Radford ante.*)

PRACTICAL CONCLUSIONS CONCERNING OCCASIONS WHEN LIEN ARISES

In spite of this uncertainty in legal circles, certain practical conclusions may be drawn. Lien implies physical possession. In *National Westminster Bank Ltd.* v. *Halesowen Pressworks & Assemblies Ltd.*, The Times, January 27, 1972, Viscount Dilhorne supported the opinion of Buckley, L.J., that once a cheque is cleared it ceases to be a negotiable instrument and it also ceases to be in the possession of the bank. Any lien that the bank may have had on the cheque disappears and the money or credit which the bank obtains becomes its own property as 'no man can have a lien on his own property'. To be subject to lien the securities must be received and handled by the bank in the ordinary course of its business, there being no express or implied agreement between the customer and the bank inconsistent with lien. Thus in *Westminster Bank Ltd.* v. *Zang* (1965) 1 All E.R. 114 the bank was considered to have forfeited their lien on the cheque, which was the basis of the case, by releasing it to solicitors of another party so that action could be taken on it.

Lien arises in the normal course of business and a bank will only seek to exercise its rights where the customer becomes in some way indebted to it. Cheques, bills, mandated dividends and kindred documents left with a bank for collection are undoubtedly received in the normal course of business and are subject to its lien. Moreover, by virtue of Section 27 (3) of the Bills of Exchange Act, 1882, where the holder of a bill has a lien on it, he is deemed to be a holder for value to the extent of the sum for which he has a lien. In *Re Keever* (a Bankrupt) *Ex parte the Trustee of the Property of the Bankrupt* v. *Midland Bank Ltd.* (1966) 3 All E.R. 631 the bank claimed to have a lien over a cheque thus preventing it being attached by a Receiving Order. The claim was contested on the grounds that there was no consideration for the lien, but it was held that an existing loan or overdraft was sufficient for this purpose. Ungoed-Thomas, J., said, 'It would seem to me that the existence and continuation of an overdraft constitute consideration for a lien. Further, however, Section 27 (1) and (3) of the Bills of Exchange Act, 1882, provide:

(1)   Valuable consideration for a bill may be constituted by:

(*b*)   An antecedent debt or liability. Such a debt or liability is deemed valuable consideration whether the bill is payable on demand or at a future time.

(3)   Where the holder of a bill has a lien on it arising either from contract or by implication of Law he is deemed to be a holder for value to the extent of the sum for which he has a lien.'

Again, in *Barclays Bank Ltd.* v. *Astley Industrial Trust Ltd.* (1970) 2 W.L.R. 876 the bank received five cheques to the value of £2,850 drawn by Astley Industrial Trust Ltd., for the credit of Mabon's Garage Ltd. Their account was £4,673 overdrawn against a limit of £2,000 at the time the cheques were received and acting in reliance upon the credit the bank decided to pay two cheques to the value of £345 which they would otherwise have dishonoured. The £2,850 was in respect of alleged Hire Purchase transactions which were subsequently found to have been fraudulent and the directors of Mabon's Garage Ltd. were prosecuted and convicted and the business went into liquidation. The cheques were dishonoured on presentation, the defendants having countermanded payment.

The bank claimed, *inter alia*, that they had a lien on the cheques (which was not contested) and by virtue of Section 27 (3) of the Bills of Exchange Act, 1882, they were holders for value. Milmo, J., decided in favour of the bank and held that the bank acquired a lien on the cheques and were holders for value to the extent of Mabon's overdraft by reason of Section 27 (3). Moreover, having taken the cheques in good faith and without notice of any defect in title, they had satisfied the conditions of Section 29 (1) and this made them holders in due course.

Bearer bonds and other securities left with the bank to enable it to collect the proceeds of coupons will also be subject to the lien. In *re United Service Company* (1870) 6 Ch. App. 212 it was held that where railway share certificates were deposited with a bank and the dividends collected for a commission charge, the certificates were received in the ordinary course of the bank's business and subject to the bank's lien.

If a customer instructs the bank to purchase or lift certain securities the bank will have a lien on them, whether or not they are negotiable, for the amount due from the customer, but where payment is made on behalf of a stockbroker customer against the delivery of certificates or certified transfers in favour of his client, the bank can exercise no right of lien over the securities because they are known to be the property of the client and cannot be retained against the debt of the broker.

Finally, it may be that when securities deposited to secure a specific loan remain in the possession of the bank after it has been repaid, they will be subject to the bank's lien for the other debts due to the bank by the depositor (*Re London & Globe Finance Corporation* [1902] 2 Ch. 416). Nowadays, however, a charge would be taken over the securities expressed to cover all possible liabilities present and future without need to fall back upon the general lien.

Where securities are deposited without a formal charge but expressly to cover an indebtedness of a customer, the bank normally obtains an equitable mortgage by deposit.

Pledge is also an express contract for security, but lien, as previously emphasised, arises quite informally from the normal course of business irrespective of any express intention by the borrower.

EXPRESS LIEN

Sometimes a bank may obtain a borrower's signature to a document described colloquially as a general letter of lien, whereby the customer acknowledges that all his securities which may from time to time be deposited with the bank are held as security for his indebtedness. Such an acknowledgment may be helpful, for example, in the case of a customer who frequently changes the securities held by the bank and it is inconvenient to obtain specific charges over every item, but, strictly speaking, the document evidences the customer's intention to create a charge and each deposit of security gives the bank an equitable mortgage by deposit. It is really a formal security and not a question of banker's lien arising out of the ordinary course of business. On the other hand, such a letter is clear evidence that the securities are subject to the bank's lien and it cannot later be contended by the customer that they were deposited for a special purpose inconsistent with lien. Similar letters may be employed where a bank is regularly accepting bills for customers to finance their import of goods, but legally a distinction has to be drawn between an alleged letter of lien and an agreement to pledge or a letter of hypothecation. These differences will be explored when the question of advances against produce is considered.

IMPLIED PLEDGE

Lien does not normally confer a right of sale. It is merely a right to retain the goods until the debt is paid. A banker's lien, however, was described in *Brandao* v. *Barnett, ante*, as an implied pledge and it is generally considered that the remedies of a pledgee apply, where appropriate, to securities subject to the lien of a bank. This means that in the event of default by the customer the bank has a power of sale without resort to the Courts. Such power of sale is generally restricted to fully negotiable securities and it can be exercised without the express approval of the customer after reasonable notice has been given of the bank's intention to dispose of the securities to recover the debt. What is reasonable notice is a question of fact according to the circumstances of the case. In *Deverges* v. *Sandeman* [1902] 1 Ch. 579 a month was regarded as reasonable notice, but no banker in practice is likely to hurry the realisation of negotiable securities which are subject to its lien. The borrower will be granted every opportunity to repay his debt before the lender resorts to his legal rights. There is little point in arguing whether or not this implied power of sale applies to non-negotiable securities because in any event application would have to be made to the Court, or the co-operation of any trustee in bankruptcy obtained, before a valid title could be given to a purchaser.

In summary it can be said that in case of need a banker may retain, and even sell to recover a debt, securities of the borrower which are received in the ordinary course of business in circumstances which are not inconsistent with lien, but the prudent course is always to obtain a complete charge over all securities which are available to support any borrowing. Lien is an informal security to fall back upon as a last resort. Far better to obtain formal security with unquestionable rights and valid title.

Part Two: Guarantees

Chapter III Introductory

DEFINITIONS—THE VALUE OF THE GUARANTEE

A guarantee is probably the simplest form of banking security, more easily obtained than any other and yet frequently most difficult to realise. It is an intangible security which may or may not be of adequate value when it is most needed. Few guarantors ever expect to be called upon to honour their contract and it is therefore imperative that the lending banker should exercise the greatest care in obtaining the guarantee and thereafter in ensuring that it is at all times worth what is required from it. The best advice from experience is perhaps not to lend relying solely on a guarantee unless the bank is completely satisfied that the guarantor is really undoubted for the amount required and that he is of such unquestionable standing that no attempt will be made to avoid the responsibility. The initial warning concerning such security is given in Chapter XI of Proverbs, verse 15: 'He that is surety for a stranger shall smart for it, and he that hateth suretyship is sure'. These biblical words so often apply in practice and it behoves the practical banker not to rely too freely upon a popular and simple form of security so easily obtained but so difficult to realise.

DEFINITIONS—A GUARANTEE AND AN INDEMNITY

Legally, a *guarantee* may be defined as an undertaking or promise whereby one person (called the guarantor or surety) agrees to be answerable for the payment of a debt or the performance of some act by another person who must be legally bound to pay the debt or to perform the act concerned. It is a collateral security of secondary liability involving three parties: the guarantor, the principal debtor (whose debt is guaranteed) and the lender or creditor (being the bank from our standpoint). The simplest form of guarantee would be 'If you, Northtown Bank, advance £X to your customer, Z (the principal debtor), and he does not repay you, I will see that you are paid—signed S. (the guarantor)'. The guarantor is liable upon the default of the principal debtor and if the guarantor meets his obligation he may sue the principal debtor for repayment.

The cynical lender from experience may prefer to define a guarantee as 'where one man that can't pay gets another man who can't pay to say he will'. This humorous definition nevertheless serves as a salutary practical warning to the practical banker.

A contract of *indemnity* differs from a guarantee in that the promisor engages to be primarily liable for the debt or obligation. To undertake that 'If you lend £20 to G, I will see that you are paid' would be to accept primary responsibility under a contract of indemnity, but the statement 'If you lend £20 to G and he does not pay you, I will' is a contract of secondary liability which arises only upon the failure of G to repay and it is a guarantee. An indemnity is of greater value where lending to an infant or other customer who may not be legally liable for the debt. Actually an indemnity need not be in writing to be enforceable, but the prudent banker is hardly likely to rely upon any oral promise as security for accommodation. A guarantee to be enforceable has to be evidenced by a written memorandum (Section 4, Statute of Frauds, 1677).

ESSENTIALS OF A GUARANTEE

The best banking approach to the subject of guarantees is to recognise at the outset that there are three clear essentials:—

1. The *value* of the guarantee, which must be maintained throughout the period of the advance to the customer.
2. The *validity* of the guarantee, which means in general that the guarantor's mind must run with his pen at the time he signs the guarantee, and that nothing shall happen to enable the guarantor later to avoid liability on the grounds of mistake, duress, or undue influence.
3. The *form* of the guarantee which must cover all possibilities, limiting the common law rights of the guarantor and permitting wide freedom to the banker in dealing with the borrower. Each bank has a form of guarantee printed for general use. At first sight it is a verbose and unduly lengthy document, but every phrase and condition is essential, as will be seen when typical clauses are examined.

The subject will, therefore, be examined in three clear stages—value, validity and form—each of which is of vital importance to the complete security.

VALUE OF THE GUARANTEE

The real value of any guarantee depends entirely upon the financial ability of the guarantor to meet the liability with reasonable promptitude when called upon to do so. The undoubted standing of the guarantor must apply not only when the contract is signed, but throughout the term of the overdraft facility. In effect, an advance against an unsupported guarantee is an unsecured advance to the guarantor and should be treated as such throughout. Fortunes can still change overnight, so that a vigilant watch must always be maintained on the financial position of any guarantor upon whom reliance is placed.

Where the guarantor is a customer of the lending banker, the problem is easily solved because the extent of his liability can be recorded and constant close touch kept with his means, the withdrawal of items from security, or safe custody, being duly noted. Where the guaranteed advance is taken at a different branch to that where the guarantor keeps his account, the officials of each branch should keep each other closely advised concerning the position at their respective branches, any major change in the fortunes of the guarantor being promptly communicated to the lending branch. Without complete co-operation on these lines unnecessary risks are accepted and carelessness in maintaining proper records may cause losses.

Where the guarantor banks elsewhere, the lending banker will wish to know the name and address of his bankers in order to make an enquiry concerning his ability to undertake such liability. There should be complete confidence and a spirit of helpfulness between all banks in this respect. Without such co-operation within the same business, the lending bank is taking an unnecessary risk and the guarantor's bank may be in its shoes on a later occasion and have reason to regret any excess anxiety previously displayed in the safeguard of the standing of its guarantor customer. On the one hand, the lending bank's enquiry should be for the exact amount required and disclose quite clearly the nature of the guarantee liability. It is foolish and misleading to attempt a form of insurance by enquiring for an amount larger than that of the guarantee because the guarantor's bank thereby has an inflated idea of its customer's commitments and qualifies its report accordingly. The banker replying to the enquiry should realise that on this occasion it is on the other side of the fence and the reply can be complete and helpful without incurring any risk of breach of secrecy. The lending banker proposes to accept a risk relying perhaps entirely upon the report received from the guarantor's bank and, if any doubt exists, the matter can always be discussed over the telephone (with suitable precautions) to avoid committing facts to paper. If the reply is 'undoubted as guarantor for £X' or 'considered good for your figures and purposes,' there should be no possible doubt that the guarantor is in fact completely reliable for the amount having regard to his known resources and other commitments. Where the slightest doubt exists, caution should be advised in the reply and there is little need to use indefinite and guarded language between bankers. The reply is given and received in the strictest confidence between bank and bank and the nature of the contents cannot be revealed to the guarantor at either end. Nevertheless, in practice some banks still employ an ancient language or remote expressions which usually result in the enquiring banker interpreting the position as far worse than it actually is. Most guarantors are considered to be 'respectable and trustworthy in the way of business,' but the lending banker really wants to know whether its security is worth the amount stated. The reply 'we cannot speak for your figure' or 'the given figure is larger than we normally see passing through the account' or 'his resources appear to be fully employed' can only mean that the subject of the enquiry is unsuitable as a guarantor and he can be relied upon merely 'for what worth.' If the bank replying to the enquiry would not be prepared to lend an equivalent amount to the guarantor without security, its customer cannot be very reliable as a guarantor to the other bank, and it is dangerous to attempt to whitewash this fact. It is not a question of protecting the guarantor customer (although he should be warned in friendly manner if he freely and optimistically enters into too many guarantee liabilities) but rather a matter for protection of the lending bank in a complete spirit of co-operation within the banking business. For example, are the words 'is good' and 'should be good' intended to have the same meaning.

As soon as the agreed advance has been fully taken, it may often be difficult in practice to obtain repayment immediately upon any adverse changes in the standing of the guarantor. Nevertheless, to be forewarned is to be forearmed and it is clearly prudent to ensure by regular enquiry that there has been no change in the position. The frequency of such renewal enquiries will depend upon the facts, varying perhaps from quarterly intervals to a prudent maximum of an annual report. Moreover, the enquiry should be suitably marked to show that it is a renewal of a previous enquiry, otherwise the guarantor's bank may jump to the conclusion that it is an additional liability. If the fresh report is qualified or weaker than the previous opinion, the lending banker is warned and may be able to take speedy steps to protect its position. In this respect the guarantor's bank should always record the nature and source of such enquiries and, as a matter of courtesy, send prompt advice to the lending bank in the event of the death or bankruptcy of the guarantor. In similar manner, when a guarantee is no longer required the lending banker should advise the guarantor's bank to enable it to amend its records. These are all common-sense, practical features between bank and bank and branch and branch, but they are, alas, sometimes forgotten in the heat and burden of the day.

JOINT AND SEVERAL GUARANTEES

The legal position and liability of joint and several guarantors will be discussed later, but from the standpoint of value the risk is naturally spread amongst all the signatories to the guarantee, and each one of them is liable for the full amount thereof. It is, therefore, prudent to enquire for the full amount against each and every guarantor, although the enquiry should reveal that it is a joint and several guarantee with a stated number of other guarantors, to give the replying bank an opportunity in case of need of stating that, although unable to speak for the full amount, the customer may be considered good for a stated proportion thereof. Again, it is a question of complete confidence and co-operation between bank and bank.

Advances are often made to private limited company customers against the joint and several guarantee of its directors and the value of the guarantee depends entirely upon the extent of the free resources of the directors outside the company. If most of their funds are invested in the borrowing company, there will be nothing available upon its failure when the guarantee is most needed. Nevertheless, a bank may take a guarantee from the directors, merely for what it may be worth, as tangible evidence of the confidence of the directors in the future of the business. If they are content to accept personal liability notwithstanding their limited private means, they must have confidence in the future or be unbounded optimists, whereas if there is any doubt they will seek to avoid personal liability to the bank.

Similarly, a holding company may guarantee the bank indebtedness of one of its subsidiaries and the value of such a guarantee may be impaired if there is a very close and interdependent trading interest between the two companies. Failure of the subsidiary may jeopardise the financial standing of the parent concern, particularly where large amounts are due by the subsidiary to its parent, and the guarantee will be of little value when it is most needed.

CONCLUSION

The real value of any guarantee, therefore, turns upon all the facts of the case, which demand close examination, always bearing in mind that no guarantor ever expects to have to pay and, when called upon to do so, will inevitably be pained and surprised. The beautifully worded and printed document which has yet to be discussed is quite useless unless it is backed by hard cash, and the ease with which such security can often be obtained is a quicksand for the unwary. No amount of legal provision will produce cash from a guarantor who is incapable of meeting his liability.

Chapter IV The Validity of the Guarantee

POSSIBLE AVOIDANCE OF LIABILITY, DISCLOSURE, SIGNING, TYPES OF GUARANTOR, GUARANTEES BY FIRMS, COMPANIES, INFANTS, ETC.

VALIDITY OF THE GUARANTEE

A guarantee may be avoided if the guarantor can prove that he or she entered into the contract by mistake or misrepresentation, or under duress or through undue influence. It is, therefore, imperative always to ensure that a guarantor understands the general nature of the liability so undertaken and enters into the engagement and signs the guarantee entirely of his own free will. There must be no suggestion of persuasion from the bank or from the principal debtor. Far too many people sign a guarantee without realising the nature and extent of the liability they have thereby undertaken. Ignorance of the contract will not enable a guarantor to avoid responsibility, but attempt may be made to prove mistake or misrepresentation or otherwise to wriggle out of the liability. Care must, therefore, be exercised in practice to remove any such source of trouble when payment is required, and the practical pitfalls call for close examination.

POSSIBLE AVOIDANCE OF LIABILITY

MISTAKEN IMPRESSION OF SIGNATORY TO GUARANTEE

It has long been held that a guarantor must realise that he is signing a guarantee, otherwise he might contend that he thought he was entering into a contract of a completely different nature. The view has been taken that there is a danger he might enter a plea of *non est factum*, based on the old principle enunciated in *Foster* v. *Mackinnon* (1869) L.R. 4C P. 704. 711–712 to the effect that a blind or illiterate person was not bound by a document which they were induced to believe was a document of a completely different type. In *Carlisle & Cumberland Banking Company* v. *Bragg* (1911) 1.K.B. 489 the bank called upon its customer, Rigg, to find a guarantor for his overdraft. He approached Bragg and prevailed upon him to sign the bank's guarantee form on the pretext that it was an insurance proposal. The guarantor succeeded in avoiding liability, being unaware of the transaction behind the document which he signed in the belief that it was something quite different from a guarantee. 'The principle involved, as I understand it, is that a consenting mind is essential to the making of a contract, and that in such a case as this there is really no *consensus*, because there was no intention to make a contract of the kind in question.' Kennedy, L.J., in the Court of Appeal. Although the jury found Bragg had simply been negligent in signing the document without reading it, he was still able to avoid his liability on the ground that he thought the document was of a different character from what it was. This point was supported, in general terms, by the judgment in *Muskham Finance Ltd.* v. *Howard & Another* (1962) The Times, December 1, but it was acknowledged in *Howatson* v. *Webb* (1908) 1 Ch. 1., that, providing a person realised he was signing a guarantee, he could not avoid responsibility by pleading that he did not read the terms of the guarantee and realise its nature.

Recently, however, the decision in *Carlisle & Cumberland Banking Company* v. *Bragg* has been strongly criticised and it can no longer be regarded as good law. It has been overruled by the case of *Saunders (Executrix of the Estate of Rose Maud Gallie, deceased)* v. *Anglia Building Society* ((1970) 3 W.L.R. 1078), formerly reported under *Gallie* v. *Lee*, which merits study in some detail. The facts of the case were these. Gallie, an elderly widow, handed the deeds of a house in which she had a leasehold interest to her nephew. She did so by way of gift, knowing that her nephew wanted to borrow against the deeds and that his business associate Lee would be involved with him in the raising of the money. Lee induced Gallie to sign a document, telling her it was a deed of gift of the house to her nephew. Having broken her spectacles, she was unable to read the document, which was in fact an assignment of the house by her to Lee for £3,000. Her nephew witnessed her signature, having agreed with Lee that Lee should raise money on the house and repay him by instalments. In the event, Lee mortgaged the house to the Building Society for £2,000, which he used to repay his debts. He defaulted on the mortgage instalments and the Building Society sought to obtain possession of the house.

Gallie pleaded *non est factum* against Lee and the Building Society and asked for the contract to be declared void and for the deeds to be returned to her. In the High Court, Stamp, J., held that the plea was established and decided in her favour, but the decision was reversed unanimously in the Court of Appeal (1969) 1 All E.R. 1062. Russell and Salmon, L.J.J., examined the *non est factum* rule and considered it should be applied narrowly, particularly when the claim is made against an innocent third party. In this case they both held that the claim was not substantiated because it appeared that Mrs. Gallie would still have signed the document had she known what it really was. She wanted to place the property at the disposal of her newphew, she trusted Lee and would have accepted whatever explanation he had to offer.

'. . . . the plea has never yet been held available to anyone unless he was able to show that, had he known the true character or class of the document in question, he would not have signed it. . . . For my part, I would certainly not extend the doctrine. Indeed I would confine it strictly to facts to which I am compelled to apply it by binding authority.' Salmon, L.J.

Lord Denning was even more categoric.

'Whenever a man of full age and understanding, who can read and write, signs a legal document which is put before him for signature—by which I mean a document which, it is apparent on the face of it, is intended to have legal consequences—then, if he does not take the trouble to read it, but signs it as it is, relying on the word of another as to its character or contents or effect, he cannot be heard to say that it is not his document. By his conduct in signing it he has represented, to all those into whose hands it may come, that it is his document; and once they act on it as being his document, he cannot go back on it, and say that it was a nullity from the beginning. If his signature was obtained by fraud, or under the influence of mistake, or something of the kind, he may be able to avoid it up to a point—but not when it has come into the hands of one who has in all innocence advanced money on the faith of its being his document, or otherwise has relied on it as being his document.'

He claimed that his reasoning was not inconsistent with previous decisions of the Court of Appeal, with the one exception of *Carlisle & Cumberland Banking Company* v. *Bragg*, which he regarded as inconsistent with many others and, therefore, could be disregarded.

Again, in the further appeal to the House of Lords it was unanimously decided that the plea of *non est factum* failed. Lord Wilberforce gave it as his opinion that the plea could only succeed when the element of consent to the document is totally lacking, so that the transaction the document purports to effect is essentially different from the transaction intended. He amplified this statement in several ways, but suffice it to note he considered that if a man of ordinary education and competence chooses to sign a document without informing himself of its purport and effect, he cannot escape the consequences to innocent third parties. Moreover, he considered this also applied to a person signing a document who failed to take ordinary precautions against being deceived and that the decision in *Carlisle & Cumberland Banking Company* was wrong. He conceded that with persons who are blind, illiterate or lacking in understanding it was impossible to define a solution which would meet all cases. If consent was truly lacking the law might feel obliged to give relief, but even here it would require signers to act responsibly according to their circumstances.

Welcome though this decision is, it still behoves the banker to act with care and a guarantee should never be given to the borrower or any other interested party to be executed outside the bank. A guarantee should always be signed in the presence of a banker or solicitor who can ensure that the guarantor realises the nature of the contract into which he is entering. If the guarantee cannot be conveniently signed in the presence of the *lending* bank, it is usually sent to the *guarantor's* bank with suitable explanation so that the surety may call to sign it in the presence of his own bankers. In such event, the risk of forgery of the guarantor's signature is automatically removed.

PRESSURE OR UNDUE INFLUENCE ON SIGNATORY TO GUARANTEE

It is up to the customer to persuade the guarantor to accept such onerous responsibility and under no circumstances should the bank create the impression in the mind of the guarantor that he is signing the guarantee at the request of the bank. The guarantor must act throughout of his own free will without any pressure or coercion from the bank. Where a joint and several guarantee is obtained from directors before accommodation is granted to their limited company, care is needed to avoid any suggestion of pressure. It may well be a fact basically that no advances will be made without the guarantee, but the directors must act of their own free will in the matter. As business men, it would normally be difficult for them to prove otherwise. According to Fry, J., in *Davies* v. *London & Provincial Marine Insurance Co.* (1877) 8 Ch. D.469: 'a contract of suretyship is one in which I think that everything like pressure used by the intending creditor will have a very serious effect on the validity of the contract.'

Undue influence may arise where the relationship between the guarantor and the borrower is such that 'the will of the one is not as freely exercisable as the will of the other,' in which event there may be a presumption at law that the contract was not fairly made and can be avoided at the option of the guarantor who was so influenced. For example, undue influence is presumed between parents and their children; doctors and their patients; solicitors and their clients; and may arise, in special circumstances, between husband and wife. Care is, therefore, necessary when there is any likelihood that a potential guarantor may be under the influence of the borrower. In practice, cases are probably limited to guarantees by a wife to secure the overdraft of her husband and the risk is removed, as will be seen later, by insisting that the guarantee is signed in the presence of the wife's solicitor or an independent solicitor. The point must be borne in mind, however, where, for example, an impecunious doctor introduces an elderly male patient as guarantor for his borrowing. The nature of the transaction and the extent of the liability should be made quite clear to the guarantor and, in case of doubt, the services of a solicitor obtained to explain the position to him.

The relationship between husband and wife is not the same as that between parent and child, solicitor and client, etc., and undue influence cannot be presumed. There is no general rule of universal application that the rule of equity as to confidential relationship necessarily applies between husband and wife so as to throw on the bank the onus of disproving undue influence. There may, however, be circumstances, unknown to the bank, which enable the contract to be avoided by the wife on the grounds of undue influence. Such risks are normally removed in practice by having a guarantee signed by any lady in the presence of her solicitor and they need not be pursued here. Any reader interested in the legal position is advised to compare *Bank of Montreal* v. *Stuart & Anor* [1911] A.C.120, with *Howes* v. *Bishop & Wife* [1909] 2 K.B. 390.

If the guarantee is signed by the guarantor in the presence of the bank or its agent, there can be little risk of pressure or undue influence as he presumably signs of his own free will after listening to an outline of the transaction. There may, of course, be some threat held over him by the borrower, but this is unlikely to be of avail when the guarantee is signed willingly in the presence of the bank's officials. Where the guarantee is foolishly entrusted to the customer to obtain the signature of the guarantor, it might be completed under duress, or undue influence.

MISREPRESENTATION—EFFECT ON SURETY'S POSITION

Misrepresentation occurs where a party to a contract makes a material statement of fact concerning the contract which is untrue. An innocent misrepresentation is an untrue statement of fact likely to influence the decision of the guarantor who, if he is misled and so induced to sign the guarantee relying upon the statement, may avoid liability. A fraudulent misrepresentation is an untrue statement made by a person who knew it to be false, or who did not believe it to be true, or who made the statement recklessly, not caring whether it was false or true, and will likewise enable the guarantor to repudiate liability. The banker, when dealing with a guarantor, is unlikely to be guilty of fraudulent misrepresentation, but care may be necessary to avoid innocent misrepresentation by failing perhaps to correct

33

C

an obviously wrong impression in the mind of the guarantor concerning the nature of the advance which is to be granted. This aspect of the matter will be discussed later under the heading of disclosure, but to illustrate the avoidance of a guarantee by misrepresentation it is well to examine *Mackenzie* v. *Royal Bank of Canada* [1934] A.C. 468.

Mrs. Mackenzie, at the request of her husband and after discussions with the manager of the bank, signed a general hypothecation form in 1920, whereby her holding of Ottawa Dairy Co., Ltd., shares worth about $10,000 were 'general and continuing collateral security for payment of the present and future indebtedness and liability of Mackenzie Ltd.', a company in which her husband was interested, and she agreed 'that the bank may grant extensions, take up securities, accept compositions, grant releases and discharges and otherwise deal with the customer and with other parties and securities as the bank may see fit without prejudice to' her liability. She alleged that her husband had given her to understand that this security was needed to cover fresh advances and the manager of the bank had commented favourably upon the future of the company. In May, 1921, the company became bankrupt under Canadian law and the debt was eventually discharged by the bank taking over assets which had been charged to it by the company, there then being no debt of the company secured by the original hypothecation of the Dairy shares. In September, 1921, however, both Mr. and Mrs. Mackenzie signed a letter to the bank stating that they agreed to the bank filing an affidavit, etc. and continuing 'we hereby agree that your so doing shall not in any way release us from our obligation under guarantees to the bank, nor shall our personal securities be in any way affected until the amount due to the bank by Mackenzie Ltd. has been actually paid'.

Thereafter the company was reconstructed and the assets of the old company were sold by the bank to Mackenzie for $125,000 and he in turn sold them to the new company at the same figure. The bank advanced the purchase price to this new company against the security of the assets and called for a guarantee from Mrs. Mackenzie for $200,000 which she signed on the bank's standard form at its office, together with a hypothecation form to cover the indebtedness of the new company. She was assured by the bank manager and her husband that her Dairy shares were still bound to the bank, that they were gone in any case, but that this was an opportunity of recovering them. After she had signed the guarantee and letter of hypothecation, she was handed a form to be taken to a solicitor evidencing that he had given her independent advice. She went to a solicitor who accepted her version of what she had done and signed the form.

Mrs. Mackenzie eventually sued the bank to recover her shares, claiming that she had been induced to charge them by undue influence of her husband and by misrepresentation. Her success before the trial Judge was reversed upon appeal and she appealed to the Privy Council, which found for her, on the grounds of misrepresentation by the bank. The judgment included these words:

'A contract of guarantee, like any other contract, is liable to be avoided if induced by material misrepresentation of an existing fact, even if made innocently. In this case it is unnecessary to decide whether contracts of guarantee belong to the special class where, even in common law, such an innocent misrepresentation would afford a defence to an action on the contract. The evidence conclusively established a misrepresentation by the bank with the

necessary inference, whether expressed or not, and their Lordships accept the plaintiff's evidence that it was expressed, that the shares were already lost, and that the guarantee of the new company offered the only means of salving them. It does not seem to admit of doubt that such a representation made as to the plaintiff's private rights and depending upon transactions in bankruptcy, of the full nature of which she had not been informed, was a representation of fact. That it was material is beyond discussion. It consequently follows that the plaintiff was at all times, on ascertaining the true position, entitled to avoid the contract and recover her securities. There were subsequent renewals of the guarantee before the plaintiff was advised of the true facts, but counsel for the bank very properly conceded that they would be in the same position as the original guarantee. There is no difficulty as to *restitutio in integrum*. The mere fact that the party making the representation has treated the contract as binding and has acted on it does not preclude relief. Nor can it be said that the plaintiff received anything under the contract which she is unable to restore.'
This case provides ample warning to the practical banker on the consequences of misrepresentation at the time the guarantee is signed.

DISCLOSURE OF INFORMATION TO PROSPECTIVE SURETY

How much information concerning the borrower and the nature of the advances must the lending bank reveal to the guarantor when he is about to sign the guarantee? Is there just cause for voluntary revelations concerning the customer and his requirements and, if the bank fails to disclose the facts, can the guarantor wriggle out of his liability? On the one hand, there are the risks perhaps of mistake or misrepresentation, to which reference has already been made. On the other hand, the bank has a duty of secrecy to its customer. Everything depends upon what happens at the interview with the guarantor and the initial warning comes from Sir Edward Fry in *Davies* v. *London & Provincial Insurance Co.*—'very little said which ought not to have been said, and very little omitted which ought to have been said, will suffice to avoid the contract'. Several clear principles can, however, be laid down and guidance obtained as ever from the past unhappy experiences of bankers.

A guarantee is not a contract *uberrimae fidei* (of the utmost good faith), whereby failure to reveal all the relevant information renders the contract voidable, and it is normally unnecessary for a bank to volunteer any disclosure concerning the customer's character, dealings, or financial position. Unless, therefore, the intending guarantor asks questions or makes statements which make it evident to the bank that he has a mistaken impression of the position, there is no need to volunteer information. This general principle is well established at law by the following cases.

In the case of *Hamilton* v. *Watson* (1845) 12 *Cl. & Fin.* 109, it was decided that the banker had no responsibility to disclose the customer's financial position to a guarantor, however material such information might appear to be. The only duty was to reply to any questions raised by the guarantor. In the words of Lord Campbell—'I should think that this might be considered as the criterion whether the disclosure ought to be made voluntarily, namely, whether there is anything that might not naturally be expected to take place between the parties who are concerned in the transaction, that is, whether there be a contract between the debtor and the creditor, to the effect that his position shall be different from that which the surety might naturally expect; and, if so, the surety is to see whether that is disclosed to him. But, if there is nothing which might not naturally take place between these parties, then, if the surety would guard against particular perils, he must put the question, and he must gain the information which he requires'.

Again, to quote Sir Edward Fry in *Davies* v. *London & Provincial Insurance Co.* (1877) Ch. D. 469—'Where parties are contracting with one another each may, unless under a duty to disclose, observe silence, even in regard to facts which he believes would be operative upon the mind of the other, and it rests upon those who say that there was a duty to disclose to show that the duty existed. It has been argued that the contract between the surety and the creditor is one of those contracts which I have spoken of as being *uberrimae fidei*, and it has been held that such a contract can only be upheld in the case of there being the fullest disclosure by the creditor. I do not think that that proposition is sound in law. I think, on the contrary, that *the contract is one in which there is no universal obligation to make disclosure.*'

These views were upheld in the more modern case of *Cooper* v. *National Provincial Bank Ltd.* [1946] K.B. 1., where the guarantor sought to avoid liability on the grounds that the bank had failed to disclose material facts. A Mrs. J. P. M. Rolfs, whose husband was an undischarged bankrupt, borrowed from the bank against guarantees for £650 and £600 by Cooper, each expressed to secure the account of 'June Phyllis Maud Rolfs, wife of Lionel Malcolm Rolfs, trading as Vale Farms Co.' Apart from disclosing that the account for Vale Farms Co. had been overdrawn a few hundred pounds for some time, the manager of the bank volunteered no other information to the guarantor before he signed the guarantees, and the latter asked no questions. He later brought an action against the bank claiming that the guarantees be declared void and set aside because before they were signed the bank failed to disclose to him: (1) that Mr. Rolfs had power to sign on the account; (2) that at all material times Mr. Rolfs was an undischarged bankrupt; and (3) that the account had been operated irregularly because the payment of cheques properly issued had been countermanded. In defence, the bank maintained that there was no obligation on it to make such disclosures and counter-claimed for the amount due under the guarantees. Lawrence, L.J., referred to and applied the test cited by Lord Campbell in *Hamilton* v. *Watson*, quoted above, and decided that the bank was under no duty to make these disclosures:—

'The submissions for the plaintiff seem to me to be diametrically opposed to what was there said by Lord Campbell. If, said Lord Campbell, the rule was that everything should be disclosed that was material for the surety to know, it would be necessary for the bankers to state how the account had been kept, whether the debtor was in the habit of overdrawing, whether he was punctual in his dealings; whether he performed his promises in an honourable manner. Lord Campbell held that it was unnecessary for the bank to make these disclosures. As to whether the debtor was in the habit of overdrawing, the plaintiff admitted that the manager of this branch of the defendant bank told him that the account had been overdrawn some hundred pounds for some time. The other issues stated by Lord Campbell were directed to the way in which the account had been operated. To state whether the debtor, the customer of the bank, was punctual in his dealings and whether he performed his promises in an honourable manner would cover a statement about these cheques which had been drawn and delivered but which the debtor had ordered the bank not to pay. Lord Campbell puts the criterion as to whether there should be a voluntary disclosure as being whether there is a contract between the debtor and the creditor, that is, between the customer and the bank, to the effect that her position shall be different from that which the surety might naturally. expect. It does not seem to me that there was here any contract between Mrs Rolfs and the bank which made the position between them one which the surety, the plaintiff, would not naturally expect. There is nothing unusual in a wife giving her husband authority to draw on her account. Moreover, that authority was not a matter of contract between the bank and herself: it was a unilateral authority given by her to her husband. The fact that her husband to whom she gave this authority to draw on her account was an undischarged bankrupt does not make the authority so unusual that it ought to have been communicated by the bank to the intended surety. If it could have been said that the account which was to be guaranteed was not really the account of Mrs. Rolfs but was, in truth, the account of Mr. Rolfs, an undischarged bankrupt, and the bank then took a guarantee from a surety of the nominal account of Mrs. Rolfs, it might be, possibly, that the bank, aware of these facts, ought first to have disclosed them. But the bank neither knew that this was so, nor had any reason to think so. Not only was the fact that the Vale Farms Co. account was really an account of Mr. Rolfs not proved in evidence before me, but the facts which were proved before me all tended to show that the account, although it was operated on by Mr. Rolfs and although the scheme of the farming venture for which the account was used was that Mr. Rolfs should manage the farms, was Mrs. Rolfs', and that the funds to be used for the purchase of the farms were those of Mrs. Rolfs in so far as they were not the funds of the bank.

'Mrs. Rolfs' account was overdrawn and she had authorised her husband, who was an undischarged bankrupt, to draw on the account. Further, a number of cheques had been drawn on this account, yet orders had been given by the drawer not to pay them. But, in my opinion, there was no duty on the bank to disclose any of these facts, since there was nothing in the contract between the bank and their customer, Mrs. Rolfs, which was unusual or which might not reasonably have been anticipated by the plaintiff, the surety. The fact that the account was overdrawn was disclosed. The orders given by the drawer of the cheques to the bank not to pay them were merely the method of operation of the account by the debtor, and the authority given by a wife to her husband to draw on her account is, in my opinion, not unusual, even where he is an undischarged bankrupt. It was not Mr. Rolfs' credit which was being guaranteed, it was his wife's and the facts known to the bank did not show that the account was, in reality, that of Mr. Rolfs, nor did the facts proved in evidence show this.'

Where, however, it is clear to the bank from the observations of the guarantor that he is under a misapprehension, there is a duty to correct him. For example, suppose that A is borrowing from the bank to finance the purchase of a new car for his private use and introduces B, his friend, as guarantor. If B in the course of conversation when he calls at the bank to sign the guarantee expresses his willingness to assist *A* to buy new machinery for his manufacturing business, there is a clear duty upon the bank to explain that the purpose of the advance is not to buy machinery but to purchase a new car. In *Royal Bank of Scotland* v. *Greenshields* [1914] S.C. 259, it was stated 'the only circumstances in which a duty to disclose would emerge and a failure to disclose would be fatal to the bank's case would be where a customer put a question or made an observation in the hearing of the bank agent which would inevitably lead anyone to the conclusion that the intending guarantor was labouring under a misapprehension as to the customer's indebtedness'. It is, therefore, incumbent upon the bank to correct any obviously wrong idea which the guarantor may show concerning the position.

Once the guarantee has been signed, there is no duty upon the bank to warn the guarantor of any change in the position. As will be seen later, the guarantee is expressed to cover any indebtedness of the borrower incurred whenever or for whatever reason the customer may overdraw, and it was decided in *National Provincial Bank of England Ltd.* v. *Glanusk* [1913] 3 K.B. 335 that failure on the part of the bank to disclose to an existing guarantor of an overdrawn account that it suspected that the borrower was defrauding the guarantor did not avoid the guarantee. In this case Lord Glanusk guaranteed the indebtedness of his agent who was also his brother-in-law. The latter opened a new account designated 'capital account' and transferred £1,000 therefrom by cheque in favour of another bank. The bank suspected that the money was being used to meet the personal debts of the drawer and it transpired that the transfer was fraudulent, but it was held that there was no obligation upon the bank to reveal that it was suspicious of the facts. In practice, however, it may often be prudent and equitable, although not legally essential, to warn the guarantor of any material weakening in the position of the borrower.

If the guarantor at the time of signing the guarantee asks questions concerning the borrower, care is necessary to ensure that they are correctly answered and that such disclosure does not amount to a breach of the banker's duty of secrecy concerning the customer's account. A too inquisitive guarantor should be held at bay until the permission of the customer can be obtained for undue revelations and the best course is then to arrange a tripartite conference between customer, guarantor and banker. It is doubtful whether, by introducing the guarantor, the customer *impliedly* consents to disclosure within the ambit of *Tournier* v. *National Provincial & Union Bank of England Ltd.* [1924] 1 K.B. 461. Far better to be discreet and obtain the express consent of the customer before making any detailed revelations.

Two further cases are worthy of brief mention to impress the legal position on the mind of the reader. In *Lloyds Bank* v. *Harrison* (1925)—Court of Appeal case not reported—a Mr. Buckle borrowed from the bank against a mortgage to finance his timber purchases and the bank called for additional security. Harrison was introduced as guarantor and signed a guarantee for £300. When action was brought by the bank against the guarantor, he contended *inter alia* that the bank had not made a sufficient disclosure to him of the borrower's position, which was serious. The bank had stipulated that the customer should accept only such business as would reduce his stock of timber and had insisted on the dismissal of four employees to reduce his wage bill. This was alleged to be tantamount to taking control of the customer's business and non-disclosure of such essential facts, it was claimed, released the guarantor. The bank succeeded at the Birmingham Assizes and the decision was upheld upon appeal. Both Sir E. M. Pollock, M.R., and Bankes, L.J., applied the test originally laid down by Lord Campbell in *Hamilton* v. *Watson (supra)* and Sargant, L.J., in supporting them said:—

'It must be remembered that in this case, as in most cases, the surety is approached in the first instance by the principal debtor, and is brought to the bank as a person who is willing to accept a certain responsibility in connection with the banking affairs of the principal debtor. Speaking generally, I should think the bank would be wrong in disclosing, without some very special direction by the customer, the whole particulars of the state of account of that customer to the surety. It may be expected that the customer who is bringing his friend along as a surety has explained the general nature of his position, and has explained it properly.

'Then, taking the test of *Hamilton* v. *Watson (supra)*, which is undoubtedly the leading case upon the subject, Lord Campbell pointed out very clearly what an extraordinary and unpractical obligation would be cast upon bankers if they were to be forced to disclose to a person becoming a surety for a cash account all the circumstances of the business relations of the customer whose account was proposed to be guaranteed. Of course, in every case there must be a large number of particular circumstances which do not occur in other cases, but, to adopt the language of Lord Campbell, there is no obligation on the banker to disclose anything that might naturally take place between the parties.

'Now, in this case what had taken place between the bank and the customer was this, that the customer apparently had been over-trading; he had exceeded slightly the overdraft of £750 which had been granted to him, and the bank made it a term of their continuing to keep his account and do business with him that he should provide a guarantee to the extent of £300, and that he should, to speak generally, restrict his business and curtail his over-trading. But they did not, apart from that, supervise or control his business in any ordinary sense of the term. That being so, is the circumstance that they have made an arrangement of that sort between themselves and their customer something which might not naturally be expected to be the case as between the banker and the customer? In my judgment it is just the kind of thing that might be expected as between the banker and the customer. And I will add this: it is an arrangement which I think would have the tendency of diminishing rather than increasing the liability of the proposed surety'.

In *Westminster Bank Ltd.* v. *Cond* (1940) 46 Com. Cas. 60, the guarantor attempted to avoid liability on the grounds that the guarantee was obtained by misrepresentation or concealment. Actually, eight years had elapsed since the signing of the guarantee and there was controversy with regard to what took place at the interview, but the guarantor did not enquire whether the account was already overdrawn and the manager did not voluntarily disclose the position. In reply to an enquiry concerning the customer's prospects, the bank manager said that he did not think much difficulty would be experienced in making repayment. In finding for the bank, Tucker, J., in his detailed review of the facts said:—

'Mere non-disclosure of a material fact is not sufficient to give relief, and in the case of a bank guarantee it has been clearly laid down that the bank manager is under no duty to disclose the existence of a subsisting overdraft, unless he is asked a question which would necessitate an answer dealing with that matter; but I think it is also clear that it is the duty of a bank manager, when he is asked a specific question, to give a true, honest and accurate answer to any question which is directed to him which can be in any way material to the giving of the guarantee'.

This exhaustive review of the legal background serves to emphasise that the greatest care is necessary when obtaining the signature of the guarantor to the guarantee. The endless legal phraseology of the document itself will be of little value if the guarantor's mind does not run with his pen and, as many guarantors will seek some loophole to try to wriggle out of the liability, patience and close attention is always necessary at the outset to ensure that the guarantee is valid. It is not a routine task but one demanding skill and knowledge and any attempt to rush the completion before the guarantor can regret his action is fraught with danger. The trouble arises when the security needs to be realised and carelessness can result in endless argument, even though legal action may not ultimately be necessary to recover the amount required.

PRACTICAL CONCLUSIONS RE POSSIBLE AVOIDANCE OF LIABILITY

To avoid any question of mistake, misrepresentation, or concealment of material facts, the guarantee should be executed in the presence of two or more senior officials of the bank, who should witness the guarantor's signature, and, in case of need, they can confirm what took place at the interview.

It must be made clear to the guarantor that he is signing a guarantee whereby he accepts full responsibility for the indebtedness of the principal debtor, subject always to the limitation of his liability to the stated amount of the guarantee, which sum the guarantor should preferably insert in the document himself.

There is no obligation on the bank to volunteer information, but questions raised by the guarantor have to be answered fully and truthfully, the permission of the customer being obtained where there may be any suggestion of a breach of the bank's duty of secrecy.

If it is apparent at the interview that the guarantor is under any wrong impression or has any doubt concerning the relative facts, the matter should be clarified beyond question. Do not gloss over the slightest suggestion of misunderstanding, but do not voluntarily hold forth at length on features which have not been raised by the guarantor. If any discussion arises concerning material facts, a suitable record of what was said should be made for future reference purposes.

When witnessing a guarantee given by a customer to secure an account at another branch or at another bank, do not express opinions or gloss over questions on points which cannot be answered without reference to the lending branch. If necessary, defer the completion of the guarantee until the required information can be obtained.

It is sufficient to describe the general nature of the guarantee liability and there is no need to enter into a detailed explanation of all the clauses in the document. The guarantor is presumed to know the contents of the guarantee when he has signed it and failure to read it is no excuse for avoidance of liability. But questions concerning specific clauses and conditions demand complete answers, so that the form of guarantee must be known and understood.

Above all, avoid any suggestion that the bank is persuading the guarantor to give the guarantee, or that completion of the document is merely a matter of form (perhaps just to satisfy the whim of a remote Head Office) and no liability is ever likely to arise.

VALIDITY OF SIGNATURE TO GUARANTEE

It may seem too obvious to mention that steps should always be taken to verify the guarantor's signature and yet a case of forged guarantees for appreciable amounts occurred only a few years ago. If the guarantee is signed in the presence of the guarantor's bank it can naturally verify the signature, but when the guarantor is a stranger and calls upon the lending bank at the instigation of the borrower to sign the guarantee the authenticity of his signature should promptly be verified by reference to his own banker, from whom enquiry has in any event to be made concerning his financial standing. This routine check is essential, otherwise any fraudulently minded person might pretend to be a reputable party of undoubted standing and sign a guarantee in such name to enable an accomplice to obtain accommodation against a worthless security. Beware of such a patent risk where the guarantor is not known personally to the bank accepting the guarantee or witnessing his signature.

TYPES OF GUARANTOR

To complete this review of the essential steps to ensure the validity of a guarantee, the requirements of certain types of guarantors have to be considered. The legal limitations on the capacity of the following guarantors to contract demand special precautions which are additional to, and not instead of, the general features which have already been discussed.

LADY GUARANTORS

Any lady who has attained eighteen years of age may accept full responsibility to the extent of her personal estate and, contrary to many beliefs, she is presumed at law to understand a business transaction and can be held liable without having the document first explained to her by a solicitor. The only occasions where a lady may be in a different position legally from that of a male guarantor are when she agrees to guarantee the account of her husband or the account of some limited company or other business in which he is interested. The risks of undue influence in such cases are much higher, but otherwise the possibility of mistake, misrepresentation, and the precautions to be taken by the bank to overcome such possibilities are precisely the same legally whichever the sex of the guarantor may be. After all, many ladies nowadays would resent any suggestions that they were unable to understand a business transaction or incapable of appreciating the nature of a bank guarantee. They certainly have no special protection on such grounds at law.

In practice, however, the prudent banker still adopts the view that a lady needs some legal guidance when faced with a guarantee and, to establish beyond doubt that she appreciates the nature of the contract and the extent of her liability, it is usual to have the guarantee signed by the lady, married or single, in the presence of her solicitor or an independent legal adviser who it cannot later be alleged was an agent of the bank. Such precautions may not be essential at law, but in practice they avoid any arguments or undue trouble when the banker requires payment from the lady concerned. She can hardly allege mistake or misrepresentation, quite apart from undue influence, if the guarantee was executed in the presence of her solicitor who explained the transaction and liability to her. Moreover, if the rule is that all guarantees by ladies should be witnessed by a solicitor, the occasional case where the possibility of undue influence may arise will assuredly be covered. It is, however, taking the practice too far to expect the signature of a spinster to be witnessed by a solicitor when she signs a joint and several guarantee for the account of a limited company of which she is a director. Care may be necessary where man and wife are the only directors of a limited company and the wife's interest is relatively small. As a director engaged in the business, she may have difficulty in proving undue influence, but advice from a solicitor when signing the guarantee may nevertheless be a prudent practical precaution. No banker expects to have to bring action against the guarantor to obtain payment, and whilst the Courts may quickly dispose of any plea by a lady guarantor of mistake, it is better to place the matter beyond doubt at the outset, removing in practice any loophole for attempted avoidance of liability. The general rule in practice, therefore, is to have every guarantee by a lady witnessed by her solicitor and to make few exceptions in approved cases. Precaution is always better than cure, and such a general rule avoids the occasional risk of mistake or undue influence.

JOINT AND SEVERAL GUARANTORS

From the standpoint of validity, the important point with joint and several guarantees is that all those who have agreed to be guarantors must sign before any of them can be held liable. Where the bank is relying solely on such security, no advance should therefore be granted until all the parties named in the guarantee have actually signed it. In *National Provincial Bank of England* v. *Brackenbury* (1906) 22 T.L.R. 797, four persons were to be joint and several guarantors but one died before he could sign the guarantee. The bank had granted accommodation relying upon due completion of the guarantee, but it was decided that the three who had signed it were not liable. To avoid dispute where one of several guarantors fails to complete the document, a letter should be obtained from all the others agreeing to be liable despite the missing signature. The safest and usually simplest course in practice is to start afresh and to obtain a new guarantee from the signatories to the original.

GUARANTEES BY A FIRM

A partner may only bind his firm in the ordinary course of business and, as the giving of guarantees will be outside the normal business of the average partnership, *all* partners should be required to sign a guarantee by a firm. The signing of a guarantee by one partner in the firm name or on behalf of the firm will not bind his co-partners (*Brettel* v. *Williams* (1849) 4 Ex 623). In practice the joint and several guarantee of all partners should be obtained to cover the position.

GUARANTEES BY A LIMITED COMPANY

A limited company can only do such things as it is empowered to do by its memorandum of association and, whilst certain powers may be implied in the course of business, the power to give guarantees must be expressly granted in the objects clause of the memorandum. There can be no implied power for a company to guarantee the debt or obligation of a third party and guarantees given without express power will be *ultra vires* the company and void *ab initio*.

When offered the guarantee of a limited company, the banker must, therefore, examine the memorandum of association of the potential guarantor to ensure that there is an express power to give guarantees. Unless the power is clearly laid down therein the guarantee should not be relied upon. In case of need, a memorandum can now be amended within Section 5 of the Companies Act, 1948, to cover the point. Whether or not the power is sufficient depends entirely upon the exact wording of the relative objects clause and in the absence of an independent objects clause, the transactions may have to be related to the general business of the company. The phrase 'to subsidise or otherwise assist' was held in *In re Friary Holroyd and Healey's Breweries Ltd.* [1922] W.N. 293 to include the giving of a guarantee, but it is preferable to see words which leave the power beyond doubt.

In order to justify—in a legal sense—the giving of a guarantee by a company it may sometimes be necessary to show that some benefit has accrued to the surety. For example, a guarantee may be offered by a company which has no business relationship with the borrower and in such a case, even if the giving of guarantees was within the objects of the former, the undertaking might not be enforceable if there is no direct or indirect benefit. To avoid the possible difficulty of proving such advantage, some authorities have suggested that the payment of 'an appropriate fee' to the company giving the guarantee is advisable. Although the case was concerned with different issues, the findings in *Parke* v. *Daily News Ltd.* (1961) 1 W.L.R. 493; (1962) *The Times* June 6 are of interest in this regard.

If the company is fully empowered to give guarantees, any guarantee must be executed in the manner laid down, if any, in the articles of association. Usually it can be given under the seal of the company or under hand by officials duly appointed to do so by resolution of the board. A certified copy of such resolution should be held by the bank and should include a specimen of the guarantee which the stated directors are authorised to sign. This is to avoid any argument later that the guarantee actually signed differed from that which was approved by the board.

Close attention must be given to all these legal points if the validity of a limited company guarantee is to be beyond question.

GUARANTEES BY INFANTS

An infant is legally incapable of entering into a guarantee liability (Section 1, Infants Relief Act, 1874), and the contract cannot be ratified after majority. It is, therefore, advisable to ensure that any youthful guarantor is over eighteen years of age: (Family Law Reform Act 1969 Section 1).

GUARANTEES TO SECURE BORROWING BY INFANTS

A guarantee to secure the indebtedness of an infant will be invalid because it is expressed to cover a debt which is not legally enforceable. Under Section 1 of the Infants Relief Act, 1874, loans to an infant are void and it is the essence of a guarantee that there should be a valid obligation of a principal debtor. See *Coutts & Co.* v. *Brown-Lecky & Ors.* [1947] K.B. 104.

To overcome this, some banks have inserted in their forms of guarantee a clause which renders the third party liable as principal debtor if the borrower is under any incapacity (*Yeoman Credit Ltd.* v. *Latter* (1961) 1 W.L.R. 828). Alternatively, a bank may decide to lend to an infant in joint account with an adult, the adult being fixed with liability for any borrowing permitted on the joint account.

It is also of interest to note that there is an exception to the general rule that immediately an infant comes of full age he or she has full contractual capacity. The exception arises in the case of a person who has recently come of age and guarantees a parent or someone who has stood in that relationship. Owing to the nature of the special relationship undue influence is presumed to exist, even if the child is married and living away from home, and exactly when the domination ceases is for the Courts to decide in the light of the facts of each case: (*Lancashire Loans Ltd.* v. *Black* (1934) 1 K.B. 380).

Part Two: Guarantees (continued)

Chapter V The Form and Contents of the Guarantee

CONSIDERATION—AMOUNT OF GUARANTOR'S LIABILITY—DEMAND AND DETERMINATION

The last essential of a valid, enforceable and satisfactory guarantee to a bank is the form thereof, and consideration of this requisite entails a review of the common law rights of a guarantor and of all the special clauses required to ensure complete security to the bank and reasonable protection to the customer borrowing, usually, on a fluctuating overdraft. A contract of guarantee must be in writing and every bank nowadays has its own printed forms of guarantee which have been drafted and redrafted by legal experts in the light of experience over many decades. They are lengthy documents replete with legal phrases, but every clause is essential and every known contingency is covered. Although they may differ slightly in detail with varying phraseology, they all cover the same essentials and the usual features may, therefore, be discussed under separate headings, with reasons quoted for the inclusion of each clause.

One word of warning at the outset. Every clause is important and has been drafted in a particular manner for a special reason. *No amendment of or addition to the printed document should ever be made* without the complete approval of the legal adviser of the bank. To alter or in any way interfere with the provisions is to court disaster, as will be seen when the relatively recent case of *Westminster Bank Ltd.* v. *Sassoon* (1926) *The Times*, November 27 is examined later. The printed form demands the greatest respect. It is the work of legal experts over the years and cannot with safety be tampered with by a practical banker or by a guarantor wishing to limit or amend his liability. The reason for the introduction of each clause and its interpretation and effect upon the guarantor and the borrower will be analysed fully as the picture unfolds.

THE PARTIES TO THE GUARANTEE

At the outset the guarantee will be addressed to the lending bank and space will be left in which to insert the name and address of the borrowing customer, described thereafter as 'the Principal'. There will then follow a space in which the full name and description of the guarantor can be inserted. When completed, the three parties to the contract are all clearly described and defined—the lender, the principal debtor, and the guarantor.

CONSIDERATION CLAUSE

From the strict legal standpoint, it is not necessary to record in a guarantee the consideration for which it is given (Section 3, Mercantile Law Amendment Act, 1856), but a bank guarantee usually includes a clause describing why the guarantor has undertaken the liability. This may, or may not, refer to borrowing by the principal. It is quite sufficient to state that it is given in consideration of the bank opening and conducting or continuing an account for the principal for so long as the bank may deem fit, but it is perhaps more usual to refer to the making or continuing of advances or otherwise granting credit for so long as the bank may think fit. It is important to realise that the consideration should not be expressed as the lending of a stated sum as it often is in a loan arrangement between private persons. For example, a clause which read 'In consideration of your advancing £1,000 to XYZ, I hereby guarantee' would be liable to be upset if the bank advanced more or less than the quoted amount. To ensure that the guarantee would be binding upon the guarantor, the bank would have to lend precisely £1,000 to the stated customer (see *Burton* v. *Gray* (1873) 8 Ch. App. 932, discussed below).

Past consideration will not support a guarantee, except when it is given under seal, and it is therefore essential that the consideration clause should not refer merely to the making of advances because it might not cover advances already granted before the execution of the guarantee. On the other hand, forbearance to sue or the grant of extended time for payment at the request of the guarantor constitute valid consideration and may even be implied from the taking of the security (*Clegg* v. *Bromley* (1912) 3 K.B. 491). Such risks are usually avoided by the expressions 'opening or continuing an account' or 'continuing advances', but the decision in *Provincial Bank of Ireland* v. *Donnell* [1934] N.I. 33, is worthy of note in this respect. Mr. Donnell had an overdraft of £1,270 from the bank secured *inter alia* by two life policies, on one of which there was an annual premium of £24 12s. 0d. The overdraft was dormant from October, 1923. In November, 1924, Mrs. Donnell guaranteed under hand payment of the life policy premiums, the consideration in the form being expressed to be in consideration of advances 'heretofore made or that may hereafter be made from time to time' by the bank to Mr. Donnell. At this stage the bank had no intention of lending any more to its customer. The life policy premiums were duly paid up to December, 1931, and a fresh guarantee in the same terms was taken from Mrs. Donnell in January, 1931. There was no threat by the bank to sue Mr. Donnell and no talk of any agreement not to sue him. When he defaulted in payment of the premium due in December, 1931, Mrs. Donnell paid it on request from the bank, but when she failed to meet her guarantee for the 1932 premiums the bank sued her on the guarantee. It was decided that the guarantee was void because the existing debt did not form consideration necessary to support the guarantee. A past or executed consideration, unless moved at the guarantor's request, is not binding without some new consideration. An agreement by a creditor to forbear to sue for a past debt is a sufficient consideration. The bank contended that the words 'in consideration of advances heretofore made' meant 'in consideration of your not suing my husband for advances already made to him', but Andrews, L.J., declined to accept this argument, stating 'one ought to be slow in implying consideration in favour of the bank whose document the guarantee is, especially when one remembers that when the guarantee was signed they did not stand to the defendant in the relationship of debtor and creditor'. Even if there was in fact a forbearance to sue, there was no evidence that it arose from any express or implied request by Mrs. Donnell. Moreover, there was no agreement binding on the bank to make fresh advances. This case is a graphic illustration of the care required in wording the consideration clause in any bank guarantee.

LIABILITY OF GUARANTOR DEFINED
The liability of the guarantor will then be defined at length and it will be found that he undertakes and agrees to pay *on demand* all advances or other liabilities whatsoever owing to the bank by the principal anywhere on any account whether solely or jointly, plus interest, commission and other banking charges including legal expenses. In other words, the guarantor accepts responsibility for every possible amount which the principal may owe to the bank when demand is made, subject to a limitation on his maximum liability which, for preference, should be inserted in the guarantee by the guarantor in his own handwriting. The limitation may read '*Provided always that the total amount for which I shall ultimately be liable under this guarantee shall not exceed one hundred pounds, plus interest thereon at the rate of . . . . per cent per annum from the date of demand by the bank for payment*'.

Why does this limitation of the guarantor's liability appear in a separate sentence after so many words have been used to describe that the guarantee is for the whole debt of the principal? It would certainly be much more simple to quote a fixed liability. There are two reasons why the whole debt is guaranteed subject to a limitation on the amount recoverable.

In the first place, as mentioned above, a guarantee expressed 'in consideration of the bank advancing £100 to XYZ, I guarantee the due repayment thereof' could be upset if the bank did not comply with the precise wording thereof and lend exactly £100 to its customer. The limitation is in the wrong place. In *Burton* v. *Gray* (*ante*) it was alleged that Burton had signed a letter in the following terms 'In consideration of your banking company' ending to Mr. Frederick Burton' (brother of the plaintiff) '£1,000 for seven days from the date I deposit with you the several documents mentioned in the schedule . . . as a security'. Actually the bank allowed its customer to draw a number of cheques but the resulting overdraft was less than £1,000. It was held that, as the bank had not fulfilled the condition precedent and the period of the overdraft had not been limited, the depositor of the securities was not liable. Obviously no bank desires to be tied to advance a stated sum and the liability of the guarantor cannot be qualified in this manner.

Secondly, and this is of much greater importance, the guarantee for the whole debt is required to safeguard the bank's position in the event of the bankruptcy of the principal debtor, and also to avoid the common law rights of a guarantor who meets his liability under a guarantee for part only of the principal's debt to the bank. These rights of a guarantor may be summarised at this stage. They are strictly applied at law and, therefore, carefully and completely removed by the bank in express terms contained in the guarantee. To quote the Earl of Selborne, L.C., *In re Sherry* (1884) 25 Ch. D. 692, 'A surety is undoubtedly and not unjustly the object of some favour, both at law and in equity. It is an equity which enters into our system of law that a man who makes himself liable for another person's debt is not to be prejudiced by any dealings without his consent, between the secured creditor and the principal debtor'.

In the absence of special provisions in the guarantee to the contrary, the guarantor when he meets his liability under the guarantee steps into the shoes of the creditor and obtains all the rights and remedies which the creditor possessed. He may sue the principal debtor in the name of the creditor (*Swire* v. *Redman*, (1876) 1 Q.B.D. 536) or after obtaining an assignment of the debt he may sue in his own name. The guarantor upon payment is also entitled to any securities which the borrower may have given to the lender (*Ex parte Crisp* (1744) 1 Atk. 133), whether he was aware of such securities at the time when he gave the guarantee or not (*Forbes* v. *Jackson* (1882) 19 Ch. D. 615). Moreover, where the guarantor contracts to be responsible for only part of the amount due to the creditor, he inherits all the rights of the creditor in respect of that amount upon payment of his liability and is thereby entitled to share *pro rata* in any security which the lender may hold for the entire indebtedness (*Goodwin* v. *Gray* (1874) 22 W.R. 312). These rights extend to collateral, as well as direct security held by the bank. Such complications obviously cannot be allowed to outstand and interfere between banker and customer so they have to be removed expressly in the guarantee.

Upon bankruptcy of the principal debtor the guarantor can prove in his estate for payments made under his guarantee and, as there cannot be two proofs for the same debt, the bank could not prove for the same amount. The proof of the bank would, therefore, have to be reduced by the amount received from the guarantor, and the dividend ultimately collected would be correspondingly smaller.

Apart from express terms in the document excluding these rights from the guarantor, the formula whereby the whole debt is guaranteed subject to a limitation on the maximum liability of the guarantor means that unless and until he pays the entire indebtedness of the principal to the bank he cannot claim any other securities which the bank may hold, or he cannot make any proof in bankruptcy. Two examples will serve to emphasise the value of this provision before reference is made to case law on the subject.

Suppose Southtown Bank lent £2,000 to Z secured by quoted shares worth £1,600 and the guarantee of M for £500 expressed to be for that amount only. If M pays up under his guarantee, he will be entitled to one-fourth of the shares held by the bank. Thus M takes £400 security and reduces the bank's holding to £1,200, which, with £500 cash from M, leaves a deficiency of £300. If M contracted in the guarantee to be liable for the entire indebtedness of Z provided always that the liability ultimately enforceable against him would not exceed £500, he could not touch the other security until he repaid the whole debt of Z to the bank.

Now take the case of customer P, whose bank debt when he was adjudicated bankrupt amounted to £1,200 secured only by the guarantee of Q expressed to be for £600. After meeting his liability to the bank, Q proves for £600 in the bankrupt's estate and the bank's proof has to be reduced from £1,200 to £600. A dividend of 50p in the £ is eventually paid and the bank collects £300, plus £600 already received from Q, and sustains a loss of £300. If the guarantee had been drawn in such terms that Q guaranteed the entire debt of P, subject to a maximum liability of £600, the bank's position would have been much better. Unless Q paid off the whole debt, he could not compete with the bank in the bankruptcy, and the bank would be able to prove for £1,200, receiving a dividend of £600, plus £600 from Q, so suffering no loss.

The importance of this full liability formula is thus evident and it was tried and upheld in *In Re Sass ex parte National Provincial Bank of England Ltd.* [1896] 2 Q.B. 12. Mr. Sass borrowed £755 from National Provincial Bank, which held as security the guarantee of a Mr. Stourton expressed to be for the entire debt but subject to a maximum liability of £300, plus charges. The customer was adjudicated bankrupt and, when the bank served demand on the guarantor, he promptly paid £303 to discharge his liability. This amount was credited by the bank to a security-realised account and held in suspense whilst it lodged a proof for £755 against the estate of the bankrupt customer. The trustee contended that the proof should be reduced by £303, being the amount the bank had already received from the guarantor, but it was held by the Court that the proof for £755 was correct and had to be accepted. In the words of Vaughan Williams J., 'the surety here became a surety for the whole of the debt. It is true that his liability was to be limited; but still, notwithstanding that his suretyship was in respect of the whole debt, and he, having paid only a part of that debt, has in my judgment no right of proof in preference or priority to the bank to whom he became guarantor'. (*Also see 'Re Houlder'* [1929] 1 *Ch.* 205 *and Ulster Bank Ltd.* v. *Lambe* [1966] *N.I.* 161).

In actual fact most bank forms of guarantee emphasise the rights of the bank in the event of bankruptcy by introducing special clauses expressly excluding the guarantor from competing with the bank for any dividend. Such clauses merely make the position clearer to the guarantor, who in any event, where he guarantees the whole debt, cannot prove in the bankruptcy of the debtor unless he first liquidates the debt of the principal to the bank.

NEED FOR DEMAND ON GUARANTOR

These liabilities of the guarantor are expressed to be payable *on demand* thereby ensuring that the guarantee cannot be statute barred until six years have elapsed from the date when demand is made upon the guarantor. This is a most essential feature and if it were omitted the bank would have to take a fresh guarantee every six years with the consequent problems of diary records and trouble to the guarantor. In *Parrs Banking Co* v. *Yates* [1898] 2 Q.B. 460, the bank sued a guarantor who pleaded the Statute of Limitations, 1623, contending that as no fresh advances had been made by the bank for more than six years before the issue of the writ the claim was barred. The guarantee, although a continuing security, did not include an undertaking by the guarantor to pay upon demand and it was decided that the cause of action on the guarantee arose as to each item of the account as soon as it became due and consequently the Statute of Limitations began to run in favour of the guarantor in respect of each debit from the date it appeared in the account. Compared with this decision, the on-demand-clause was upheld in *Bradford Old Bank Ltd.* v. *Sutcliffe* [1918] 2 K.B. 833, where it was stated by Pickford, L.J.: 'In my opinion there was no cause of action till after demand, and the plea of the Statute of Limitations therefore fails'.

The bank obtains the right to determine the guarantee by calling for payment and the guarantor agrees to pay upon demand, usually undertaking also to pay interest at 5 per cent. per annum from the date of demand to the time of payment. There is no obligation upon the banker to sue the debtor or realise other security before calling upon the guarantor. According to Lord Eldon in *Wright* v. *Simpson*

49

D

(1802) 6 Ves. 714, 'It is his (the guarantor's) business to see whether the principal pays and not that of the creditor'. In short, the guarantor's liability is determined when demand is served on him.

DETERMINATION BY GUARANTOR

How and when may the guarantor seek to determine his liability? The guarantee has to be a continuing security to cover the ultimate indebtedness of the borrower and it would obviously complicate business dealings and embarrass the customer if the guarantor retained any right to determine his liability on demand to the bank. Suitable provision has, therefore, to be made in the guarantee to ensure that reasonable time can be given to the borrower to complete outstanding dealings and make other arrangements before the guarantor can close down on the position. The normal period is three months, and the relative clause in the guarantee may read '*I agree that this Guarantee shall be binding as a continuing security on me until the expiration of three calendar months' written notice given to the bank of my intention to discontinue and determine it and in the event of my death the liability of my estate will continue until the expiration of three calendar months' written notice given to the bank by my executors or administrators of their intention to determine the guarantee*'.

What is the legal and practical effect of any clause on these lines? To start with the operation of the Rule in *Clayton's Case* is excluded by the use of the words '*continuing security*'. This is essential, otherwise every payment into the account after completion of the guarantee would reduce the liability of the guarantor and every payment out would be unsecured by the guarantee. As the bank usually advances on current account, it is the final balance which has to be secured when the guarantee is determined. The legal effect of the remainder of the clause is beyond question if the words are construed as they are intended to be read. The account of the customer can be continued for the period of notice and the guarantor will be liable for the balance outstanding at the end of the period. Whether a bank in practice always relies on this strict interpretation of the clause depends usually on the facts of the case, but normally it will give some thought to the equitable rights of the guarantor which were recognised in *Hollond* v. *Teed* (1848) 7 Hare 50. The right of the guarantor to determine his liability is clearly limited by the stipulation for three months' notice and, where it is laid down that on the death of the guarantor three months' notice is necessary from his personal representatives, such provision is binding upon his estate (*Coulthard* v. *Clementson* (1879) 5 Q.B.D. 42).

In practice, difficulty may arise because the bank may think it inequitable to allow the borrower to take full advantage of the special notice period. Suppose that A has an arrangement to borrow up to £1,000 at any one time from Southtown Bank against the security of Z's guarantee for the entire debt, subject to a limit of £1,000 on his liability. When A's account is debit £150, Z gives notice of determination of his guarantee. To stop the account forthwith may completely upset outstanding business commitments of A which he has entered into safe in the knowledge of his overdraft limit at the bank. The bank can hardly dishonour cheques issued or about to be drawn in respect of such *bona fide* commitments. On the other hand, it would be most inequitable for Z if the bank allowed A to draw right up to £1,000, regardless of any business engagements, as soon as notice of determination was received from Z. An equitable medium course can usually be steered by arrangement between the debtor and the guarantor. In this example, no doubt, Southtown Bank would interview A upon receipt of the notice from Z and agree to pay all cheques drawn and to be drawn in respect of commitments already undertaken, but decline to grant further accommodation for fresh transactions. The acknowledgement of the notice from Z would call attention to the guarantee provisions and emphasise that his liability outstands until three months have elapsed from the date of receipt of the request for determination. It is unwise to accept the notice as operating forthwith, notwithstanding the fact that the debt of the customer to the bank is repayable upon demand. Fortunately, delicate situations do not often arise in practice because the borrower is so often at or near the agreed maximum indebtedness when the guarantor gives notice to determine his liability. The provision whereby three months' notice is required from the personal representatives to determine the liability of the deceased guarantor is legally binding, but in practice rarely relied upon. The debtor's account will be stopped upon, or shortly after, receipt of notice of the guarantor's death, providing such action does not unduly embarrass the borrower in respect of current business transactions.

To complete this discussion of the way in which a guarantee may be determined, reference can be made to *Westminster Bank Ltd.* v. *Sassoon* (1926) *The Times*, November 27, which furnishes a graphic warning of the dangers of altering the printed form of guarantee, to which reference was made at the start of this chapter. Mrs. Giulia Sassoon agreed to guarantee the indebtedness of the Marquis Guido Serra di Cassana to Westminster Bank on the understanding that her liability was limited to £1,700 for one year. The guarantee form was, therefore, altered by the addition of the following words at the end 'This guarantee will *expire* upon June 30, 1925'. Payment was not demanded by the bank until October, 1925, when it called for £1,673. The intention of the bank was, of course, to limit the liability of the guarantor to the balance outstanding on the customer's account at June 30, when the account was actually stopped. Mrs. Sassoon contended that she could not be liable for any claims made after that date and, when Rowland J., decided that it was a continuing guarantee and gave judgment for the bank, with costs, she appealed. The Court of Appeal likewise rejected her argument, upholding the view that it was a continuing guarantee and she was liable for the balance at the given date. There was a provision that the guarantee could be terminated by the guarantor giving three months' notice, but there was nothing to limit the period of her liability in the way she contended. A more careful amendment would have avoided the need for troubling the Court to interpret this guarantee.

Part Two: Guarantees (continued)

Chapter VI The Form and Contents of the Guarantee— continued

PROVISIONS REGARDING ARRANGEMENTS WITH CUSTOMER—CLAYTON'S CASE—LEGAL INCAPACITY OF PRINCIPAL

In addition to the main clauses in a guarantee which were discussed in Chapter V, many important subsidiary and definitive clauses are usually added to bind the guarantor and to place the bank's position beyond doubt. These may embrace any of the points considered in this chapter.

RESERVATION OF RIGHT TO VARY THE POSITION AND CONTRACT WITH THE BORROWER

At common law any variation of the terms of the contract between the banker and the borower or principal debtor would enable the guarantor to claim to be released from his liability. In other words, any action by the bank which would weaken the position of the guarantor in relation to the debtor would be grounds for avoidance of his obligation. The rights of the guarantor to other securities held by the bank have already been explained and, if a bank released securities to the borrower without the permission of the guarantor, he would lose his right of taking over such security or of obtaining any contribution from a co-surety or collateral depositor. In such event, he would be entitled to a reduction of liability *pro rata* to the extent to which his own protection had suffered. In the same way, if the bank grants time to the borrower in which to repay the debt without the consent of the guarantor, the rights of the latter have been varied and he can claim to be discharged from his liability, even though he may not have been prejudiced by the action of the bank (*Bolton* v. *Buckenham* [1891] 1 Q.B. 278). By granting time to the borrower for repayment, the bank would upset the right of the guarantor to decide whether to meet his liability and then to attempt to recover from the principal debtor. If the latter has been given special permission to defer repayment, the right of the guarantor to recover from this is correspondingly affected, and on such grounds the guarantor might contend that he is discharged from liability under the guarantee. According to Blackburn, J., in *Polak* v. *Everett* (1876 1 Q.B.D. 669, if this right of a guarantor 'be suspended for a day or an hour, not injuring the surety to the value of one farthing, and even positively benefiting him, nevertheless by the principles of equity, it is established that this discharges the surety altogether'.

Many cases happen in practice when the bank wishes to come to some special arrangement with the borrowing customer regardless of the legal rights of the guarantor. It may be necessary to release direct or other collateral security without any reduction in the peak borrowing, or to agree to a voluntary composition to avoid the expense of the bankruptcy of the borrower (thereby denying to the guarantor his right upon payment of his liability to make the debtor bankrupt), or to 'give time' to the customer in which to repay the debt. Variations of this kind do arise and it would obviously be impracticable if the banker had always to discuss the position with the guarantor and to obtain his express consent to the proposed action. Apart from the delays which would inevitably occur, the bank's position might be prejudiced by the refusal of the guarantor to approve the proposals. To place the position beyond doubt and to leave the bank free from the fetters of the guarantor's common law rights, express provision is usually made in the guarantee to ensure complete freedom of action and choice to the bank. A clause on the following lines overcomes all the difficulties and removes the normal rights of the guarantor.

I hereby agree that the Bank shall be at liberty without any further consent from me and without thereby in any way affecting my liability under this guarantee at any time to determine enlarge or vary any credit to the Principal and to vary exchange abstain from perfecting or release any other securities bills notes mortgages charges liens received or to be received from the Principal or any other person or persons and to grant time to and to compound with or accept composition from and make other arrangements with the Principal or any persons liable on any such other securities held or to be held by the Bank.

In other words, the bank obtains a free hand to deal as it may wish with the borrowing customer and with any other guarantors or depositors of tangible collateral security. The value of a clause on these lines may be illustrated by reference to *Perry* v. *National Provincial Bank of England* [1910] 1 Ch. 464, which confirms that a guarantor may contract out of the rights afforded to him by law. Here, the guarantor, Perry, had mortgaged certain deeds to the bank to secure the indebtedness of a partnership customer and the bank, without reference to him, released the customers from liability under an arrangement whereby it obtained instead debentures in a limited company incorporated to take over the assets of the original borrower. Perry then claimed his release from liability on the grounds that, as the bank had forgiven the principal debtor, his guarantee liability was finished. The mortgage by Perry to the bank, however, included terms enabling the bank 'to vary exchange or release any other securities held or to be held by the bank for or on account of the moneys thereby secured . . . and to compound with give time for payment of and accept compositions from and make any other arrangements with the debtors,' and the bank contended that its rights against him thereby remained. It was decided upon appeal that Perry continued to be liable to the bank, the decisive factor being the terms of the clause which has just been quoted. In the words of Buckley, L.J., 'There is an agreement and declaration that the bank should be at liberty to do certain things, including to compound with the debtor without forfeiting their rights under the instrument. The effect I apprehend is this. The surety mortgages his property to secure the principal debt, and the bank may, if they please, compound with the borrower, by which I understand that they may accept from him a sum less than the amount of the debt upon the terms that they shall not sue for the balance, and this deed provides that that may be done without affecting the bank's right against the surety'. Perhaps the following words from the judgment of Sir H. H. Cozens-Hardy

Master of the Rolls, are even more helpful—'it is perfectly possible for a surety to contract with a creditor in the suretyship instrument that notwithstanding any composition, release or arrangement the surety shall remain liable although the principal debtor does not'.

The need to ensure that variations in the contract between the bank and the principal debtor are covered was further illustrated in the Privy Council case of *National Bank of Nigeria* v. *Awolesi* (1965) reported in THE BANKERS' MAGAZINE for January 1965.

With such a clause the bank thus retains a completely free hand and the guarantor contracts out of his common law rights. It is as well to mention this aspect generally to the guarantor at the time when the guarantee is signed, as many may not realise the purport of the clause. Failure to understand the terms of the guarantee will not, however, in itself, excuse the guarantor from liability because he is presumed to know the contents and implication of the contract he has signed.

COVENANT NOT TO TAKE SECURITY FROM THE DEBTOR

Clearly where a bank lends £1,000 to X against the security of a guarantee for £1,000 by Y and the latter thereupon obtains say £1,000 Savings Bonds from X as security for his liability the financial strength of the customer has been weakened by the security given to Y and, if the bank later lends a further £500 to X without fresh security, its position will be prejudiced by Y in the event of the failure of X. To avoid this risk, however remote it may appear to be, and to stop the guarantor from protecting himself at the expense of the bank, a special clause is usually incorporated in the guarantee whereby the guarantor promises not to accept security from the debtor without the approval of the bank and further covenants that if he nevertheless does accept security the amount of the claim of the bank against him will be increased by an amount equivalent to the decrease in the dividend received by the bank from the debtor's estate as a result of the guarantor's breach of the contract.

A clause to cover this point may read somewhat as follows:—'*I declare that I have not taken and that I will not take from the principal either directly or indirectly without the consent of the Bank any security whatsoever in respect of any liability hereby undertaken by me and I further agree that in the event of my taking any such security the amount of my liability under this guarantee shall be increased by an amount equivalent to that which the dividend payable by the Principal to the Bank is thereby reduced, or the security so taken without the consent of the Bank shall be security to the Bank for any liability hereunder and shall be charged by me to the Bank for that purpose*'.

The trouble in practice is that few guarantors are aware of this specific arrangement at the time when they sign the guarantee and the covenant is therefore frequently broken. It is not unusual to find that a guarantor has obtained some form of security from the debtor, but no case has yet been reported of action by a bank on the clause because its position has been so prejudiced by the guarantor. But the clause is there and could be enforced. The practical solution is surely to call the attention of the guarantor to this special undertaking at the time when the guarantee is signed.

RIGHT OF SET-OFF AGAINST GUARANTOR

Where the guarantor is a customer of the lending banker, it is useful when the guarantee liability is determined to have immediate recourse to any credit balance on the account of the guarantor and, to avoid the need for a special arrangement outside the guarantee, a clause will usually be included in the document whereby the bank so long as any moneys remain owing under the guarantee has a lien on all moneys now or hereafter standing to the credit of the guarantor with the bank, whether on current or other account. This avoids the need for obtaining a special letter of set-off from the guarantor customer.

CHANGES IN CONSTITUTION OF PARTIES

During the course of the advance the constitution of the borrowing customer or principal debtor may change. There may be an alteration in the partners in a firm or trustees or joint account borrowers may change. In the normal course the bank will stop the borrower's account in such circumstances to retain the liability of the deceased or outgoing parties, but to cover inadvertent omissions in this respect and to protect the bank against any changes in the constitution of the principal debtor which may occur without the knowledge of the bank, a special clause is inserted in the guarantee reading perhaps—'*If it shall so happen that the Principal herein named shall be a firm or limited company or other corporation or any committee or association or other unincorporated body or debtors on a joint account then the guarantee shall continue to be effective notwithstanding any death, retirement, addition or other change as completely as if the persons constituting such firm, limited company or other body, committee, association or unincorporate body at the date of the Principal's default or at any time before that was or were the same as at the date of the guarantee*'. This is a protective clause inserted in abundance of caution to remove any doubt and to protect the bank against failure to adopt the normal precaution of breaking the account.

To cover the possibility from the other side that the lending bank may subsequently change its name or amalgamate, a declaration is usually inserted to the effect that the expression or description of 'the bank' wherever used in the guarantee shall include and extend to its successors and assigns.

SECURITY ADDITIONAL TO THE GUARANTEE

Another protective clause often inserted to overcome any doubts or practical errors is a statement that the guarantee is *in addition to and not in substitution for* any other guarantee for the principal given by the same guarantor to the bank. This avoids any contention by a guarantor that his second or later guarantee was intended to replace the one or those already held by the bank. As a guarantor frequently gives more than one guarantee for the same account, the phrase is valuable, but it is usually better business tactics to obtain a fresh guarantee for the total liability on all guarantees given and promised.

AVOIDING THE OPERATION OF THE RULE IN CLAYTON'S CASE UPON DETERMINATION

The operation of the Rule in *Clayton's Case* during the term of the guarantee is removed by making it a continuing security for the ultimate balance owing upon determination (by the clauses explained in Chapter V), but when the guarantee is properly determined in accordance with the terms thereof and the bank omits to stop the account, any credits received afterwards will reduce the liability of the guarantor, whilst fresh withdrawals will not be his responsibility. To cover the risk of error in this respect, some banks have introduced a special provision into the guarantee form and the efficacy of such a clause was proved in *Westminster Bank Ltd. v. Cond* (1940) 46 Com. Cases 60. In this case Westminster Bank served demand for payment upon the guarantor on August 29, 1933, but it did not stop the borrower's account and action was not brought to recover the amount of the guarantee liability until just before the expiration of six years from the date of demand. The guarantor contended that by the application of the Rule in *Clayton's Case* to the unbroken account, payments to the credit received after the date of demand had discharged his liability.

After referring to Lord Selborne's interpretation of the Rule in *Clayton's Case* in *In re Sherry* (1884) 25 Ch.D. 692 (see below) Tucker, J., said:—

'In the particular case with which I am now dealing the account was not ruled-off, but it was one unbroken account and continued as one unbroken account; and, as at present advised—it is not necessary for me to give any decision on the matter—*were it not for the terms of this particular guarantee* I should be inclined to the view that the rule in *Clayton's Case* might quite well have applied to the present circumstances; that is to say, one unbroken account remaining on and not ruled-off, and no fresh account started. I think it may well be that in such circumstances the payments should or would have been regarded as appropriated according to the priority in order of entries on one side and the other of that account. That being the position, and a position well known to all persons concerned with banking, this particular guarantee under which the bank are suing contains these words: "*In the event of this guarantee being determined either by notice by me or my legal representatives, or by demand in writing by the bank, it shall be lawful for the bank to continue the account with the Principal notwithstanding such determination, and liability of myself or my estate for the amount due by the Principal at the date when the guarantee is so determined shall remain, notwithstanding any subsequent payment into or out of the account by or on behalf of the Principal*". I think that those words are apt to prevent the application of the rule in *Clayton's Case*. I cannot help thinking that they were expressly so to do, and I think that they have achieved that object. The result is that the guarantor becomes liable for the amount due from the principal debtor *when the guarantee was determined*. Once that sum has been ascertained, that represents the liability of the guarantor'.

Judgment was, therefore, given for the bank.

Nevertheless, where a clause of this kind designed, expressly to combat the application of the Rule in *Clayton's Case* is contained in the guarantee, it is far better in practice to stop the account promptly upon determination of the guarantee and so to place the position beyond doubt and avoid possible acrimony. The prudent banker will merely look upon the clause as an insurance against failure to follow the established procedure and not accept it as a reliable reason for omitting to break the account. It is there as a memorial to the ingenuity of the draftsmen in protecting the bank against all known risks and is of proved worth in case of need.

To establish beyond doubt the right of the bank upon proper determination of the guarantee to open a fresh account for the subsequent transactions of the principal, specific reference to the matter is often included in the guarantee. For example, if the guarantor gives due notice of determination of his liability, the account of the borrower will be stopped on the day when the liability is determined and a fresh account opened for future operations, such account being conducted on a creditor basis in the absence of additional security satisfactory to the bank. This action prevents the operation of the Rule in *Clayton's Case* enabling the debtor to appropriate credits to the new account. It is a well established method of procedure and, strictly speaking, needs no emphasis in the guarantee.

The practice was recognised and supported in *In re Sherry, London & County Banking Co.* v. *Terry* (1884) 25 Ch. D. 692, where, upon the death of John Sherry, the guarantor of Edward Terry, his son-in-law, the bank stopped its customer's account, the balance of which was debit £677 17s. 2d. and all subsequent transactions were passed by Edward Terry through a new account. There was no express provision in the guarantee covering this arrangement. The new account soon ran into debit and continued overdrawn, but sufficient credits were applied to it to wipe out the dormant debt on the stopped account. When Edward Terry went bankrupt, the bank looked to the estate of the late guarantor to meet most of the debt on the old account, there being two guarantees of the deceased totalling £500. The executors repudiated liability on the grounds that as the guarantee was 'to cover all moneys which shall at any time be due', it covered both the accounts and the breaking of the old account was not effective. They, therefore, contended that by virtue of the Rule in *Clayton's Case* all credits received after the death of the guarantor had to be applied in reduction of the liability of his estate. The bank admitted that the guarantee was determined upon the death of the guarantor, but claimed that by breaking the account the subsequent credits had been appropriated by the customer to the new account, thereby preventing the application of the Rule in *Clayton's Case*. The bank succeeded in the Court of Appeal and the following extracts from the judgment indicate the view taken concerning the right of the bank to open a fresh account:—

'The question is whether there is anything in the contract to prevent the bank from carrying out these payments to the new account. There is certainly no express contract, and in my opinion there is no implied contract to that effect. The balance which the surety guarantees is the general balance of the customer's account, and to ascertain that, all accounts existing between the customer and the bank *at the time when the guarantee comes to an end* must be taken into consideration.' Cotton, L.J.

'A surety is undoubtedly and not unjustly the object of some favour both at law and in equity, and I do not know that the rules of law and equity differ on the subject. It is an equity which enters into our system of law, that a man who makes himself liable for another person's debt is not to be prejudiced by any dealings without his consent between the secured creditor and the principal debtor. If, therefore, it could be shown that what has been done here was done without the consent of the surety in prejudice of an implied contract in his favour, I quite agree that he ought not to suffer from it. But there being no express contract, on what ground is it to be said that there is an implied contract? I am unable to find any such contract, unless we are to hold that the mere fact of suretyship takes away from the principal debtor and the creditor those powers which they would otherwise have of appropriating payments which are not subject to any particular contract with the surety.' Lord Selborne, L.C.

Nothing has happened to change this view expressed in 1884 and it is the established practice of a bank to open a fresh account for the customer upon the proper determination of the liability of any guarantor. Nevertheless, most bank guarantees expressly provide for such developments and a clause on the following lines covers all the features discussed under this heading. '*In the event of the determination of my liability under this guarantee the Bank shall be at liberty without thereby affecting their rights hereunder to open a new account or accounts and to continue any then existing accounts with the Principal and no moneys credited to such accounts by or on behalf of the Principal and subsequently withdrawn by him shall on settlement of my liability on this guarantee be appropriated towards or have the effect of repayment of any of the moneys due from the Principal at the time when this guarantee is determined, unless the persons paying in such moneys directs the Bank in writing at the time to appropriate them to that purpose.*' This test places the whole position beyond doubt and can be explained to the guarantor as and when required.

UNDERTAKINGS OF GUARANTOR TO STAND ASIDE

Although the formula whereby the guarantor undertakes to be liable for the entire debt of the principal subject to a limitation on his maximum liability means that the guarantor cannot claim in the bankruptcy of the customer in competition with the bank unless and until he has liquidated the whole of the indebtedness to the bank (see Chapter V, pages 47 and 48), it is usual to emphasise these limitations of the guarantor's rights in separate clauses. Moreover, it is prudent to arrange that the guarantor will not sue the customer for amounts paid up under the guarantee until the bank has recovered its entire debt. Suppose that a bank has lent £2,000 to X against the guarantee of Y for £1,000 and when demand is made upon Y for payment he promptly meets his liability and brings an action against X for £1,000. The prospect of the bank recovering the unsecured balance of £1,000 will be correspondingly prejudiced. A complete admission by the guarantor can be embodied in a clause somewhat as follows to make it quite clear that the guarantor has contracted out of the common law rights which he would otherwise enjoy:—

'*Notwithstanding that my ultimate liability under this guarantee is limited to the amount hereinbefore stated this guarantee shall be construed and take effect as a guarantee of the whole of the balance that may become due to the Bank from the principal and until repayment of such balance I will not take any steps to enforce any right or claim against the principal and I am not entitled as against the Bank to any right of proof in the bankruptcy or liquidation of the principal or other right of a guarantor discharging his liability in respect of the principal debt unless and until the whole of the moneys and interest due to the Bank have been completely repaid.*'

LEGAL PROOF OF AMOUNT OF DEBT DUE

In those less fortunate cases where action has to be brought against the guarantor to recover the amount of his liability, it may be necessary to prove the amount of the debt and to prove that effective demand has been served upon the guarantor. Explanatory clauses are, therefore, introduced to clarify these points.

The question of the amount of the debt is disposed of by providing that '*any admission or acknowledgment in writing by the principal or any person on behalf of the principal of the amount of the indebtedness of the principal to the bank of any judgment or award obtained by the bank against the principal or proof in bankruptcy or company's winding up which is admitted or any statement of account furnished by the bank the correctness of which is certified by the bank's auditors shall be binding and conclusive on and against me my executors and administrators.*'

In the absence of these express provisions, admissions made by the principal debtor after determination of the guarantor's liability would not be acceptable as evidence against the guarantor, there being no privity of contract between the borrower and the guarantor. It has even been held that a guarantor cannot be bound by a judgment obtained against the principal (*Ex parte Young* (1881) 17 Ch. D. 668). Sometimes in order to avoid the necessity of obtaining the co-operation of the customer, the bank retains the right in the guarantee to furnish the evidence itself, the guarantor agreeing that a copy of the account of the principal for a given period prior to the date of determination, duly certified by officers of the bank, shall be conclusive evidence of the amount due.

Proof of demand where needed against a recalcitrant guarantor can be covered by a clause on the following lines:—'*Any notice or demand hereunder shall be deemed to have been duly given if sent by prepaid post letter to the last known address or to the address herein given of the person to whom or to whose executors or administrators such notice is to be given, and shall be assumed to have reached the addressee in the course of post. In proving such service it shall be sufficient to prove that the letter of demand was properly addressed and delivered to the Post Office.*' In practice, demand is usually served on a guarantor by registered post with proof of delivery obtained from the Post Office as will be seen later.

These two clauses are self-explanatory and are of importance only when the bank's legal advisers are instructed to sue the guarantor.

LEGAL INCAPACITY OF PRINCIPAL AND ULTRA VIRES BORROWING

Where a bank has lent against the security of a guarantee to someone contractually incapable of accepting liability for a debt, there cannot be a valid enforceable guarantee. The essence of a guarantee obligation is that there is a valid obligation of a principal debtor. If the principal cannot be liable then the guarantor cannot be liable. The position in respect of infant borrowers was mentioned in Chapter IV and to overcome the possible incapacity of the principal, a special provision is inserted in some forms of bank guarantee. The usual course is to turn the guarantee into a contract of indemnity, making the guarantor liable instead as principal debtor. Here is a typical clause—'*As a separate and independent stipulation, I agree that all sums of money not recoverable from the undersigned on the footing of a guarantee, whether by reason of any legal limitation disability or incapacity on or of the principal whether known to the bank or not shall nevertheless be recoverable from the undersigned as sole or principal debtor*'. The need for this clause emerged particularly following *Coutts & Co.* v. *Browne-Lecky & Ors.* [1947] K.B. 104, but whether it is generally required in all standard guarantee forms is a moot practical point.

Some banks also seek by a special clause to insure against the risk that the guarantor may try to avoid liability on the grounds that the money borrowed by the customer, being a limited company, was in excess of its borrowing powers and therefore void. It is generally held that a guarantor would in any event be liable on the guarantee providing the parties acted in good faith and believed the borrowing to be *intra vires*. The view depends on *Garrard* v. *James* [1925] Ch. 616, but doubt can be removed if the guarantor admits in the guarantee that '*any moneys shall be deemed to be owing notwithstanding any defect or insufficiency in the borrowing powers of the principal or in the exercise thereof which might be a defence as between the principal and the bank*'.

Chapter VII The Determination and Enforcement of the Guarantee

PAYMENTS BY THE BORROWER—FRAUDULENT PREFERENCE—RETENTION OF THE GUARANTEE

So far the value, validity and form of a guarantee have been discussed and the stage has been reached where a valid obligation has been entered into by satisfactory guarantor in approved form. To complete the practical and legal picture, it is now necessary to decide when and how a guarantee can be determined and what action should be taken to protect the bank's position and to enforce its security.

At law a contract of guarantee may be determined by the bank, the guarantor, or by an act of the principal debtor. The consequences of mistake or misrepresentation have already been explored under the heading of validity, whilst the effect of any variation of the terms of the contract between the bank and the borrower, the grant of time to repay or the release of the debtor, changes in the constitution of the parties concerned, and the release of securities belonging to the principal debtor were covered when the form of a bank guarantee was analysed. Any of these developments would suffice to determine the guarantee but it will be realised that such risks are usually removed by express provision in the guarantee itself, and they need not be discussed further at this juncture. The remaining ways in which the guarantee may be determined result from a specific action on the part of one of the parties. The bank may demand payment, the borrower may repay the bank debt or the guarantor may offer cash to settle his liability. On the other hand, the guarantor or the debtor may die, be adjudicated bankrupt, or become mentally incapacitated. Any of these happenings may occur and give rise to practical problems which can now be considered in detail.

PAYMENTS BY THE BORROWING CUSTOMER

Security is taken as an insurance in case the borrower may be unable to repay his indebtedness to the bank, but the bank does not grant the advance relying entirely upon the security. The intention is that the borrower will repay in the normal course of business and this is what normally happens. The discharge of the debt releases the guarantor from all liability assuming that the customer does not wish to borrow again from the bank and there is no question of a fraudulent preference.

The bank guarantee is drawn to cover all advances made at any time. It is a continuing security covering the ultimate indebtedness of the borrower and is not, therefore, automatically determined if and when the account goes into credit. Sometimes a guarantee may be given, to the knowledge of the bank, to cover a particular transaction and when the account reverts to credit the guarantor may expect to be released from liability but, in the absence of any express arrangement or the actual determination of the contract by notice from one of the parties, he will by the terms of the guarantee remain liable for any future advances. For example, suppose that customer B arranges overdraft accommodation up to £500 to finance his purchase of a new machine and G, another customer of the lending bank, guarantees the indebtedness. Six months later, the advance is repaid from trading receipts and B's account thereafter remains in credit. No action is taken by G and the guarantee remains undisturbed. After an interval of twelve months, B approaches the bank for another £500 overdraft to assist him in buying a lorry, and the practical question arises as to whether reference should be made to G to obtain his confirmation that the guarantee can remain as security for the fresh indebtedness. Legally, the position is beyond doubt because the guarantee is drawn to cover all moneys owing by B at any time, but it may be expedient to remind the guarantor of his liability in case he originally intended the guarantee to be limited to the finance of the machinery purchase, which was completed months previously. It may often, therefore, be equitable to ensure that the guarantor is content to allow his liability to continue and not to rely willy nilly upon the legal rights contained in the guarantee itself. This practical approach is perhaps of greater importance when the surety is also a valued customer of the lending bank.

Where the borrower repays the advance and seeks the release of the guarantee because fresh advances will not be required, the course to be adopted by the bank is straightforward providing there is no possible risk of fraudulent preference, the incidence of which is explained below. The guarantee can be placed with the bank's expired securities and the guarantor advised that his liability thereunder is at an end.

FRAUDULENT PREFERENCE

The risk of loss to the bank through fraudulent preference where a guarantee is held as security is much more real than many realise and to appreciate the dangers it is necessary to explore the question in detail.

A fraudulent preference is defined in Section 44 of the Bankruptcy Act, 1914, as 'Every conveyance or transfer of property, or charge thereon made, *every payment made*, every obligation incurred, and every judicial proceeding taken or suffered by any person unable to pay his debts as they become due from his own money *in favour of any creditor*, or of any person in trust for any creditor, *with a view of giving such creditor or any surety or guarantor for the debt due to such creditor, a preference over the other creditors . . .*', and when the debtor is adjudged bankrupt on a petition presented within six months (previously only three months but extended by Section 115 (3) of the Companies Act, 1947) of such fraudulent preference, the payment or transfer is void against the Trustee.

Section 320 of the Companies Act, 1948 (previously Section 265 of the 1929 Act) applies the same principles to limited companies in that any payment made to prefer any creditor of a company *or any guarantor of the debt due to such creditor* may be held to be fraudulent and void as against the liquidator of the company.

There are four essentials before fraudulent preference can be proved and the relative transaction avoided by the trustee in bankruptcy:

1. The debtor must be made bankrupt.
2. The payment or act in question must have been completed within six months of the date of the petition.
3. At the time when the transaction in question was effected the debtor was unable to meet his liabilities as they became due.
4. The *dominant motive* or intention in the mind of the debtor when making the payment was to prefer the particular creditor or surety, thereby affording him preferential treatment to the other creditors.

The first two points can easily be decided, but the onus of proving the last two conditions rests on the trustee, who cannot rely on the evidence of the bankrupt and may have great difficulty in proving the intention to prefer. Pressure from the creditor concerned will generally suffice to disprove any suggestion of preference, but even then the test must be 'what was the dominant motive in the mind of the debtor?'—the threat of the creditor or the desire to prefer him to the other creditors.

THE BASIC PRINCIPLES OF FRAUDULENT PREFERENCE

The principles of fraudulent preference can best be explained by reference to a simple example. Suppose worthless Tim Broke succeeded in borrowing £10 from each of his three associates, Tom, Dick and Harry, but such loans failing to bridge his ever widening gap, he realised within six months of obtaining these loans that his bankruptcy was inevitable. Just before the crash his total resources amounted to £9, and he decided, of his own free will, to pay this amount to his creditor, Dick, his closest lifelong friend. The Official Receiver (there being no need for any trustee to wind up the estate of Tim Broke) could, and no doubt would, treat and prove the payment of £9 as a fraudulent preference. Assuming no other assets or other creditors, it was wrong in principle to pay £9 to Dick. The three creditors for £10 each were entitled to an equal share of what little remained from the wreck. Instead of the best friend, Dick, getting £9, each of the three associates should have received £3. This is only fair and in essence illustrates the basic principles of fraudulent preference. Upon insolvency of the debtor all creditors, other than those secured on the assets of the debtor or granted preferential rights prescribed by law, shall rank equally together.

The intention of a debtor to prefer may even be imputed from the action of an employee who, perhaps realising the position, may of his own accord arrange the payment of a particular creditor before the normal time or turn for such payment. In *re Drabble Brothers* [1930] 2 Ch. 211 is a case in point. In that case the employee of a firm of builders in the normal course of his duties decided what payments should be made under running contracts which the firm had with merchants and drew the necessary cheques for signature by the partners. For his own purposes he arranged the issue of a cheque to a certain creditor with the result that the creditor was paid earlier than would normally have been the case. The firm was adjudicated bankrupt on a petition presented within three months of the payment, and it was decided that the payment was void as a fraudulent preference. Although there was no intention on the part of the bankrupts themselves to prefer the particular creditor, yet, having delegated control of their finances to their employee, his knowledge and intention as their agent must be imputed to them.

PREFERRING THE GUARANTOR

It is difficult to imagine an impecunious borrower being so concerned about the bank as to ensure voluntarily the repayment or reduction of his bank debt at the expense of his other creditors. Alas, it is usually the other way round and repayments are obtained by the bank only after pressure so prolonged as to remove any possible thought of fraudulent preference. But Section 44 of the Bankruptcy Act refers not only to *the preference of a creditor but also the preference of any surety or guarantor.* This inclusion is the banker's real source of trouble and, again, it is helpful to resort to a simple case with quite blatant facts to illustrate the practical danger.

Suppose that X has for several years enjoyed overdraft accommodation from the South Bank up to an agreed maximum of £1,000, secured by the guarantee of his mother-in-law, Mrs. Y, for £1,000. The bank records show clearly that X is a hungry borrower who for years has operated always close to and often a little beyond the limit of £1,000. Suddenly, for no apparent reason, the nature of the account completely changes. Instead of the usual steady drawings, X over the course of two or three weeks makes practically no payments to creditors but applies all receipts in reduction of his overdraft, with such success that within one month the account is operating on a creditor basis. X then calls and requests the cancellation of the guarantee of Mrs. Y as he no longer wishes to borrow from the bank. Without thought, the guarantee is cancelled by South Bank and X thereafter promptly files his own petition in bankruptcy and is soon adjudged bankrupt. The trustee naturally examines the bank account of the bankrupt and wonders why the whole nature of the account changed so strangely during the month immediately prior to the petition. His enquiries will soon lay bare the facts and a strong case of fraudulent preference emerges. Why did X collect all he could from his debtors and yet stop payments to creditors? Surely to repay the bank and so obtain the release of his mother-in-law's guarantee before the crash occured. He dare not go bankrupt and leave his mother-in-law liable on her guarantee to the bank, so he exerts himself ostensibly to prefer the bank but really to prefer his mother-in-law, the surety. On the given facts it is reasonable to assume that the repayment of the bank debt would be void as a fraudulent preference and the bank would have to reimburse the estate to the extent of such payments. But having cancelled the guarantee, the bank, prior to the limited protection now afforded by Section 92 (4) of the Companies Act, 1947 (discussed fully below), had no redress against the mother-in-law and had to be content with whatever dividend might ultimately be paid from the bankrupt's estate. This example is certainly fictitious but it is not a fairy story because similar facts arose in reported cases which can now be examined.

In the course of in *re G. Stanley & Co. Ltd.* [1925] 1 Ch. 148 Mr. Justice Eve stated that he was convinced the real object of Section 44 was to enable the trustee to recover the payment from the person actually preferred. Action was in this case brought against the guarantor and not the bank, and the Judge overruled the preliminary objection of the respondent that no order for repayment could be made against him as guarantor. Unfortunately, such principles were not allowed to prevail and subsequent actions based on similar grounds were brought against the lending banker.

In *re J. S. Lyons ex parte Barclays Bank Ltd.* v. *The Trustee* (1934) 152 L.T. 201, the bankrupt, a wine and spirit merchant, had an overdraft limit of £2,000 with Barclays Bank Ltd., secured by the guarantee of his father. There was evidence that from and after March, 1932, the bankrupt knew that he was insolvent. By the end of August in that year Mr. Lyons had stopped payments to the general body of his creditors but proceeded to apply to the credit of his account with Barclays Bank all moneys collected from his debtors. By such means he gradually reduced the overdraft by £698 4s. 5d., leaving a debit balance of £1,301 at the date of the petition in October, 1932. The trustee, on examining the bank account, asked for a declaration against the bank and the guarantor that the various payments which, during the given period, had resulted in a reduction of £698 4s. 5d., constituted a fraudulent preference of the bank and/or the guarantor. In the lower Court Mr. Justice Clauson decided that the fair inference to be drawn from the facts was that the bankrupt had acted with the dominant intention of relieving his father of his liability under his guarantee. The payments were, therefore, deemed to be fraudulent and void and the bank was ordered to repay £698 4s. 5d. to the trustee. No order was made against the guarantor. Barclays Bank, however, appealed from this decision and succeeded because the facts were too indefinite in the opinion of the higher Court to prove fraudulent preference.

The words of the Master of the Rolls, in giving judgment, are of considerable practical interest. He said that the bankrupt's banking account was an ordinary business account into which cheques were paid and on which cheques were drawn. Mr. Justice Clauson had said that the account was operated in such a way that the only possible inference was that an effort was being made by the bankrupt to prefer his father. But was that so? The bankrupt continued to operate the account after September 12 in exactly the same way as he had done before that date, when there was admittedly no intention to prefer anyone. He paid money in and drew money out. To deduce from that that the only explanation was that the debtor was minded to relieve his father from liability was to misread the evidence and not to look at it in its proper perspective. It overlooked the essential nature of a fraudulent preference, as indicated by Lord Tomlin in *Peat* v. *Gresham Trust Limited* 50 T.L.R. 345 at page 349; [1934] A.C. 252 at page 262 as follows:—

'The onus is on those who claim to avoid the transaction to establish what the debtor really intended, and that the real intention was to prefer. The onus is only discharged when the Court upon a review of all the circumstances is satisfied that the dominant intent to prefer was present. That may be a matter of direct evidence or of inference, but *where there is not direct evidence and there is room for more than one explanation it is not enough to say there being no direct evidence the intention to prefer must be inferred.*'

Therefore, continued the Master of the Rolls, the appeal would be allowed and the order made by Mr. Justice Clauson discharged.

Thus the bank here was given the benefit of the doubt. Facts suggesting possible fraudulent preference are not enough. The intention of the debtor has to be proved by the trustee beyond doubt. On similar grounds but more definite facts, the trustee did succeed against Lloyds Bank Ltd. in the case of *In re M. Kushler Limited* nearly a decade later [1943] 2 All E.R. 22. The principles are exactly the same although here the payments were made by a limited company

65

E

prior to winding-up.

M. Kushler Ltd. was a private company incorporated in 1934 with its issued capital held entirely by Morris Kushler and his wife, who were also the only directors of the company. Lloyds Bank granted the company overdraft acommodation up to £800, secured by the guarantee of Morris Kushler and four policies for £900 nominal on his life. On May 10, 1941, the account was debit £609 3s. 9d. On May 12 the directors were advised that the company was insolvent and must be wound up. Between May 12 and 21 a total of £730 8s. 4d. was received by the company and credited to the banking account, thereby liquidating the overdraft and relieving Kushler of liability under his guarantee. On May 14 the directors issued notices calling a meeting of creditors, and on the 23rd of the same month a resolution was passed for the voluntary winding-up of the company. The liquidator thereafter took out a summons for a declaration that all payments to the bank between February 23 and May 23, 1941, or so much of these payments as went to extinguish the company's overdraft, constituted a fraudulent preference to the bank, contrary to Section 265, of the Companies Act, 1929, for an order that the bank should repay these sums. Later, the claim was reduced to the payments made between May 10 and 23, 1941, and the special facts proved in evidence, relied on as showing a fraudulent intention to prefer the bank, may be summarised as follows:—

1. that between May 10 and 23 substantially no payments were made by the company to existing trade creditors;

2. that Messrs. Debenham & Co. had been pressing for payment of their February account of £88 1s. 6d. since the beginning of April, that at the request of Morris Kushler they consented to wait if half the amount was paid by the end of April, but that in fact no part of it had been paid;

3. that the bank never pressed for reduction of the overdraft, and up to May 23, 1941, would have allowed the company to operate up to the limit of the permitted overdraft;

4. that, although on May 14 there was still an overdraft, no notice of the creditors' meeting was sent to the bank; and

5. that, at the meeting of creditors on May 23, Morris Kushler, in answer to a creditor's question, falsely said that the guarantors of the company's bank account were two persons called Cohen and Waldman, and omitted to say that he himself was the guarantor.

In the lower Court the bank succeeded. Bennett, J., decided that the onus of proving fraudulent preference rested on the liquidator. In view of the fact that on May 12 the company had been advised that it was insolvent it might be said that the company stopped payment to creditors in order not to prefer any of them, and paid the money received by the company into the bank without contemplating the consequences as regards the overdraft. That being a possible explanation, it was not open to him, in view (again) of Lord Tomlin's judgment in *Peat* v. *Gresham Trust Ltd.*, and of the absence of direct evidence of intention to prefer, to hold that the liquidator had proved a fraudulent preference. The liquidator was not content, however, and appealed with success. The Master of the Rolls, Lord Green, considered what inference ought to be drawn from the evidence, and, after due reference to Lord Tomlin's speech, a distinction was drawn between the facts here and those of *In re J. S. Lyons*. It was decided that the inference of an intention to prefer in the Kushler case was overwhelming and Lloyds Bank thus felt the impact of fraudulent preference.

The above two cases have concerned payments made to release or reduce the liability of a guarantor, but any form of collateral security will usually suffice where it can be proved that the intention was to obtain the release of that security, or, at least, to reduce the amount of the debt secured by it. This aspect of the problem was examined at length in *Re Conley* (*trading as Caplan & Conley*) *ex parte the Trustee* v. *Barclays Bank Ltd.*, and the *same parties* v. *Lloyds Bank Limited* [1938] 2 All E.R. 128. Briefly, in these cases the bank held as collateral security for advances to the bankrupt War Loan and Building Society shares deposited by the wife of the bankrupt and by his mother. Shortly before his failure the bankrupt, by various means, paid large sums into his accounts so that they both were in credit. In a few days thereafter the wife and mother obtained release of the securities and subsequently the customer was adjudicated bankrupt. It was basically the same story, but instead of a guarantee the securities in question were merely deposited with the bank, and neither the wife nor the mother gave any covenant or undertaking of any kind to pay any sum to the bank. The question, therefore, was whether the deposit of the securities without any contract to pay the bank was sufficient to make the depositors sureties, or guarantors, within the meaning of Section 44 of the Bankruptcy Act, 1914. It was first thought that because the depositors did not in the memorandum of deposit accept any personal liberty for the borrower's debt to the bank, they were outside the provisions, but the nature of their liability was examined at great length upon appeal and the decision reversed. What ultimately happened is obscure, but it was well established that the depositor of collateral security is a guarantor within the meaning of Section 44.

PRACTICAL LESSONS AND PREVENTATIVE MEASURES

These cases have been examined at length in order to drive home the principles, and the practical lessons can now be drawn. The basic features to cause anxiety are three in number. First, there must be a debit account secured by a guarantee or some other form of collateral security. Secondly, the nature of the account changes; instead of operating in heavy manner, there is a marked decrease perhaps almost a cessation of withdrawals, but credits continue to flow in until the overdraft is much reduced or repaid and, thirdly, (if such stage is reached) an approach is made for release of the collateral security. Throughout this quite short period of metamorphosis there must surely be a feeling of surprise and disbelief in the breast of the manager controlling the bank account. How and why has the borrower who previously experienced such stringency suddenly repaid the bank?

If the danger is realised in the course of repayment there may be time in which to exert pressure for repayment as a possible proof against the voluntary action of preference by the borrower. But where the red light only glows with sufficient strength when request is made for the release of the collateral security, the salvation of the banker must rest in the retention of the security under some pretext. Inability to obtain the security from the safe may give breathing space in which to verify the facts and, if need be, seek legal advice concerning the position. Assuming there are reasonable grounds for preventative action, the banker can decline to release the security and await action against him for wrongful detention. The relative charge or guarantee may provide for six months' notice of determination upon which the banker may rely, or the circumstances may warrant open resistance by informing the customer that, as the facts suggest the possibility of fraudulent preference, the bank is not prepared to release the security until six months have elapsed. If plans have in fact been made to prefer the surety, the crash is not likely to be held off for many weeks because there will be a host of pressing creditors hungry for payments which were diverted in previous weeks to the bank account. Relying upon the old adage that a bird in the hand is worth two in the bush, this precautionary action merits consideration, notwithstanding the right of indemnity introduced by the Companies Act and discussed in the ensuing paragraphs. After all, when the banker wishes to rely on the indemnity, the party liable thereon may no longer be in a position to meet the cash liability. Much better to retain, if at all possible, the tangible security in its original form.

WHY CANNOT THE BANKER BE PROTECTED?

From what has been said and from the examples cited, it is clear that the voluntary act of preference by the debtor is directed towards the collateral depositor or guarantor and certainly not for the direct benefit of the bank. Why then should the bank bear the risk of subsequent loss? The hardship of the position has long been recognised by bankers and in 1944, when submitting their Memorandum to the Company Law Amendment Committee, the Committee of London Clearing Bankers drew attention to the banker's vulnerability in this respect. Blame was attributed to the words 'or any surety or guarantor for the debt due to such creditor' which were contained in Section 265 of the Companies Act, 1929, as well as Section 44 of the Bankruptcy Act, 1914. It was contended that the cases in which banks were involved arose out of the intention upon the part of the company, or private debtor, to prefer a surety or guarantor and not from any desire to prefer the bank. It was, therefore, quite inequitable that claims should be made against banks who were thus involved in undeserved losses to substantial extent. To correct the position it was suggested that the appropriate sections should be amended to ensure action against the party actually preferred, and not against the innocent banker caught between the debtor and the preferred party.

These suggestions were examined at length and many questions thereon appear in the Minutes of Evidence, but unfortunately the findings of the Amendment Committee were a disappointment to the banking world. Although the period within which transactions might be avoided as fraudulent preferences was increased from three months to six months before the date of the petition, thereby increasing the risks to banks, there was no recognition that the party really preferred was the collateral depositor or guarantor and not the bank receiving the cash. The only improvement from the bank standpoint lay in the introduction of a right of indemnity against the guarantor or third party to cover cases where the guarantee has been cancelled or the security released by the bank prior to proof of preference and repayment by the bank to the trustee or liquidator, as the case may be, of the amount preferred.

As far as bankruptcy is concerned, the amendment is contained in Section 92 (4) of the Companies Act, 1947, which came into force on July 1, 1948. In the winding-up of a company the relative provision is to be found in Section 321 of the 1948 Act:—

'(4) On any application made to the Court with respect to any payment on the ground that the payment was a fraudulent preference of a surety or guarantor the Court shall have jurisdiction to determine any questions with respect to the payment arising between the person to whom the payment was made and the surety or guarantor and to grant relief in respect thereof, notwithstanding that it is not necessary so to do for the purposes of the winding-up and for that purpose may *give leave to bring in the surety or guarantor as a third party as in the case of an action for the recovery of the sum paid.* This section shall apply, with the necessary modifications, in relation to transactions other than the payment of money as it applies in relation to payments.'

Thus, in effect, the party actually preferred may be linked with the bank as defendant in the action by the trustee to prove fraudulent preference and recover sums paid in such manner. In this way the released guarantor or collateral depositor who has recovered his security may nevertheless be held liable and have to reimburse the bank or pay the trustee direct if the means for payment are still within his control.

In an abundance of caution some banks have introduced a special clause into the guarantee providing that no payment which may be avoided as a fraudulent preference and no release given on the faith of such payments shall prejudice the bank's right to recover from the guarantor to the full extent of the guarantee. This clause in effect retains the liability of the guarantor notwithstanding the payments into the account from the principal debtor, but to be able to rely upon it the guarantee presumably has to be held intact after the repayment of the advance. To release the guarantee or to cancel it would destroy the protection of the clause.

RETENTION OF THE GUARANTEE BY BANKER

In practice, the problem often arises as to whether the bank can retain the guarantee after settlement of the indebtedness or when the guarantor pays the amount to which his guarantee is limited. It is a sore point on many occasions. The guarantor meets his liability or the overdraft is otherwise liquidated and the guarantor or his legal advisers ask the bank to return the guarantee to them or demand that it should be cancelled. The bank is conscious of all the provisions therein and is reluctant to cancel them in case the need arises to rely upon such provisions. It is always a delicate situation. As an acme of perfection, the bank should, whenever possible, retain the guarantee unimpaired but, in practice, this is not always possible. Where the guarantor discharges the entire debt of the customer, it is immaterial to the bank whether the guarantee is retained or not, but where the customer's debt exceeds the amount of the guarantee the bank will normally wish to retain the guarantee as evidence of the undertaking of the guarantor not to sue the customer or to prove in his bankruptcy until the entire debt has been liquidated. The usual course, therefore, is to retain the guarantee as evidence merely advising the guarantor that his cash liability has been satisfied. On the other hand, unless the guarantee expressly provides that upon discharge it is to remain the property of the bank, it is probable that the guarantor can insist upon the delivery of the guarantee to him. If the document is cancelled by appropriate words written across it, the provisions cannot later be produced as evidence against the guarantor. Where there is a threat of possible fraudulent preference, it is clear that nothing should be done to damage the effect of the terms of the guarantee and the bank should insist on retaining it unimpaired. Everything depends upon the facts of the case, but normally the banker will be wise to arrange to hold the guarantee, merely acknowledging receipt of monies received from the guarantor subject to all the provisions of the document.

Part Two: Guarantees (continued)

Chapter VIII The Determination and Enforcement of the Guarantee—*continued*

DETERMINATION BY GUARANTOR—INCAPACITY OF
GUARANTOR—DEATH OR BANKRUPTCY OF CUSTOMER—
DEMAND FOR PAYMENT—INCOME TAX CLAIMS
BY GUARANTOR

VOLUNTARY PAYMENT BY GUARANTOR

It occasionally happens that the guarantor voluntarily seeks to meet his liability and proffers payment to discharge the guarantee. In such event, the attitude of the bank will depend upon the balance of the borrower's account and the arrangements made for overdraft accommodation. If the debt exceeds the amount of the guarantee, there can be no harm in accepting the cash from the guarantor provided it is credited to a special guarantee security account to preserve the collateral position and the guarantor realises that he cannot proceed against the principal debtor to recover his money but must stand aside in accord with the terms of the guarantee, which should be preserved intact as evidence of the contract. The common law rights of a guarantor in this respect and the provisions inserted in a bank guarantee to contract out of them were discussed in pages 47 to 51 and can be applied here. The collateral position has to be preserved to ensure that, in the event of the bankruptcy of the borrower, the bank can prove for the full amount of the debt ignoring the cash received from the guarantor. In other words, the guarantee contract in these circumstances continues fully supported by cash and interest will usually be allowed on the balance at a special set-off rate according to the rate charged on the debit monies.

Where the debt is less than the amount of the guarantee at the time when the guarantor proffers cash in settlement, everything depends upon the arrangement with the borrower and the action of the bank may vary according to the standing of the parties. On the one hand, the guarantor is subject to the terms of the guarantee requiring written notice (usually three months) of determination and he cannot summarily decide to pay off the balance. On the other hand, the indebtedness of the borrower is repayable upon demand and, if it so wishes, the bank can easily determine the position by calling in the advance, regardless of any outstanding commitments of the customer. The best course is usually to temporise until a satisfactory arrangement can be made with all parties. The guarantor has perhaps to be reminded of his obligation to give notice of determination whilst the prospect is referred to the customer. Legally, the guarantor remains bound until the expiration of the notice if and when it is properly served upon the bank, but the customer will not be allowed to profit at the guarantor's expense. An example will help to clarify the problem from the practical standpoint.

Suppose that customer X, a retail trader, enjoys overdraft accommodation up to a limit of £1,000 secured only by the guarantee of Z for £1,000. When the account is debit £400, the guarantor seeks to discharge his liability. If the bank then accepted £400 cash from Z and summarily cancelled the overdraft arrangements, X might be seriously embarrassed, being unable to find cash to pay for goods ordered and even delivered. Clearly, some consideration has to be given to the outstanding commitments of X and the bank will not usually be prepared in such circumstances to grant unsecured facilities to bridge the gap. The first step, therefore, will be to remind Z of the need for notice, pointing out that he will continue to be liable under the guarantee for the fluctuating indebtedness up to the stated date. The matter can then be referred to X to see whether arrangements can be made to reach a mutually satisfactory practical solution. It may be that X does not require any further accommodation, in which event £400 can be accepted from Z and credited direct to the account of X, which thereafter will be maintained in credit. On the other hand, a figure of £600—£700 may suffice to meet outstanding commitments and Z may be disposed to find this sum to conclude the matter. But where X insists on retaining his full limit of £1,000, he may be called upon to justify the use of the available margin unless the account has always fluctuated freely with frequent and recent balances up to £1,000 debit. A happy solution can usually be reached when the guarantor is anxious to pay up. The trouble usually is to find a guarantor so willing to settle in cash. Needless to add, where the payment from the guarantor meets the entire liability of the customer, there is no point in preserving the collateral position and the guarantor can exercise whatever rights he may wish to recover his money from the principal debtor.

It should not be forgotten that where a guarantor elects to discharge the entire liability of the customer to the bank he is entitled to step into the bank's shoes and take over all security, direct and collateral, regardless of whether he knew of the security when he repaid the debt.

DETERMINATION BY GUARANTOR

Instead of proffering payment voluntarily to support the borrower, the guarantor may decide to determine his liability to reduce his commitments or because he has lost confidence in the debtor. There is little difference in practice between this happening and the circumstances described above, although more difficulty may be experienced in reaching a friendly settlement. When the customer's account is at or in excess of the arrangement, it can be stopped forthwith and no embarrassment will be caused to either party. The customer has then to open a fresh account which has to be maintained in credit unless and until other approved security is available to cover any agreed indebtedness. The extent of the guarantor's liability is immediately determined and, if he meets it, the cash will be applied to a guarantee security account to preserve the collateral position (unless the proceeds of the guarantee suffice to discharge all the customer's liabilities to the bank) and an opportunity taken to remind the guarantor that by the terms of the guarantee he cannot seek to recover from or obtain security from the principal debtor until the whole of the bank debt has been liquidated.

When the account is well within the arrangement, the same problems arise in practice as those referred to under the previous heading. Legally, the guarantor has to give notice before his liability can be determined and the account of the customer can be continued for the period of the notice, the guarantor being liable for the balance outstanding at the end of the period. Usually, however, some thought will be given to the equitable rights of the guarantor and steps taken to prevent the customer taking advantage of the position. The guarantor has first to be warned that by the terms of the guarantee notice is required to determine his liability and a date can be fixed for such purpose. An approach will then be made to the customer to reach an amicable settlement which enables him to clear outstanding commitments but stops him entering into fresh engagements relying on the guarantee. If the customer is unsatisfactory and the bank wishes to protect the guarantor, who may be a much more important customer, it can always elect to determine the position forthwith by demanding repayment from the borrower, all advances being subject to normal banking conditions. Upon determination, whenever the date may be agreed, the amount received from the guarantor will be credited to a guarantee security account to preserve the bank's rights against the customer and the guarantor will be reminded that he cannot exercise any rights against the principal debtor until the whole of the bank debt has been repaid.

DEATH OF A GUARANTOR

In the absence of express provision to the contrary in the guarantee itself, the guarantee will be determined as soon as notice of death of the guarantor reaches the bank. Strictly speaking, where the guarantee binds the personal representatives of the deceased guarantor by a clause expressed somewhat as follows 'in the event of my death the liability of my estate will continue until the expiration of three calendar months' written notice given to the bank by my executors or administrators of their intention to determine the guarantee', the account of the borrower can be continued unbroken until the expiration of such notice. The validity of this provision was tried and proved in *Coulthard* v. *Clementson* (1879) 5 Q.B.D. 42 and the liability of the deceased estate for further advances pending notice from the executors appears to be supported by *Egbert* v. *Northern Crown Bank* [1918] A.C. 903. In practice, however, the account will usually be stopped and notice of the actual liability given to the personal representatives as soon as reliable news of the death of the guarantor reaches the bank. Equity demands such a course to protect the estate of the deceased and to enable his executors to determine the liability for estate duty purposes. If there is any conflict of interests, the need to determine the liability promptly is obvious. For example, if the borrower is also the sole executor of the deceased guarantor, it would be unwise to continue the account in case he took advantage of his position and drew up to the full amount of the guarantee before sending notice of determination to the bank. Apart from this obvious case of danger, the estate of the guarantor may be bequeathed to needy parties or devised on trust and it would be unwise to jeopardize the interests of the beneficiaries by continuing the account (*Harris* v. *Fawcett* (1873) 29 L.T. 84).

Again, much depends on the state of the account at the time the bank receives notice of the death of the guarantor. If it is at or beyond the agreed maximum, it will be stopped immediately without embarrassment to the customer who will be called upon to pass subsequent entries through a fresh account maintained strictly on a creditor basis. If the debit balance exceeds the amount of the guarantee, the account can likewise be stopped and fresh advances made to any agreed extent against the other security. The power to open a fresh account and to divert credits to it is expressly stated in most guarantee forms, but, in any event, it is well established and recognised in practice (*In re Sherry, London & County Banking Co.* v. *Terry* (1884) 25 Ch. D. 692). Complications arise in practice only where the balance of the account is well within the agreed maximum and less than the amount of the guarantee. Suppose customer B has an overdraft limit of £500 secured only by the guarantee of G for £500 and the account is debit £200 when notice of G's death is served upon the bank. Is it incumbent upon the bank to stop the account forthwith regardless of any cheques issued or about to be drawn by B to settle outstanding debts? Sure peremptory action would clearly embarrass B and would appear to be an undue protection of G's estate at his expense. The practical solution is to allow B a reasonable time to meet outstanding commitments, relying upon the notice clause in the guarantee and then to determine the position. Everything will depend upon the standing of the customer concerned, but care should be exercised to ensure that all outstanding cheques at least have been met before the amount of the guarantee liability is advised to the personal representative of the deceased guarantor. It would be folly to quote the amount of the liability immediately upon receipt of notice of death and then be faced with large cheques presented for payment through the clearing next day. Some reliance has to be placed on the notice clause unless the bank is content to ignore the position of the customer and return his cheques out of hand because of the death of the guarantor. As soon as the position can be determined, the account is stopped and remains dormant until the guarantee liability is discharged by the estate or satisfactory arrangements are made for the deposit of fresh security to enable the bank to release the guarantee. Any payments from the guarantor's estate are treated in the same way as all proceeds of collateral security and held in guarantee security account unless they suffice to discharge the entire indebtedness of the customer to the bank.

MENTAL INCAPACITY OF GUARANTOR

In the unhappy event of mental incapacity of a guarantor, the account has to be stopped immediately the bank has notice of it. The legal effect of mental incapacity is the same as that of death of a guarantor, but the provisions in a bank guarantee covering further advances made after death do not apply. In *Bradford Old Bank Ltd.* v. *Sutcliffe* (1918) 23 Com. Cas. 299, the continuing guarantee to the bank provided that three months' notice had to be given by the guarantor, his executors or administrators, to determine liability. To the knowledge of the bank, one of the guarantors became insane but the account was continued unbroken. It was decided that the Rule in *Clayton's Case* applied and all credits after the notice of lunacy reduced the liability of the insane guarantor and he could not be liable for fresh advances. The clause requiring notice did not provide for lunacy. Thus, a bank cannot continue advances against a guarantee when it knows that the surety lacks contractual capacity and a provision can hardly be introduced into a guarantee form to cover this sad prospect. If a guarantee is determined by mental incapacity of the guarantor, notice of the liability thereunder has to be given to the Court of Protection.

BANKRUPTCY OF GUARANTOR

An equally unhappy position arises from the standpoint of the bank when the guarantor becomes bankrupt. The position is not only determined, but the value of the security is in jeopardy. Legally, it appears that the liability is determined immediately the bank has notice that the guarantor has committed an act of bankruptcy, but in practice the first news of bankruptcy proceedings will usually come from the Official Receiver when a Receiving Order has been made. In any event, as soon as the bank has reliable notice that the guarantor is involved in bankruptcy proceedings the account has to be stopped to avoid the operation of the Rule in *Clayton's Case* and to determine the amount for which the bank can prove against the bankrupt's estate. The amount required, being the balance of the account, plus interest to the date of the Receiving Order or the amount of the guarantee, whichever may be the larger, should then be advised to the Official Receiver or, where appointed, the trustee in bankruptcy, for the guarantor's estate. At this stage the liability is contingent and an attempt will be made to recover the balance from the customer or to obtain other approved security to cover the position. If these efforts are fruitless, a proof can be filed against the guarantor's estate and any dividend thankfully collected. Needless to add, further advances should not be granted relying upon the guarantee after the guarantor has obtained his discharge.

This concludes the review of what may happen in practice when a guarantee is determined at the instigation of the guarantor. In similar manner, the guarantee contract can be determined upon the death, bankruptcy or mental incapacity of the principal debtor.

DEATH OF BORROWING CUSTOMER

Upon reliable notice of the death of the borrower, his account will be stopped and the liability of the guarantor is automatically determined. Any cheques paid after death but before notice reaches the bank will be covered by the guarantee. At the outset it will normally be prudent to advise the guarantor in tactful manner that, consequent upon the unfortunate passing of the principal debtor, his liability has been determined at £X and interest will accrue thereon at a stated rate to the date of payment. The guarantor may then elect to discharge his liability. If the amount suffices to repay all the indebtedness of the deceased to the bank, it can be applied to the account to close it and the guarantor will be free to take what action he may wish to recover from the deceased's estate. In such event, the guarantor steps into the shoes of the bank and is entitled to any direct or collateral security which may be held. If the guarantee is for a smaller amount than the total indebtedness of the deceased, all payments from the guarantor should be applied to a guarantee security account to preserve the bank's full claim against the deceased's estate. By the terms of the guarantee, the guarantor cannot make any attempt to recover from the estate until the bank has recovered the entire debt, but it may be necessary to remind him of this arrangement. The guarantee has to be preserved intact until the debt has been liquidated. Sometimes a guarantor, being aware of other security held by the bank, may elect to pay the entire debt of the deceased, notwithstanding the lower limitation of the guarantee liability, so that he may take over all the bank's security and so perhaps strengthen his position.

More frequently in practice the guarantor prefers to wait until the bank has realised any direct security and collected as much as it can from the estate of the deceased customer. In such circumstances, it is prudent to make it quite clear to the guarantor that he will be liable for interest accruing on the outstanding debt and it may be wise to serve formal notice upon him to place the matter beyond doubt. Some time may elapse before the personal representatives of the deceased can wind up the estate and care may also have to be exercised to ensure that the guarantor's financial position does not deteriorate in the meantime. In fact the patience of the bank will depend upon the net value of the deceased's estate and the known standing of the guarantor. In most cases the problem can be solved quite happily because of the relationship between the guarantor and the deceased, always assuming that the bank granted the advances against a reliable guarantee, but particular care may be necessary where the guarantor is the executor of the deceased customer.

BANKRUPTCY OF BORROWING CUSTOMER

The value of the special provisions in a bank guarantee is most evident when the borrower is adjudicated bankrupt. The guarantor accepts responsibility for the entire indebtedness of the customer with a limitation on his maximum liability and cannot, therefore, prove in the bankruptcy unless he first repays the whole debt. Normally, the guarantor will also expressly convenant not to intervene in the bankruptcy until the bank has been repaid. These two provisions enable the bank to treat all payments from the guarantor as collateral proceeds and to ignore them in its proof of debt against the bankrupt estate. Any payment made by the guarantor before bankruptcy should, of course, be placed to a separate account. If the proceeds are applied direct to the customer's account, they will reduce the amount of the debt and the bank can prove only for the balance outstanding when the receiving order is made. In maintaining the collateral position the bank relies on the undertaking of the guarantor to stand aside and, where the guarantor meets the full amount of the guarantee, it has to be preserved intact to prove that the bank has not waived this part of the contract. In *Mackinnon's Trustees* v. *Bank of Scotland* [1915] S.C. 411, payments received from a guarantor before the bankruptcy of the borrower were applied by the bank to a suspense account and interest on the balance was set off against interest on the customer's overdraft, but the guarantee did not contain any special provision whereby the guarantor covenanted to stand aside in the event of the bankruptcy of the principal debtor. It was decided that the bank could prove only for the net amount after deduction of the monies received from the guarantor. This furnishes sufficient warning of the need for preserving the guarantee if the bank wishes to retain its full proof in bankruptcy.

In practice, payments are usually received from the guarantor after bankruptcy and the position is quite clear. The bank will advise the Official Receiver or trustee of the full amount due from the bankrupt customer and give details of any direct security which may be held. The guarantee need not be disclosed. In due course, a proof can be lodged for the whole debt, less the value or proceeds of any direct security, and the dividend collected on that amount. The guarantor cannot intervene and must rest content in the knowledge that, if there is any surplus after the bank has received the dividend, it will be returned to him. If the guarantor wishes to prove in the bankrupt estate, he must first repay the entire bank debt and he can then step into the shoes of the bank and collect what he can from any direct security and by way of dividend. There cannot be two proofs for the same debt and the guarantor cannot attempt to prove for his guarantee payment at the same time as the bank is proving for the full indebtedness of the customer. The legal position was discussed at length in pages 47 and 49. From the practical angle there are two points to be watched. The collateral position has to be preserved throughout by applying the guarantor's moneys to a suspense account and the guarantee has to remain intact to retain the convenants of the guarantor.

DEMAND FOR PAYMENT ON GUARANTOR

A guarantee may be determined by the bank when it decides to enforce the security and it is now appropriate to give consideration to the points at issue.

The guarantor undertakes to repay upon demand and there is no legal obligation upon the bank to sue the customer or take any steps to recover the debt before calling upon the guarantor. In fact, a reasonable attempt will be made to obtain payment from the customer, upon whom formal demand will usually be served before turning to the guarantor, but sometimes where the customer dies or is adjudicated bankrupt or, in the case of a limited company customer liquidation proceedings occur, it is prudent to serve formal demand upon the guarantor to determine his liability and to give him an opportunity for prompt payment to avoid additional liability for interest.

Demand is made in writing upon the guarantor at his last known address or the address stated in the guarantee and should be sent by registered post to obtain proof of delivery. If the indebtedness of the customer exceeds the amount of the guarantee, demand will be limited to the latter amount, plus interest at the rate stated in the guarantee to the date of payment. Where the debt is less than the guarantee, the amount demanded will be the balance of the account, including interest and commission to date, plus interest thereon at the agreed rate until payment is made.

Thereafter, everything depends upon the guarantor. If he pays up promptly, all is well, but sometimes the bank may have to accept payment by instalments. If the guarantor tries to avoid his responsibilities and ignores further requests from the bank, the matter has to be placed in the hands of the bank's solicitors, who may have to institute legal proceedings to recover the amount. It is at this unhappy stage that the doubtful value of a guarantee as banking security is realised.

INCOME TAX CLAIMS BY GUARANTORS

Finally, a brief word concerning the rights of guarantors to obtain a rebate of income tax on any interest which they may pay to the bank when meeting their liability under the guarantee. It will be appreciated that a *borrower* is entitled to a certificate from his bank on Form 38 E-1 or 38 E-2 showing the amount of interest he has *actually paid* on any overdraft or loan so that he can produce it to the Inland Revenue to seek rebate of tax.

Occasionally, a guarantor who has discharged his liability approaches the bank for an interest certificate to cover the amount of interest unpaid by the customer but included in the total debt which the guarantor has liquidated under the guarantee. An unqualified certificate cannot be issued to any guarantor for interest so paid because a rebate of tax can be claimed only for interest paid by the party to whom the advance was made. Payments by the guarantor are not within Section 200 (1) of the Income Tax Act, 1952, quoted in full above.

The question was argued at length in *Holder* v. *Inland Revenue Commissioners* (1932) A.C. 624 where guarantors paid-off the debt of Blumfield Ltd. to Midland Bank and part of the amount paid was interest debited half-yearly to the account of the company. Actually no less than £17,861 comprised interest added to the guaranteed account from 1920 to 1926 and the guarantors sought to recover tax on this amount. The claim failed. It was held that, when interest is debited half-yearly by the bank, it is capitalised and the guarantors, therefore, paid principal and not interest, but in any case, even if the payment by the guarantors was interest then payment under the guarantee was not a payment of interest within the Act. According to Lord Dunedin 'interest payable on an advance from a bank means interest on an advance made to the person paying. The guarantor does not pay on an advance made to him, but pays all interest due by the person to whom the advance is made, but his debt is his debt under the guarantee, not a debt in respect of the advance made to him'.

Therefore, if a guarantor presses for a certificate of interest paid, the bank must not issue Form 38 E-1 or 38 E-2, but should instead certify in the form of a letter how much has been paid, by whom, in what capacity and the circumstances. It is then up to the Inland Revenue to decide whether or not any rebate is due to the guarantor.

Chapter IX The Joint and Several Guarantee

To complete this review of guarantees, it is appropriate to consider the special matters relating to joint and several guarantees. Some reference has already been made to such undertakings—as on page 28 under *value* and on page 42 under *validity*—but these various points are here gathered together as a matter of convenience.

VALUE OF THE GUARANTEE

Where two or more persons are disposed to support the borrowing of a customer, it is obviously preferable to obtain their signature to a joint and several guarantee whereby each one of them will be liable for the full amount although the risk is spread amongst them. The advantages of joint and several liability over mere joint liability are well known. With joint liability, under the doctrine of survivorship the estate of a deceased guarantor is released and the bank has only one right of action on the contract, but with joint and several liability the estate of a deceased guarantor remains liable and the bank has as many rights of action as there are guarantors. A joint guarantee is, therefore, never accepted in banking practice.

To ascertain the value of such security, it is always wise to enquire for the full amount against each and every guarantor, but the enquiry should disclose that it is a joint and several guarantee with a stated number of co-guarantors in order to afford the replying bank an opportunity, in case of need, of pointing out that, although unable to speak for the full amount, the customer may be considered good for a given proportion of the total liability. The most frequent joint and several guarantee accepted in practice is taken from the directors of a private limited company to secure advances granted to their company and its value naturally depends upon the free resources of the directors outside the company. At worst, it can be taken as tangible evidence of the confidence which the directors have in the future of the business which they control.

VALIDITY OF THE GUARANTEE

It is essential from the standpoint of validity that all those who have agreed to execute the joint and several guarantee must sign it before any of them can be held liable. No advances can, therefore, be granted relying solely on such

79

security until all the parties named in the guarantee have actually signed it. In *National Provincial Bank of England* v. *Brackenbury* (1906 22 T.L.R.797), four persons were to be joint and several guarantors but one died before he could sign the guarantee. Although the bank had made advances relying on the guarantee, it was held that the three parties who had signed it were not liable. To avoid dispute where one of several guarantors fails to complete the guarantee, a letter should be obtained from the remainder agreeing to be liable notwithstanding the missing signature. In practice, the safest and simplest course is to start afresh and to obtain a new guarantee only from those who have already executed the original.

FORM OF THE GUARANTEE

All the clauses found in an individual guarantee, which have been discussed at length in previous chapters, will be incorporated suitably in a joint and several guarantee to apply equally and severally to all the guarantors, who will expressly contract to be jointly and severally responsible for the amount required. In addition, to overcome the possibility that the release of one guarantor may discharge the remainder, a clause may be introduced providing that the bank is at liberty to release any one of them or to accept any composition or make other arrangements with any one of the guarantors without thereby prejudicing its rights against the remainder. In short, the bank retains freedom to deal with any guarantor without disturbing its full rights against the others.

Similarly, a clause may be found requiring notice of determination (usually three months) by *each* guarantor or by his personal representatives, thereby ensuring that one guarantor or his executors cannot alone determine the guarantee. They must all join together in sending notice of determination. In *Egbert* v. *National Crown Bank* [1918] A.C. 903, a joint and several guarantee provided that the liability was to continue 'until the undersigned, or the executors or administrators of the undersigned, shall have given the bank notice in writing to make no further advances on the security of this guarantee'. It was decided that one guarantor could not determine this guarantee and, to quote Lord Dunedin, '. . .this clause stipulates that the guarantee is to remain in force until there is notice given by *each and all* of the guarantors, the executors of any deceased co-signatory coming in his place'.

DETERMINATION OF A JOINT AND SEVERAL GUARANTEE

Upon the *death* of one joint and several guarantor, the action taken by the bank will depend upon the terms of the guarantee and the facts of the case. The death of one surety does not, in any event, determine the continuing liability of his co-sureties (*Beckett* v. *Addyman* (1882) 9 Q.B.D. 783) and where a clause similar to that discussed above is included in the guarantee, the estate of the deceased will remain liable until notice is received from his executors *and* from all the other guarantors. In the absence of such notice from all parties, there is no legal need to break the account of the principal debtor. In practice, however, the bank may decide to determine the position to enable the executors to wind up the deceased's estate and it may be possible to release the estate, relying on the remaining guarantors or obtaining fresh security to support the position. To place the matter beyond controversy (which can so easily arise with guarantors despite the soundness of the bank's legal position), the simplest practical solution, where the deceased's estate can be released, is to obtain a fresh guarantee from the survivors. Sometimes a new guarantor will be found to replace the deceased. To continue to rely upon a joint and several guarantee for many years after the death of one of them is to invite trouble, however watertight the bank's position may be upon interpretation of the clauses of the guarantee.

In the event of *bankruptcy* of a joint and several guarantor, much depends upon whether the bank wishes to prove against the bankrupt estate or is content to rely upon the liability of the solvent sureties. In the former event, the account has to be stopped immediately to determine the several liability of the bankrupt. In the latter case, the prudent course will be to take a fresh guarantee from the other guarantors to guard against the prospect that, despite any clause enabling the bank to release one guarantor without reference to the others, it might be held that any release obtained through bankruptcy was not a release by the bank and therefore outside the provisions of the guarantee. In practice, it is usual to break the account promptly upon reliable advice of bankruptcy proceedings against a joint and several guarantor and not to grant further advances until approved fresh security has been taken.

Should a joint and several guarantor unhappily be found to be mentally incapable, the safest course is to stop the account as the party suffering from the mental disorder certainly cannot be held liable for future advances (*Bradford Old Bank Ltd.* v. *Sutcliffe* (1918) 2 K.B. 833).

It is needless to add, where the bank finds it necessary to demand payment of a joint and several guarantee, it will call upon each guarantor to find the full amount required, being either the amount of the debt or the amount of the guarantee, whichever is the smaller sum. Each guarantor may then proffer his alleged share of the liability and, in accepting such contributions for the credit of a guarantee security suspense account, it is incumbent upon the bank to emphasise that the liability is several and the amount is merely accepted by way of instalment and not in discharge of all liability. Sometimes all the guarantors pay their required share, but more often one or more of them cannot find anything and the bank has to return to the attack to enforce further payments from the original contributories. The full rights of the bank must, therefore, be preserved with care until its debt is satisfied in full.

F

Part Three: Life Policies

Chapter X Types of Policy and their Acceptability as Security

Compared with the average guarantee a life policy, providing it has an adequate surrender value, is a much more tangible, reliable and acceptable banking security. A satisfactory title can easily be obtained to the policy. Its value is readily ascertainable and does not fluctuate with market conditions. The security can easily be realised when required and in the unhappy event of the untimely death of the assured the full nominal value of the policy will be payable. For this reason they are most acceptable as supporting security for advances granted to partnership and private company customers where the continued success of the business of the borrower depends upon the knowledge, personal ability or drive of the assured, upon whom the bank relies to earn the profits to repay the indebtedness. If death intervenes the proceeds of the policy will correct what might otherwise have been a position involving some risk.

The chief disadvantages lie in the fact that the policy may lapse through the non-payment of premiums, but so long as the bank does not permit the customer to overdraw in excess of the surrender value of the policy any risk is negligible on these grounds because future premiums can be paid by the bank to the debit of the customer's account to keep the policy alive. The surrender value will not be increased by the full amount of the premium payment but the policy can always be surrendered if the bank thinks fit. As will be explained later, it is up to the bank to safeguard its position. There are also remote risks that the policy may be vitiated by the suicide or the breach of other conditions by the assured, but these restrictions are nowadays rarely found in policies and the banker is in any event forewarned when the contract is examined. The only serious disadvantage is that the bank may be criticised by the widow and dependants of an assured if it collects the proceeds of a policy upon which they were relying to provide for their future. Such criticism is obviously unfounded because the borrower in his lifetime used the policy to support his requirements in what he presumably regarded as the best interests of his family. The bank can hardly be blamed for any unhappy outcome.

Basically, life policies fulfil the most essential canons of sound banking security. They are stable in value and easily realisable at all times. With these general introductory remarks all the legal and practical problems which arise in taking, maintaining and realising such security can be explored in detail.

NATURE OF LIFE ASSURANCE CONTRACTS

A life assurance may be defined as a contract whereby the insurer in consideration of a certain premium, which may be payable in one amount or by annual payments, undertakes to pay to the beneficiary of the policy a sum or annuity upon the death of the life assured. The capital sum may be payable either at death or at the end of a certain number of years, whichever first happens. There are many types of life policies to meet particular requirements and the following general classes may be distinguished:—

1. *Whole Life Policies*, which provide for the payment of the amount of the policy, with or without profits according to the terms thereof, upon death. They do not mature until death and are, therefore, taken out primarily to provide for the dependants of the assured. The longer the assured may live the larger the total amount of premiums paid unless there is a limit on the number payable.

2. *Endowment Policies*, which provide for the payment of the sum assured, with or without profits as the case may be, on a certain date *or* at death, whichever occurs first. During the term of the policy full cover is available in the event of death, but if the assured survives to the stated date the amount can be collected and used as a nest-egg perhaps for retirement. From the banking standpoint, the advantage of this type of policy lies in the fact that the maturity date is certain. It is acceptable security in normal times for a bridging operation where, for example, a customer aged 58 years wishes to borrow to buy a house for retirement and has an endowment policy maturing on his 60th birthday.

3. *Family Protection Policies*, is a general term for special types of whole life or endowment policies designed to protect the widow and children in the event of the untimely death of the husband. In addition to the payment of a capital sum at death, provision is made for the payment of an annuity to the person entitled to the proceeds of the policy. There are many variations, but the terms can soon be seen when the policy is studied by the banker.

4. *Term Assurance Policies*, are not satisfactory banking security because they provide for payment of the amount of the policy *only if death occurs during the stated period*. They have no surrender value. Such policies may be taken out by anyone wishing to cover the risk of death duty liability on an *inter vivos* gift or settlement. If the assured survives the seven-year period all is well. If he dies, the proceeds of the policy will be available to meet the death duties.

5. *Pure Endowment Policies*, are also unsuitable from the banking standpoint because there is no life cover. The amount assured is payable only if the assured survives the specified period. Sometimes the policy provides that if the assured dies before the maturity date all premiums paid to date are returnable. These policies are comparatively rare but should be recognised if offered as security.

6. *Industrial Policies*. These are a special type of life or endowment policy, usually for small amounts subject to weekly or monthly premiums entered upon payment in a policy book. They will be considered fully later.

When entering into a contract of assurance, the assured is called upon to complete a questionnaire disclosing information required by the assurance company and he has to reply fully and accurately to all questions raised by the company. Full disclosure is essential because *a contract of assurance is a contract uberrimae fidei* (of the utmost good faith) and may be vitiated by any fraudulent or innocent non-disclosure of essential facts. In *London Assurance* v. *Mansel* (1879) 11 Ch. D. 363 the defendant in his proposal for assurance wrote 'Insured now in two offices for £16,000 at ordinary rates. Policies effected last year' in reply to the questions 'Has a proposal ever been made on your life at any other office or offices? If so, where? Was it accepted at the ordinary premium, or at an increased premium, or declined?' It transpired after the acceptance of the proposal that the assured's life had previously been declined by several offices and it was decided that the assurance company could set aside the contract. Another instance where it was held that there had been incomplete disclosure was *Godfrey* v. *Britannic Assurance Co. Ltd.* (1963) *The Guardian*, May 15. Apart from innocent mistakes made in stating the age of the assured in the proposal, which can easily be remedied (see later), it is fortunately rare to hear of the avoidance of a contract of assurance through non-disclosure of essential facts. It is nevertheless a risk, however remote, over which the lending bank has no control.

A life policy is not always on the life of and in favour of the same person. It may be in favour of a third party and another basic feature of assurance contracts is that, where a policy is taken out by a third party, it may be avoided by the company if the third party did not have an *insurable interest* on the life assured at the time the policy was issued (Life Assurance Act, 1774). When faced with a third party policy taken out a decade previously, it may be a little difficult for a bank to verify that the third party originally had an insurable interest. Fortunately, the problem rarely arises because no established assurance company to-day will issue a policy unless it is satisfied that there is an insurable interest and, in any event, if the company later discovered that there was no insurable interest, it would be unlikely to take advantage of the defence in the 1774 Act to the detriment of a bank holding the policy *bona fide* as assignee. The provision was introduced to stop gambling on the lives of third parties, but it was decided in *Worthington* v. *Curtis* (1875) 1 Ch. D. 419 that the defence of failure of an insurable interest availed only if and when the company elected to plead it. The policy is not, therefore, automatically avoided and the practical risk to a bank to-day is correspondingly remote.

A guarantor or a creditor has an insurable interest in the life of his debtor always providing the debt was not extinguished when the policy was taken out. The fact that the debt is repaid before the maturity of the policy is not material. It follows that if it so wished a bank could take out a policy on the life of a borrowing customer. The question hinges upon whether the third party would suffer financial loss in the event of the death of the person whose life he wishes to insure. If so, he has an insurable interest. It has been decided that in the following cases an insurable interest can be presumed without need for evidence to support it:—

(*a*) Insurance by a wife on the life of her husband (Section 11 Married Women's Property Act, 1882).

(*b*) Insurance by a husband on the life of his wife (*Griffiths* v. *Fleming* [1909] 1 K.B. 805).

But a parent has no insurable interest on the life of a child, or *vice versa*, in the absence of some pecuniary interest. (*Halford* v. *Kymer* (1830) 10 B. & C. 724). Fortunately, the third party policies offered to a bank as security usually come within the two cases set out above and the presence of an insurable interest is unquestionable. Unusual policies can always be treated on their merits as circumstances dictate.

IS THE LIFE POLICY ACCEPTABLE AS SECURITY?

When offered a life policy as security, the first step is to examine the policy in detail and the officer entrusted with this important duty will consider all the following questions:—

1. *By whom is the policy issued?* The standing of the company responsible for payment of the capital sum at maturity is obviously important. Where it is issued by a well known British life company no question arises because the exceptional strength of their financial position is common knowledge. But the policy may be issued by a company domiciled abroad with no office in this country and, apart from the need for enquiry concerning its standing, the prospect of difficulty arising in collecting the proceeds of the policy has to be considered. Exchange control and exchange risks may cause difficulty. Most policies accepted by banks as security nowadays are, however, issued by companies of high repute.

2. *What type of policy is it? How much will be payable and when?* An endowment policy will be preferred to a whole life policy and there may be variations in the cover which affect the bank's position. For example, the capital sum payable at death may be reduced progressively with the age of the assured. Any doubts concerning when and how much is payable at maturity should be settled by enquiry from the company. The term of an endowment policy may be important because, apart from the possibility of surrender, the period yet to run may indicate the maximum period of the advance to the customer. In like manner, with a pure life policy the age and normal state of health of the assured may be material. The prudent banker will not, however, be relying solely on the proceeds of the policy for repayment. Nevertheless, the capital amount and whether it is payable with or without profits within a reasonable time is obviously important.

3. *When was the policy taken out? What is the amount of the premium and when is it payable? Are the premiums paid to date? What is the current value of the policy?* The surrender value of the policy usually increases more rapidly as the policy nears maturity, and in the first few years after issue its value will be a mere fraction of the total premiums paid to date. The surrender value can be ascertained by enquiry from the company, but the bank may have to estimate the value when the advance is urgently required and a safe guide with life and endowment policies is to take one-third of the premiums paid up to five years from the date of issue and 50 per cent. of the premiums for a policy which has run for a longer term. Such a rough estimate usually leaves ample margin to protect the bank. Production of the last premium receipt is essential to prove that premiums have been paid to date, and it is often prudent to consider whether the amount of the premium is reasonable in relation to the known financial means of the party responsible for its payment. The bank has no wish to finance the premiums and the future of the security depends upon the regularity of such payments. They may be payable in monthly or quarterly instalments and the due dates have to be diarised suitably to obtain the premium receipts. The best course in practice is to obtain the customer's instructions for payment by the bank under standing order, thereby removing the need for repeated enquiry for the receipts. Sometimes a paid-up policy is deposited as security. It is an ideal security because it steadily increases in value without further payment and no trouble is involved to the bank to ensure that its value is maintained. It can virtually be forgotten until maturity.

4. *Has the age of the assured been admitted?* The importance of this requirement is

often missed and trouble arises when the policy monies are claimed. The annual premium payable depends amongst other things upon the age of the assured when the policy is taken out and the proposal form calls for details of the date of birth. The companies naturally require proof of this material factor but unfortunately few, if any, insist upon production of the birth certificate before they issue the policy. No monies will, however, be paid under the policy until the company is satisfied that the age of the assured was correctly stated at the outset. Mistakes in ages are not uncommon and the risk to the bank is that if the proposer understates his or her age (an acceptable feminine failing) higher premiums will be payable and, when meeting the claim at maturity or upon surrender of the policy, the company will deduct from the capital sum the total of premium amounts thus unpaid during the period since the issue of the policy. The reduction in the amount payable may be material and it is, therefore, essential that the bank should be satisfied that the age of the assured has been admitted. If the assured has duly produced his birth certificate to the company, the policy will be endorsed 'age admitted' or there will be a slip attached. In the absence of this evidence (and it is frequently missing) the prudent banker will take prompt steps in the best interests of the assured as well as itself to obtain the birth certificate and to send it to the company with the policy for endorsement. It is foolish to delay this precaution and, if the assured cannot find his birth certificate and he was born in England or Wales an application should be made to the Registrar General, General Register Office, Somerset House, London, W.C.2, quoting name, place and date of birth on form P.A.S. 8(h), when a short birth certificate will be issued upon payment of a fee of fifteen p. It is surprising how frequently a bank has to attend to this matter on behalf of a customer.

Incidentally, when accepting as security a policy on the life of a lady who has married since the issue of the policy, a certificate of her marriage should be obtained and registered with the company to establish her identity. This will save trouble when any claim materialises.

5. *Are there any restrictions or special conditions which may affect the value of the policy to the bank?* Although rarely found, the terms of the policy have to be studied to be sure that no qualifications are made concerning, for example, air travel or residence in hot climates, etc. abroad. Sometimes the life may have been accepted without a medical examination subject to a reduced payment if death occurs within a given time. Again, the assured may have undertaken not to engage in employment or sport of a dangerous nature. Any restrictions of this type have obvious disadvantages from the bank's standpoint and have to be interpreted in relation to the facts of the case. There may be a suicide clause providing that if the assured commits suicide the policy will be invalidated, but there is usually a time limit and often a proviso to protect the interests of *bona fide* third parties. Any restrictions of this kind demand close attention, unless there is a protective clause on the following lines to cover the bank: 'Provided always that this assurance shall not be avoided as regard any person who shall have a *bona fide* pecuniary interest herein under assignment or charge but shall remain in force to the extent of that interest only.'

There is a principle that no criminal should be allowed to benefit from his crime and where a man murders someone whose life he has assured, he cannot collect the policy moneys. In like manner, as suicide is a crime, if a man insures himself and then commits suicide whilst of sane mind, his executors or administrators cannot recover the proceeds of the policy. Any express undertaking by the company to pay notwithstanding sane suicide would not be upheld because it is contrary to public policy.

The suicide problem was last considered by the House of Lords in *Beresford* v. *Royal Insurance Co. Ltd.*, [1938] 2 All E.R. 602. In June, 1925, Major Rowlandson took out five policies on his life for £50,000 paying the premiums regularly to 1934, when he became insolvent with heavy debts to personal friends and a loan of £6,791 from Royal Insurance Co. Ltd., against the policies, being the total of their surrender value. He was unable to pay the premiums and shot himself. It was clear from letters and interviews that he committed suicide so that the policy moneys would be available to meet his debts. The following condition appeared in the policies:—'If the life or any one of the lives assured (being also the assured or one of them) shall die by his own hand, whether sane or insane, within one year from the commencement of the insurance, the policy shall be void as against any person claiming the amount hereby assured or any part thereof, except that it shall remain in force to the extent to which a *bona fide* interest for pecuniary consideration, or as a security for money, possessed or acquired by a third party before the date of such death, shall be established to the satisfaction of the directors,' and there being no doubt concerning the true construction of the contract (nine years had elapsed since the date of the policy), the question hinged on whether it was enforceable in a court of law. It was decided that it was contrary to public policy for the contract to be enforced against the company and the claim of the administrators was dismissed. The rights of third parties were not considered, but certain comments were made *obiter* and the following extracts from the judgments are of interest:—

'The remaining question is whether the principle applies where the criminal is dead and his personal representative is seeking to recover a benefit which only takes shape after his death. It must be remembered that the money becomes due, if at all, under an agreement made by the deceased during his life for the express purpose of benefiting his estate after his death. During his life he had power to complete testamentary disposition over it. I cannot think the principle of public policy to be so narrow as not to include the increase of the criminal's estate amongst the benefits which he is deprived of by his crime. His executor or administrator claims as his representative, and, as his representative, falls under the same ban.

'Anxiety is naturally aroused by the thought that this principal may be invoked so as to destroy the security given to lenders and others by policies of life insurance which are in daily use for that purpose. The question does not directly arise, and I do not think that anything said in this case can be authoritative. But I consider myself free to say that I cannot see that there is any objection to an assignee for value before the suicide enforcing a policy which contains an express promise to pay upon sane suicide, at any rate so far as the payment is to extend to the actual interest of the assignee. It is plain that a lender may himself insure the life of the borrower against sane suicide; and the assignee of the policy is in a similar position so far as public policy is concerned. I have little doubt that after this decision the life companies will frame a clause which is unobjectionable: and they will have the support of the decision of the Court of Queen's Bench in *Moore* v. *Woolsey* (4 E. & B. 243), where a clause protecting *bona fide* interests was upheld. It was suggested to us that so far as the doctrine was applied to contracts it would have the effect of making the whole contract illegal. I think that the simple answer is that this is a contract to pay on an event which may happen from many causes, one only of which involves a crime by the assured. The cause is severable, and the contract, apart from the criminal cause, is perfectly valid.' Lord Atkin.

'I feel the force of the view that to increase the estate which a criminal leaves behind him is to benefit him. To enforce payment in favour of the assured's representative would be to give him a benefit, albeit in a sense a post-mortem benefit, the benefit, namely, of having by his last and criminal act provided for his relatives or creditors. And no criminal can be allowed to benefit in any way by his crime.'

'I return to the simple question—ought the courts to enforce a contract to pay a sum of money to a person's representatives in the event of his committing *felo de se*. In my opinion I am bound to answer this question in the negative, both on principle and, so far as the courts of this country are concerned, by authority. I should add that I desire to reserve my opinion as to the position of third parties who have *bona fide* acquired rights for value under such policies.' Lord MacMillan.

From this it seems reasonable to assume that the rights of a bank as mortgagee of a policy would not be prejudiced by the suicide of the assured while sane, if the policy included an express proviso to pay in such event, because there is no offence against public policy. Where an insured commits suicide when he is insane, the right of his personal representatives to collect the proceeds of the policy is unquestionable unless, of course, there is any express condition to the contrary included in the policy. The whole problem is not a risk that the lending banker can ignore but it is to be hoped that such unfortunate circumstances will rarely arise to embarrass the bank.

6. *Can the policy holder assign his interest?* Apart from industrial policies which are often unassignable without the approval of the company the beneficiary of a policy can normally assign or mortgage his interest in a policy, but the point demands consideration in case there is any express prohibition.

7. *Who is entitled to the proceeds of the policy? Can all interested parties join in the charge to the bank?* A life policy taken out by a borrower on his life and in his favour presents no difficulty in this respect, but a policy in favour of a third party, who must be of full age if he is to charge the policy to the bank, calls for special consideration. All interested parties must join in the charge and it is clearly essential when examining the policy to decide by whom the deed is to be executed. A few general examples can be drawn.

A policy taken out by X on his life and in his favour is his to charge as he may wish and X alone need charge it to the bank. A policy taken out by Y on the life of Z (in whom he has an assurable interest) is the property of Y, who can charge it to the bank without the approval of Z. Greater complications arise with settlement policies within Section 11 of the Married Women's Property Act, 1882, whereby a trust is created in favour of a third party, usually the wife of the assured. Where A takes out a policy on his life in favour of Mrs. A. she has an immediate vested interest in the policy and, if she predeceases her husband, the policy passes to her personal representatives as part of her estate (*Cousins* v. *Sun Life Assurance Society* [1933] 1 Ch. 126), and attracts estate duty. If A dies first, the proceeds are payable to Mrs. A and do not comprise part of A's estate for duty liability.

To obtain a valid charge on this type of policy Mrs. A must be a party thereto and it is desirable that her signature to any mortgage should be witnessed by her solicitor to prove that she was under no pressure or undue influence from her husband. Particular care is necessary where a policy is drawn in favour of the wife of the assured without actually naming her. Unless clearly limited to 'my present wife' a second or subsequent wife may be entitled to the proceeds of the policy at maturity, and it is impossible for a bank to obtain a valid charge. For example, a policy drawn in favour of 'his wife and children' without mention of actual names has been held to be for the benefit of the widow at death, and all children by any marriage and whenever born who survive the assured (*In re Browne's Policy* [1903] 1 Ch. 188]. It is obviously impossible to get all interested parties present and future to join in a charge over a policy of this kind. Again, a policy taken out by P for the benefit of his wife, Mrs. P, and the children of their marriage is in favour of the named wife if she survives P and all children of their marriage whenever born who survive him (*In re Seyton* (1887) 34 Ch. D. 511). Unless the children are all more than 18 years of age and there is no medical possibility of further issue, it is virtually impossible to obtain a valid charge over this kind of policy. There are many variations and particular care is necessary with policies on the lives of infants. They are generally suspect from the banking standpoint.

A policy taken out by a minor in his own favour obviously cannot be charged by the infant (Section 1 Infants Relief Act, 1874). A policy taken out by a parent upon the life of a child where no trust is created in favour of the child can be charged by the parent because no legal estate is created for the child. In *Tibbetts* v. *Engelbach* [1924] 2 Ch. 348, a father, in the proposal form, described himself as the proposer 'for his daughter Mary Noel, aged one month' and a policy was issued payable at the end of the endowment term to the daughter if she survived. In the event of her death before the given date all premiums were repayable to the proposer. She survived but her father died and his personal representatives claimed that the policy monies were part of his estate. They succeeded because the daughter had no interest in the policy merely because it was expressed payable to her. She was a stranger to the contract and the father had not constituted himself trustee for his daughter of the policy or of its proceeds. Such a policy taken out by a parent for the benefit of his child when he or she reaches a stated age can, therefore, be validly charged as security by the parent, but where the policy is taken out as agent for the child creating a trust in the child's favour, the power of the parent to mortgage the policy as security for his account is doubtful (*In re Webb* [1941] Ch. 225). The crucial test is whether the infant has any legal or beneficial interest in the policy or its proceeds and, as the position is usually obscure, such children's deferred policies should not normally be relied upon as security.

The care required in scrutinising the policy to decide who are the interested parties and whether they can create a valid charge is thus clear and, as all interested parties have to join in the charge, the importance of the task needs no further emphasis. Where any doubt arises concerning who is an interested party, legal advice may be necessary or the bank may resort to the assurance company for guidance, but policies of this kind with their many variations should be avoided wherever possible.

Chapter XI The Creation of the Security

EQUITABLE AND LEGAL MORTGAGES

Being satisfied from the examination of the policy that it is acceptable as bank security, the next step is to obtain a satisfactory charge over it and to protect the bank's position against the risk that other parties may have or seek to obtain an interest in the policy.

EQUITABLE MORTGAGE OVER A LIFE POLICY

A life policy can be taken as security in quite an informal manner by the mere deposit of the policy with or without a memorandum evidencing the intention of the parties. Although it is cheap and simple, an equitable mortgage by the deposit of the policy has many weaknesses, but occasions do arise in practice where it is better to take a policy on security receipt only as informal cover for indebtedness rather than to remain unsecured. As a chose in action no formality is required to obtain an equitable mortgage of a policy, but in view of the disadvantages compared with a legal mortgage, a bank does not normally rely on this method or use any standard form of memorandum of deposit for policies.

An equitable mortgage is valid against a trustee in bankruptcy in the event of the failure of the mortgagor, but the limited equitable interest does not entitle the bank to sue on the policy in its own name or to give a valid discharge for the proceeds. The policy cannot be surrendered without the co-operation of the assured or the approval of the Court and at maturity the company will require the discharge of the assured or of his personal representatives in the event of his death. In other words, the power of the bank to deal with the security depends throughout upon the co-operation of the assured, who will usually be unwilling to sacrifice his life cover just to repay the bank debt.

Notice of an equitable mortgage can be given to the company, but priority of equitable charges is determined by the order in which they are created in the absence of notice (*In re Weniger's Policy* [1910] 2 Ch. 291) and by virtue of the Policies of Assurance Act, 1867, companies are under no legal obligation to recognise equitable interests.

The fact that the bank obtains possession of the policy has, however, the obvious advantage that it will be difficult for the assured to charge it elsewhere and, upon maturity the company will not pay over the proceeds without the production of the policy or a satisfactory indemnity to cover any failure to deliver it. If the assured or his personal representatives or a trustee in bankruptcy will not co-operate by signing the discharge and authorising payment of the proceeds direct to the bank, there is an impasse and no money will be paid out by the company until the parties reach agreement. An equitable charge is thus better than no charge at all and can serve to bridge a gap where a difficult customer declines to create a legal mortgage in favour of the bank. Care must always be exercised to ensure that proof is available that the policy was taken as security. In the absence of a memorandum of deposit, the receipt given for the policy or any correspondence regarding the transaction should show that it was deposited as security. This is to obviate any suggestion by a trustee in bankruptcy or a personal representative that the policy was left with the bank for safe custody only.

LEGAL MORTGAGE OVER A LIFE POLICY

The most complete and normal method of obtaining a charge over a life policy is by way of legal mortgage whereby the assured *assigns* all his rights in the policy to the bank subject to his equity of redemption. The Policies of Assurance Act, 1867, gives the right to assign policies of assurance and enables an assignee to sell in his own name and thereby to give a valid discharge for the proceeds. The assignment has to be in writing either by endorsement on the policy or by a separate instrument. The assignee must give written notice to the assurance company, receipt of which it has to acknowledge in writing. In effect, therefore, the benefits of the policy are mortgaged to the bank and retained until repayment of the advance, when the policy can be reassigned to the assured. All these points can now be considered in turn.

1. *Form of Legal Mortgage*

Each bank has its own standard printed forms to cover the legal mortgage of life policies by various parties and the reader is advised to study the form in use in his bank in relation to the general provisions discussed below. There will usually be direct charges to cover policies charged by an assured for his own overdraft and collateral charges needed when the assured deposits the policy to secure the indebtedness of a third party, but all the main clauses will be on similar lines.

The mortgage opens with what is known as the assignment clause whereby, in consideration of the granting of banking facilities to, or continuing the account of, the named borrower, the assured assigns the entire policy (usually described in a schedule) to the bank, together with all bonuses and additions, as security for all indebtedness or other liabilities of the customer on any account either solely or jointly with other persons. The security is expressed to be a continuing security to avoid the operation of the Rule in *Clayton's Case* and the bank is expressly authorised to give a valid discharge for the entire proceeds of the policy notwithstanding that the balance owing at maturity may be less than the amount payable by the company. It is provided that if the customer repays all his debts and liabilities to the bank it will, at his request and at his expense, reassign the policy to the mortgagor.

The assignor engages to pay punctually the premiums and any other moneys payable under the policy and to lodge the premium receipts with the bank. An assurance company usually grants thirty days of grace for the payment of premiums and, if arrangements are not made for the payments to be made by the bank under standing order, a card diary has to be maintained to check the production of the required premium receipts by the given dates. It is further agreed that if the premiums are not paid the bank may pay them to the debit of the customer's account.

The bank is empowered at any time to sell or surrender the policy without the consent or concurrence of the mortgagor, or to convert it into a paid up policy and, for this purpose, it may exercise all the powers conferred upon mortgagees by the Law of Property Act, 1925, excluding the restriction of three months' notice of repayment required by Section 103 of that Act. The bank also reserves the right to consolidate its mortgages by expressly excluding the operation of Section 93 of the Law of Property Act, 1925. The indebtedness secured by the mortgage is always repayable upon demand and, although the bank reserves the right to sell or surrender the policy without the approval of the mortgagor, ample notice will normally be given in practice before taking such drastic action. Nevertheless, the power is there and is useful when the mortgagor disappears or ignores communications from the bank.

2. Notice of Assignment to the Company

Immediately upon completion of the mortgage, the next step is to give notice of the charge to the assurance company to comply with Section 3 of the Policies of Assurance Act, 1867, and so to secure full rights under the policy and to record the date of the bank's interest. Such notice entitles the bank to sue on the policy in its own name and makes the company liable to the bank should it pay the proceeds of the policy to another claimant. Priority also depends upon the date of the receipt of the notice by the company and the bank will have priority over any earlier assignees who have failed to register their interest, always providing that the bank had no actual *or constructive* notice of any such earlier charges when it granted its advances (*Newman* v. *Newman* (1885) 28 Ch. D. 674). Failure to give notice may, therefore, seriously jeopardise the bank's position.

The notice has to be in writing, quoting the date and nature of the assignment, and is usually sent in duplicate with the request that one copy is returned to the bank duly receipted by the company. By virtue of the Policies of Assurance Act, 1867, the company is obliged to acknowledge receipt upon request and can charge a fee not exceeding twenty five p. for such service. Some companies are content to charge less and some give the service free. A list of these charges is given in *The Banker's Almanac and Year Book*. Included in the notice to the company will be an enquiry as to whether any notice of previous charges or interest have been received or if the company itself has any charge over the policy. In other words, the bank has to be satisfied that it has complete priority before granting accommodation relying on the life policy as security. Frequently the opportunity is taken to ascertain the surrender value of the policy if such information has not been obtained before the execution of the charge.

If the assurance company in reply to the enquiry from the bank discloses prior charges over the policy, it is necessary to ascertain whether they have been duly discharged. Any earlier mortgages will form part of the chain of title to the policy and should be filed with the policy, together with the relative reassignments. All these documents have to be produced to the assurance company before any claim on the policy can be paid. Difficulty will arise if they have been lost or destroyed and the company will require a satisfactory indemnity before payment. If the enquiries reveal prior charges outstanding, the bank is obviously fixed with notice that its charge is subject to the prior charge and, if it is content nevertheless to rely on the second mortgage, notice has to be given to the first mortgagee. On the other hand, if the bank has possession of the policy, it is unlikely to find that there is a prior charge in favour of a mortgagee who has released it.

This thought brings to mind the need for a warning where a bank is asked to grant advances against the security of a policy which the customer has lost or mislaid. Such cases are troublesome but not unknown and the risk of course, is that the policy may already be charged elsewhere. With an undoubted customer the only difficulty will be the collection of the proceeds of the policy when the company will call for an indemnity from the bank. But where there is a prior charge which has not been registered with the company, it might be held that the absence of the policy was constructive notice to the bank of a prior charge, the policy being held by the assignee. If so, this constructive notice would operate against the bank and it could not obtain priority merely by reason of the fact that it had registered its own charge with the company.

3. *Maintenance of the Security*
Having examined the life policy, obtained the legal mortgage and registered the charge with the company, there being no prior charges current the bank can rest content in the knowledge that the security is complete. To protect the bank's position thereafter a record system has to be introduced to ensure that:—

(a) The premiums are promptly paid on their due dates.

(b) Prompt action is taken in the event of the failure of the customer to pay the premiums. According to the circumstances, the bank may decide to pay the premiums to the debit of the account to keep the policy alive, or it may exercise its right to sell or surrender the policy or to convert it into a fully paid policy.

(c) The security is revalued at reasonable intervals (normally every three to five years) by obtaining the surrender value from the company. No charge is made by the assurance company for this information.

(d) All premium receipts and any bonus notices are filed with the policy in the bank safe.

(e) The maturity date of an endowment policy is suitably diarised to enable the proceeds to be collected without delay.

(f) Prompt action is taken upon the receipt of notice of a second charge created on the policy (*see below*).

4. *Notice of a Second Charge*
It will be difficult for a mortgagor to create other charges on a policy which is retained in the possession of the bank (and it should never be released on any excuse until the advance has been repaid), but in the unlikely event of notice to the bank of a second charge, the account has to be stopped forthwith to avoid the operation of the Rule in *Clayton's Case*.

If the account is continued, all credits received after the notice will reduce the debt secured by the charge to the bank and subsequent withdrawals will be fresh advances ranking after the rights of the second mortgagee. If the indebtedness is repaid after the notice, the policy after reassignment should be delivered to the second mortgagee and not released to the mortgagor.

5. *The Release or Realisation of the Life Policy*

Upon repayment of the advance or other satisfactory arrangement for the release of the policy, it will be reassigned to the mortgagor usually by the completion and sealing of the reassignment clause printed in the bank's standard charge. Strictly speaking, Section 115 (1) of the Law of Property Act has removed the need for a reassignment and a receipt for the moneys secured will suffice instead if it is endorsed on the mortgage signed by the bank and it states the name of the person paying the money. Unless the mortgagor particularly wishes to free the policy from the charge, it is a good idea in practice to retain it undisturbed until maturity. The policy is then in the safe keeping of the bank and available as security without further trouble or expense if any need to borrow should arise in the future.

Where the policy is released, it is as well to remind the mortagor that the charge to the bank and the reassignment now form part of the chain of title to the policy and they must be preserved with it for production to the assurance company when a claim is made. The legal mortgage to the bank cannot be destroyed, however anxious some customers may be to remove the evidence of the past borrowing. When the reassignment is completed, the assurance company should be advised by the bank withdrawing the original notice of charge.

No formality is necessary to release a policy held merely by way of equitable mortgage because no legal interest has been granted to the bank. Any memorandum of deposit can be cancelled and need not be kept with the policy.

Where the advance becomes unsatisfactory during the life of the policy, steps may have to be taken to enforce the security. Failure of the borrower to repay or reduce the debt and failure to pay the premiums to maintain the policy may force the bank to exercise its rights set out in the mortgage. In addition to the removal of the life cover, the surrender of a policy entails financial loss to the mortgagor because the surrender value will usually be much less than the total of premiums paid to date. Every attempt will therefore be made to avoid such a drastic step, but occasions do unhappily arise when no alternative remains if the bank's position is to be protected.

An attempt may first be made to prevail upon the mortgagor to borrow from the assurance company itself against the policy, if in fact sufficient can be raised from this and any other sources to satisfy the bank. By this means the policy can be kept alive and a long term lender takes the place of the short term bank lender. Most assurance companies will lend from 80–90 per cent. of the surrender value of the policy and all that is necessary is for the bank to obtain the instructions of the customer to deliver the policy and the mortgage direct to the assurance company in return for the proceeds of the loan. Another alternative to avoid undue loss to the assured is to sell the policy to a friend or to a house which specialises in the purchase of life policies and reversionary interests as an investment. It often happens that a price can be obtained which is much higher than the current surrender value and, providing the power of sale has arisen according to the terms of the mortgage (usually failure of the borrower to repay upon demand), the bank can, if need be negotiate such a sale itself. The policy is assigned to the buyer, who thereafter pays the premiums and awaits realisation of his investment at maturity. The fact that the assignee has no insurable interest in the life insured does not upset the contract (*M'Farlane* v. *The Royal London Friendly Society* (1886) 2 T.L.R. 755) and there are often advertisements in the legal press by companies prepared to buy policies as an investment. To a certain extent they speculate upon the expectancy of life of the assured.

Sometimes a policy can be exchanged into a paid up policy for a lower amount without reduction in the surrender value. This possibility can be explored where the customer cannot meet the premiums, but the surrender value is sufficient to cover the bank debt. The policy will then steadily increase in value as the maturity date approaches without further liability for premiums. Much, of course, depends upon the period which has yet to run to maturity and the willingness of the bank to carry the advance for this maximum period.

As a last resort, the bank may have to surrender the policy. The power to do so is contained in the mortgage and any conditions therein have to be followed. Usually the bank has the right to surrender without reference to the customer, but every latitude will normally be granted in practice. The actual process of surrender is quite simple. Application has to be made to the company, which will supply details of the amount payable and the discharge required. The mortgage and policy can then be produced to the company to enable it to verify the title, and payment will be made thereafter against the receipt executed by the bank, usually under seal. The mortgage itself does not, of course, have to be discharged. It is of interest here to remind the reader of the difficulties which will obviously arise when the bank wishes to surrender a life policy, if the age of the assured has not been admitted to the company. The co-operation of the customer may be difficult to obtain in such circumstances and the company will not pay out until the point can be settled.

6. *Maturity of Policy*

When the assured dies the banker can claim upon the company for the proceeds of the policy, sending it with the legal mortgage (undischarged) and the death certificate to the company to prove the bank's title. Payment will then be made against an appropriate receipt for the amount due. As the title to the policy has been assigned to the bank, there is no need to await production of Probate of the deceased's will or to trouble his personal representatives in the matter. In like manner, the proceeds of an endowment policy can be collected when it matures during the lifetime of the assured. The due date will be diarised and about a month beforehand the question of payment can be taken up with the company, who will forward the required form of receipt. This receipt can be executed by the bank in advance and sent with the policy and legal mortgage to the company in good time to permit of payment promptly on the due date. Again, the payment is made direct to the bank as mortgagee without reference to the assured.

Although it is legally possible to take one legal mortgage of several policies issued by different companies and maturing on different dates, it is much more convenient in practice to take a separate mortgage over each policy. As explained above, the mortgage deed has to be produced to the company when a claim is made under the policy. If there are other policies charged in the same deed, it cannot be retained by the company and the bank has to execute an undertaking to produce the deed if and when it may later be required. To avoid this multiplication of documents executed by the bank and to keep the chain of title to each policy intact, it is far better to use separate deeds.

Incidentally, if the bank has notice of a second mortgage on a policy and there are surplus proceeds available when a claim is paid by the company, the surplus has to be held in trust for the second mortgagee.

When the bank has relied upon an equitable mortgage of a policy, the process of surrender or realisation at maturity is far from simple unless the assured, or if he has died his personal representatives, are co-operative. The policy cannot be surrendered without the approval of the depositor or an order from the Court and the latter method is a relatively expensive and protracted process. Few customers are likely to co-operate in such event. At maturity the legal title remains in the assured or his personal representatives and they have to execute the discharge to the company. If they decline, there is stalemate, but usually they are anxious to facilitate the payment of the bank debt to avoid further liability for interest accrued. Similarly, when an assured is adjudicated bankrupt his trustee will join in the receipt for the surrender of the policy in order to speed the discharge of the bank debt, particularly if any surplus proceeds or other securities are likely to be released for the benefit of the bankrupt estate.

7. Industrial Policies

Finally, a brief word of warning concerning industrial policies which are life assurances issued by industrial companies for small amounts subject to weekly or monthly premiums, usually collected by an agent of the company who acknowledges their receipt by an entry in a policy book. These policies are not acceptable as bank security because they have negligible, if any, surrender value and are rarely assignable without the approval of the issuing company. It is a difficult task to verify the payment of weekly premiums by production of the receipt book and expensive to the assured if the bank undertakes to pay the premium under standing instructions. Such policies, which are governed by the Friendly Societies Acts, should therefore be accepted for what they are worth and not relied upon as security. The depositor is obviously scraping the proverbial barrel if he has to resort to these policies in an attempt to raise funds.

G

Chapter XII Quoted Securities

BEARER STOCKS—SHARE WARRANTS—INSCRIBED STOCKS

The next type of security for consideration is stocks and shares, which is a general term covering many securities which are normally most acceptable to a banker. There are quoted shares which may be bearer, registered or inscribed, or in the temporary state of scrip certificates or allotment letters. There are unquoted shares which are usually registered but can be in the other classes. Types and classes of quoted shares abound, but apart from the question of valuation, the means by which they can be taken as security depends upon whether they are bearer, inscribed or registered shares. It is convenient, therefore, first to deal with quoted securities under these three headings, leaving unquoted shares for separate consideration.

As the story unfolds it will be appreciated that quoted shares are usually a near perfect type of bank security. The value of such security may well fluctuate sharply at times, but the current price can always be ascertained quickly and the shares held can, generally speaking, be sold in a ready market. Providing an adequate margin is maintained to combat any reasonable fall in market price, the risk of loss through an undue depreciation in the value of the security is negligible. A valid title can be obtained simply and cheaply and there is no cause for investigation of a complicated title as in the case of land. Certain disadvantages arise with special types of stocks, but generally speaking this class of security is ideal for bank lending.

QUOTED SHARES

Valuation
The first essential, as always, is to decide the value of the security and to introduce a system whereby any material fall in its value is quickly realised so that action may be taken promptly to protect the bank's position.

The prices of the more popular stocks and shares are quoted in the financial columns of the daily press, but a more complete source of information is *The Stock Exchange Daily Official List*, which is published by the Council of the London Stock Exchange and records the nominal quotations on the day of issue and actual prices at which deals were done during the day. The prices at the close of the market may differ from the prices ranging during the morning or afternoon and this distinction has often to be explained to customers who, after reference to the closing prices, think their shares have been bought at a higher price or sold at a lower price than that prevailing in the market. If there are no deals in a stock on any particular day, the list gives the price and date of the last recorded transaction. Prices are quoted in this list for about ten thousand stocks and shares, all listed in groups under appropriate headings. Since the last war securities which are rarely dealt in are excluded from this official daily list and will be found in *The Monthly Supplement of Quoted Securities Temporarily Removed from the Stock Exchange Daily Official List*. Where shares are not quoted on the London market, they may be dealt in officially on one of the Provincial Stock Exchanges, of which there are now eleven, including the Northern Stock Exchange and the Scottish Stock Exchange, these last being in each case a federation of exchanges existing in a number of separate business centres. The Northern Stock Exchange, for example, embraces, *inter alia*, exchanges in Manchester, Liverpool, Leeds etc., all of which publish their own *Official List*. Some of the provincial exchanges specialise in the shares of local industries which are not quoted outside their area. For example, at Oldham, there is a specialist market for cotton spinning mill shares. The best initial source of reference to find out where a particular share is quoted and also to formulate a picture of the capital structure, dividend history and trading activities of a quoted public company is the *Stock Exchange Official Year-Book*, which is published annually in two volumes. A reasonably up-to-date copy of this standard publication should be kept in all bank branches as it is a mine of information on shares. If the price of any share cannot be readily traced or it is rarely dealt in, the branch broker will always be willing to guide the bank, quoting the latest price and reporting on the nature and extent of the market in the shares. For security purposes, the shares should always be valued at the lower limit of the latest quotation, being the worst price the shares would be likely to realise at the time of going to press on the given date. The higher price quoted in the *Official Lists* is the limit at which the shares might have been purchased at the same time.

Having ascertained the lowest market value for the shares, the next step is to decide how much margin is required to protect the bank against any unforeseen fall in the market price. Apart altogether from changes in the trading fortunes of the company concerned, prices can fluctuate according to the impact of political and international events or general monetary conditions upon the market, which is frequently affected by factors which have no direct bearing upon the trade or prospects of the company whose shares are charged to the bank. It is impossible to look far ahead in the market with any degree of certainty. A company may announce record trading results at a period when the market is unduly depressed by political uncertainty and its shares will nevertheless drop in value because there are few, if any, buyers with sufficient confidence in the future to risk investment at that stage. Whilst buyers can hold-off there may be sellers who have to dispose of their shares because the cash proceeds are urgently needed and the market temporarily has an excess supply of the shares compared with the demand for them, with the result that the price falls. In a period of acute depression or in any general emergency, the whole market may collapse, whereas particular troubles may only materially affect certain classes of shares.

It is obviously impossible for a banker to decide what future developments are likely to depress the value of any shares charged as security, but a general view can be taken according to the class of stock or share because the prices of some fluctuate more widely than those of others in boom or slump conditions. The wider the fluctuations, the more speculative will be the shares and the bank will call for a much greater margin between the total market value and the maximum amount to be advanced.

The margins required by any bank will necessarily vary according to the type of shares (based on the market history), the nature of the overdraft facility and current conditions, but the following broad conclusions can be drawn as a general guide.

The minimum margin will be expected for stocks of or guaranteed by the British Government (which are by far the largest proportion of those issues known as *Gilts*) bearing a fixed rate of interest and repayable on a given date. Undated gilts may in certain conditions call for a slightly higher margin. The price of the longer dated or undated (*i.e.*, no date fixed for obligatory repayment) gilts will usually fluctuate more widely than the shorter dated stocks which will be repayable at par within a few years. Normally, the market price of gilts will vary according to the market value of money. When Base rates rise and other money rates follow, the price of fixed interest government securities will fall in order to increase their yield, in keeping with the rise in market rates. Similarly, when money rates fall the market price of gilts will rise to reduce the yield. All this, of course, assumes that nothing else happens to disturb the general trend. In the absence of a substantial fall in money rates, Government Stocks carrying a low rate of interest are unlikely to rise in value above par, but with the exception of undated issues they do not usually drop too severely in price, and are relatively more stable over varying conditions. A margin varying perhaps between five and fifteen per cent., according to the period a stock has to run before maturity, may, therefore, be deemed sufficient for the bank's purpose.

For convenience, some banks may follow the practice of the Stock Exchange and include County, Corporation and Public Board issues with Dominion and Colonial Government Stocks within the gilt bracket. Others may call for a slightly larger margin in view of the fact that over periods such stocks fluctuate a little more widely in value than British Government Stocks.

The next group demanding a higher margin of anything between say fifteen to thirty per cent., comprises good class industrial and commercial stocks and shares. In this class the bank will usually include for convenience fixed interest stocks (preference shares, loan stocks and debentures) whose price may vary with money rates in the same way as Government Stocks *and* with the fortunes of the company concerned, as well as ordinary shares (known as *equities*) whose value varies largely with the trading results and prospects of the business, as well as with money rates. The market prices of these shares can fluctuate widely with general and particular trading conditions, but in periods of inflation their value normally increases, always providing their results keep pace with the general trend. The extent of the margin required by the bank may, therefore, vary according to the size, history, and trading prospects of the company, although in daily practice it is hardly feasible to allocate a particular margin to each share. A more general view has to be taken erring necessarily on the side of caution. The shares of long established industrial giants, with immense reserves, dealing in essential markets with a successful history (known as *blue chips*), have a wider market than other commercial and industrial shares, and a smaller margin may suffice. The shares of the lesser known and unproved concerns may call for a larger margin, particularly when trade conditions are deteriorating.

The third and last general class which can be distinguished from the security standpoint is the extensive range of more speculative shares, such as rubbers, teas and mines which fluctuate much more widely in price, being subject to many local as well as general influences. A mine may be uneconomic to work or it may be exhausted, and weather can damage a crop, so that unknown and unexpected contingencies can suddenly react upon the market price of such shares. A margin of perhaps thirty per cent. up to fifty per cent. may, therefore, be deemed prudent for speculative shares in this class.

The practical course, therefore, is first to consider the type of share offered as security. Is it fully paid or partly paid? Is it a fixed interest stock or an ordinary share with dividends declared according to trading results? Is it dated (in which case how long dated?) or undated? By whom is the stock issued and what is the standing and history of the issuer? In other words, is it a gilt, a blue chip, medium industrial, or a speculative share? How wide is the market? Are there frequent daily dealings in the stock or share or have buyers to be found by negotiation? What are the highest and lowest dealing prices recorded over a reasonable period? This information, which as far as the more popular securities are concerned can be obtained from monthly booklets issued by many stockbrokers and from the end pages of *The Financial Times*, gives an indication of the fluctuation in the particular market. After all this data has been marshalled and considered, the bank can decide the extent of the margin required for the class of share and, after deducting it from the value of the shares at current selling price, the worth of the security to the bank is estimated. Thereafter, it is essential to revalue the shares at reasonable intervals, and to introduce a card index system whereby the impact upon the bank's position of a serious fall in the market price of a given share can quickly be determined. Suppose for some reason the shares of X Ltd. dropped thirty per cent. in the market value overnight. If the branch banker can refer to an index showing the names of all borrowers who have charged X Ltd. shares as security, it will be a simple and speedy task to review the security position of those customers. In the absence of such a system, all the security book entries would have to be examined to trace the accounts likely to be affected by the drop in the price of X Ltd. shares. It is unwise to rely upon memory to protect the bank's position in such an event. A general substantial fall in market prices will obviously call for a complete revaluation of all quoted shares held as security. It would be unwise to wait until each overdrawn account came up for its periodic review.

Being satisfied concerning the value of the proposed security, the next step is to decide how the bank can best obtain a valid charge over the stocks and shares. This broadly depends upon whether they are bearer, inscribed or registered securities.

BEARER STOCKS

Bearer securities issued by a first class concern are the best form of banking security because they can so easily be charged and realised without expense, but, compared with the days before the last war comparatively few are in existence. Any company, other than a private company, may issue bearer securities for fully paid shares or stock if it has the express power to do so in its articles of association (Section 83 of the Companies Act, 1948). When issued by a limited company, the instrument would be called a 'share warrant', enabling one holder to transfer it to another by mere delivery. The holder is not a registered holder of the shares and, as the company cannot have any record of the warrant holders, coupons are usually attached for cutting and presentation to the company or to its bankers when a dividend is declared. Sometimes the actual warrant has to be presented in order that it can be marked for dividend and the proceeds paid to the holder. Few companies in this country favour the issue of share warrants to bearer. They are costly to issue, being subject to £3 per cent. stamp duty, and the company does not know who are its shareholders. Most American and Canadian shares are, however, transferable by delivery (*see later*) and foreign government bonds are generally bearer securities.

The Finance Act, 1963—in Section 71—provided that a registered holder of a British Government stock could exchange it for a bearer document, subject to certain conditions and this may be a growing source of securities in this form.

When the last war broke out, a strict control was introduced to cover the issue and transfer of bearer securities and they now remain subject to the Exchange Control Act, 1947. Section 10 of this Act provides that no person may issue in the United Kingdom any bearer bond or coupon without the permission of the Treasury and Sections 15 and 16 lay down that all bearer securities have to be held by an *authorised depositary*. No capital or interest payment can be made on the bonds except to, or to the order of, the authorised depositary and no transfer can be effected without producing evidence to the depositary proving that the transfer is legal. The whole point of the control is to prevent the export of bearer securities. They are held largely by the banks as authorised depositaries and, as they cannot be withdrawn or transferred to the order of other customers without satisfactory evidence of the transaction, they cannot be smuggled abroad or used to defeat the Exchange Control. From the standpoint of simplicity of transfer this modern development is obviously a complication and a handicap to dealings. An exception is granted in the case of bearer securities issued provisionally pending surrender to the issuer for registration or inscription. Such documents during their short life need not be deposited with an authorised depositary (The Exchange Control (Deposit of Securities) Exemption Order, 1947).

Legally, a bearer security may be defined as a bond or share warrant or debenture which is payable to bearer, the full title in which passes by mere delivery, and so long as the transferee takes it in good faith and for value and without notice of any defect in the title of a transferor, he obtains an indefeasible title with the right to sue on the instrument in his own name. In other words, these documents are negotiable instruments and, apart from certain American and Canadian Share Warrants (*see later*), are recognised as such by the Courts. According to Bingham, J., 'In my opinion the time has passed when the negotiability of bearer bonds, whether Government bonds or trading bonds, foreign or English, can be called in question in our Courts' (*Edelstein* v. *Schuler* [1902] 2 K.B. 144). Their negotiability is now, of course, subject to the restriction that they have to be held by an authorised depositary on behalf of the owner and cannot be transferred by him except to another authorised depositary upon the production of satisfactory information to permit the movement.

To obtain a valid title to a bearer bond as security, a banker obtains a pledge by the deposit of the bond. The essence of pledge is possession and the bonds are delivered to the bank to be held as security on the understanding that they will be redelivered to the owner when the liability has been liquidated. The bank as pledgee may sell the bonds if the borrower fails to discharge his debt. All that is necessary, therefore, is that the bank should take the bonds *as security* in good faith and for value without notice of any defect in the title of the pledgor.

The first step when offered such bonds as security is to examine them closely to ensure that they are complete and regular in order to constitute a good delivery to a buyer if they have to be realised. They should be properly stamped and free from ink markings or other alterations. The Stock Exchange Rule 135 (1) provides that a bond or certificate is to be considered perfect, unless it be much torn or damaged, or a material part of the number or wording be obliterated. All unpaid coupons should be attached, and as it will be the duty of the bank to collect the proceeds of these coupons when they are payable, a diary record has to be maintained and care taken not to miss the press announcement of the payment. Nowadays the bonds will normally already be in the possession of the bank as an authorised depositary when they are offered by the customer as security. The question of their regularity is, therefore, a simple matter to settle.

The next step is to obtain the signature of the depositor to a memorandum of deposit evidencing his intention to pledge the bonds as security and expressly empowering the bank to sell if the borrower fails to repay upon demand. The mere deposit of the bonds with intent to pledge them is sufficient, but this memorandum places the matter beyond doubt and the depositor cannot later contend that he left them with the bank for safe custody only. The contents of a typical memorandum of deposit will be discussed in Chapter XIII. Occasionally a banker may have to rely on a pledge of the bonds without an accompanying memorandum signed by the pledgor. It is then of the greatest importance to ensure that there can be no suggestion that the bonds were passed to the bank to be held mainly as an authorised depositary or for safe custody. If they are already held in this way, the original receipt should be recovered and a fresh security receipt issued or other written evidence obtained to place the position beyond question in the future.

Providing the bank takes the bonds in good faith and for value and without any knowledge of a defect in the title of the pledgor, it will have a valid title even though the depositor had no title or a defective title thereto. Whilst the bank cannot shut its eyes to facts brought directly to its knowledge, constructive notice alone will not affect its position. This rule can be illustrated by reference to *London Joint Stock Bank* v. *Simmons* [1892] A.C. 201 where it was the established practice of a firm of stockbrokers to borrow from the bank against stocks and shares and bonds. This security changed frequently over the years. A partner, without the knowledge of his co-partner and unknown to the client who owned the bonds, pledged to the bank foreign bonds payable to bearer. The bank received them as security in the ordinary course of business not knowing or enquiring whether the bonds were the property of the partner. Later, when the partner absconded and the firm suspended payment, the bank realised the security to recover the advances. The client who owned the bonds brought an action against the bank claiming their value. He succeeded in the lower Court and in the Court of Appeal, but the House of Lords reversed the decision. The bank had acted in good faith and was entitled to the proceeds of the bonds. The following words of Lord Herschell serve to emphasise the strength of the bank's position when relying upon bonds which are negotiable instruments:—

'It is surely of the very essence of a negotiable instrument that you may treat the person in possession of it as having authority to deal with it, be he agent or otherwise, unless you know to the contrary, and are not compelled, in order to secure a good title to yourself, to enquire into the nature of his title or the extent of his authority . . . I should be very sorry to see the doctrine of constructive notice introduced into the law of negotiable instruments . . . I desire to rest my judgment upon the broad and simple ground that I find, as a matter of fact, that the bank took the bonds in good faith and for value. It is easy enough to make an elaborate presentation after the event of the speculation with which the bank managers might have occupied themselves in reference to the capacity in which the broker who offered the bonds as security for an advance held them. I think, however, they were not bound to occupy their minds with any such speculations. I apprehend that when a person whose honesty there is no reason to doubt offers negotiable security to a banker or any other person, the only consideration likely to engage his attention is, whether the security is sufficient to justify the advance required. And I do not think the law lays upon him the obligation of making any enquiry into the title of the person whom he finds in possession of them; of course, if there is anything to arouse suspicion, to lead to a doubt whether the person purporting to transfer them is justified in entering into the contemplated transaction the case would be different, the existence of such suspicion or doubt would be inconsistent with good faith. And if no enquiry were made, or if on enquiry the doubt were not removed and the suspicion dissipated, I should have no hesitation in holding that good faith was wanting in a person thus acting.'

There were no circumstances to excite suspicion or to put the bank upon enquiry and, as it gave value and took the bonds in good faith and in the honest belief that they belonged to the broker or that he had authority to deal with them, the bank had a valid title to the negotiable instruments. The practical warning arising out of this case is not to search for defects but to be on guard where there is any direct notice of a possible deficiency in the title or authority of the pledgor.

The realisation of such security is also a simple process. If the borrower fails to repay upon demand, the bonds can be sold in the market and transferred to the authorised depositary acting for the buyer. When an overdraft is repaid and the security has to be released, the bonds can be transferred to safe custody and the memorandum cancelled. They have to be retained by the bank as an authorised depositary unless they are transferred to another depositary at the behest of the owners.

AMERICAN AND CANADIAN SHARE WARRANTS

Virtually all share warrants issued by American and Canadian Companies are made out in the name of a registered holder, with a composite form of transfer and power of attorney on the reverse which can be executed in blank by the registered holder. The object of the power of attorney is that the holder of the warrant may appoint an attorney to act for him in the country of registration when a transfer has to be registered. As soon as the composite transfer and power of attorney is signed in blank by the registered holder, the warrant becomes transferable by delivery and is regarded as a bearer security. To comply with American custom, the signature of the registered holder must be exactly as on the face of the warrant, including any prefix or suffix. The signature has to be attested and, if the registered holder is not a 'good marking name' (*see later*), his signature has also to be guaranteed by a banker or broker. Although such documents may be freely sold in the market and are accepted as a bearer security, they are not fully negotiable instruments in the legal sense because the holder cannot sue on the instrument in his own name unless he is the registered holder.

Share warrants of this type issued by the Pennsylvania Railroad Company were under consideration in *London & County Banking Co. Ltd. v. London River Plate Bank Ltd.* (1887) 20 Q.B.D. 232 when the judge expressed the opinion that, as the instrument could not be sued upon by the person holding it *pro tempore*, it could not be negotiable. It was handed over by the transferor with a blank power of attorney but the holder could not sue until it was transferred into his name on the register. 'If the right of suing upon an instrument does not appear upon the face of it to be extended beyond one particular individual, no usage of trade, however extensive, will confer upon it the character of negotiability.'

It is the custom in this country to have these shares registered in the name of a specialist firm of London brokers, a finance house, or banks who are described collectively as 'good marking names'. They receive the dividends as registered holders and pay them over to the holders of the certificates (less a small handling charge) upon application. At one time the warrant was 'marked' on the back with a rubber stamp each time a dividend was claimed from the 'marking house'. Whilst this system is still operated, the more usual practice is now for the authorised depositary holding the warrant to 'mark' it only with the date of the last dividend claimed before it is released to another authorised depositary, thus indicating that all dividends have been claimed up to the date shown. A list of about four hundred 'marking houses' will be found in *The Stock Exchange Official Year-Book* and, unless a warrant is in one of these names it is not a good delivery on the Stock Exchange. Some of the nominee companies of the joint stock banks appear in the list of 'good marking names'. All these warrants in whatever name they may be registered have to be deposited with an authorised depositary, in accord with the Exchange Control Act, 1947.

When offered this type of security, the bank has to be satisfied that the warrant is in a 'good marking name', regularly endorsed, and, unless the share is of no par value, properly stamped. It is then readily saleable and can be taken as security by way of deposit with a memorandum of deposit. The bank thus obtains an equitable mortgage. It cannot obtain a pledge because, as explained above, the warrants are not negotiable instruments. A legal mortgage could be obtained by registering the shares in the name of the bank's nominees. Where the warrants are registered in the name of the depositor, it is preferable to have them transferred into a 'good marking name' to make them readily saleable and to remove any risk that the issuing company may have a lien on the shares for some indebtedness of the registered holder to the company. If left in the name of the depositor, his endorsement will be required (the formalities of which have already been described) before the warrant is accepted as security. It is a cumbersome procedure to have the shares registered in the name of a nominee company unless that company is 'a good marking name' and it is of little practical value because these share warrants are not a good delivery when registered in the name of a limited company unless each warrant, in addition to endorsement either under seal or by attorney, is stamped with the signed guarantee of the registered holder that all the necessary documents have been filed with the registrar or transfer agent to evidence who may transfer the shares on behalf of the company. The endorsements have also to be guaranteed by a banker.

A bank's title to security of this kind was challenged in *Fuller* v. *Glyn Mills Currie & Co.* [1913] 2 K.B. 168, where some Canadian Pacific Railway ordinary stock was charged to the bank by a firm of stockbrokers who subsequently failed. The warrants were registered in the name of a Mr. Harmsworth, and endorsed in blank by him. The true owner of the stock, one of the clients of the stockbrokers, brought an action to recover it from the bank, but it was decided that as there had been nothing to put the bank upon enquiry concerning the authority of the stockbrokers to deal with the warrants the bank's title could not be impugned. By leaving the blank endorsed warrants in the possession of the brokers, the owner had represented to the bank or any other party who accepted them that the brokers had authority to deal with them and he was therefore estopped from claiming against the bank. To obtain a valid title to such warrants, a bank has thus to receive them in good faith and for value without direct notice of any defect in the title of, or want of authority on the part of, the depositor.

INSCRIBED STOCKS

Brief reference can be made at this stage to inscribed stocks which are now almost extinct. An inscribed stock may be defined as one where the title of the owner is evidenced solely by an entry or inscription in the books of the registrar acting for the body which has issued the stock. Instead of a certificate issued to the holder of registered stock, the owner of inscribed stock received a stock receipt, or certificate of inscription, which was valueless except as a memorandum of the transaction and did not have to be surrendered on sale. The legal title to inscribed stock could be transferred without production of this receipt and the only way in which a bank could obtain a valid charge was to have the stock transferred into the name of its nominees. Inscribed stock was transferred by the attendance of the owner or his attorney at the office of the registrar to sign the stock out of his name into that of the transferee. The stockbrokers acting for the seller normally attended as his attorney. It was a cumbersome process which has fortunately been superseded and the production of a stock receipt by a customer nowadays calls for an investigation of its origin and raises the question as to whether it has been replaced by a registered certificate.

Prior to 1939, the holders of certain Government Stocks had the option of taking inscribed stocks, the registers being maintained by the Bank of England. When war broke out the registers had to be removed outside London for safety and the problem of the personal attendance of a seller or his attorney arose. Inscribed stock was then made transferable in precisely the same way as registered stock (The Government & Other Stocks (Emergency Provisions) Act, 1939) subsequently amended by the Emergency Powers (Repeal) Act 1959 as to certain Dominion Stocks.

As from January 1, 1943, all inscribed stock for British Government securities was converted automatically into registered stock (The Government Stock Regulations, 1943), and stock certificates had to be issued to all persons subsequently acquiring such stocks. Holders of inscribed stock were invited to apply for stock certificates, which are issued free of charge. It was provided that the certificates constituted *prima facie* evidence of the title of the person specified therein to the amount of stock of the description so specified. Similar regulations were made in 1949 converting all local authority inscribed stocks into registered stocks as from January 1, 1950. There remain only a few inscribed stocks, issued by Commonwealth countries, and it is rare indeed for the practical banker to encounter them today.

Chapter XIII Quoted Securities—continued

REGISTERED STOCKS—CREATION OF A LEGAL
MORTGAGE—USE OF NOMINEE COMPANIES

A share has been defined as 'the interest of a shareholder in the company
measured by a sum of money, for the purpose of liability in the first place, and
of interest in the second, but also consisting of a series of mutual covenants entered
into by all the shareholders *inter se*' (Farwell, J., in *Borland's Trustee* v. *Steel Bros.*
[1901] 1 Ch. 279). It is personal property transferable in the manner provided by
the articles of the company. Each share in a company having a share capital has
to be distinguished by its appropriate number, provided that, if at any time all the
issued shares in a company, or all the issued shares therein or a particular class,
are fully paid up and rank *pari passu* for all purposes, none of those shares need
thereafter have a distinguishing number so long as it remains fully paid up and
ranks *pari passu* for all purposes with all shares of the same class for the time being
issued and fully paid up (Section 74 of the Companies Act, 1948). If so authorised
by its articles, a company limited by shares may convert all or any of its paid-up
shares into stock (an original issue of stock cannot be made) and the term 'share'
in the Companies Act includes 'stock', except where a distinction is expressed or
implied.

Every company is required to keep a register of its members and to enter
therein the names and addresses of the members, and in the case of a company
having a share capital a statement of the shares held by each member, distinguishing each share by its number so long as the share has a number, and of the amount
paid or agreed to be considered as paid on the shares of each member. The date
when each person became a member and the date when any person ceases to be a
member have also to be registered. No notice of any trust, express or implied, or
constructive shall be entered on the register, or be receivable by the registrar, in
the case of companies registered in England. This restriction contained in Section
117 of the Companies Act, 1948, is of considerable importance from the banking
standpoint, as will be explained later.

Every company, within two months after the allotment of any of its shares,
debentures, or debenture stock and within two months after the date on which a
transfer of any such shares, debentures, or debenture stock is lodged with the
company has to be complete and deliver a certificate or certificates evidencing the
title of the member to the shares in his name. The form of the certificate will
usually be described in the articles of association, which normally provide that it

has to be issued under the seal of the company, signed by at least one director and countersigned by the secretary. A certificate does not have to be stamped.

Section 81 of the Companies Act, 1948, provides that a certificate, under the common seal of the company, specifying any shares held by any member, shall be *prima facie* evidence of the title of the member to the shares. The certificate is not, therefore, conclusive evidence of title and it is possible for someone to prove that he is legally entitled to the shares described in a certificate issued to another person. Transfers may be forged with the result that they are transferred out of the name of the holder without his authority. When the fraud is discovered the true owner can have the transferee's name struck off the register and have his own name restored as the registered owner of the shares. Apart from this risk of forgery, which will be discussed in greater detail later, the banker can accept the share certificate as evidence of the title of the customer or depositor to the shares described therein.

The brief statement of the essential legal principles which are laid down in the Companies Act, 1948, serves as an introduction to the problems which confront the lending banker when taking registered shares as security. There are three practical methods of obtaining a charge:—

1. By way of legal mortgage.
2. By way of equitable mortgage, purely and simply.
3. By way of equitable mortgage which can be converted into a legal mortgage by the bank without recourse to the mortgagor. A form of half-way house which is most popular.

The advantages and disadvantages of each kind of charge and the way in which it is obtained can now be explored in detail.

LEGAL MORTGAGE OVER QUOTED SECURITIES

To obtain a legal mortgage, the shares have to be transferred out of the name of the mortgagor into the name of the bank, or its nominees, subject to the equity of redemption of the mortgagor upon repayment of the advance. The legal estate in the shares is thus vested in the bank which then has a virtually unassailable title.

It is first necessary to obtain the certificate for the shares as evidence of the title of the depositor. This should be examined to ensure that the shares are actually registered in the name of the person or persons who propose to deposit the security, any differences between their known name and the name in the certificate being queried. The customer or a third party may seek to charge shares which do not belong to him and the bank will be fixed with notice if the name on the certificate differs from that of the mortgagor. The shares will be clearly described in the certificate and it is essential to note whether they are partly paid or fully paid up. A security receipt will usually be issued for the certificate.

A *memorandum of deposit* will then be taken signed by the shareholder and, as the same form is normally used for equitable mortgages as well as legal mortgages, it can be conveniently analysed at this stage. The memorandum will recite that, in consideration of the bank granting accommodation to, or continuing the account of, the stated customer, the stock and shares described in the schedule have been charged as security for all monies owing by the customer, either solely or jointly. The security will be expressed to be a continuing one to avoid the operation of the Rule in *Clayton's Case* and the bank will be empowered to realise the securities in the event of the failure of the borrower to repay upon demand. This latter provision is essential to enable the bank to act promptly when the need arises (*Deverges* v. *Sandeman* [1902] 1 Ch. 579). In practice, of course, reasonable notice will usually be given to the mortgagor before the shares are sold. So that the document may also be used in those cases where the shares remain in the name of the depositor, a covenant is often included whereby the depositor agrees to execute any transfers which may later be required in order to vest the shares in the name of the bank or of a buyer. The practical value of this clause is doubtful because borrowers are usually reluctant to co-operate when the bank wishes to complete its security.

Arising out of the experiences of the Bank of Scotland in *Crerar* v. *Bank of Scotland* [1921] S.C. 736, it is prudent nowadays to include a provision whereby the depositor agrees that upon his redemption of the shares he will be content to accept delivery of stock or shares of 'the same class or denomination' as those which were originally charged to the bank. Miss Crerar charged to the Bank of Scotland 2,775 J. & P. Coats Ltd. ordinary shares which were transferred into the name of the bank's nominees. Fifteen years later when the indebtedness was repaid, Miss Crerar claimed that she was entitled to have retransferred to her name the identical shares which she had originally charged to the bank. The bank throughout had ignored the individual numbers of the original shares and it will readily be appreciated that it held at all times a large block of these well-known shares in its nominees' names as security for advances to many customers. It would be quite accidental if the bank transferred back to the mortgagor shares of the same numbers as those originally deposited. For reasons known only to herself, she wanted the actual shares she had charged. The Court of Session upheld her contention that the bank was bound to identify the shares deposited by each customer, but the bank succeeded because she had by her conduct acquiesced in the course it had adopted. It is difficult to see what point there can be in insisting upon the return of specified shares, but in the absence of acquiescence by the mortgagor the bank might be in difficulty. Technically perhaps the shares were identifiable and a pledgor upon satisfaction of his debt has the right to recover the specific article pledged. To remove any risk of argument, however, a clause on the above-mentioned lines will cover the position.

As well as signing the memorandum, the depositor of the shares is usually called upon to initial the schedule describing them immediately beneath the final item. To avoid the need for a fresh memorandum whenever securities are changed, a bank may take an omnibus form of charge from a borrower who is frequently changing his investments. Instead of detailing specific items, the memorandum will be expressed to cover all the securities which may at any time be lodged by the customer. Such a charge should be used with discretion and care exercised to avoid any contention that certain stocks are merely deposited with the bank for safe custody and are thus outside the charge. A form of general charge usually has to be used for stockbrokers' loans because the securities may change daily. This type of memorandum will cover all stocks and shares of any class from time to time deposited with the bank or transferred into the names of its nominees to be held as security for all monies owning by the customer to the bank.

The memorandum of deposit evidences the intention of the parties and can, therefore, be used in all cases, whether the bank is obtaining a legal mortgage or is content to rely merely upon an equitable mortgage. The legal mortgage is completed by registration of the shares in the name of the bank or its nominees and this is the next step for consideration.

The shares of a limited company are transferred in the manner laid down by the Articles of the company. Table 'A' of the Companies Act, 1948, Article 23, provides that 'any member may transfer all or any of his shares by instrument in writing in any usual or common form or any other form which the directors may approve'. Thus a company may require a special form of transfer to be executed under hand, or if the Articles so stipulate, executed under seal. However, most companies simply require the common form of transfer executed under hand. The common form of transfer was simplified by the Stock Transfer Act, 1963 and only the transferor is now required to execute the present transfer whereas formerly both transferor and transferee were required to sign. A few companies, notably those registered in South Africa, still require the old common form of transfer to be used and such companies are marked in the *Stock Exchange Daily Official List*. The precise requirements with regard to the transfer of shares in all public companies are to be found in the *Stock Exchange Official Year-Book*, to which reference may be made in case of doubt. Some banks, insurance companies, and a few undertakings with a long history require a special form of transfer which can be obtained from the secretary upon request. The point is that the bank has to obtain the form of transfer required by the articles of the company concerned.

The shares will be described in the transfer and a purely nominal figure, usually twenty-five p, inserted as the consideration to obtain exemption from *ad valorem* stamp duty. The transfer then attracts a fixed duty of fifty p, a certificate being given by the bank on the reverse side that the transfer is exempted from Section 74 of the Finance (1909–10) Act, 1910. British Government Stocks registered at the Bank of England or at the Post Office are, of course, exempt from all stamp duties (The Stamp Act, 1891) but special forms of transfer may be required.

THE USE OF PERSONAL NOMINEES AND NOMINEE COMPANIES

To obtain the legal mortgage, the stocks or shares have to be registered in the name of the bank or its nominees. The legal ownership thus rests in the lending bank, leaving the borrower with his equitable right to redeem the shares upon satisfaction of all his liabilities to the bank. It would be a cumbersome process to take all shares into the name of the bank, which might then have an enormous holding of say a popular Government Stock comprising amounts charged to the bank by innumerable borrowers and its own investment holding of the given stock. But assets would then be confused with security and the problems of dividing one dividend between all the parties would be immense. Designations might be introduced to distinguish between various holdings, but the complications of such a system are too numerous to make it practicable. Instead the stock will be taken either into the names of personal nominees of the bank or into the name of a nominee company.

It is still the practice of some banks to use personal nominees, whereby the shares are transferred usually into the joint names of the branch manager and a head office official. The advantage of this method is that it spreads the holdings in any particular stock between many names and thereby simplifies the branch record system, the application of dividends, and the holding of the certificate. A nominee company can hardly be incorporated for every branch and a nominee company acting for a large number of branches has to maintain complicated records of the branch and mortgagor for whom the shares are held in order to split the dividends between the beneficial owners. The disadvantages of personal nominees arise from human frailties. Officials may be promoted to remote branches, or retire or die with the resulting need for the trouble and expense of transfer to fresh nominees. Inevitably one of the nominees is on holiday when his signature is required. For the short term transaction, however, personal nominees are probably more convenient than nominee companies, but the lending banker can never be sure that the shares will remain as security for a short period, and the officials may change before the shares can be transferred back to the mortgagor.

Nominee companies were incorporated by the banks primarily for the purpose of holding shares as security, although they may also be used for the convenience of customers who are not borrowing. The directors are usually appointed from the ranks of local senior officials and there are always sufficient available to execute transfers into or out of the company's name. Changes in the board do not affect the receipt of dividends or the completion of transfers under the seal of the company. The advantages of perpetual succession are obvious, but record and labour problems arise when dividends have to be split between many mortgagors and proxies and balance sheets of the companies have to be distributed between them. For example, if one hundred customers of Southtown Bank individually charged their holding of Imperial Chemical Industries Ltd. ordinary shares as security and they were all registered in the name of Southtown Bank (Nominees) Ltd., that company would receive one warrant for the net dividend payable on the total holding registered in its name, together perhaps with only one print of the annual report and balance sheet of I.C.I. Ltd. The dividend would then have to be split between the hundred customers according to their individual interest and, as a matter of courtesy, the bank would probably wish to provide each customer with a print of the balance sheet and directors' report. The record system, clerical work and calculations entailed in this process need no further emphasis. These disadvantages often outweigh the drawbacks attendant upon personal nominees.

To complete the legal mortgage, the stamped transfer duly signed by the mortgagor is forwarded to the registrar of the company, together with the share certificate. (In those cases where it is necessary, the transfer must in addition be signed by the bank's personal nominees or sealed by the nominee company). In the very rare circumstances where a registration fee is charged, a postal order for the appropriate amount must be forwarded. In due course a certificate will be received by the bank evidencing that the shares are registered in the name of its nominees and its legal title is then complete. The share certificate will then be held in security until such time as the indebtedness is repaid and the shares can be transferred back into the name of the customer or other depositor by precisely the same process in reverse.

ADVANTAGES OF A LEGAL MORTGAGE AS SECURITY

A legal mortgage is the only perfect form of security and the following two advantages accrue to the bank by obtaining a complete charge in the manner described above.

1. The bank as legal owner of the shares can realise them if the need arises after due notice to the mortgagor but without his co-operation. All dividends are paid to the bank as registered holder of the shares and any rights accruing on the shares, including bonus issues, vest in the bank. This latter aspect is usually expressly covered by a clause in the memorandum of deposit signed by the mortgagor. In other words, the mortgagor cannot interfere and the bank can at all times protect its position by retaining complete control over the security.

2. Provided that at the time when the shares are transferred into the names of the bank's nominees it had no notice of other equitable interests, the legal title of the bank will have priority. This rule is founded on the old principle that where equities are equal the law prevails. In other words, the holder of the legal estate has priority providing it was obtained in ignorance of earlier equitable rights. An example may serve to clarify this advantage. If X holds shares in P.Q.R. Ltd. as a personal trustee for his nephews, Y and Z, the share certificate will be in his name with no reference to the trusteeship (Section 117, Companies Act, 1948, *ante*). Y and Z have an equitable interest as beneficiaries of the trust. If X then charges the shares to a bank as security for his personal indebtedness and the bank obtains a legal mortgage by registration of the shares in the name of its nominees without knowledge of the prior interests of the nephews, it will have a good title notwithstanding the breach of trust. As will be seen later, if the bank had been content to rely merely upon an equitable mortgage of the shares, the prior equitable interest of Y and Z would prevail before the bank.

To obtain priority as legal mortgagee it is, of course, imperative that the bank should have no knowledge and no reasonable grounds for suspicion that there are other interests in the background at the time when the shares are taken into its nominees' names. In *Coleman* v. *London, County & Westminster Bank Ltd.* [1916] 2 Ch. 353, debentures in a private company were issued to Mrs. Coleman, who settled them upon trust for herself for life with remainder to her three sons equally. The trustee did not register the debentures in his name and Mrs. Coleman later obtained possession of the debentures and deposited them with the bank under a memorandum of deposit as security for the indebtedness of the issuing company. The debentures were registered in the name of Mrs. Coleman and the bank, without knowledge of the settlement, left them in her name, merely giving notice of their interest to the trustee of the debentures who it so happened was also trustee of the settlement. At a later date the bank heard of the settlement and they immediately obtained a transfer from Mrs. Coleman and registered the debentures in the bank's name. After the death of the mortgagor, an assignee of one of the beneficiaries under the trust brought an action against the bank to recover the debentures in which she claimed to have a prior interest. She succeeded because her equitable interest was prior to the equitable mortgage to the bank and the bank could not improve its position by obtaining a legal title after it had notice of the prior equitable interest.

DISADVANTAGES OF A LEGAL MORTGAGE AS SECURITY

Most of the disadvantages of a legal mortgage are restricted to particular types of securities, but it is well to schedule them all to complete the picture.

113

H

1. *The risk of a forged transfer*

When a bank lodges a transfer with a company, it thereby vouches that it is genuine and as transferee it remains indefinitely liable to indemnify the company against any loss it may incur if the transferor's signature proves to be a forgery. If B steals a share certificate from A and forges A's signature in order to transfer the shares to C, who acting in good faith buys them from B, and the company registers C as the owner of the shares, A can nevertheless claim to be reinstated on the register as the true owner when the fraud is discovered. C, as transferee, has to indemnify the company for any loss it may sustain in rectifying the position. Some companies, however, now insure against the risk of forged transfers or build up a reserve fund under the Forged Transfer Acts, 1891–92.

The case of *Sheffield Corporation* v. *Barclay and Ors.* [1905] A.C. 392, illustrates this risk. Two trustees, Timbrell and Honeywill, were the registered joint holders of a substantial amount of Sheffield Corporation Stock. As security for his personal indebtedness to Barclays Bank, Timbrell transferred the holding by way of legal mortgage into the name of the bank's nominee, Mr. E. E. Barclay, forging his co-trustee's signature to the transfer. When the advance was repaid, the stock was sold to two third parties who were duly registered as the owners. The fraud was discovered when Timbrell died and the surviving trustee, Honeywill, brought an action against Sheffield Corporation for rectification of its register, the recovery of dividends paid subsequent to the registration of the forged transfer and other relief. It cost the Corporation £11,000 to buy an equivalent amount of stock to register it in the name of Honeywill, and it then turned to the bank to indemnify it against its loss. It was decided by the House of Lords that the bank was liable to indemnify the Corporation because by sending forward the forged transfer for registration it had impliedly warranted it to be genuine. The question of forged transfers was last explored at length in *Welch* v. *Bank of England, Francis & Praed & Ors.* [1955] 1 All E.R. 811, but space will not permit a detailed discussion of this case here. The liability of the bank outstands for an indefinite period because the period under the Limitation Act, 1939, does not start to run in its favour until the cause of action arises when the company has to rectify the register.

The risk of a forged transfer should be remote if the bank knows the party mortgaging the shares. Transferors should always be called upon to sign the transfer in the presence of the bank or of its agent and it is obviously unwise to hand a transfer to a joint shareholder in order that he may obtain the signature of his co-owner. For this reason also it is prudent always to query any discrepancy between the known name of the mortgagor and the name shown in the certificate. The customer, John Davies, may not be the same person as John Davis, the registered owner of the shares which are proffered as security.

2. *Partly-paid shares*

If the bank becomes the legal owner of partly-paid shares, it will be liable to meet any calls made on the shares and by virtue of Section 212 of the Companies Act, 1948, this liability may outstand for twelve months after the shares are transferred out of the name of the bank's nominees. Upon the winding-up of a company, if the existing members are unable to pay the unpaid liability on shares when called by the liquidator, anyone who has been a shareholder within the previous year can be called upon to contribute the unpaid amount provided that it is needed to meet the debts of the company incurred whilst he was a member. Fortunately, partly-paid shares are relatively rare nowadays and the solution rests with the bank in that such shares should be left in the name of the depositor.

3. *Legal mortgage may not be possible*

In some cases the articles of a company may restrict its members to private persons or to people engaged in a particular trade and the directors may, therefore, decline to register the bank's nominees. These restrictions are more often found in the case of private companies, which will be discussed later. Sometimes the borrower may be charging as security the shares of a company of which he is a director and, as they represent his qualification holding as required by the articles, it is impossible to transfer them out of his name unless he resigns from the board.

4. *Expenses entailed*

Every time a legal mortgage is taken over shares, it costs the customer stamp duty of fifty p, i.e. as a nominal consideration, unless they are free from stamp duty. In a few cases a registration fee is also charged and the same expenses recur when the shares are retransferred upon repayment of the debt. From the standpoint of the bank, the cost of running the nominee company is much more material, but this is the price of complete security and it is clear that the advantages of a legal mortgage over stocks and shares vastly outweigh the disadvantages.

Chapter XIV Quoted Securities (*continued*)

REGISTERED STOCKS—CREATION OF EQUITABLE MORTGAGE

A simple equitable mortgage is obtained merely by the deposit of the share certificate with intent to charge, a security receipt usually being issued to show, in case of need, that it was taken by the bank as security and not held in safe custody for the customer. To place the position beyond doubt, a memorandum of deposit should also be signed by the depositor, as written evidence of the purpose of the lodgment of the share certificate and to show when the bank may exercise its rights to realise the security. This memorandum is not, however, essential to obtain an equitable charge. According to Cozens-Hardy, J., in *Harrold* v. *Plenty* [1901] 2 Ch. 314, 'The deposit of the certificate by way of security for the debt seems to me to amount to an equitable mortgage, or, in other words, to an agreement to execute a transfer of the shares by way of mortgage'. There are occasions when a bank has to be content with security taken in this informal manner, but it is not a method to be encouraged because of the difficulties which arise if it proves necessary to realise the shares.

An equitable mortgage merely gives the bank a right against the mortgagor to have a legal mortgage executed or to share in the proceeds of sale. The certificate can be retained until the debt is repaid and, if the customer fails to meet his liability, the bank can apply to the Court for an order for foreclosure and sale. Such process is tedious and expensive. Obviously it is unwise to rely upon a security which cannot be realised without the assistance of the Court or the co-operation of the customer, and to overcome these weaknesses without taking initially a legal mortgage over the shares, a bank usually strengthens its position by obtaining undated, unstamped transfers and giving notice to the company.

THE TAKING OF UNDATED, UNSTAMPED TRANSFERS

A completed transfer naming the nominees of the bank as transferee has to be stamped within thirty days with the nominal duty of fifty pence and could be held until such time as the bank wishes to register the stocks in the name of its nominees. The registrar of the company might query the transfer if it is dated several years previous to presentation to the company, but there is no reason why registration should be declined however stale the transfer may be. Apart from any reluctance on the part of the depositor to have the shares transferred out of his name, there is little point in holding a completed stamped transfer and it is preferable in such circumstances to have the shares registered in the name of the bank's nominees, thereby obtaining a legal mortgage with all its advantages.

A half-way house, suitable for temporary advances to satisfactory borrowers, which avoids the immediate payment of stamp duty and yet places the bank in a position to turn the equitable charge into a legal mortgage whenever it wishes, is to take an undated, unstamped transfer wherever this course is legally possible. Some banks complete the transfer in every particular except the date. If anything occurs to endanger the bank's position, the transfer can then be dated, stamped and registered without delay. Other banks may omit to insert the name of any transferee so that a direct sale can be made to a purchaser, where circumstances permit without the intervention of nominees.

These incomplete transfers are generally known as 'blank' transfers but, strictly speaking, this term is limited to a transfer which lacks a material particular. The omission of the name of the transferee will make the document a blank transfer, but the mere failure to date the instrument is not a material omission and it is perhaps more correct to describe it as an undated, unstamped transfer. As soon as it is dated, the transfer has to be stamped within thirty days thereof and, as the object is to avoid unnecessary expense to the customer, care is necessary to avoid the insertion of a date until, if ever, registration is desirable.

The memorandum of deposit taken from the customer when the shares are deposited usually expressly authorises the bank to complete and register an undated, unstamped transfer whenever it wishes to do so, but in any event the delivery of an instrument under hand empowers the transferee to fill in the blanks and it operates as a valid transfer (*Ireland* v. *Hart* [1902] 1 Ch. 522). The banker also has an implied authority to complete the transfer arising out of the nature of the transaction (In *re Tahiti Cotton Company* (1874) L.R. 17 Eq. 273). But where the articles of a company require transfers to be under seal, an undated, unstamped transfer is useless because a deed has to be complete in every respect when it is delivered. If the customer seals and delivers an incomplete transfer, it will be void for uncertainty and the blanks cannot be completed afterwards except by an agent of the transferor authorised under seal so to act. The only safe course when stocks or shares proffered as security have to be transferred by a deed is to take a complete transfer duly stamped and to hold it unregistered if the bank is content for some acceptable reason to delay the normal completion of its legal mortgage by registration.

The type of transfer required by a company or other issuer of quoted stocks can be ascertained from *The Stock Exchange Official Year-Book*. The articles of most companies adopt the standard form of transfer in common form, which is under hand. Article 22 of Table 'A' in the first schedule of the Companies Act, 1948, prescribes that any member may transfer all or any of his shares by *instrument in writing* in any usual or common form or any other form which the directors may approve. The rule is always to follow the form required by the articles, but where no seal is required a transfer under seal will be valid providing that it is regular in all other respects. The usual transfer is under hand, but there are exceptions such as companies subject to the Companies Clauses Consolidation Act, 1845. The point has, therefore, always to be verified by reference to *The Stock Exchange Official Year-Book* or direct to the company itself.

The legal title to shares can be obtained only by way of a valid transfer and the completion of a transfer previously held unstamped and undated cannot be a valid instrument where transfers have to be executed under seal. The transfer may well be accepted without question by the company in their ignorance of what has transpired, but the bank's title could be upset when the facts became known. These risks were brought out in *Powell* v. *London & Provincial Bank* [1893] 2 Ch. 555, where a fraudulent executor obtained possession of certain stock in a statutory company which belonged to a marriage settlement and deposited it with his bankers as security for his overdraft. He assured the bank that he was the absolute owner of the stock and executed a blank deed of transfer which he signed, sealed and delivered to the bank. The stock remained in his name until a year later, when the bank completed the transfer and had the stock registered in its name. The fraudulent customer absconded about four years after and the trustees of the marriage settlement then claimed that the bank held the stock in trust for them and it had no beneficial interest therein. The Court of Appeal decided that the bank had acquired no legal title and its equitable interest was subject to the prior interest of the trustees of the marriage settlement. The stock was that of a statutory company under the Companies Clauses Consolidation Act, 1845, and every transfer of stocks or shares had to be by deed, duly stamped. The blank transfer which was executed under seal was not an effective deed and the bank could not, therefore, obtain the legal estate in the stock.

The following extract from the judgment of Bowen, L.J., explains the position: 'It seems to me that the deed never was as against the parties to this suit the deed of the grantor. A deed in order to be a deed must be sealed and delivered, and although we have heard a very ingenious argument which seems to rest on the assumption that a deed can be a deed before it is delivered, I never heard of it before. The sealing and delivery are essential parts of a deed. When was this deed ever delivered as a deed? At the time of its supposed delivery it was in blank. When was it redelivered, if at all? The redelivery must be done by the grantor or by somebody who acts for him. The grantor in this case never saw the deed again . . . it is well known law that an agent cannot execute a deed, or do any part of the execution which makes it a deed unless he is appointed under seal.'

In order to prove at any time that it is the legal owner of stocks a bank has to be able to show that the transfer which was registered was valid when it was registered. Where a deed is required, it has to be a perfect deed when registered, otherwise the registration will not suffice to protect the bank. It follows that where statute or the articles of a company prescribe that the transfer of the shares has to be by deed, a transfer should be taken complete in every respect, stamped and registered with the company. In other words, a legal mortgage should always be obtained where the stocks or shares are transferable by deed. (See also *France* v. *Clark* (1884) 26 Ch. D. 257 and *Société Géneralé de Paris* v. *Walker* (1885) 11 A.C. 20.)

NOTICE OF LIEN TO COMPANY

In an attempt to strengthen the bank's position, a notice may be sent advising the company of the bank's charge over the stated shares and enquiring perhaps whether the company has received notice of any other charges on the shares or whether it has a lien itself on the shares. The notice is usually forwarded in duplicate with the request that the copy should be returned, duly completed, by way of acknowledgment. All this effort will rarely bring forth much helpful response from the company. The notice may be ignored or a formal reply will be received drawing attention to Section 117 of the Companies Act, 1948, which provides that no notice of any trust, expressed, implied or constructive, can be entered on the register, or be receivable by the registrar, in the case of companies registered in England. A company may, therefore, disregard the bank's equitable interest and continue to treat the registered holder as the absolute owner of the shares and entitled as such to transfer them. The fact that the company has been advised of the bank's charge does not place it under any obligation whatsoever to see that the registered holder does not deal with the shares in a manner prejudicial to the bank. In like manner, Section 30 of the National Debt Act, 1870, provides that the Bank of England cannot take any notice of the rights of parties to Government Stocks other than those of the registered holders, and notices of lien can, therefore, be ignored.

Unless a company keeps an unofficial register of notices of lien, such an advice by the bank will not alone protect it against the risk that a fraudulently minded customer might obtain a duplicate share certificate and dispose of the shares held by way of equitable mortgage by the bank. It is believed that some companies do keep an unofficial record of these notices to which they can refer when an approach is made for a duplicate certificate, but they are under no obligation to do so and cannot be liable if they fail to refer to any such record. Apart from this pious hope, the legal value of a notice of lien is limited to those cases where a company by its articles has a lien on its shares for any moneys owing to it by the shareholder.

A distinction has to be drawn between the company as a trading concern granting credit to buyers who may also be shareholders and as a registering body recording the names and holdings of its shareholders. The application of Section 117 of the Companies Act is limited to this latter capacity in that the company is protected in registering a transfer of shares by a registered holder, but when credit is granted by the company to a shareholder on the security of his shares, the interest of the company is subject to any prior equitable interest of a third party in the shares if the company had notice of the existence of such interest. Notice of lien served on a company in this respect is akin to notice of a second mortgage served upon a banker holding a first mortgage as security for fluctuating advances. The company's lien cannot have priority for any debts incurred by the shareholder after receipt of the notice of lien from the bank.

The articles of association of a company may provide that it shall have a first and paramount lien on its shares for all amounts due to the company by a shareholder. Article 11 of Table 'A' of the 1948 Act reads as follows:—
'The company shall have a first and paramount lien on every share (not being a fully paid share) for all moneys (whether presently payable or not) called or payable at a fixed time in respect of that share and the company shall also have a first and paramount lien on all shares (other than fully paid shares) standing registered in the name of a single person for all moneys presently payable by him or his estate to the company; but the directors may at any time declare any shares to be wholly or in part exempt from the provisions of this regulation. The company's lien, if any, on a share shall extend to all dividends payable thereon'. It will be noted that this lien applies only to partly paid shares. A lien on fully paid shares can be established by special articles, but where the shares have an

official quotation on the London Stock Exchange the company cannot claim any lien thereon. It is a condition of the official quotation by the rules of the Stock Exchange that no lien will be claimed by the company on its fully paid shares.

Where a company has a lien on its shares, the receipt of notice of the lien of the bank determines the position and any fresh indebtedness incurred by the shareholder to the company ranks for security in the shares after the lien of the bank. In such circumstances, the notice of lien has a tangible value in protecting the bank's interest and the position can best be illustrated by reference to *Bradford Banking Company Ltd.* v. *Henry Briggs, Son & Co.* (1886) 12 App. Cas. 29. The articles of the Briggs company provided that it should have a first and paramount lien and charge, available at law and in equity, upon every share for all debts due from the holder of the shares. Mr. Easby, a customer of Bradford Banking Co., deposited his shares in Briggs as security for advances granted to him and the bank gave notice of their lien to the company. In acknowledging receipt of the notice, the company warned the bank of its prior lien. When the customer failed, he owed a large amount to the Briggs company, which claimed a prior lien on the shares to cover amounts lent after the receipt of the bank's notice.

It was decided by the House of Lords that, as the company were aware of the bank's interest, its lien was subject to the prior rights of the bank in respect of amounts lent after receipt of the notice. The articles made the company in effect the first mortgagee of the shares of any shareholder who was indebted to it and, upon receipt of the notice of the second mortgage to the bank, it could not make further advances ranking prior to the bank's interest in the shares. The company claimed that by virtue of Section 30 of the Companies Act, 1862 (now Section 117 of the 1948 Act), it could under the lien clause in the articles assert a prior lien, but this contention was not upheld. The notice of lien from the bank was not a notice of a trust which the company was forbidden to recognise by statute. In the opinion of Lord Blackburn, the company had such knowledge that the shareholder had ceased to be the owner of the shares as would make it unjust to allow him credit on the shares. The bank was not trying to fix the company with notice of a trust but to affect it as a trader with due notice of the bank's interest. The principle is thus clear and, wherever a company has a lien on its shares, notice of the bank's interest should be promptly given to it. In the words of Stirling, L.J., in *Rainford* v. *James Keith & Blackman Co.* [1905] 1 Ch. 296, 'where the company in which the shares are held sees fit to deal with the shares for its own benefit, then that company is liable to be affected with notice of the interest of a third party.'

What happens in practice? If the system demands that notice of lien shall be given to every company regardless of whether it has any lien on its shares, it will ensure that notice is always given when actually required. There will be no errors of omission but much wasted effort and expense unless the notices are recorded unofficially and the bank advised as a matter of courtesy if and when any transfer is presented. Some banks, therefore, restrict notices of lien to those cases where the company has a lien on its shares. Even then the number of instances where the shareholder is likely to be indebted to the company is relatively small. Particular care is necessary where there is a known trading connection between the shareholder customer and the company. For example, a retailer may often owe money to a wholesale house from which he buys goods and whose shares he holds as an investment. Similarly, the licensee of an hotel may hold shares in a brewery company to which he is indebted for supplies of liquor. The primary test is whether the shares are fully paid and officially quoted. If not there may be a lien clause in the articles of the company and it will be prudent to serve notice of the bank's interest in the shares.

It is worthy of mention here that some companies provide in their articles that the company shall have a paramount lien on its shares for all liabilities incurred by the shareholder before and after receipt of notice of lien from a third party. Whether this clause would prevail is open to doubt but it is certainly not completely ruled out by any of the judgments in the *Bradford Banking Company* case already explained.

THE GIVING OF A NOTICE IN LIEU OF DISTRINGAS

There is a more formal and effective means of protecting the bank's interest in shares held as security which are not registered in the names of the bank's nominees. A notice in lieu of distringas can be served upon the company under Rule 4 of Order 46 of the Supreme Court, whereby any person claiming to be interested in shares registered in the name of someone else may file notice in a specified form on affidavit in the Central Office of the Supreme Court or at a District Registry. An office copy of the affidavit and a sealed duplicate of the notice will be supplied and can then be served on the registered office of the company. Thereafter the company has to give eight days' warning before registering any transfer of the shares and the bank can intervene to protect its interests, usually by obtaining an injunction in the High Court. As this system is complicated and relatively costly in fees, it is rarely if ever resorted to by a bank. If the customer and the transaction do not warrant acceptance of the risks of an equitable mortgage, the advance should not be granted unless a legal mortgage can be obtained over any shares offered as security). The effect of this old form of writ (distringas meaning 'that you distrain'), is therefore, of technical interest only to the practical banker.

The usual course with approved customers where a legal mortgage is not essential is to take the shares on a memorandum of deposit with an unstamped, undated transfer, giving notice of the bank's lien, where desirable, to the company. Before summarising the advantages and disadvantages of this system, it will be appreciated that where the advance is repaid the security can be released to the customer in simple manner by returning the shares to him and cancelling or scrapping the memorandum of deposit and undated, unstamped transfers. Where notice of lien has been served, it should be withdrawn by suitable letter in case any objections are raised by the company when the customer subsequently disposes of the shares. On the other hand, where the bank's position deteriorates and the need arises to realise the security, all that is necessary is to fill in the blanks in the transfers, stamp them, and register the shares in the names of the bank's nominees. The bank then has a legal mortgage with the powers and means of sale already discussed under that heading. In the absence of an undated, unstamped transfer, the bank has to rely on the co-operation of the customer or resort to the Court before a sale can be made. Where the customer dies before the shares can be registered in the name of the bank's nominees, the executors of the deceased will usually pay off the debt to obtain the release of the shares, or sign fresh transfers

121

after probate has been registered with the company to facilitate the sale by the bank so that the proceeds may be applied in repayment of the loan. When bankruptcy intervenes before registration the trustee will sign fresh transfers to enable the security to be realised. Wherever possible, of course, the bank should complete its legal mortgage before the happening of such events so that it has a free hand to deal with the security promptly without awaiting the registration of probate or proving to the company the power of the trustee in bankruptcy to act. Emergencies of this kind call for speedy action on the part of the branch banker.

THE ADVANTAGES OF AN EQUITABLE MORTGAGE SUPPORTED BY AN UNDATED, UNSTAMPED TRANSFER

From the practical standpoint, the half-way house method which has been described gives the bank the means of combining all the potential advantages of a legal mortgage, subject to the risks scheduled below, with the avoidance of expense to the customer. Every time a legal mortgage is taken over shares the customer has to pay 50p stamp duty, unless the transfers are free from duty, also in a few cases a registration fee, and the same costs recur when the shares are transferred back into the name of the customer or third party who has charged them as security. If there are many changes in the holdings charged to the bank (the customer may often switch his investments during the life of the advance), these expenses will mount up. They can all be avoided in approved cases by relying upon an equitable mortgage and holding unstamped, undated transfers. This risk of liability for calls on partly paid shares is also removed if the bank does not become the legal owner of the shares.

Generally speaking, the advantages all lie in cheapness and simplicity. The bank's position is reasonably protected without the labour and cost involved in transferring the shares into the names of its nominees and the resulting complications of splitting dividends and distributing balance sheets and notices from the company. These very practical benefits are, however, subject to the following legal risks and a legal mortgage should obviously be taken where any doubts arise.

DISADVANTAGES OF AN EQUITABLE MORTGAGE

The disadvantages of an equitable mortgage, despite the ease with which it can be converted into a legal mortgage if an undated, unstamped transfer is held, can be summarised as follows:—

1. Unknown to the bank, there may be prior equitable interests which will upset the position. For example, the borrower may hold the shares as a trustee but the share certificate will be in his sole name and no note of the trusteeship will appear in the share register of the company (Section 117 of Companies Act, 1948, *ante*). If the bank relies upon an equitable mortgage of the shares, the prior equitable interests of the beneficiaries of the trust will prevail and it will not be any use registering the shares in the name of the bank's nominees as soon as it has notice of these prior interests (*Coleman v. London County & Westminster Bank* [1916] 2 Ch. 353, discussed on page 113). Where a legal mortgage is taken without notice of other equitable interests, the legal title of the bank will ensure priority. The risk of a prior equitable interest has to be accepted with an equitable mortgage of shares,

but the average borrower will be sufficiently known to limit this possibility.

2. A fraudulently minded shareholder may dispose of the shares held by the bank as security by obtaining a duplicate certificate and selling the shares on the market. If a notice of lien has been sent to the company and noted informally in its records, this risk may be removed, but the company is under no legal obligation to adopt these safeguards. In *Rainford* v. *James Keith & Blackman Co. Ltd.* [1905] 1 Ch. 296, a shareholder called Casmey lodged his share certificate with Rainford as security for a loan and signed a transfer which was held unstamped and undated. Casmey later sold the shares to a Mr. Younie and gave a declaration to the company that the certificate was held by a friend but not as security for a debt. The transfer was registered despite the fact that the certificate bore the following words 'without the production of this certificate no transfer of the shares mentioned herein can be registered' and a fresh certificate issued to the buyer. When Rainford sent his transfer to the company with the original certificate for registration in his name, the company declined to accept it because the shares had already been transferred to Younie. It was decided that the company was not liable to the plaintiff. The note on the certificate was held to be merely a warning to the shareholder to take care of it and the words did not constitute a representation that the shares would not be transferred without production of the certificate. Such deliberate frauds are admittedly rare, but the risk is always present unless a company makes and refers to an unofficial record of the bank's notice of lien.

This danger brings to mind the care which a banker should always exercise before joining in an indemnity to a company on behalf of a customer who has lost a share certificate. It is not a mere formality to facilitate the issue of a duplicate certificate and these indemnities should be provided only for undoubted parties after the bank has verified the position by question and answer. A thorough search for the missing certificate should first be insisted upon and every avenue explored to prove that it has really been lost. A forgetful customer may long ago have deposited the original certificate elsewhere as security for the debt of a friend and the facts may have escaped his memory.

3. The bank cannot realise the shares unless and until the transfer is completed, stamped and registered. Its position may be jeopardised during the interim period, but this is a practical risk which can reasonably be accepted in approved cases. Where the shares have to be transferred under seal, a blank transfer is, of course, useless.

4. If the company makes an issue of bonus shares, the certificate for the additional shares will be despatched direct to the customer, who may not co-operate by charging the bonus shares to the bank. The fact that bonus shares have been issued may even escape the notice of the bank until it revalues its security. Unless profits increase proportionately, the value of the shares in a company will normally be reduced when a free bonus issue is made by capitalisation of reserves. Suppose, for example, that when the £1 shares of O.P.O. Ltd. are quoted on the market at £2 each, yielding 10 per cent. on a regular dividend of twenty p per share, the directors decide to issue from reserves one bonus share for every share held, but they

indicate that there is unlikely to be any increase in the net profits earned by the company. Thereafter the dividend will be at the rate of ten p per share and the market price will probably drop to £1 per share. Customer Q, who has charged five hundred shares in O.P.O. Ltd. to Northtown Bank by way of equitable mortgage, is no worse off because he receives direct five hundred bonus shares and, instead of holding the original five hundred shares worth £2 each, he now has altogether one thousand shares worth £1 each, but the value of the bank's security has been halved automatically and it will normally require the deposit of the bonus shares to make up the deficit. It is a question of watching the market notices in the financial press so that prompt action can be taken where necessary. Where the shares are registered in the name of the bank nominees, any bonus shares will be issued direct to the nominees and no risk arises.

A similar weakness arises in those few cases where the bank relies upon the dividend from the shares to reduce the bank debt or to pay the half-yearly interest charges. Unless mandated to the bank, the dividends will be paid direct to the customer who may negotiate the warrant elsewhere. The cure for this evil is simple. The blank transfer merely has to be completed and registered to ensure that future dividends are paid direct to the bank.

5. Finally, there remains the risk that the company may have a lien on its shares for amounts due by the shareholder to the company. The method employed to safeguard against this possibility and the attendant practical problems have been explained at length.

The disadvantages of a legal mortgage were set out in Chapter XIII and the practical banker has to weigh the advantages and disadvantages of both methods of charge in the balance before deciding which is best suited to the particular circumstances. If there is any doubt concerning the liquidity of the advance or the reliability of the customer, a legal mortgage is obviously desirable. In other cases the bank may be content for the time being with an equitable mortgage with an undated, unstamped transfer. It is a question of judgment and policy.

Chapter XV Unquoted Shares and Kindred Securities

NATIONAL SAVINGS CERTIFICATES—BRITISH SAVINGS BONDS—
PREMIUM SAVINGS BONDS—BUILDING SOCIETY SHARES—
LETTERS OF ALLOTMENT

UNQUOTED SECURITIES

Unquoted shares fall into two distinct classes from the standpoint of banking security. There are firstly the shares of a few public companies which are not quoted on any stock exchange and, secondly, the shares of private companies. Both classes are generally unsuitable as banking security because they are difficult to value with any accuracy and often difficult to realise. In the case of private company shares, it may also be impossible to obtain a legal mortgage. Apart from the problems of valuation and of sale in a narrow market, unquoted shares in a public company may be taken as security in precisely the same manner as quoted shares, but the restrictions which have to be placed upon the transfer of shares in a private company introduce many complications calling for special consideration. What follows, therefore, largely concerns shares in a private company.

Section 28 of the Companies Act, 1948, defines a private company as a company which by its articles:—

1. restricts the right to transfer its shares; and
2. limits the number of its members to fifty, not including persons who are in the employment of the company and persons who, having been formerly in the employment of the company, were while in that employment, and have continued after determination of that employment to be, members of the company; and
3. prohibits any invitation to the public to subscribe for any shares or debentures of the company.

For a full survey of the privileges and advantages of a private company compared with a public company the reader is referred to '*The Accounts of Limited Company Customers*'. When offered such shares as security, the chief point to be explored by the banker is the precise nature of the restriction on the transfer of the shares. This calls for a study of the articles. If a print is not available from the customer (the private company often banks with the same branch as the shareholder who is tendering the shares as security), a search can easily be made at Companies' House. Any kind of restriction imposed by the Articles on the transfer of the shares will be sufficient for the purposes of the Act, but some articles are more restrictive than others. The relative clause for private companies in Table

'A' of the 1948 Act reads as follows: 'The directors may, in their absolute discretion and without assigning any reason therefor, decline to register any transfer of any share, whether or not it is a fully paid share'. This restriction is very wide and the directors can decline to register the nominees of the bank or any purchaser as holders without quoting reasons for their decision. Some companies may have articles which state specifically that only persons engaged in the same trade as the company may be shareholders. The usual object, apart from preserving the company as a private company, is to keep the shares in the hands of the existing members and their families and any attempt by an outsider to obtain an interest in the company can be summarily stopped by the directors. Thus, where the banker can obtain a legal mortgage, the market for the sale of the shares is very narrow. They can never be regarded as acceptable banking security, but some reliance has at times to be placed upon them and all the pitfalls have therefore to be discussed.

VALUATION OF UNQUOTED SHARES

In valuing any unquoted shares, due allowance has always to be made for the problems which will arise in finding a buyer. Quite apart from the trading history and earning capacity and inherent financial strength of the company, a discount has inevitably to be made for the narrowness of the market. If the shares can be sold only to a limited class of persons, the price which they are prepared to pay will be lower than that which could be obtained from the general public, unless, of course, there is a suitable buyer to whom the possibility of control of the company has special attractions. The extent of any restriction on the transfer of the shares has, therefore, to be borne in mind in assessing a prudent security value.

The primary means of valuation will be to examine the last available balance sheet of the company and to study the trading results and dividend history over the past few years. Every member of any private company will have copies of the annual accounts (Section 129 (4) Companies Act, 1948) and a customer is hardly likely to decline to produce them to the bank if he is anxious to borrow against the security of the shares. In the case of a public company, the information can be obtained from Companies' House if circumstances so demand.

From the available figures the average dividend paid on the shares over the past four or five years can be calculated and a prudent price assessed by comparison with the yield on quoted shares of a similar class. For example, suppose that the average market yield for light engineering shares is 7 per cent. and the banker is valuing shares in Z Ltd., a private company engaged in this type of business. Over the past five years the average dividend paid by Z Ltd. has been 12 per cent. The bank might take the view that if quoted shares are yielding 7 per cent., unquoted shares should yield an additional 2 per cent. having regard to their restricted market for sale. On this basis an unquoted share yielding 9 per cent. would be worth par and, as the £1 shares of Z Ltd. pay 12 per cent. dividend, they can be valued at say £1-33p each to yield 9 per cent.

An alternative or complementary method of valuation is to assess the net surplus available for the share capital on a brake-up basis. All the assets are valued at an estimated auction or forced sale figure and any balance remaining after payment of all the liabilities and any preference capital is divided by the number of ordinary shares to give their estimated value. The reliability of this method largely depends upon the extent of the bank's knowledge of the assets of the company. Nevertheless, it is a practical means of reaching a prudent minimum valuation as a general guide.

Sometimes the value of unquoted shares can be determined by reference to the secretary of the company who may be willing to disclose the prices at which any shares have been bought and sold in recent months. Occasionally, the shares may have been valued for probate purposes within the past twelve months and the figure will be a helpful guide to the bank. In both cases a reasonable margin will be deducted from the price quoted to cover the prospect of a sale to a less willing buyer.

METHOD OF CHARGING UNQUOTED SHARES

If the shares are of sufficient value for the bank's purpose, they may be taken as security by way of legal mortgage if the articles will permit the registration of the bank's nominees as shareholders. This may not be possible with many private company shares and the bank has to be content with an equitable charge for what it may be worth. In many cases the borrower is a director of the company and most reluctant to allow the shares to be transferred out of his name. Moreover, he may object to the service of notice of lien upon the company and expect the bank to shoulder the risk that the company may have a lien on the shares for amounts due by the shareholder to the company. In other words, the security has to be held in an incomplete manner relying largely upon the integrity of the borrower and looking upon the shares as mere evidence of his means available in case of need to repay the debt providing he will co-operate with the bank and a buyer who is acceptable to the directors can be found at a satisfactory price. Frequently, the shares have first to be offered to the existing members of the company at a price agreed by the auditors. They may, or may not, be in a position to bid for the shares and the price may eventually have to be reduced to find a buyer within the permitted class.

The difficulties which can arise may be illustrated by reference to *Hunter* v. *Hunter & Ors.* [1936] A.C. 222. S. Hunter guaranteed to Lloyds Bank the overdraft of a company called A. M. Cawthra & Co. Ltd., of which he was chairman, and supported his guarantee *inter alia* by the deposit of 800 shares in a private company, Thomas Hunter Limited, the shares being deposited under a memorandum in the usual terms as security for the repayment on demand of the liabilities of S. Hunter to the bank.

S. Hunter was the registered holder of 1,146 shares in all of Thomas Hunter Limited, and the remaining shares in that company were held by members of the Hunter family who were also directors of the company, but S. Hunter himself was not on the board.

The articles of association of Thomas Hunter Limited restricted the rights of transfer and provided that 'no member shall be entitled to transfer any share otherwise than in accordance with the following provisions . . .'; the provisions which followed contained the usual machinery whereby a member desirous of selling his shares should give a sale notice to the secretary of the company, that the price should be fixed by the auditors of the company, and that the secretary should thereupon offer the shares to the other members of the company, subject to a pre-emptive right in favour of T. H. V. Hunter, the managing director.

There were also provisions for transmission of the shares by reason of the death or bankruptcy of any member.

In October, 1930, the bank, being dissatisfied with the overdraft of A. M. Cawthra & Co. Ltd., made formal demand upon S. Hunter for payment under his guarantee, but following upon this demand negotiations took place between S. Hunter and the bank, with the result that S. Hunter deposited further security, including the balance of his shares in Thomas Hunter Limited, and it was arranged that the bank's nominees should be registered as the holders of both the additional shares and those originally deposited. In due course the shares were registered in the names of the bank's nominees, the transfers being passed by the directors without any special formalities, presumably because the provisions of the articles for sale notices, etc., did not appear to them to be applicable in the circumstances.

A year later the bank, still being dissatisfied with the overdraft of A. M. Cawthra & Co. Ltd., informed S. Hunter in writing that either he must take steps to realise his shares in Thomas Hunter Limited or the bank would itself deal with them. S. Hunter did not effect a sale of the shares, with the result that the bank proceeded to realise them by giving to the secretary of the company the requisite notice under the articles of association and procuring the auditors of the company to fix the price. The steps taken were all in regular form, and T. H. V. Hunter, pursuant to the pre-emptive right conferred upon him by the articles, exercised his right of purchase.

Six months later two actions were commenced, the first by Mrs. Hunter, a shareholder in Thomas Hunter Limited, and the second by S. Hunter himself, claiming that the transfer of the 1,146 shares of Thomas Hunter Limited to the nominees of the bank, and the subsequent transfer by the nominees of the bank to T. H. V. Hunter, were null and void as contrary to the articles of association, and accordingly that the register of the company should be rectified by restoring the name of S. Hunter as the holder of the 1,146 shares. In addition, S.Hunter in his action claimed that he was entitled to redeem his shares, upon the ground that the bank had purported to sell the shares without their power of sale as mortgagees having arisen.

The House of Lords held in S. Hunter's action that the notice of October, 1931, that the bank would sell the shares was not equivalent to a demand for payment of S. Hunter's indebtedness, and that the original formal demand was not effective in view of the subsequent events, *viz.*, the giving by S. Hunter, and the acceptance by the bank, of further security, which amounted to waiver by the bank of the demand previously made. It was, therefore, held that the bank's power of sale had not arisen and that S. Hunter was entitled to redeem his shares, together with the dividends paid thereon since the sale.

The Lord Chancellor said that in reaching this conclusion he felt some regret, because he had no doubt that S. Hunter had full notice of what the bank were doing and that if he had objected at the time the bank would undoubtedly have served a formal demand which he could not have met, but the Lord Chancellor added—'The right of sale is a very drastic remedy and it is essential for the due protection of borrowers that the conditions of its exercise should be strictly complied with'.

Upon the same point Lord Blanesburgh said that the question had 'become one of principle not only of major importance in this action to the Appellant but of deep interest generally to borrowers on security to whom it would too frequently be disastrous if there were permitted any relaxation of the rule whereby invariably and strictly a lender is held to the fulfilment of every condition made by the instrument precedent to the exercise by him of any power of sale over the mortgaged property. The condition in this instance was a very small protection to the Appellant. So much the stricter was the Bank's duty to fulfil it'.

Mr. Justice Bennett and the Court of Appeal, in the action brought by Mrs. Hunter, decided that a transfer by way of mortgage was not a transfer which was permitted by the articles of association, in so far as the articles provided that no member should be entitled to transfer his shares except in accordance with the specific provisions of the articles, which made no mention of transfer by way of mortgage, and it was ordered accordingly that the name of S. Hunter be restored to the register. In the action by S. Hunter the Court of Appeal held that T. H. V. Hunter and the bank were entitled, if they so desired, to treat the sale of the shares to T. H. V. Hunter as a sale of the equitable interest only in the shares, and, therefore, that although the name of S. Hunter must be restored as the registered holder of the shares, S. Hunter should execute a declaration of trust in favour of T. H. V. Hunter. There was no appeal to the House of Lords in Mrs. Hunter's action.

Although the decision of the House of Lords that the bank's power of sale had not arisen was sufficient to settle the appeal to the House of Lords of S. Hunter in his favour, their Lordships dealt with the question of the validity of the transfer of the shares to the bank's nominees and subsequently by the bank's nominees to T. H. V. Hunter, and confirmed the decision of Mr. Justice Bennett and the Court of Appeal as to the invalidity of those transfers. Upon the question of the sale of the equitable, as opposed to the legal, interest in the shares they disagreed with the Court of Appeal upon the ground that a mortgagee of shares cannot split up the interest of the mortgagor and agree to sell either the whole or part of the mortgagor's equitable interest divested of the legal title. Moreover, it was pointed out that if the bank had been selling the equitable interest in the shares none of the provisions of the articles of association as to the restriction on possible purchasers, or as to the method of fixing a price, would have been effective, and it would have been quite a different transaction from a sale of the shares.

The Lord Chancellor pointed out that the construction placed upon the articles of association would not prevent a mortgage of the shares or their sale by the mortgagees in default of payment of the mortgage debt, although the sale must be effected in accordance with the terms of the articles. He said that the bank could have taken from S. Hunter letters addressed to the auditor and to the secretary respectively in blank, or they could have taken a power of attorney to write such letters in his name and on his behalf. The Lord Chancellor also made a further suggestion that he did not think the disregard of the provisions of the articles of association rendered the transaction *ultra vires* the company, and therefore the transfers could have been regularised by the assent of all the shareholders.

This case certainly brings out the importance of examining the articles of association of any private company whose shares are to be taken as security to decide whether and in what way a valid charge can best be obtained. If the banker is to rely upon such security, it is by no means a simple task to take a satisfactory charge over the shares, and the practical conclusion to be drawn from this brief survey is that unquoted shares should be avoided wherever possible as banking security. Where they have to be taken for what they are worth, they should be valued in the most pessimistic manner and the articles of the company should be studied in detail to decide how best to obtain the most effective charge which the provisions will permit. In any event, the problem of realisation will often be complex and the sale prolonged.

NATIONAL SAVINGS CERTIFICATES

Although National Savings Certificates are in practice a popular form of banking security for personal indebtedness, they are not, strictly speaking, beyond criticism because it is impossible to obtain a watertight charge. They are not transferable and a legal mortgage cannot, therefore, be obtained. Moreover, their terms of issue expressly provide that no claim by a person holding a certificate in respect of a loan can be recognised by the Director of Savings.

The method of charge is to obtain the deposit of the certificates with the standard form of memorandum evidencing the intention of the customer, together with an official form of request for repayment signed in blank by the depositor of the certificates. To realise such security the name of the bank can be inserted in the repayment form which is then forwarded to the Director of Savings with the certificates and the proceeds will, in due course, be paid direct to the bank. The danger is that, whilst the banker is holding the certificates, the depositor may obtain duplicates, or may obtain repayment by representing that the original certificates have been lost. The certificates held by the bank will then be useless. At one time the Department for National Savings acknowledged and recorded notices of deposit received from banks to ensure that duplicates were not issued or repayment made to anyone who had charged his certificates as security. In 1950, however, the Director of Savings advised the banks that this arrangement had to be withdrawn except as regards notices already accepted. The only protection to-day is that when asked to issue duplicate certificates the Department for National Savings, before complying with the request, enquires whether the originals have been deposited with or left in the custody of any third party. The same rules apply to notices of charge in respect of other stocks on the National Savings Stock Register (see below).

When dealing with a reliable customer, there is little practical risk in relying upon National Savings Certificates as security. They can easily be realised when required and a valid equitable title is obtained against a trustee in bankruptcy if the customer happens to fail. The current value of such security can always be ascertained from tables or from the Department for National Savings and they steadily increase in value with the passage of time.

BRITISH SAVINGS BONDS

These Bonds have taken the place of National Development Bonds, which themselves succeeded Defence Bonds. British Savings Bonds may be bought for £5 and multiples thereof and the National Savings Department issues each bondholder with a bond book, which must be produced when bonds are bought or sold. Interest is paid without deduction of tax and withdrawal of funds before maturity is subject to one month's notice; if funds are left until maturity a small premium is paid.

As with National Development Bonds and Defence Bonds, banks cannot obtain a legal mortgage over British Savings Bonds. They are not transferable without the consent of the Director of Savings and this is not forthcoming in the case of transfer by way of sale or mortgage. However, banks are able to obtain an equitable charge by having the bond book deposited on a memorandum of deposit and the customer should be asked to sign a repayment form. As with National Savings Certificates, the bank relies upon the integrity of the depositor not to attempt to deal with the bonds by representing that he has lost the bond book in order to claim a duplicate. Nevertheless, some comfort can be taken from the case of *R. v. Chief Registrar of Friendly Societies, ex parte Mills* (1970) 3 All E.R. 1076. In this case the applicant had charged £500 National Development Bonds over which the Westminster Bank had taken an equitable charge. The customer had signed the encashment application form in favour of the bank, and when the Westminster Bank were unable to obtain repayment of the overdraft, it sought encashment of the bonds. The applicant wrote to the Director of Savings countermanding her encashment order and the bank was told that the dispute would have to be referred to the Chief Registrar of Friendly Societies for his decision under the terms of the National Debt Act, 1958. The Chief Registrar decided that payment should be made to the bank.

Appeal was made to the Divisional Court and the point at issue was not whether the bank had a good equitable title, but whether the Registrar had any jurisdiction under the National Debt Act to determine a case. It was argued that the Registrar could only settle a dispute through the Director of Savings and a person entitled to the bonds (i.e. the bank in this case). Once the encashment order was countermanded the bank were no longer 'entitled' to the bonds. The Divisional Court accepted this argument and found in favour of the bank only because they considered themselves bound by an earlier authority, a decision of the Court of Appeal in 1926.

PREMIUM SAVINGS BONDS

Some general comments may not be out of place here concerning Premium Savings Bonds which yield no interest but entitle the holder to participate in weekly and monthly draws for prizes paid free of tax. The conditions of issue expressly state that the bonds are not transferable. Past opinion has been that these bonds are not acceptable as security and that they should only be held as evidence of means. However, it appears to be fairly common practice now to take them if nothing else is available. The validity of the holding may be confirmed by application in the form of a letter to the Bonds and Stock Office.

On the death of the holder the personal representatives can claim repayment of the bonds on Form S.B.4, which can be obtained from any Post Office.

OTHER STOCKS ON THE NATIONAL SAVINGS STOCK REGISTER

To facilitate investment by small investors, British Government stocks up to a maximum of £5,000 nominal value in any one purchase may be bought through the National Savings Bank at slightly less commission than would be payable if the stocks were purchased in the market through a stockbroker. Instead of being registered in the books at the Bank of England, the holder of such stocks is registered on the National Savings Stock Register and a certificate is issued by the Department for National Savings.

To obtain a legal mortgage over stock on the National Savings Stock Register, a special form of transfer has to be obtained from the Director, Bonds and Stock Office, Lytham St. Annes, Lancs., and when completed by the depositor the stock can be transferred into the names of the bank's nominees. Apart from obtaining the transfer form and registering with the Department for National Savings, the system is basically the same as when obtaining a legal mortgage of British Government stocks registered at the Bank of England. A memorandum of deposit will normally be taken to prove the intention of the parties.

An equitable charge will be obtained by the deposit of the certificate under a memorandum of deposit and the customer should complete an application form for the sale of the stock (obtainable from any Post Office transacting National Savings Bank business), which is held undated until such time as it may be necessary to realise the security. As with National Savings Certificates, the Department for National Savings will not record or acknowledge any notice of deposit or lien from a bank, so there is no point in sending one.

BUILDING SOCIETY SHARES

Occasionally a customer may offer building society shares as security for temporary overdraft facilities, preferring to borrow from the bank to avoid disturbing his investments. The title to the shares will often be evidenced by an entry in a share passbook which is deposited with the bank and a memorandum of deposit taken in the usual manner from the customer. It is doubtful, however, whether a valid charge can be obtained because the rules of most building societies prohibit or severely restrict the transfer of their shares. Many societies will not register limited companies as shareholders. Where the rules permit, a legal mortgage should preferably be obtained by transfer of the shares into the names of the bank nominees, always providing that the shares are fully paid. Nevertheless, it may prove difficult to realise the shares because a buyer cannot be found or the society may not be prepared to repay the balance. Fortunately, many of the larger societies nowadays repay shares on demand or at reasonable notice and it is possible to realise the security.

It is a question of studying the rules to decide whether the shares can reasonably be accepted as cover for the proposed borrowing. A mere equitable mortgage by deposit with perhaps a blank transfer or withdrawal form accepts the risk that the shareholder may obtain a duplicate passbook and then withdraw the capital. Again, it depends upon whether the society is prepared to record and acknowledge any notice of lien from the bank. Generally speaking, it is better to prevail upon the customer to withdraw his money from the building society instead of borrowing from the bank against the shares.

A distinction has to be drawn between shares and deposits in a building society. They are both usually evidenced by entries in a passbook, but in any exceptional case where deposits are taken by a bank as security they have to be legally assigned to the bank with due notice to the society. The rules may forbid such an assignment and the safer course is to insist upon the withdrawal of the deposit, which will entail no capital loss to the customer.

LETTERS OF ALLOTMENT

Whenever a public company makes an issue of shares, a prospectus is issued inviting its members, or the general public, to subscribe by application for the shares, tendering the amount stated to be payable upon application. The directors then allot the shares and letters of allotment are sent to the successful applicants. The legal position was described by Baggallay, L. J., in *Re Scottish Petroleum Company* (1883) 23 Ch. D. 413 as follows 'to constitute a binding contract to take shares in a company when such contract is based on application and allotment, it is necessary that there should be an application by the intending shareholder, an allotment by the directors of the company of the shares applied for, and a communication by the directors to the applicant of the fact of such allotment having been made.'

Where a company makes a bonus or free rights issue to existing members, allotment letters for fully paid shares will be sent to shareholders for the number of shares to which they are entitled without need for any application on their part. When the public or merely existing members are invited to apply for fresh shares, the prospectus usually calls for payment in instalments. For example, twenty-five per cent. of the purchase price may be payable on application, a further twenty-five per cent. on allotment, and the balance of fifty per cent. two months' after allotment, and the price of such partly paid shares in the market will vary with the amount paid-up.

The letter of allotment records how much has been paid up and remains payable on the shares stated therein and on the reverse side there will be a form of renunciation which the allottee can complete if he wishes to transfer the shares before the date fixed for registration. The holder thereby renounces his rights in favour of the person who completes the registration form, which is usually printed on the reverse side of the allotment letter.

Occasionally, a customer may proffer an allotment letter as security, being in need of accommodation before the shares can be registered in his name and a certificate issued. It has first to be examined to ensure that it is in favour of the depositor, fully paid and properly stamped. The form of renunciation has then to be signed by the allottee and the letter deposited with the usual memorandum of deposit. It is then equivalent to a bearer security and the bank can complete the acceptance form within the given time and send the allotment letter to the company to have the shares or stocks registered in the names of its nominees. Alternatively, the shares can be sold and the allotment letter, with renunciation in blank, delivered to the purchaser so that he can complete the form of acceptance. The last date upon which renunciation will be accepted by the company will be recorded clearly in the allotment letter and the need for care in diarising this date is obvious.

Where the bank is content to rely upon an equitable mortgage, the allotment letter will be taken without renunciation, together with a memorandum of deposit and undated, unstamped transfers (where legally possible). When the allotment letter is required by the company for exchange into a definitive certificate, it will be sent forward by the bank, together with a request addressed to the company by the shareholder, for the delivery of the certificate direct to the bank. Alternatively, the bank may be content to rely upon the customer to bring the share certificate into the bank immediately it is received. Nowadays, with bonus issues, share certificates are often issued direct to shareholders, in the absence of any renunciation, without delivery of the allotment letter to the company. It is a question of studying the detailed provisions printed in the allotment letter.

In practice, a banker normally handles allotment letters as agent for the customer as part of a general investment service, paying instalments upon the customer's authority as and when they fall due and ultimately collecting the definitive certificate when it is available for safe custody. The dates when action has to be taken on the allotment letters have always to be diarised with care, otherwise the bank may be liable for any loss sustained by the customer through its negligence.

In recent years a renounceable type of certificate has been introduced as an alternative to the allotment letter. This is designed to avoid the necessity of having to obtain a definitive certificate in replacement for the allotment letter. The renounceable certificate is, in fact, a combination of allotment letter and certificate for, after the date indicated, the document is treated as a definitive certificate and transfer of ownership can be made by the usual methods. It can, nevertheless, be renounced in the same way as an allotment letter and the date by which this must be done will usually be quoted on the front of the certificate. The relevant forms of renunciation will be printed on the reverse side and full instructions on their completion will be found normally on an attached perforated slip.

Part Five: Land

Chapter XVI Introductory

Although it is not the normal function of a banker to finance directly the purchase of property on a long-term basis, land in its various forms is frequently taken as security for advances and, in approaching what is a lengthy and somewhat complex subject, it is prudent at the outset to define the basic terms and to outline the method of attack.

LAND DEFINED

Land comprises the surface of the earth together with all things of a physical nature above and below the surface, including all types of buildings, and chattels attached to the buildings, trees, growing crops and minerals. It thus covers many vastly different types of banking security from the virgin building site, woodland or fertile farmland to the humble dwelling house, stately mansion, hotel, factory or office block. The legal definition is derived from the maxim that whatever may be attached to the soil becomes part of it (*quiequid plantatur solo, solo cedit*). Whether a chattel has been affixed to land as to become part of it is a question of fact. The test usually is whether a chattel has been fixed for its more convenient use as a chattel or whether it is fixed for the more convenient use of the land or building. For example, bricks stacked on a vacant site by a builder are not fixtures, but a wall built of stones laid one upon another without mortar is a fixture. (*Holland* v. *Hodgson* (1872) L.R.7). Legal niceties of this kind rarely trouble a banker, however, and the nature of land taken as security is simple to describe.

ADVANTAGES AND DISADVANTAGES OF LAND AS SECURITY

The advantages and disadvantages of land as banking security can briefly be described as follows:—

1. Although unlikely to fluctuate widely in value over a long period, the land may be difficult to value with any degree of accuracy and realisation may be a protracted and expensive matter if there are no willing buyers in the market. Generally speaking, property has steadily increased in value over the past fifty years, but much depends upon the type of property under consideration. The valuation and forced sale of a modern dwelling house, or of good investment property is quite different from the valuation and market for the disposal of a factory, mill, hotel or other

specialised building. The value of any type of property cannot, however, be ascertained by the banker with the same speed and accuracy as the worth of a quoted share or life policy held as security. Moreover, in order to ensure that the value of the land is maintained, an inspection has be to made at reasonable intervals, involving time and travelling expenses.

2. Unless the title to the land is registered, the services of a solicitor are required to examine the title and to furnish a report to the bank. The chain of title may be complicated and defects may be discovered which limit the value of the security.

3. The costs to the borrower are higher in the case of land than they are with many other types of security. There will be search fees and solicitors' costs for the examination and report upon title and, perhaps, the expenses involved in the periodic inspections of the property.

4. The security will depreciate in value unless it is well maintained. Repairs and decorations are essential over the years and difficulty may arise if the mortgagor neglects the building. The need always to verify that property is fully insured against all known risks is a further trouble to the bank.

5. Lastly, there is a pronounced tendency in practice for some advances granted against property (particularly dwelling-houses) to develop into long-term mortgage loans. A bank is not a building society and care has to be exercised to keep the advance liquid. It is a question of control and not, strictly speaking, a disadvantage inherent in the security.

Notwithstanding these disadvantages compared with more marketable securities land in all its forms is acceptable banking security providing there is ample margin in the value and a satisfactory title can be obtained. All the practical and legal problems which confront the bank when taking such security can best be discussed in the order in which they normally arise in practice, and the following main headings can be adopted for our purpose in shaping the face of things to come in these pages:

1. The valuation of the security.
2. The question of fire insurance.
3. The title—examination and report.
4. The mortgage to the bank—legal or equitable?
5. The priority of charges and searches required.
6. Repayment of the advance.
7. Remedies available to the bank as a mortgagee.
8. Second mortgages and sub-mortgages.
9. Registered land.

LEGAL ESTATES IN LAND

Without at this stage enquiring into the history and theory of the various interests in land, the following distinction can be drawn between legal estates and equitable interests in land.

According to Section 1 of the Law Property Act, 1925 (hereinafter described as L.P.A.), the only *estates* in land which are capable of subsisting or of being conveyed or created *at law* are:—

(*a*) An estate in fee simple absolute in possession.

(*b*) A term of years absolute.

An estate may be described simply as the duration of an interest in land. *An estate in fee simple* virtually means that the owner has absolute ownership of the land. It is the largest estate known to law. *An estate for life*, arises where land is limited to a tenant for his own life, or where someone becomes entitled by operation of law to hold lands for the rest of his or her life. *An estate tail* is the estate of inheritance inferior to the fee simple whereby it is inherited only by descendants of the original grantee. For example, a grant to 'X and the heirs of his body'. *A leasehold interest* is less than freehold because the estate is granted by the owner of the fee simple (known as the *lessor*) to the *lessee* for a fixed term of years, at the end of which it reverts to the original owner. Although the period of a leasehold interest may be as long as 999 years, it is not a freehold estate, and legally is a smaller interest than a life estate.

The only *interests or charges* in or over land which are capable of subsisting or of being conveyed or created *at law* are:—

(*a*) An easement, right, or privilege in or over land for an interest equivalent to an estate in fee simple absolute in possession or a term of years absolute.

(*b*) A rent-charge in possession issuing out of or charged on land being either perpetual or for a term of years absolute.

(*c*) A charge by way of legal mortgage.

(*d*) Land, tithe rent-charge, and any other similar charge on land which is not created by an instrument.

(*e*) Rights of entry exercisable over or in respect of a legal term of years absolute, or annexed, for any purpose, to a legal rent-charge.

A charge by way of legal mortgage is of the greatest interest to the practical banker, but all the above terms will be touched upon later. The point now is that all estates, interests and charges in or over land other than those listed above take effect as *equitable interests*.

Chapter XVII The Valuation and Insurance of the Property

The first practical step when taking land as security is to decide how much it is worth from the standpoint of the bank. Although the bank manager is not expected to be a professional valuer, he has to be able to estimate the value of any property within his area with reasonable accuracy. The services of a professional valuer will not normally be required in practice, because the bank is taking the security as a form of insurance in the background, relying primarily upon the borrower to repay the advance from trade or other known sources. As the advance is not made primarily against the property, any risks of error in valuation can be accepted, but prudence demands that in all cases the banker should be pessimistic in his approach to the problem.

Two distinct and yet complementary methods of valuation can be adopted and the principles apply to any type of property. The current value can be assessed as a basis and an agreed margin deducted to provide for the possible depreciation over the period of the advance, or an attempt can be made to estimate the forced sale value in the worst event. Any need for the bank to sell the property as mortgagee is unlikely to arise for some years and property values may depreciate heavily in the meantime. Whichever method may be adopted is a matter of policy, the fact remaining that the basic test is whether the security will realise sufficient for the bank's purpose if and when it has to be sold to recover the debt.

The current value of any property is the price which a willing buyer would be prepared to pay and a willing seller would be prepared to accept, depending upon the demand for and supply of properties of the size and type in the given area. In the unhappy event of a sale by the bank as mortgagee, there may be few, if any, willing buyers in the market and it would probably be necessary to sell by auction in unfavourable conditions. It is then the old story of the auctioneer trying hard to attract bids from a small band of most unwilling buyers gathered together in the local hotel on a cheerless day and, with this sorry picture in mind, the banker inspects the property and reaches a safe valuation. The banker has to be flexible in his approach, weighing in the balance many factors, but the following general practical points may be of assistance when faced with the problem of valuing such security.

DWELLING HOUSES

If the branch manager maintains close contact with local estate agent friends and watches the local press, the prices at which houses are changing hands in his district will be known to him and little difficulty will be experienced in placing a safe current value upon an established owner-occupied house, according to its size, state of repair, and situation. The larger and more remote the residence, the smaller will usually be the potential market because the number of buyers capable of financing such a purchase and maintaining a large household with servant problems is limited. Needless to say, every mortgagor will be optimistic concerning the worth and attractions of his own homestead and it may often be necessary to discount such unsolicited opinions. The initial asking price of a willing seller may be much higher than the price eventually accepted. Nowadays, the smaller compact type of house, with three or four bedrooms, and preferably with a garage, attracts more buyers, particularly when it is conveniently situated for public transport, shopping and entertainment facilities. The situation in relation to local amenities and areas subject to development is obviously an important consideration. The price which a buyer is willing to pay for an established house may be influenced by the price at which he can buy a new house of a similar size from a builder developing plots in the locality. The point is that the bank manager knows his area and the plans for the development of the area and can consider any given property within this general picture. It follows that the valuation of house property should be entrusted to the local manager to obtain the most reliable valuation. The manager of a branch outside the district is a stranger unaware of local conditions and, if he attempts to value houses relying only on his personal inspection and by drawing a comparison with the prices obtaining for similar houses in his own district, he may be wide of the mark.

The original cost price of a house may serve as an initial guide to its current value providing the date of purchase is known and considered in relation to general conditions then existing in the property market.

The inspection of the property has to be arranged without causing offence to the customer. Little difficulty arises where the owner is in occupation and the interior as well as the exterior can be inspected, but when the house is let care may be necessary to avoid disclosure to the tenant that the owner has mortgaged the property to the bank. There is a vast difference between the detailed survey of a house by a personally conducted tour under the auspices of a proud owner, with perhaps a cup of tea or stronger beverage included, and the surreptitious glances made during a slow march past fervently hoping that the lady of the house is not watching through the curtains. It is up to the initiative of the banker to obtain the closest inspection circumstances will permit, always remembering that an attractive exterior can hide an interior in dire need of repair. An inspection of the interior may, or may not, be necessary according to the extent to which the bank is relying on the security, but a well kept tastefully decorated interior often attracts buyers and increases their willingness to pay the sellers' price. The extent of the garage accommodation and the size of the garden are also factors to be considered with the size and situation of the house.

A possible risk which cannot be disregarded when valuing an owner-occupied house is that, if the advance proves to be unsatisfactory, the borrower may nevertheless continue to reside in the house which cannot then be sold with vacant possession. Any attempt to obtain repayment by prevailing upon the customer to arrange finance from a building society or a private mortgagee may be abortive because the borrower may be unacceptable to such lenders. Unless the bank adopts the unsavoury course of forcing the mortgagor out of his house by legal process, the house cannot be sold unless a buyer can be found who is content to accept the owner as a tenant. In such an event, the price paid would be much lower than the price obtainable for vacant possession.

INVESTMENT PROPERTIES

Apart from inspecting investment properties to consider their size, condition and situation, the banker has to calculate the net income yield derived from them after meeting all outgoings.

To value such property, the banker has first to ascertain the actual gross rental yield of the buildings which may, or may not, be subject to legal control. Where the local supply of similar properties has been materially increased by new buildings, an allowance may be necessary for voids likely to arise if part of the building cannot be let. This applies more particularly to office accommodation. The next step is to assess the total outgoings and expenses payable by the landlord in accord with the terms of the leases to tenants. These will include the cost of repairs, usually limited to the exterior except where the landlord expressly accepts responsibility for interior repairs and decorations; all rates which are not payable by the tenant; the cost of insuring the property; and management expenses where agents have to be employed to collect the rents and arrange lettings, etc. When the total of the actual or estimated annual outgoings is deducted from the annual gross rental, the net rental forms the basis of valuation and, subject to any defects in situation, state of repair or other drawbacks likely to reduce the selling price, the security can be valued at, say, ten years' purchase of the net rental, according to the type of building and the current level of interest rates. On the other hand, if the manager's estimate of the forced sale value of the dwellings with vacant possession is less than the value calculated from the net rental, the lower figure will be the prudent one to adopt for security purposes.

Blocks of flats and office buildings, as well as cottages and dwelling houses, can all be valued on this net yield basis as investment properties. In the case of flats the rentals, which are usually inclusive of rates, may be increased by a service charge for lifts and other amenities. Outgoings to be met by the landlord will often include heating, service, garden upkeep and management expenses as well as insurance and repairs. The age, state of repair and situation of the building also has to be reviewed with the likely demand for such accommodation in the district. If a recent professional valuation of an office building or block of flats can be obtained, it will be a useful guide to the bank. In any event, a complete picture of all the receipts and payments of the building should be obtained from, and discussed with, the mortgagor.

SHOPS

The valuation of shop property is essentially a task for the branch manager who can apply his close knowledge of local conditions to the problem. Generally speaking, the value of the shop in the property market depends upon its earning capacity which largely varies according to its size and position. The following features will normally be considered. Is the shop well situated in the centre of a busy shopping area, near a bus route or railway station or is it tucked away in a quiet side street with no prospect of passing trade? Is the property capable of conversion for use by another retail business, or is it limited to a given trade? Is there adequate space for customers, display areas and windows? Is there any housing accommodation above the shop and adequate storage space at the rear? Is the shopping area developing with increased demand for retail services resulting from new houses being built in the district, or is trade drifting elsewhere? What rentals are similar-sized shops commanding in the district? Local planning schemes have to be known in case they may ultimately affect the site of the shop and change the centre for the retail trade. In the light of all these points and the general condition of the shop, a safe estimate can be made of the minimum amount likely to be realised upon a forced sale of the shop in the worst possible conditions.

INDUSTRIAL BUILDINGS

When faced with the unenviable task of placing a value upon a factory, warehouse, or other specialised industrial building offered as security, the inexperienced bank valuer cannot expect to do more than make an intelligent guess or estimate of the lowest price which would be realised in the unhappy event of having to sell the building to another manufacturer upon the failure of the owner. Such properties are strictly unsuitable as banking security because they are so difficult to sell when the need arises. The market is severely restricted and conditioned by general trading conditions, but it often happens that many limited company trading and manufacturing customers have their factory only available as fixed security for trade borrowing and the banker has to rely upon it to some extent in support of the floating charge taken on all the other assets of the borrower. Innumerable features may influence the value of an industrial building and an up-to-date professional valuation is of little assistance because it will quote the current worth between willing buyer and willing seller. Such a property usually has to be sold in the worst conditions when few buyers are interested. In any event, industrial buildings are rarely bought and sold and there is very little indication of current price levels to assist the local manager. The following points for consideration may nevertheless be of assistance.

As a starting point in approaching the problem the area and original cost of the building can usually be ascertained from the title deeds. The price paid by the customer has then to be considered in relation to the date of purchase. It may be, of course, that extensive additions or alterations may have been made since then or parts of the land may have been sold off and adjustments will have to be made in this starting price. A glance at the balance sheet of the mortgagor will show the valuation of the property at cost, less depreciation to date, but the effect of inflationary spiral in the years since the purchase date may mean that these figures bear little relationship to current values. Nevertheless, this information furnishes a background for the manager who can then make a detailed inspection of the property and consider the following points.

Is it a modern building with attractive lighting conditions and facilities, well maintained and well situated for the transport of finished goods outwards and raw materials inwards? Is there an adequate supply of labour living near to the factory or will anyone buying the factory have to arrange to transport labour from a remote housing estate? Can the building be adapted without difficulty or undue expense for the production of a different class of goods than those made by the present owner? This is a most important consideration. If the customer fails or otherwise cannot continue the manufacture of his goods in the factory, it will usually mean that there is a surfeit of supply in his line of business, and his competitors are unlikely to be interested in buying the factory to produce the same type of articles. The more specialised the factory the fewer will be the buyers attracted to any auction. A prospective buyer has to decide which is the cheaper and more efficient plan. On the one hand, he can buy virgin land well situated and erect a factory thereon to meet his precise needs at a known total cost. On the other hand, if he buys the existing factory he has to convert it to suit his requirements, and the price he is prepared to pay, plus the estimated cost of alterations, must be considerably less than the cost of a new factory if he is to forgo the advantages of a new building erected to meet his exact wishes. The adaptability of any industrial building is, therefore, a material factor when valuing it and a specialised building, such as a steel foundry or brick works, may be virtually unsaleable. The general test is whether the building comprises large floor spaces which can easily be divided if required to suit the buyer. If it is not adaptable, a valuation on the basis of the current price of factory floor space per square foot may be quite inappropriate. Sometimes the site value of the land may be important regardless of the condition and type of building at present erected on it.

The customer will naturally have an exaggerated opinion of the worth of his factory because he will value it on a going concern basis. It is a totally different question when the building has to be sold as a shell by auction and patience may be required before anyone can be attracted to offer to buy it. The safest course is, therefore, to estimate the current value according to age, condition, situation, size and type and then to deduct a large margin to reach a safe minimum which will be realised in the worst conditions. Prudence obviously demands that the banker should err on the low side. It may be many years before the bank, as mortgagee, unhappily has to sell the building and it may then be in a poor condition because, when funds are short, repairs and renewals will be deferred.

AGRICULTURAL LAND
When valuing a farm as security, the bank manager will rely on his inspection of the farm and his knowledge of prices current in the area. The chief factors for consideration will be the acreage, the fertility of the land and its situation in relation to markets, with due regard to the age, size and condition of the farm-buildings. The quality of the land, with adequate water supply, but good drainage to prevent flooding, will be important according to the area suitable for grazing or cultivation. Part of the farm may be scrubland or woodland or it may specialise in growing hops or fruit. There is a wide variation in the value of agricultural land per acre according to its situation and use, and it is up to the local manager to know the land and to study local prices, maintaining a record of prices obtained at recent sales as a guide for valuation purposes. The same principles apply throughout and the banker must decide what the farm might realise if and when it had to be sold by auction with few buyers around.

LEASEHOLDS

In all the above cases where the land is not freehold the length of the unexpired period of the lease will influence the value of the security regardless of the type of building. It is, therefore, essential to consider whether the title is freehold or leasehold and, in the latter event, to determine the unexpired term of the lease. In general the less time the lease has to run the lower will be the value of the property, which may also be influenced by restrictive covenants contained in the lease. In the case of investment properties, the ground rent payable is an added expense to be included with the other outgoings of the landlord when calculating the net rental yield.

Opinions will inevitably differ concerning the security value of any given property and their accuracy may rarely be tested because the advance is repaid in the ordinary course of business without resort to the security. Nevertheless, the prudent banker fixes a safe value upon which he can rely as a bare minimum in the worst event, and it is thus possible to appreciate the risk accepted when granting the advance. There is no uniform rule or method other than the general need for pessimism and caution, it being safer to under-value rather than over-value. But excessive caution in valuing property may lead to loss of business. A reasonable balance has to be preserved.

FIRE INSURANCE

After valuing the security, the banker next obtains from the mortgagor the fire policy covering the building, which should be for an amount in excess of the forced sale value estimated by the bank. However exact the valuation may be and however complete the charge, the security will be worthless if the buildings are not at all times fully insured against the risk of loss or damage by fire. It is well to establish this principle at the outset and it is surprising in practice how many cases of under-insurance arise.

Sometimes a policy is taken out in the joint names of the bank and of the borrower. The policy should be studied closely to ensure that it affords adequate cover for the property concerned. For example, plate glass insurance will be required for shops or other buildings with large windows. Where doubts arise, reference to the insurance company will usually prove helpful and guidance can then be given to the mortgagor where extensions of the amount or type of cover are deemed desirable.

In 1960 an extremely useful agreement was made between The British Insurance Association and the Clearing Banks whereby it became no longer necessary to obtain an endorsement of a bank's interest on fire policies issued by certain insurance companies. All that is now required in such cases is to notify the insurance company concerned of the bank's interest. This agreement was amended in 1964 so that a 'scheduled insurer' participating in the scheme now undertakes that, in respect of any policy in which a bank's interest has been notified, it will, instead of endorsing the policy with a note of the bank's interest:

(a) advise that bank if the policy is not renewed as soon as practicable after such non-renewal comes to its knowledge.

(b) advise that bank if the cover in which the bank is interested is reduced or if any risk hitherto covered is restricted or cancelled.

(c) pending the receipt of instructions from the bank, keep the interest of that institution in the policy in force up to the full sum insured etc.

There are about two hundred insurance companies now taking part in the scheme and it therefore relieves the banker of a considerable burden. Once the company has been advised of a bank's interest no further action by the bank is required other than to record the fact that the company participates in the scheme and to ensure that an acknowledgment from the company is received.

Even so, not all risks are removed. Unknown to the bank, a customer may take out an additional fire insurance with another company upon the building charged to the bank and, in the event of a claim, the liability would be shared between the two companies and the company which was unaware of the bank's interest might pay its portion of the claim direct to the borrower (*Halifax Building Society & Another* v. *Keighley & Another* [1931] 2 K.B. 248). Naturally, for those insurance companies not participating in the scheme referred to above, it is still necessary to have the policy endorsed in favour of the bank in order to fix the insurance company with notice of the bank's interest and so to prevent the payment of claims direct to any mortgagor, who might convert them to his own use.

Whilst the property is held as security, it is imperative to ensure that the fire policy is kept alive by the prompt payment of renewal premiums. The provisions of the mortgage will include an undertaking by the borrower or mortgagor to insure the property with an approved company and to pay the premiums as they fall due and, in the event of default, the bank, as mortgagee, is empowered to insure and to charge the premiums to the borrower's account.

Part Five: Land (continued)

Chapter XVIII The Title—Examination and Report

Being satisfied that the land to be taken as security is of sufficient value and that it is adequately insured against all risks, the next step is to obtain the deeds relating to the property and to have the title examined by the branch solicitor, who will make a report for the guidance of the bank. Whilst a solicitor is normally called upon to undertake this highly specialised work, at the expense of the borrower, the practical banker should have an elementary knowledge of the general principles of the law relating to land. It is an immense subject and the following outline is necessarily limited to the bare essentials in an attempt to present a simple picture to the practical reader who may occasionally have to glance through a parcel of deeds deposited by an impatient customer anxious to overdraw his account before the solicitors can examine the title and present their report.

HISTORICAL DEVELOPMENT OF THE SYSTEM OF TITLE
The oldest part of our law is the law relating to land, which, generally speaking, after the Norman Conquest was the sole form of wealth. The system of land law emerged, founded on custom and developed by court decisions, based on *feudalism* with the different types of tenure. Feudalism here means that the land is not owned by the person in possession or apparent holders, but it is held by them from some one else. Thus after the Norman Conquest, William confiscated the land of the English landowners and distributed it amongst his followers and others in return for money payments. All land became the property of the King, from whom tenants directly, or indirectly, obtained their interest in the land and the doctrine of land tenure became universal. In return for service, which might be pecuniary, military or agricultural, persons held land and sub-tenancies were rapidly created whereby each transferee became the tenant of his immediate transferor.

Without delving deeper, it is of interest to note that the estate vested in the lord holding the land was called a *fee* and to-day a freehold title is described as a *fee simple*. The retainers of the lord, whose holding was known as a *manor*, obtained land in return for services. Those who were *free* men, apart from certain liability for military service, became holders of free land, hence the origin of *freehold*. In due time, the practice arose of letting off this free land at a price for a given period on the understanding that the land reverted to the original owner, or his heirs, at the end of the term. This form of tenure was the origin of our *leasehold* of to-day.

Other retainers who were not free held parts of the manor subject to their giving certain services. Their rights were more uncertain and the transfer of their holdings was subject to the consent of the lord. This form of title became known as *copyhold* because it was evidenced by a copy of the entry in the Manorial Court Rolls which set out the service and payment due by the *copyholder* to the lord. Copyhold tenure was abolished by the Law of Property Acts 1922 and 1925 and converted into freehold.

REFORM OF THE LAND LAW

In 1922 an attack was made on the many antiquated rules and hindrances to the transfer of land arising from the past development of the law from a feudal origin, but three years elapsed before the drafting and redrafting could be completed and eventually the following seven statutes were passed in 1925:—

Law of Property Act
Settled Land Act
Trustee Act
Land Charges Act
Administration of Estates Act
Land Registration Act (N.B. Registered Land: *see* Chapters XXIV to XXVI)
Universities and College Estates Act.

When we add to these statutes the amendments and various Town and Country Planning Acts, etc., passed since 1925, it will be seen how complicated the law relating to land remains to-day. It is a matter for the legal expert and difficult to present a simple picture to the practical banker.

LEGAL ESTATES IN LAND

For our purpose, the law now recognises two classes of legal estates:—

1. *Freeholds*, or estates in fee simple, absolute in possession.

2. *Leaseholds*, or terms of years absolute, whereby the owner of the fee simple (called the *lessor*) grants an estate in the land to another person (called the *lessee*) for a fixed term of years. At the end of the lease the property reverts to the lessor.

These are the only two legal estates in land, but interests or charges may exist. Interests or charges in or over land capable of subsisting or being conveyed or created *at law* were listed in chapter XVI, the most significant of which to the practical banker is the *charge by way of legal mortgage*. All estates, interests and charges other than those listed were classified as equitable interests and the practical distinction lies, as we shall see, in the different natures of the mortgages and the different remedies available to the respective mortgagees.

EVIDENCE OF TITLE

In the historical development briefly described above the original lord of the manor received from the King a deed which evidenced his title to the land. He, in turn, granted a deed to the freeholder to show his title to the land and gradually, as the land was bought and sold, the practice developed for the seller to execute a deed transferring or conveying his title to the buyer, who also took over the original deed of grant. In the course of years, therefore, the history of any piece of land could be traced from all the deeds evidencing the title from owner to owner, starting with the original grant and passing by conveyance or upon death by deed of assent to subsequent owners.

A bulky parcel of deeds to-day may go back centuries, but it is sufficient if a good root title of fifteen years can be traced (Section 23 Law of Property Act, 1969). With the parcel of deeds there will usually be found an *abstract of title*, which is in effect a summary of all the documents in the chain of title and a recital of all the births, deaths, marriages and other important events affecting the title. When anyone purchases land, he can insist upon the vendor producing all the evidence necessary to prove that the title which he has contracted to sell is vested in him. The history of the land is set out in the abstract of title and the accompanying deeds prove the position. In addition to the abstract, the vendor is called upon to verify its contents by producing the actual documents extracted or suitable evidence of the contents of those which are not available to prove all facts which are material to the title.

The abstract should start with a *good root of title* evidencing beyond doubt the ownership of the land not less than fifteen years ago. It should be a document which purports to deal with the absolute ownership and which is valid without reference to an earlier document. The best and most usual example of a good root of title is a conveyance by way of sale, but a legal mortgage is also generally acceptable on the assumption that the mortgagee would ensure at the time when the mortgage was created that the mortgagor had a good title. On the other hand, a general, as distinct from a specific, devise of land does not constitute a good root of title because it does not identify the property. Starting from a good root of title, all the other documents affecting the legal estate will be listed in date order with appropriate recitals, and it is quite a simple matter to follow the devolution of the property to the customer or third party who intends to mortgage it to the bank as security. Thus Bluestone may have been conveyed to A in 1946 and when he died in 1950 his personal representatives by written assent passed the title to his son, B, who mortgaged it to X in 1955, repaid the loan in 1960, when the mortgage was discharged and sold it to Miss C in 1962. When Miss C married Mr. D in 1965, the change of name is recited in the abstract, and the subsequent conveyance in 1970 to the customer E completes the chain of title for the freehold property when the deeds are passed to the bank. In the case of leasehold properties the title must be traced back to the original lease of the property. The examination and report upon the actual documents is a matter for the expert and the branch solicitor will soon draw the attention of the bank to any defect.

This brief introduction can be concluded with a practical warning. If the branch solicitor reports upon the title, all queries raised should be settled to his satisfaction and to the bank's satisfaction before the advance is granted. It is pointless to employ and pay an expert and then ignore the advice given. In other words, reports on title have to be studied and followed. They are *not* routine notes which can be ignored in the rush of daily business.

Part Five: Land (continued)

Chapter XIX The Nature of the Mortgage to be Taken

LEGAL OR EQUITABLE

The next step is to decide what type of mortgage to take over the property. Ignoring, for the time being, the special clauses usually introduced into a bank mortgage form, it is essential to realise the basic difference between a legal mortgage and an equitable mortgage. A banker has to decide from the facts of the proposal and his knowledge of the borrower whether to be content with a mere equitable charge or whether to insist upon a legal mortgage. As a counsel of perfection, a legal mortgage should always be taken and it must not be forgotten that there are very few lenders, apart from banks, who would ever dream of relying upon an equitable mortgage as security for a loan. A simple comparison is helpful at the outset before detailing the remedies available to each type of mortgagee.

A mortgage can be defined as a conveyance of property as security for the payment of a debt or for the discharge of some other obligation. The person who conveys the property by way of security is called the mortgagor, whilst the lender who acquires an interest in the property is known as the mortgagee, and the debt for which the security is created is known as the mortgage debt.

A *legal mortgage* of a *freehold* can be effected by either:—

(a) a demise (the grant of a lease) for a term of years absolute, subject to a provision that the term shall cease if repayment is made on a fixed day (known as the provision for cesser upon redemption); or

(b) a charge by deed expressed to be by way of legal mortgage, known as a 'legal charge', which is shorter and simpler in form than a mortgage by demise and equivalent to a mortgage by way of a lease for 3,000 years.

A *legal mortgage* of a *leasehold* can be effected by either:—

(a) a sub-demise (sub-lease) for a term of years absolute, subject to a provision for cesser on redemption, the term being at least one day (usually ten days) shorter than the term vested in the mortgagor; or

(b) a charge by deed expressed to be by way of legal mortgage.

An equitable mortgage is created in much less formal manner. There may be an agreement to create a legal mortgage, or the title deeds may merely be deposited with the lender with intent to treat the land as security. Usually there is some agreement in writing evidencing the intention of the parties. It is a comparatively simple document setting out the facts and it may or may not include an undertaking by the mortgagor to create a legal mortgage on the property when called upon to do so.

ADVANTAGES OF LEGAL MORTGAGE

A legal mortgage gives the lender rights against the property itself without the need for reference to the borrower. All the remedies set out below are available in the given circumstances and can be exercised by the mortgagee without seeking the consent of the Court. All this in addition to the right of personal action against the borrower. With bank advances it is often essential to be able to sell the property or to appoint a receiver to collect the rents without seeking the consent of the customer who has disappeared abroad. By taking a legal mortgage at the outset the bank obtains the strongest position and is able to act promptly against the property without recourse to the borrower should the need ever arise.

The only *disadvantage* which arises with a legal mortgage is that it forms part of the title to the property and the mortgage deed, duly discharged, has to be retained with the deeds after the mortgage debt has been repaid. This is no real hardship in modern conditions, and the banker should be able to persuade the borrower that anyone who may subsequently purchase the property will not be interested in the fact that the seller had borrowed against the security of the property. It is no blot on the family escutcheon to mortgage the house.

DISADVANTAGES OF AN EQUITABLE MORTGAGE

If the banker decides exceptionally to rely upon an equitable mortgage, the following weaknesses are accepted:—

1. The bank has no right against the property itself and cannot deal with or intervene in anything concerning the property without the co-operation of the mortgagor or the approval of the Court. In particular, there is no power of sale.
2. The bank's rights are limited to a personal right against the owner mortgagor, who may have to be forced by invoking the aid of the Courts, with unavoidable delays and unnecessary expense.

An equitable mortgage is occasionally accepted for the alleged short bridge-over advance to keep the mortgage off the title, but unexpected developments can always occur to delay repayment and to freeze the liquid loan, and experience shows that no one is more unwilling to create a legal mortgage than the borrower who has undertaken so to do in an equitable charge. Far better to start well at the outset by obtaining a legal mortgage and legislating for every possibility, however remote and unexpected it may appear to be, before the advance is granted. All other lenders call for a legal mortgage and the occasions when a bank is prepared to accept less should be few indeed.

EQUITABLE MORTGAGE UNDER SEAL

Where a customer declines to create a legal mortgage, some banks use an equitable mortgage under seal incorporating a power of attorney clause whereby the mortgagor irrevocably appoints an official of the bank to sell the property as his agent, or a declaration of trust clause whereby the mortgagor agrees that he holds the property upon trust for the bank and he empowers the bank to replace him by some other person as trustee. In either case the bank is able to deal with the legal estate without the co-operation of the mortgagor, but there seems to be little point in resorting to these devices as a legal mortgage is much more simple and complete.

POWERS AND REMEDIES OF LEGAL MORTGAGE

To bring out the many advantages of a legal mortgage, it is convenient to describe the remedies available to the bank as legal mortgagee, emphasising at the outset that, except where stated, they can be exercised without the consent of the mortgagor and without the approval of the Court.

1. *Right to Sue on the Mortgage Debt*

A mortgage usually includes an express covenant by the mortgagee to repay the principal sum on demand or on a definite date, meantime paying interest at an agreed rate. The mortgagee can always sue on this covenant for what worth when the right arises. An action to recover the amount of the mortgage debt is statute barred unless it is brought within twelve years from the date when the right to receive the money accrued.

Every creditor has a right to sue his debtor to recover the amount owing and the same right accrues to an equitable mortgagee. An unsecured creditor may sue in order to levy execution against the debtor's property, but there is usually little point in a secured creditor adopting this course because he already has his security in the property of the mortgagor. Unless, therefore, the bank is only partly secured and it contemplates forcing the borrower into bankruptcy, it is unlikely to exercise this first right which is available to legal and equitable mortgagees alike.

2. *Power of Sale*

This is by far the most important and helpful remedy from the standpoint of the bank.

Subject to any stipulation to the contrary in the mortgage, every legal mortgagee has power to sell the mortgaged property, wholly or in part, by public auction or by private contract, as soon as the mortgage debt has become repayable but remains outstanding. Although the power of sale arises when the mortgage debt becomes due, it cannot be exercised until *one* of the following things has happened:—

(*a*) Notice requiring repayment of the mortgage debt has been served on the mortgagor, and default has been made in payment of the money, or part thereof, for three months after such service.

(*b*) Some interest is in arrear and remains unpaid for two months after becoming due.

(*c*) There has been a breach of some provision (other than the covenant to repay the debt and interest) contained either in the mortgage deed or in the Law of Property Act, 1925, and which imposes an obligation upon the mortgagor. A typical example would be where the mortgagor breaks a covenant to keep the property in a reasonable state of repair.

The three occasions are set out in Section 103 of the Law of Property Act, 1925, but they are often varied expressly by the mortgage deed. For example, to speed the power of sale, a mortgagor to a bank normally contracts that the bank can sell if he fails to repay the debt one month after demand has been served upon him. This variation will be considered fully when a bank mortgage form is analysed. The point is that in the given circumstances the mortgagee may sell the property to recover the debt and the power is given to him for his own benefit and not in the capacity of trustee for the mortgagor. All that a bank is expected to do when exercising its power of sale is to act prudently. According to Sir George Jessel, M. R. in *Nash* v. *Eads* (1880) 25 Sol. J. 95, 'Of course there were some limits to the powers of the mortgagee. He, like a pledgee, must conduct the sale properly, and must sell at a fair value, and he could not sell to himself. But he was not bound to abstain from selling because he was not in urgent want of his money, or because he had a spite against the mortgagor.' And again more recently in *Cuckmere Brick Co. Ltd. and Another* v. *Mutual Finance Ltd.* ((1971) 2 All E.R. 633) it was held that although a mortgagee is not a trustee for sale for the mortgagor, and may prefer his own interest when there is a conflict of interests, he must still take reasonable care to obtain the true value of the property he is selling.

The Matrimonial Home

The position with regard to the matrimonial home is governed by the provisions of the Matrimonial Homes Act, 1967. In the case of *National Provincial Bank Ltd.* v. *Ainsworth* (1965) A.C. 1175 the decision of the House of Lords had destroyed the concept that a deserted wife had an equity in the matrimonial home; that she could continue in occupation despite the claims of a mortgagee. Broadly speaking, the purpose of the Act was to re-establish these rights and it provides that the spouse who is not the owner or tenant shall have certain rights of occupation; if in occupation a right not to be evicted without a Court Order, or if not in occupation, a right to enter and occupy, but only with the leave of the Court. Section 2 (1) provides that such rights of occupation are a charge on the estate or interest of the other spouse and by Section 2 (6) the charge can be registered in the Land Charges Registry, Class F. With registered land a notice or caution is registered under the Land Registration Act, 1925.

Numerous cases have been brought to decide whether a spouse without a legal title can acquire a beneficial interest in the home, either through cash payments or through services provided. The position has been clarified by the Matrimonial Proceedings and Property Act, 1970, which provides that any substantial contribution, in money or money's worth (e.g. improvements to the property), confers a beneficial interest in the absence of agreement to the contrary. Of course, these matters are the concern of the two spouses affected, but the banks as mortgagees can be interested inasmuch as under this Matrimonial Proceedings and Property Act the holder of such a beneficial interest can register it as a Class F land charge.

When a banker takes a charge over the matrimonial home it would be unreasonable to expect him to pry into the affairs of husband and wife in an effort to determine the nature and extent of each spouse's interest. In *Caunce* v. *Caunce* (1969) 1 All E.R. 722 Stamp J., held that unless the bank had constructive notice of an equitable interest it took the property free of that interest. Counsel for the wife had argued that the bank should have automatically made enquiries, whereupon the wife would have disclosed her interest, and that therefore the bank in fact had 'constructive notice' of her interest. This argument was rejected and it was stated that where a vendor or mortgagor owns and occupies the property the purchaser or mortgagee is not affected by notice of any equitable rights of anyone also living on the premises and whose presence is consistent with the title offered; for example, a wife living with her husband. The words of defence counsel for the bank were quoted with approval, which were to the effect that it was not in the public interest that bank mortgagees should be snoopers and busybodies in relation to wholly normal transactions of mortgages.

It is possible that the bank may be offered as security a house on which a Class F charge has been registered. This will not usually be acceptable security unless the spouse entitled to the charge agrees in writing to give the bank's charge priority, as provided for in Section 6 (3) of the Matrimonial Homes Act. If a spouse's rights are registered as a Class F charge *after* the creation of a mortgage this does not of itself constitute notice to the mortgagee. Thus a banker is under no obligation to search the register periodically, nor should he do so, because if he as mortgagee actually receives notice of a Class F charge the customer's account should be broken and further sums should only be advanced if, as already stated above, the spouse is prepared to agree in writing to the bank's mortgage taking priority.

Under Section 1 (5) of the Matrimonial Homes Act a deserted spouse who continues to live in the matrimonial home has the right to pay off the debt and to this end can insist on being joined in any action brought by the mortgagee. This was the situation in *Hastings and Thanet Building Society* v. *Goddard* (1970) 2 All E.R. 737 where the husband had mortgaged the home and then deserted his wife. The day before he left she had registered a Class F charge and when she learned that the Building Society had obtained an order for possession, because the husband had discontinued payments to them, she claimed she should have been joined in the action. She stated that she had received no notice of the order for possession and for their part the Building Society claimed they were under no obligation to do so.

In the High Court Foster J., found for the wife, basing his decision on Section 1 (5), but the decision was reversed on Appeal. Russell L.J., maintained that the husband could only resist the order for possession by redeeming the mortgage and the Matrimonial Homes Act, 1967, did not put the wife in any better position. In this case the wife was unable to show she could redeem the mortgage and to join her as defendant would have only delayed the Building Society's undisputed right to possession. However, it was conceded that had the wife been able to show she could within a very short time repay the mortgage the proper course of action would have been to have joined her in the action. This judgment is of interest to bankers in those circumstances, albeit rare, where they are obliged in their capacity as mortgagees to seek an order for possession of the matrimonial home.

3. *Power to Appoint a Receiver*
Where it is desirable to intercept the rents or profits from a mortgaged property in order to service the interest and perhaps make some reduction in the capital debt, the mortgagee has a statutory power to appoint a receiver. Although this power arises as soon as the mortgage debt becomes due, it cannot be exercised until one of the three events described above occur to enable a mortgagee to

exercise his power of sale. In other words, the statutory power to appoint a receiver arises in precisely the same circumstances as the power of sale. The advantage of appointing a receiver lies in the fact that he is deemed to be the agent of the mortgagor, who is solely responsible for his acts and defaults (Section 109 (2) L.P.A. 1925). Where the mortgaged properties are well let but difficult to sell, it is often helpful to appoint a receiver who will realise sufficient from the rents after normal outgoings to service the debt.

4. *Right to Foreclose*

Lastly, application can be made to the Court for a foreclosure order, whereby the fee simple absolute is vested in the mortgagee and the mortgagor is deprived altogether of his equity of redemption. This right need not be explored further at this stage because it is rarely utilised in practice.

POWERS AND REMEDIES OF AN EQUITABLE MORTGAGE

An equitable mortgagee *under hand* can sue for the amount of the mortgage debt and can apply for a foreclosure order in the same way as a legal mortgagee, but he cannot sell the property or appoint a receiver without the help of the Court. In short, the two most reliable remedies of a legal mortgage are not available to an equitable mortgagee unless and until he is able to obtain the support of the Court.

The memorandum evidencing the deposit of the deeds with the bank as security will usually include an undertaking by the mortgagor to execute a legal mortgage when called upon to do so. If the borrower readily implements this undertaking upon request, all is well and the bank quickly obtains the rights of a legal mortgagee, but so many borrowers are reluctant to carry out their covenants when the need arises. If the borrower will not co-operate, the bank has to incur the expense and time of an approach to the Court.

An equitable mortgagee with a mortgage *executed under seal*, however, has a power of sale and the power to appoint a receiver (Section 101, L.P.A. 1925) and is, therefore, in very much the same position as a legal mortgagee.

This outline summary of the rights of the different types of mortgagees suffices to show that in the normal course the prudent banker always obtains a legal mortgage. The terms of this mortgage and the reasons for the introduction of special clauses into bank mortgage forms will be considered in Chapter XX.

LEASEHOLD REFORM ACT 1967

The overriding aim of this very complicated piece of legislation is to give the occupants of certain leasehold properties the right to buy the freehold on favourable terms, or in the majority of cases, to give them the option of having the lease extended by 50 years. If the leaseholder chooses a 50-year extension of the lease, the right to buy the freehold is lost as from the date the original lease expires and it cannot be exercised at any time during the 50-year period. The Act seeks to protect tenants whose leases run out and who are faced with the prospect of eviction or alternatively an exorbitant price for the freehold. Before a leaseholder can take advantage of the provisions of the Leasehold Reform Act the following conditions must be satisfied:—

(i) the lease must be of the whole house, and flats and maisonettes are thus excluded (however, an applicant leaseholder can avail himself of the provisions of this Act although he may have sub-let part of the premises).

(ii) rateable values must not exceed £400 in Greater London or £200 elsewhere and the leaseholder must be paying an annual ground rent less than two-thirds of the rateable value.

(iii) the original lease must have been granted for a period in excess of 21 years and the leaseholder must have occupied the house as his main residence for the last five years or for periods amounting to five years out of the last ten years.

The freehold is valued on the site only, that is, on the basis that the house itself already belongs to the leaseholder, and the value of the site is estimated as if the lease had been extended by 50 years. If the leaseholder chooses to have his lease extended by 50 years he must pay a revised ground rent when the extended period begins and this will be based on the letting value of the site only, for the uses to which building(s) and site have been put since the beginning of the tenancy. If the parties are unable to agree either the price to be paid for the freehold or the revised ground rent it will be fixed by the Lands Tribunal.

These provisions are of interest to bankers for two reasons. First, because leaseholders may approach them seeking help with the purchase of the freehold. Secondly, these provisions are of some consequence where bankers are mortgagees of the properties involved.

MORTGAGES

1. *Freeholds*

If the leaseholder obtains the freehold, the conveyance automatically discharges the premises from any mortgage, although the mortgagee may not, and almost certainly will not, be a party to the conveyance. Thus Section 12 (1) " . . . a conveyance executed . . . shall, as regards any charge on the landlord's estate (however created or arising) to secure the payment of money or the performance of any other obligation by the landlord or any other person, not being a charge subject to which the conveyance is required to be made or which would be overreached apart from this section, be effective by virtue of this section to discharge the house and premises from the charge, and from the operation of any order made by a court for the enforcement of the charge, and to extinguish any term of years created for the purposes of the charge, and shall do so without the persons entitled to or interested in the charge or in any such order or term of years becoming parties to or executing the conveyance."

However, the leaseholder must, in the first instance, pay the price paid for the purchase of the freehold in or towards redemption of the mortgage. Section 12 (2) states:—

"Where in accordance with subsection (1) above the conveyance to a tenant will be effective to discharge the house and premises from a charge to secure the payment of money, then except as otherwise provided by this section it shall be the duty of the tenant to apply the price payable for the house and premises, in the first instance, in or towards the redemption of any such charge (and, if there are more than one, then according to their priorities); and if any amount payable in accordance with this subsection to the person entitled to the benefit of a charge is not so paid nor paid into court . . ., then for the amount in question the house and premises shall remain subject to the charge, and to that extent subsection (1) above shall not apply".

By Section 12 (6) the bank as mortgagee will still retain the personal liability of the mortgagor under the terms of its mortgage, subject only to certain provisions which enable the court in certain circumstances to vary the terms of the mortgage where at the time the Leasehold Reform Act was passed there was a long tenancy with an unexpired period of up to but not exceeding twenty years: Section 36.

2. Leaseholds

Where the banker has a mortgage over a leasehold property and the leaseholder acquires the freehold, he may extend the mortgage over the freehold by asking the mortgagor to execute a deed of substituted security.

Where the tenant obtains an extended lease the mortgagee is entitled to the documents of title to the new tenancy. Section 14 (6) covers this:—

"Where under a lease executed to give effect to this section the new tenancy takes effect subject to a subsisting charge on the existing tenancy, and at the time of its execution the person having the charge is by reason thereof entitled to possession of the documents of title relating to the existing tenancy, then he shall be similarly entitled to possession of the documents of title relating to the new tenancy and the tenant shall within one month of the execution of the lease deliver it to him, and the instrument creating or evidencing the charge shall apply in the event of the tenant failing to deliver the lease in accordance with this subsection as if the obligation to do so were included in the terms of the charge as set out in that instrument".

Here the banker will normally require the mortgagor to pass over the documents and execute a new form of mortgage.

Part Five: Land (continued)

Chapter XX Bank Forms of Mortgage and the Powers They Provide

All banks nowadays have their own printed mortgage forms, drafted by experts and available to meet most standard requirements. All that is necessary is to choose the right form to meet the case and, after filling in the name of the mortgagor and, where the security is collateral, the name of the borrower, with the description of the land, to have it executed by the mortgagor. This is not so simple as it sounds. The contents of forms have to be known and understood in order to select the correct form and to explain to any mortgagor with an enquiring mind the effect and purpose of the clauses in the usually very lengthy deed. To this end a reasonable working knowledge of the contents is essential and a typical bank legal mortgage form will now be examined in detail.

Being a deed, the mortgage has to be signed, sealed and delivered by the mortgagor, who when signing should touch the wafer seal and recite 'I deliver this as my act and deed,' but it is questionable whether this performance is always carried out in branch banks. According to Danckwerts, J., in *Stromdale & Ball Ltd.* v. *Burden* [1952] 1 All E.R. 59, 'it appears to me that at the present day if a party signs a document bearing wax or wafer or other indication of a seal with the intention of executing the document as a deed, that is sufficient adoption or recognition of the seal to amount to due execution as a deed'. There thus appears to be little doubt that, where a mortgagee signs the mortgage and delivers it to, or leaves it with, the bank, he cannot thereafter claim that he did not execute the deed in a proper manner.

It is not, of course, incumbent upon the banker to enter into a detailed explanation of all the clauses in the document, but it is prudent to be prepared to answer in simple fashion any enquiries raised by the customer or other mortgagor, who, in any event, is at liberty to seek independent advice from his solicitor. Some features, such as the undertaking not to grant leases without the express approval of the bank, should certainly be drawn to the attention of the mortgagor, but otherwise it is largely a matter of replying to enquiries. In many cases the document will be signed without question and no attempt is made to read the clauses. So long as the mortgagor is aware of the nature of the instrument he is executing, he will be bound by its provisions. These practical experiences do not, however, excuse the banker from studying the mortgage forms and acquiring a working knowledge of the contents.

THE LEGAL MORTGAGE

CREATION OF THE SECURITY

After setting out the names and descriptions of the parties, being usually the mortgagor of the one part and the lending bank of the other part, the mortgage will state that in consideration of the bank making or continuing advances or otherwise furnishing banking facilities, the mortgagor as beneficial owner creates the mortgage in favour of the bank. With freeholds this may be by a charge expressed to be by way of legal mortgage or by a demise for a term of years absolute, subject to a provision for cesser upon redemption, as explained in Chapter XIX. The former method is shorter and simpler, it merely being necessary to state that the borrower as beneficial owner 'hereby charges by way of legal mortgage all the land described in the Schedule hereto'. Precisely the same wording can be used for a legal mortgage of leaseholds, thereby avoiding the introduction of distinctive forms for freeholds and leaseholds, and argument from a customer who objects to creating a long lease in favour of the bank.

The mortgage by demise will state that the mortgagor as beneficial owner conveys and demises to the bank all the property described in the Schedule, to hold it unto the bank for a given term (usually 3,000 or 4,000 years) from the date of the charge without impeachment for waste but subject to the proviso for redemption. It is then agreed and declared that, if the mortgagor or his successors in title shall *on demand* pay to the bank all moneys which are now owing, or at any time shall be owing, to the bank by the mortgagor on any account, whether from him solely or jointly with any other person, or from any firm in which he may be a partner, together with interest, commission and legal charges, the bank will after such payment surrender and reconvey the premises to the mortgagor free from all encumbrance by the bank. Strictly speaking, this redemption clause is unnecessary because Sections 5 and 116 of the Law of Property Act, 1925, provide that upon repayment the mortgage term is satisfied and automatically ends.

When the security is leasehold, the mortgage may merely be by deed expressed to be by way of legal mortgage, as indicated above, or a sub-lease can be taken for a term at least one day shorter than the period vested in the mortgagor. The normal course is to make the sub-term ten days shorter than the lease to allow for second and subsequent mortgages in case the need arises.

AMOUNT SECURED BY THE MORTGAGE

From the above draft wording of the cesser on redemption clause it will be appreciated that the mortgage is always drawn to cover all the indebtedness of the customer anywhere on any account, whether solely or jointly. Moreover, he personally promises to repay upon demand. There is thus a personal covenant upon which the bank can sue, apart from the security. Demand from the bank is, therefore, necessary before action can be taken so that Section 4 (3) of the Limitation Act, 1939, cannot start to operate against the bank until a demand has been served on the mortgagor (*Lloyds Bank Ltd.* v. *Margolis* [1954] 1 W.L.R. 644).

CONTINUING SECURITY

To avoid the operation of the Rule in *Clayton's Case* (1816) 1 Mer 572 against the bank when the advances are made on current account, the security is expressly described as a continuing security. A typical clause might read 'It is hereby declared that this security shall not be considered as satisfied by any intermediate payment or satisfaction of the whole or any part of any moneys owing hereunder, but shall be a continuing security and extend to cover any sums of money, which shall for the time being constitute the balance due from the mortgagor to the bank on any account herein-before described.'

REPAIRS AND INSURANCE—RESPONSIBILITY OF MORTGAGOR

In addition to covenanting with the bank to repay upon demand, the mortgagor covenants that at all times during the continuance of the security he will keep the buildings, fixtures and any machinery in a good state of repair and fully insured against loss or damage by fire in such office or offices as the bank shall approve. A natural sequel to this latter covenant is an undertaking to pay all insurance premiums promptly on their due date and to produce the policy and the premium receipts to the bank. In the event of failure to insure for a sufficient amount and to maintain the insurance, the bank is empowered to exercise the right of insurance against fire conferred by statute on mortgagees (Sections 101 and 108 of the Law of Property Act, 1925) and can insure the property itself, charging the cost to the mortgagor. The reason for this express provision is that the amount of the insurance is limited by the Act to the amount specified in the mortgage or, in the absence of any quoted figure, to two-thirds of the cost of restoring the property in the event of total destruction. It is prudent, therefore, to be able to insure for as much as the bank may deem best.

To cover the prospect of a fire claim arising, it is also usual to provide that all insurance moneys are to be applied either in making good the loss or damage or in reduction of the indebtedness so secured. This clause may be worded to cover any insurance of the mortgaged property, whether or not it is the one actually required by the mortgage, thereby embracing any additional insurance taken out by the mortgagor unbeknown to the bank (*Halifax Building Society* v. *Keighley* [1931] 2 K.B. 248).

MORTGAGEE'S POWER OF SALE

Clauses are next introduced whereby the borrower or depositor contracts out of his statutory rights as a mortgagor, and the rights and remedies of the bank are thereby strengthened. Under Section 103 of the Law of Property Act, 1925, the power of sale arises as soon as the mortgage money becomes due, but it does not become exercisable until three months after default in repayment after notice to repay has been served, or interest payments are two months or more in arrear, or there has been a breach by the mortgagor of any of the mortgage covenants. Speed of action is often essential when dealing with an unsatisfactory debt and it is too long to have to wait three months to exercise a power of sale (or the power to appoint a receiver) to recover advances which are repayable upon demand. To overcome this statutory drawback, it is usual to declare that the moneys owing shall be deemed to become due within the meaning of Section 101 of the Law of Property Act, 1925, immediately on demand for payment being made by the bank on the mortgagor and to state that Section 103 shall not apply and the bank instead shall be entitled to exercise the power of sale conferred on mortgagees by statute within one month (or immediately) after the moneys become due.

Some banks provide for one month's notice, whilst others reserve the power to act upon demand. In practice, the speed of action depends upon the urgency of the position, but sound borrowers need have no concern that the lending bank will act in a peremptory and inequitable manner.

In some forms there will also be found the statement that a purchaser shall be entitled to assume without enquiry that some of the amount secured is outstanding and that a demand has been duly made and the money has become due. Section 104 (2) protects any purchaser by providing that his title cannot be impeached because due notice of repayment was not served on the mortgagee. A purchaser has to ensure that a power of sale has arisen, but is under no duty to satisfy himself that it is exercisable.

There is one further matter which must be considered, namely, the implications of Section 36 of the Administration of Justice Act, 1970, as it affects the mortgagee's power of sale where possession is first sought. When exercising its power of sale, a bank as mortgagee will normally prefer to sell with vacant possession, in order to obtain the best price possible. If the mortgaged property is a dwellinghouse or contains a dwellinghouse (e.g. shop with living accommodation), and the mortgagor is still living in the property, the bank may well have to apply to the court for an order for possession. This will have the effect of exerting pressure on the mortgagor to make satisfactory proposals for the meeting of his liability, and, in default, it will enable the bank to obtain possession and proceed with the sale.

Section 36 of the Administration of Justice Act, 1970, provides that where the mortgagee under a mortgage of land, which consists of or includes a dwellinghouse, brings an action in which he claims possession of the mortgaged property (not being an action for foreclosure in which a claim for possession is also made) the court may exercise certain powers. These powers include the power to adjourn the proceedings or postpone the date for delivery of possession, and can be exercised provided that it appears to the court that the mortgagor is likely to be able to repay any sums due within a reasonable period.

POWER TO CONSOLIDATE

Section 93 of the Law of Property Act, 1925, lays down that a mortgagor seeking to redeem any one mortgage is entitled to do so without paying any money due under any separate mortgage made by him, but this rule can be expressly excluded by the terms of a mortgage. The doctrine of consolidation covers the cases where a borrower has created several separate mortgages on different properties as security for moneys borrowed from the same lender. This position could arise in banking practice and can best be explained by the following simple example, which ignores the fact that in modern forms of charge the security is expressed to cover all the indebtedness of the borrower on any account.

Suppose a bank lends £500 to customer X on No. 1 Loan against the security of a legal mortgage of a house worth £2,000, and later lends a further £1,000 to X on No. 2 Loan against a shop property valued at £1,500, each mortgage being drawn to cover the particular loan. A year or so later, X repays Loan No. 1 and seeks the release of the house, but by that time the value of the shop property has depreciated to £800. Prior to 1881, the bank could have treated the securities as jointly charged to cover the total debts and it could have declined X's request to redeem the house, insisting upon the repayment of both loans before the release of either security. In short, the bank was entitled to consolidate both mortgages. This right was first abolished by the Conveyancing Act, 1881, and Section 93 of the Law of Property Act retains the ban.

In case it should ever be needed and to remove any doubt on the subject, the bank mortgage form normally expressly retains the power to consolidate. This is achieved by declaring that Section 93 shall not apply and that the mortgagor and his successors in title shall not be entitled to redeem the security without at the same time redeeming any or every existing or future mortgage for the time being held by the bank on other property now or at any time hereafter belonging to the mortgagor, or his successors in title, or to redeem any other such mortgage without at the same time redeeming this security.

As a bank does not grant separate loans against distinct properties but relies upon any security to cover all sums advanced on any account of the borrower, the value of this clause is largely theoretical.

GRANT OF LEASES BY MORTGAGOR

Subject to the stated conditions (which are not material here) a mortgagor in possession is empowered by Section 99 of the Law of Property Act, 1925, to grant leases of the mortgaged property for any term not exceeding fifty years, and building leases for any term up to 999 years. Leases so granted without reference to the bank might well create an unsatisfactory encumbrance which would reduce the value of the property as security and make it difficult to realise when necessary. As it is possible to contract out of these provisions, a clause is usually inserted in the bank's mortgage whereby it is declared that neither the mortgagor nor any of his successors in title can, except with the written consent of the bank, exercise the powers of leasing or of agreeing to lease or of accepting or agreeing to accept surrenders.

It is essential to warn any mortgagor of these disabilities which he agrees to accept when he signs the mortgage. Unless the borrower is properly cautioned, he may grant leases in complete ignorance of the undertaking and, although the bank's position will not necessarily be jeopardised, much trouble and ill will can be caused. Where a lease is granted in breach of the covenant without reference to the bank, it is not binding against the bank because the terms of the mortgage expressly excluded the power of the mortgagor to grant leases binding on the mortgagee (*Dudley & District Benefit Building Society* v. *Emerson* [1949] 1 Ch. 707). (See also *Baring Bros.* v. *Hover Marine Transport Ltd.*, *Financial Times* 27 *May*,1971). But this clause will not protect the bank where the leases are granted prior to or even on the same day as the execution of the mortgage. The decisions in *Universal Permanent Building Society* v. *Cooke* [1952] Ch. 95, and in *Church of England Building Society* v. *Piskor* [1954] Ch. 553, are of interest in this respect and show how essential it may sometimes be for the bank to be satisfied that the borrower is buying the property for his own occupation and not as an investment.

ATTORNMENT CLAUSE

Finally, there will probably be an attornment clause, whereby the mortgagor attorns tenant to the bank of such of the mortgaged properties as are in his occupation at the yearly rent of a peppercorn, if demanded. Provided that the bank may at any time enter into or upon the premises and determine the tenancy thereby created without giving to the mortgagor any notice to quit, and neither the tenancy so created nor any receipt of rent shall constitute the bank mortgagees in possession or render them liable to account as such.

This last example of legal phraseology is of ancient origin and of no practical value to-day. It will probably disappear with time because its purpose to obtain a speedy process no longer applies. Needless to add, no rent is ever collected from the mortgagor. Space will not permit the luxury of a historical review of the origin of this clause.

COMPLETION OF THE MORTGAGE FORM

When filling in the schedule to the mortgage, all that is primarily necessary is to describe the property subject to the mortgage in sufficient detail to ensure that no possible doubt can later arise concerning exactly what has been charged. The phrase 'Deeds or documents relating to the freehold dwelling house situate at and known as The Wigwam, 27, Indiana Close, Utopia' should suffice, but some banks make a practice of listing all the documents in the chain of title to the property as per the abstract of title and the mortgagor is then asked to initial the end of the schedule.

Other essential precautions are necessary, including searches to ensure priority, and these questions are dealt with in Chapter XXI.

THE EQUITABLE MORTGAGE

The typical bank equitable mortgage form, or memorandum of deposit, is a comparatively short document more easily understood by the layman, and much easier to analyse. Basically, it evidences the intention of the mortgagor who declares that the deeds specified in the schedule have been deposited as security for all advances to the given customer, and the same form can be used to cover both freehold and leasehold premises.

It may open with the statement that in consideration of the bank granting or continuing advances or otherwise furnishing banking facilities for as long as it may think fit, the deeds in the schedule are deposited as security for the repayment *on demand* of all moneys due now or at any time to the bank by the borrower anywhere on any account solely or jointly with interest, commission and legal charges. An equitable mortgage can always be obtained by the mere deposit of the deeds with the intent to create a charge over them, but these words provide tangible evidence of the intention of the depositor, who cannot later dispute the purpose of the lodgment.

Next will appear the undertaking by the depositor that, when called upon to do so by the bank, he will execute at his own cost a legal mortgage of the property even though the moneys secured may not then be actually payable. The value of this covenant naturally depends upon the good faith of the depositor. If he declines to implement it, the bank can only seek the support of the Courts to enforce it.

Sometimes the memorandum will embody a declaration that the property is free of all charges and the depositor will undertake not to create any fresh

161

charges without the written approval of the bank. There may also be an agreement to keep the buildings fully insured against fire risks and to supply the bank with the premium receipts. Other clauses may be incorporated to prevent leases without the bank's consent and to allow the bank to consolidate mortgages if circumstances demand.

Altogether it is usually a simple document, but its use should be restricted to the undoubted borrower on very short term where the bank is satisfied that it would be most unreasonable to ask for a legal mortgage.

Part Five: Land (continued)

Chapter XXI Priority of Mortgages—Searches at the Registries

Having obtained the mortgage, the next step before granting the advance is to ensure that there are no other mortgagees of the property or persons with other material interests ranking prior to the bank. To achieve this object, various searches have to be made and the banker has to know when, where and how to search. But first of all it is necessary to understand the rules of priority of mortgages.

PRIORITY BETWEEN MORTGAGES

The general rule is that priority depends upon possession of the title deeds or by registration as land charges, regardless of whether the mortgage is legal or equitable. Normally the bank obtains the deposit of the title deeds and satisfies by searching that no prior charges are registered. If the deeds are held, any subsequent mortgagee will be deemed to have constructive notice of the existence of a prior charge. If the deeds are not available to the bank, their absence suggests that they have already been charged elsewhere. The first mortgagee normally holds the deeds and subsequent mortgagees, if any, protect their interests by registration at the Land Charges Registry. Failure to register a charge not supported by the deposit of the deeds, entails the risk that a later mortgagee may obtain priority. Section 199 (1) of the Law of Property Act, 1925, provides that a purchaser (which term includes a mortgagee) shall not be prejudicially affected by notice of any instrument or matter capable of registration under the provisions of the Land Charges Act, 1925, or any enactment which it replaces, which is void or not enforceable as against him under that Act or enactment by reason of the non-registration thereof. It follows that providing no entry revealing any encumbrance appears in the Land Charges Register when the search is made, the bank may ignore any other interests.

From the standpoint of priority, legal and equitable mortgages are of equal standing and every mortgage affecting a legal estate in land made after 1926, *whether legal or equitable* (not being a mortgage protected by the deposit of documents relating to the legal estate affected) ranks according to its date of registration as a land charge pursuant to the Land Charges Act, 1925. (Section 97 of the Law of Property Act, 1925.) If a mortgagee obtains the deeds and satisfies himself that there are no charges registered, he has priority. On the other hand, he could dispense with the deposit of the deeds and register his charge instead at the Land

Charges Registry, which will be notice to any subsequent mortgagee who, even though he may have the deeds, will take his charge subject to the rights of the mortgagee who registered his charge. In practice the first man in always secures the deeds and need not register his charge, leaving subsequent mortgagees to register their charges which rank after the first mortgage for priority in order of the dates of registration. In the absence of the deeds, failure to register a charge may result in a subsequent charge gaining priority by registration. The order of mortgages thus rests on the time factor depending upon the date of the mortgage which is accompanied by the deeds and the date of registration of the charges unaccompanied by the deeds.

Practical Conclusions

These rules can now be applied in the following simple manner to practical banking:—

1. The title deeds of the property should always be obtained and a search made to ensure that no prior charges are registered before the advance is granted.
2. No registration is necessary to ensure priority if the deeds are held, but they should not be released before the advance is repaid in case the mortgagor creates a fresh mortgage with the deeds elsewhere.
3. If no deeds can be obtained (for reasons acceptable to the bank) a *puisne mortgage*, being a legal mortgage without possession of the deeds, should be taken and promptly registered.

There are inevitably many complications arising out of the above simple steps which call for comment before exploring the procedure for searching.

NOTICE OF SECOND MORTGAGE

Where a bank has an undoubted first mortgage, its priority is at all times subject to notice of a second mortgage and, as soon as such notice is received, the account has to be broken to avoid the operation of the Rule in *Clayton's Case* (1816) 1 Mer. 572. If the account is continued after notice of the second mortgage, all credits will reduce the amount secured by the first charge to the bank and all future advances will rank after the rights of the second mortgagee. A new account has, therefore, to be opened upon receipt of the notice and maintained on a creditor basis in the absence of fresh security. In practice, a second mortgagee, in addition to registering his charge, gives direct written notice to the bank as first mortgagee. He would be foolish to neglect this simple safeguard because when a bank is the first mortgagee the second mortgagee cannot rely upon the fact that registration of the charge is automatic notice to prior mortgagees.

Section 198 of the Law of Property Act, 1925, provides that the registration of any instrument or matter under the provisions of the Land Charges Act, 1925, or any enactment which it replaces in any register kept at the land registry or elsewhere, shall be deemed to *constitute actual notice of such instrument or matter, and of the fact of such registration, to all persons and for all purposes connected with the land affected.* In short, registration fixes the first mortgagee with notice of the second mortgage. If this rule were applied rigidly to banks, it would be virtually impossible to lend on current account against the security of land because a search would have to be made at the land charges register before paying every cheque to make sure that no fresh charge had been registered. Fortunately, Section 94 of the Law of Property Act, 1925, overcomes the difficulty to a reasonable extent.

It firstly provides that a prior mortgagee is entitled to grant further advances ranking in priority to subsequent mortgages, whether legal or equitable, in the following three cases:—

1. Where an arrangement has been made to that effect with the subsequent mortgagees; or
2. Where he has no notice of such subsequent mortgages at the time when the further advances are made; or
3. Whether or not he had such notice, where the mortgage imposes an obligation on him to make such further advances.

This last provision for tacking is of little use to a bank because it would not be prepared to enter into any obligation to make further advances, but the protection is derived from the second provision because it is amplified by the following statements in Section 94 (2):—

In relation to the making of further advances after the commencement of this Act, a mortgagee shall not be deemed to have notice of a mortgage merely by reason that it was registered as a land charge or in a local deeds registry, if it was not so registered at the time when the original mortgage was created, or when the last search (if any) by or on behalf of the mortgagee was made, *whichever last happened*. This sub-section only applies where the prior mortgage was made expressly for securing a current account or other further advances.

It will be seen later that, in order to come within these provisions, a bank normally searches after the charge has been executed and has no need to search again before granting fresh advances. It is clear that it will not be affected with notice of a subsequent mortgage if that mortgage is registered *after* the date of the bank's charge or the date of the last search, whichever happened last. Incidentally, when a new mortgage is taken for any reason (and such course should be avoided), a fresh search is necessary because the bank will be deemed to have notice of any charges registered at the time when the fresh mortgage was created. The golden rule is having searched never to search again, otherwise the bank will be fixed with notice of charges registered since the date of the first search. The protection, however, is limited to subsequent mortgages and does not extend to other matters which can be registered under the Land Charges Act. Registration of a writ, for example, does constitute notice to the bank.

As previously indicated, all this question of second and subsequent charges registered unbeknown to the bank as first mortgagee is largely theoretical because the legal advisers acting for a second mortgagee will always ensure that notice is served upon the bank in addition to registration, and enquiries will be raised concerning the amount secured by the bank's charge. Ample notice is thus served in practice and guided by what happened in *Deeley* v. *Lloyds Bank Ltd.* [1912] A.C. 756, there will be no hesitation in stopping the account. In any event, the fact that a borrower has had to resort to obtaining more accommodation elsewhere against a second mortgage is in itself often a salutary warning to the bank. Occasionally, arrangements may be made by the customer with the bank to raise further money outside by mortgages on properties already held by the bank, and the second mortgagee may co-operate by including in his charge a clause allowing the bank to lend up to a quoted figure on overdraft with continuing security and priority. The second mortgagee naturally has to execute such a document as well as the mortgagor. Negotiations between first and second mortgages are not unknown.

RELEASE OF DEEDS

It is imperative always to retain the deeds of properties charged to the bank until the advance has been repaid or other arrangements made to replace the security. The fact that the bank holds the deeds is tacit notice to other parties that there may be a charge on them. If the mortgagor attempts to borrow elsewhere on the security of the property, the lender will ask for the deeds and draw his conclusions from the inability of the borrower to produce them. If the customer obtains the deeds from the bank on some pretext and hands them to the fresh lender, the latter acting *bona fide*, being unaware of the bank's charge, may obtain a charge which may rank before the bank. A fraudulent customer can think of plenty of excuses to persuade the bank to part with the deeds, including attempts to dispose of the property or disputes concerning boundaries, and he may then prevail upon a friend or other gullible lender to advance by way of *puisne mortgage* so that, in due course, the deeds can be returned to the bank. In such event, the second lender will find no mortgages registered and will register his own charge content in the belief that it is the only charge on the property with every priority. The example is quoted as a salutary warning of what could happen. There is no precedent to decide whether the second mortgagee in such circumstances would have priority, but it is difficult to see upon what grounds he could fail within the rules of priority which now apply. After all, it is incumbent upon the bank as first mortgagee to protect itself by retaining the deeds or registering the charge and any release of mortgaged deeds to a borrower is quite contrary to established practice.

The risk, however remote it may be, is easily avoided by insisting that the deeds remain in the possession of the bank, where they can be examined by arrangement (upon payment of a fee for preference) by anyone concerned, with the authority of the mortgagor. Where the property has been sold, the deeds can be released exceptionally to an approved solicitor against his written undertaking to hold them unimpaired on behalf of the bank and either to return them within a reasonable time or, if the sale is completed to pay the net proceeds direct to the bank. The value of such an undertaking entirely depends upon the integrity of the solicitor who should be well known to the bank, or its agents. Although it is possible for the bank to register its charge when the deeds are released, thereby obtaining protection, this course is rarely adopted in practice.

MORTGAGES UNACCOMPANIED BY DEEDS

A banker may find himself asked to lend against properties without the deposit of the relative deeds. The inability of the customer or mortgagor to produce them is an indication that they may already be charged elsewhere, but occasionally there may be a valid reason for their absence which can be verified to the complete satisfaction of the bank. In such cases the whereabouts of the deeds will be ascertained and the title of the customer to the relative property will be examined by the solicitor acting for the bank. It may be that four houses were originally conveyed to the customer by the same deed and he has mortgaged two of them to a building society and now wishes to borrow from the bank against the remaining pair. The deeds will be examined by the bank's solicitors at the building society and the acknowledgment of the society obtained assuring the bank, in writing, that they have no interest in the two free houses and hold the deeds relating to them on behalf of the bank.

If a search reveals no other charges, the bank takes and registers a *puisne mortgage* (a legal mortgage unaccompanied by the deeds) and secures priority from the date of registration, which is notice to all (Section 198 (1) L.P.A., 1925). It would be most unusual for a bank in such circumstances to be content with a *general equitable charge* (an equitable mortgage unaccompanied by the deeds) because, quite apart from the disadvantages of an equitable mortgage compared with a legal mortgage, it has further drawbacks from the aspect of priority. If the land is subject to a settlement or trust for sale and a sale is made, the purchaser can take the land free from the general equitable charge despite the fact that it is registered, and the bank would have to rely upon the trustees for repayment. Moreover, according to Section 2 (2) of the Law of Property Act, 1925, an estate owner can create a settlement or trust for sale by conveying the land to trustees upon the statutory trusts for sale. These trustees can sell the land free from any general equitable charge and the bank, as mortgagee, would be forced to recover from the trustees. Some protection is perhaps obtained from the fact that the purchase money has to be paid to a trust corporation or to at least two trustees. Nevertheless, a general equitable charge will hardly commend itself to the lending banker.

STATUTORY PRIORITIES

Finally, brief reference has to be made to two cases where the normal rules of priority can be upset by statutory provisions. Under Sections 72 and 83 (5) of the Agricultural Holdings Act, 1948, and Section 59 of the Improvement of Land Act, 1864, a charge can be created to take priority over all existing mortgages. In both cases the money secured by the charge is used to improve the land charged to the bank and the ultimate effect is not unduly harmful. The bank will usually be well aware of such developments and can treat the matter on its merits.

After surveying the rules of priority, we turn back to the banker in possession of the deeds with a completed legal or equitable mortgage about to start searching in order to ensure that before anything is lent there are no parties with prior right. Where, how and when are the searches made ?

SEARCHES

·WHERE TO SEARCH

Several searches may be necessary to discover what rights, if any, other persons may have against the land charged to the bank. Where the land is owned by a limited company, the primary search will be in the Register of Companies at Companies' House, but a search will also be made in the Land Charges Register, which is the most important search to make in most other instances. If the land is situated in Yorkshire, other than the City of York, there are special registers which have to be searched. In most cases nowadays it is also prudent to search the local land charges registers wherever the land may be. All these registers concern unregistered land. Different rules apply to registered land which will be discussed later as a separate subject. Altogether it may be a searching problem, but it cannot be regarded as a difficult task. The most reliable practical rule is, if in doubt, to search everywhere possible according to the situation and ownership of the land. There is safety in excess caution and the additional costs are negligible.

HOW TO SEARCH

The method of searching in each Registry can be outlined as follows:—

(a) Land Charges Register

There are five registers maintained at the Land Charges Department but, to avoid the need for separate searches, a central alphabetical index is kept recording the name, address and description of the owner of the land and the parish, place or district where the property is situated. It is a register of names and not of properties so that all searches are against the name of the owner at the material time. To reduce the risk of error from misspelt names or confusion between persons of the same name, the address and description of the owner is also recorded. A further check can be made from the address, etc., of the land. It is obviously an enormous register and care has always to be exercised to detail in the requisition form the correct full names and descriptions and all known addresses of those against whom a search is to be made. Where land is held in joint names by partners, trustees, or otherwise, a search will be made against each name.

The usual method of searching is to complete a requisition on Form L.C.11 and to forward it by post to the Superintendent, Land Charges Registry, Kidbrooke, London, S.E.3. This postal indent costs 15p per name, the fee being paid by stamp affixed to the form. The registrar then issues an official search certificate which reveals any entries outstanding on the registers and is conclusive evidence in favour of a purchaser or mortgagee (Sections 17(3) and 20 Land Charges Act, 1925). Where the application for a search cannot reach the Registry by the morning mail and a reply is required on the same day, an expedited search will be made upon payment of an additional fee of 15p per search. In an emergency it is possible to telephone or telegraph for a search (confirming with an application on Form L.C.11 by post) or to send a post request asking for a telephonic or telegraphic reply, all subject to additional but moderate cost.

Anyone with the time and energy to spare can make a personal search (without any authority from the owner of the land) upon payment of a fee of 15p per name. This course cannot be recommended because the Registry naturally decline to accept responsibility for any errors or omissions by the searcher. In practice, the banker always obtains an official search certificate. The application is either made by the branch bank direct to the Land Charges Superintendent or through the agency of the branch solicitor. In some banks all searches pass through Head Office channels. When received, the certificate shows the position in the register when it closes to the public on the date of issue.

As every purchaser or mortgagee of land is deemed to have notice of all the rights of third parties which appear in the register, a search has to be made whenever property changes hands. The solicitor examining the title for the bank will, therefore, expect to see a search certificate against the name of every vendor for at least the past fifteen years. If any are missing, there is the risk that some charge may remain outstanding against the property which is registered in the name of a former owner. This risk is very remote in practice because, on the one hand, the solicitor acting for the buyer is unlikely to complete without searching, and, on the other hand, any third party with a material interest in the property would hardly rest content relying entirely on his registration. Searches can always be made against former owners to remove any doubts on this score.

WHAT MAY BE FOUND IN THE LAND CHARGES REGISTER

The Land Charges Register records charges on unregistered land and it is divided into five separate registers. It should be clearly distinguished from the Land Registry, which is concerned only with the registration of titles to land and with charges created on registered land.

The five registers and their sub-divisions may be summarised as follows:—

1. *A Register of Pending Actions*

In this register all actions or proceedings pending in court relating to any interest in land are entered. For example, anyone who has an action pending which affects land may warn the world by registration so that any purchaser or mortgagee is fixed with notice of his claim, and will thus be bound by the result of the action. These entries automatically lapse at the end of five years unless renewed. All petitions in bankruptcy are entered in this register whether or not they affect an owner of land. A list of all these petitions is furnished by the Bankruptcy Office to the Land Charges Register every day and they are registered promptly against the name of the debtor.

2. *A Register of Annuities*

An annuity within the meaning of the Land Charges Act, 1925, is a rent-charge or annuity for one or more life or lives, or for any term of years or greater estate determinable on one or more life or lives created after April 25, 1855, and before January 1, 1926, and not being a rent-charge or an annuity created by a marriage settlement or will. The contents of this register are thus limited to all annuity items charged on land which were registered prior to 1926, and the register will be closed as soon as all the entries outstanding on January 1, 1926, have been removed. Charges of this kind created after 1926 are registered as Class C (iii) land charges as set out below. Few entries on this register are accordingly ever disclosed by a search.

3. *A Register of Writs and Orders Affecting Land*

Here are entered any writs and orders of the courts for enforcing judgments. All orders appointing a receiver and receiving orders in bankruptcy, regardless of whether they affect land or not, are registered in this register.

4. *A Register of Deeds of Arrangement*

All deeds of arrangement which affect land have to be entered here and require registration every five years if the trustee under the deed is still in action. Failure to register enables a purchaser acting *bona fide* to obtain a title free from the rights of the trustee.

In most of the above-mentioned cases the bank would know of such encumbrances from dealings with the customer, but the last register contains the charges which are of more direct interest. It is divided into five classes, two of which are in turn sub-divided.

5. *A Register of Land Charges*

Classes A and B comprise land charges created under an Act of Parliament, for example, the Land Improvement Act, 1864, and the Agricultural Holdings Act, 1948. Such charges rank prior to any existing, as well as future, charges but the money secured by the charge is spent on improving the land and, as previously explained, the position of a prior mortgagee is not unduly weakened.

Class C is sub-divided into four classes:—

C. (i) *A Puisne Mortgage.* All legal mortgages unaccompanied by the relative title deeds are registered in this class. As already indicated, they are normally second or third mortgages.

C. (ii) *A Limited Owner's Charge.* These are equitable charges possessed by a tenant for life or statutory owner by reason of his payment of death duties or other liabilities.

C. (iii) *A General Equitable Charge.* In this register are entered all other equitable charges which do not arise under a settlement or a trust for sale. They include equitable mortgages unprotected by the deposit of the title deeds, and annuities created after 1925 (see above).

C. (iv) *An Estate Contract,* which includes any contract by an estate owner, or by a person entitled at the date of the contract to have a legal estate conveyed to him, to convey or create a legal estate. Any agreement for the sale of a legal estate can be registered under this heading. The standard form of equitable charge used by a bank includes an undertaking by the mortgagor to execute a legal mortgage when called upon to do so and the charge could, therefore, be registered as an estate contract on the grounds that the mortgagor has contracted to give the bank a legal estate in the form of a term of years absolute. Advantage is not normally taken of this feature.

Class D is sub-divided into three classes:—

D. (i) is a charge for *death duties* whereby the Inland Revenue, if it so wishes, may register a charge for estate duty. In point of fact, it is not often the Inland Revenue avails itself of this means of registration because it is usually content to follow the proceeds of sale to obtain satisfaction of its rights. Where a search reveals no entry, there is no duty to enquire further and a mortgagor or purchaser can then assume that there are no death duties outstanding which affect the land.

D. (ii) *A restrictive covenant* created after 1925. Any agreements or covenants which restrict the use of the land are registered here unless they are made between a lessor and a lessee. Some restrictions can materially influence the market value of land and any entry in this register may require close consideration.

D. (iii) *Equitable Easements,* such as rights of way, light and drainage, created after 1925, comprise this class. They can likewise jeopardise the value of the land as security. Incidentally, where any easement is perpetual and is created by deed, it is not registered because it is a legal interest.

Class E comprises annuities charged upon land which were created prior to 1926, but were not registered until after 1925.

Finally, *Class F* comprises charges arising from the rights of occupation given to a spouse by the Matrimonial Homes Act, 1967, also beneficial interests under the Matrimonial Proceedings and Property Act, 1970.

HOW TO OBTAIN DETAILS OF CHARGES

In most cases the search certificate will bear the magic words 'no subsisting entries,' but where any charge has been registered, the type of charge described only by letter and number will be revealed in the certificate. To obtain details a further application has to be made to the Registry on Form L.C. 14, requesting an office copy of the entry for a fee of 15p. The picture is then complete and the full effect of the charge upon the bank security can be determined.

The most dangerous charges from the banking standpoint are those in the C class, particularly a C (i), puisne mortgage, or a C (iii), general equitable charge, because the bank is fixed with notice of a prior charge created by the mortgagor which presumably has not been disclosed in the previous negotiations between bank and customer. Sometimes, however, it can be proved that the entries are overdue for removal from the register because the particular mortgage is in the possession of the bank duly discharged. There is no obligation upon the mortgagee to vacate the entry, but steps should be taken to correct the register as soon as possible.

WHEN TO SEARCH THE LAND CHARGES REGISTER

The time when the search is made is of vital importance. The fact that the bank will not be affected by entries which are registered after the date of the charge or the date of the search, *whichever last happened,* has already been explained, and the golden rule is to search *after* the charge has been created and not to search again. The reasons for this practice and the legal provisions which apply to searching times can now be reviewed in detail.

It is difficult and often impossible to search on the day the mortgage is signed and any search made before the completion of the charge entails the risk that other charges may be registered in the interim period. Section 4 (2) of the Law of Property Amendment Act, 1926, as amended by the Land Charges Rules, 1972, provides that when a mortgagee obtains a search certificate and the mortgage is completed within 15 working days after the date of the certificate, he shall not be affected by any entry made in the register between the date of the certificate and the date of the charge, unless the entry was made pursuant to a *priority notice* entered before the certificate was issued. A priority notice may be lodged by any person intending to register a charge and it has to be filed at least 15 working days before the date of the charge. It follows that if the charge is then registered within thirty working days of the entry of the priority notice in the register, the registration will date back to the date of the charge. Fifteen working days' notice has to be given to protect anyone who may search before the priority notice is filed.

This breathing space of fifteen working days between the date of the search certificate and the completion of the charge certainly protects a mortgagee advancing a fixed sum, but it is doubtful whether it covers a banker advancing on current account. If a lender, such as a building society, is asked to extend a fixed loan, which it is not bound so to do by the terms of the mortgage, a fresh search will be made to ensure that no entries have appeared since the last search and another charge will probably be created. All this can be carried out without complications relying on the fifteen working days of grace, but the banker cannot pretend to search before paying every cheque and has necessarily to seek protection elsewhere.

Section 94 (2) of the Law of Property Act, 1925, as amended by the Law of Property (Amendment) Act, 1926, applies to mortgages made expressly for securing a current account or other further advances, and it is upon this provision that the banker relies in practice. It states, in effect, that the banker will not be affected by any mortgages entered on the register subsequent to the time when the original mortgage was created, or to the date of the last search, *whichever last happened*. It must be emphasised, however, that this protection does not cover the subsequent registration of pending actions, writs, etc. It is limited to the registration of mortgages.

The best course, therefore, is to have the mortgage completed and then to search, it being made clear to the customer that no advances can be taken until both operations have been carried out and the result of the search is satisfactory. This counsel of perfection may often be difficult to follow, but the risks entailed in making exceptions are patent.

(b) The Yorkshire Registries

If the land charged to the bank is situated in Yorkshire, other than within the City of York, searches have to be made in the appropriate Deeds Register. Land in the City of York is not caught by these special registers, being subject to the same provisions as those which related to unregistered land elsewhere in England.

There are three Deeds Registers in Yorkshire at Northallerton, Beverley and Wakefield, for the North, East and West Ridings respectively. They are not registers of titles, but merely documents, including mortgages, wills and conveyances, which evidence the transfer of the legal title to land in Yorkshire. The Law of Property Act, 1969, contains provisions for the eventual closure of the Yorkshire Registers, and, as this process has already begun, it will be necessary to consider the three Ridings separately.

The Deeds Register at Beverley is still accepting new entries and no date has yet been set for its closure. When dealing with land in the East Riding, it will, therefore, be necessary to register the bank's mortgage, for whilst non-registration will not, in itself, invalidate the title of the bank as mortgagee, it may well affect its priority, and all legal mortgages, with or without the title deeds, have to be registered. Even legal mortgages created by a limited company over land in the East Riding of Yorkshire have to be registered in the East Riding Deeds Register, as well as with the Registrar at Companies' House. Generally speaking, this deeds register furnishes a record of all documents relating to the ownership of land within the East Riding, which is of value whenever deeds are lost or destroyed.

An equitable mortgagee of land in the East Riding of Yorkshire is not obliged to register his charge, but to standardise the system (for all other mortgages have to be registered) and so as to obviate the risk of vital omissions, a bank may prefer to register such a charge, which will be accepted by the registrar without comment.

General Equitable charges (unprotected by the deposit of the deeds) are registered in the East Riding of Yorkshire Register of Land Charges at Beverley. This Charges Registry is in reality a branch of the Land Charges Registry in London and, for land in the East Riding, any of the charges contained in Section 5 of the Land Charges Register (see page 170), must be registered at Beverley instead of the Land Charges Register in London. However, it will still be necessary to search the Land Charges Register in London for charges registered in the four other registers (Pending Actions, Annuities, Writs and Orders, and Deeds of Arrangement).

It is no longer possible to place new entries in the Deeds Registers at Northallerton (closed 1.9.1970) and Wakefield (closed 1.10.1970), but for the time being, they should still be searched for entries dated prior to their closure. These registers provide a record of all documents relating to ownership of land within the North and West Ridings respectively, up to the date of their ceasing to accept new entries. The outstanding entries on the Charges Registers at Northallerton and Wakefield have now been transferred to the Land Charges Register in London and any mortgage which is unaccompanied by the deeds, or other interest, should be registered there.

From this survey of the contents of the Yorkshire Registers, it will be seen that, before granting advances against the security of land in the East Riding of Yorkshire, the banker has to search both the Deeds and Land Charges Registers at Beverley. For land in the North and West Ridings it will be necessary to search the appropriate Deeds Register only, at Northallerton or Wakefield. In addition, for all land in Yorkshire, a search should always be made at the Land Charges Department of the Land Registry in London, and, where appropriate, at Companies' House.

(c) The Companies Register

By virtue of Section 95 (d) of the Companies Act, 1948, particulars of *any charge* created by a limited company on land, *wherever situate*, or any interest therein (but excluding a charge for any rent or other periodical sum issuing out of land) has to be registered with the Registrar of Companies at Companies' House, City Road, London E.C.1, within twenty-one days of its creation, otherwise it will be void against the liquidator and any creditor of the company. Failure so to register means that the bank, or any other mortgagee, has no security. All charges, legal or equitable, with or without the deposit of the deeds, have, therefore, to be registered within twenty-one days of their date.

It follows that, when taking a mortgage over land belonging to a limited company, the primary search to ensure that there are no prior mortgages has to be made at Companies' House. It is a personal search which costs 5p and, as all the entries are contained on the file of the company concerned, the responsibility of obtaining an accurate picture rests on the officer making the search. Particular care is necessary where the search discloses that the company has created debentures.

It is imperative to ensure that the property being charged to the bank is not already caught by the debenture. These searches at Companies' House are normally made immediately after the registration of the mortgage to the bank, but before any advances are taken by the borrower. This is to avoid the risk that charges might be registered between the date of a search and the date of the registration of the bank's mortgage.

The Land Charges Act, 1925, Section 10 (5), provided that, in the case of a land charge created by a limited company for securing money, registration at Companies' House under the Companies Act was sufficient in place of registration under the Land Charges Act, and that it was to have effect as if the land charge had been registered thereunder. This rule has been amended by the Law of Property Act, 1969, Section 26 which enacts that the provision in the Land Charges Act, 1925, is not to apply to any charge created by a company, other than one created as a floating charge, on or after 1st January 1970.

In practice, therefore, when taking a charge over land from a limited company, the bank should search the Registers Department at the Land Charges Registry, but registration of the mortgage in that Department is only necessary in those cases where the title deeds are not deposited with the bank. Floating Charges do not require registration at the Land Charges Registry, but they must be registered at Companies' House within 21 days of their creation. In addition, where a company deposits as security land which is situated in Yorkshire (outside the City of York), further searches will have to be made in the appropriate Yorkshire Registers.

Finally, circumstances may demand that a search should be made in one of the following registers.

(d) Registers of Local Land Charges

All district, borough and county councils keep registers of local land charges in which are recorded charges which the local authority has acquired over any land within its area. These may include road charges covering the cost of laying drains and making up roads, restrictive covenants, such as town planning schemes, and charges in respect of repairs carried out under the Public Health Acts, or improvement grants. There may also be tree or building preservation orders and enforcement notices under the Town and Country Planning Acts. All these interests are recorded whether the title to the land is registered or unregistered.

Unlike all the registers discussed so far, these local authority registers are concerned with properties and not the names of the proprietors of the land. The charges are registered against the actual properties and, unless so registered, they are void against a subsequent purchaser or mortgagee of the property. It is possible to make a personal search, but it is always preferable to obtain an official search certificate, which only costs 50p per parcel of land. When the land is within the area of a county borough, a search in the register at the local Town Hall will suffice, but where the land is within an urban, rural, or borough council district, searches have to be made at the local district council offices and in the county council register.

The need for such local searches varies according to the type of property which is being charged to the bank. In the case of an old-established building, they may be thought unnecessary, but with land that has been recently developed or is about to be developed they are essential because of the risk of road charges and restrictive covenants. The solicitor acting for the bank branch will normally make the searches wherever it is considered advisable, but much will depend upon the value of the security in relation to the maximum amount to be lent.

TOWN AND COUNTRY PLANNING ACTS

Finally, a word of caution has to be introduced concerning the incidence of the Town and Country Planning Acts. Space will not allow a complete discussion of the effect of the planning law upon the lending banker, but readers are reminded that no development of land may now be undertaken without the express permission of the local planning authority. In this context, development includes any material change in the use of any existing buildings, as well as constructional operations. The division of a house into flats, the conversion of a dwelling house into a shop or cafe, or the change of user of a shop to sell fried fish, tripe, pets, and cats' meat, all require planning permission. If anyone contravenes these regulations by developing without the formal approval of the local planning authority, an enforcement notice can be served upon them within four years of the development demanding the restoration of the land to its original condition. This may entail further advances by the bank to enable the owner to correct the position. The need to ensure that any development or material change of use which is proposed, or has taken place since July 1, 1948, has been blessed by planning permission is thus clear, and the branch solicitor will usually deal with this problem when investigating the title.

Moreover, the Town and Country Planning Act, 1947, required every planning authority to prepare a development plan covering its area, which had to be submitted to the Minister of Town and Country Planning, and this plan may have to be examined to ensure that the land to be mortgaged to the bank has not been designated for compulsory acquisition. A search at the local authority register will not reveal these dangers, but the plans for development have to be available within the area for inspection free from charge. Nowadays these problems are usually overcome in standard fashion by sending with the formal request for an official search of the local land charges register a schedule of enquiries concerning other factors affecting the land. Local authorities will answer these standard questions upon payment of an appropriate fee.

SUMMARY

The vital importance of always searching in every appropriate register at the right time is now quite clear. In all cases, make searches as well in the *registers of local land charges* unless the property is well established.

Thus far the prudent banker has:—

1. Valued the property and had the bank's interest endorsed on the fire policy with adequate cover.
2. Ensured by obtaining an independent report from the branch solicitor that the mortgagor's title to the property is sound.
3. Taken the appropriate legal or equitable mortgage on the bank's standard form, duly executed by the mortgagor.

4. Searched all essential registers to confirm that there are no prior charges or interests affecting the value of the security.

5. Registered the charge where necessary.

At this stage, the borrower is at liberty to draw up to the agreed maximum and no further difficulty arises, unless the bank receives notice of a second mortgage, until the debt is repaid and the overdraft arrangement cancelled, or steps have to be taken to dispose of the security to recover the balances outstanding.

Chapter XXII Second Mortgages and Sub-Mortgages

SECOND MORTGAGES

Until fairly recently bankers were, generally speaking, reluctant to accept second mortgages as security. They regarded them as preferable to no security at all, but the disadvantages were obvious. The first mortgagee could exercise his remedies without considering the bank and might force the sale of the property at an uneconomic price, leaving little, if any, surplus for the bank, particularly if arrears of interest had been added to the amount secured by the first mortgage. If the bank wished to control the price obtained, it had little alternative but to repay the first mortgagee and then sell on its own account.

Today the weaknesses of this type of security still exist and the worth of a second mortgage obviously depends on the margin which is ultimately available between the amount of the first mortgage and the value of the property. However, of late there has been a sustained rise in property prices and this has frequently resulted in steadily increasing equities which are further increased in those cases where regular reductions are being made to the first mortgagee, for example a Building Society. Again, much depends on the parties concerned; a private lender may well act without regard to the interests of another mortgagee, but a Building Society has a statutory duty to obtain the best price possible and can be relied upon to co-operate with the bank.

METHOD OF TAKING A SECOND MORTGAGE

The practical steps to be taken when obtaining a second mortgage as security can be set out as follows:

1. Ascertain the amount due to the first mortgagee and whether he is under any obligation to make further advances which would rank in priority to the second mortgage to the bank. Then inspect and value the property on a forced sale basis to determine the equity available for the bank. If the margin is insufficient in relation to the amount required, there is usually little point in proceeding further.

2. Decide whether it is necessary to investigate the title to the property. As the deeds will be held by the first mortgagee, special arrangements will have to be made for the branch solicitor to examine the deeds and

177

M

report upon the title. If the first mortgagee is an experienced lender, such as a building society, the bank may rely upon the fact that the title has already been proved and a separate examination can be waived.

3. Confirm that the property is adequately insured with a reliable company and the fire policy is held by the first mortgagee. Notice of the bank's interest as second mortgagee should also be served upon the insurance company.

4. Obtain the charge by way of legal mortgage. A second equitable charge has far too many obvious drawbacks and the prudent banker always obtains the remedies of a legal mortgage. The standard bank mortgage form can be used without amendment, although reference is sometimes made to the first mortgage of given date in favour of the named mortgagee. In the case of freeholds and leaseholds the mortgagor in effect grants the bank, as second mortgagee, a term one day or more longer than that granted to the first mortgagee. The charge is executed in the same way as any first legal mortgage.

5. Search all the necessary registers according to the situation of the land and type of mortgagor as explained in Chapter XXI.

6. Register in the appropriate register(s). There being no deeds, it is a puisne mortgage and requires registration in the Land Charges Register or elsewhere to secure priority.

7. Serve formal notice of the second mortgage in writing upon the first mortgagee, requesting confirmation of the amount of his loan and that he is under no obligation to make further advances. Unless the first mortgagee is under this obligation, the notice fixes the amount secured by his charge, and further amounts cannot be lent secured in priority to the bank's charge. Incidentally, unless the first mortgage is expressed to cover advances on current account or additional loans, registration of the second mortgage is notice to the first mortgagee, but direct notice by the bank places the position beyond doubt. Any obligation to make further advances enables the first mortgagee to tack, and additional monies can be lent ranking prior to the bank (Section 94 (1) Law of Property Act, 1925, which was discussed in Chapter XXI). In other words, the value of the bank's security cannot be determined unless there is a maximum figure fixed upon the obligation of the first mortgagee.

The security is then as complete and watertight as it can be made, and many first mortgagees will, as a matter of courtesy, keep the bank in touch with any material developments likely to affect its interests.

SUB-MORTGAGES

Occasionally, a customer offers to the bank as security a mortgage of a mortgage in his favour. Thus Green may have lent £1,000 to Brown secured by a legal mortgage on the borrower's dwelling house. Green later needs temporary finance and, instead of calling upon Brown to repay, he approaches his bank for accommodation against the security of the mortgage created by Brown in his favour. Green thereby mortgages to the bank the mortgage debt of Brown and the security for that debt. Green is the sub-mortgagor and the bank the sub-mortgagee. Such security is sometimes taken from a building society customer.

The steps taken to perfect this type of security may be summarised as follows:

1. Ascertain the amount outstanding due from the mortgagor to the mortgagee under the original mortgage and then value the property to decide whether the amount is fully secured. Any shortfall in the value of the property will be the personal liability of the mortgagor, as well as of the sub-mortgagor, and their combined worth may suffice to meet the bank's requirements. Normally, however, the bank will expect the mortgage to be covered with a reasonable margin by the value of the mortgaged property, which should be adequately insured in the usual manner.

2. The title should next be investigated by the branch solicitor and his report obtained. This precaution may be waived where the sub-mortgagor is experienced in such matters, and a satisfactory report made by his solicitors at the time when the mortgage was granted is available for perusal by the bank. All the deeds and the mortgage will, of course, be held by the bank. No searches will be necessary if they were made by the sub-mortgagor when he obtained his mortgage. Care is required where amounts have been advanced in addition to the original loan in case the sub-mortgagor failed to search afresh against the mortgagor. There is always the risk of a second mortgage which could rank in priority to the additional advances made by the first mortgagee. If in doubt, the best course is always to search against both the original mortgagor and the sub-mortgagor. The latter could always create a sub-mortgage without depositing the relative deeds.

3. Obtain the charge which may be taken by way of legal mortgage or by a sub-demise for a shorter term than that held by the sub-mortgagor, plus an assignment of the mortgage debt due on the original mortgage with the customary provisions for redemption. Alternatively, a transfer of the benefit of the original mortgage can be taken within Section 114 of the Law of Property Act, 1925. This course may be more satisfactory where the original charge is expressed to be by way of legal mortgage, but in practice the standard form of legal mortgage is usually taken by most banks. A sub-mortgage of a legal mortgage of land in the East Riding of Yorkshire has to be registered in the East Riding of Yorkshire Deeds Register. Needless to add, an equitable sub-mortgage can only be entertained where the sub-mortgagor is of undoubted standing.

4. Serve notice of the sub-mortgage in writing upon the original mortgagor, calling upon him when acknowledging receipt to confirm the amount owing and embodying an undertaking to make any future repayments direct to the bank and not to his mortgagee. The acknowledgment and undertaking is usually prepared by the bank and sent with the notice for signature and return by the original mortgagor.

The remedies available to second mortgagees and sub-mortgagees are considered in Chapter XXIII in the course of a general survey of the methods by which mortgagees may obtain repayment.

Chapter XXIII The Repayment of the Advance—Releasing the Security—Procedure for Recovery on Default

In the normal course with good lending the advance will be repaid and the bank is called upon to release its security. Unless the property has been sold, or the customer wishes to charge it elsewhere, it is better, and certainly cheaper, not to disturb the mortgage in case overdraft accommodation may be required again in years to come. It does not inconvenience the customer to leave the mortgage outstanding and the deeds remain in the safe-keeping of the bank. Where circumstances demand that the property has to be freed from the mortgage encumbrance, some evidence will be required depending upon the type of mortgage held by the bank.

RELEASING THE SECURITY

WITH EQUITABLE MORTGAGE

As the equitable mortgage does not create any legal estate or interest in the land thereby charged as security, it does not become part of the chain of title and is not, therefore, an essential document to be retained with all the deeds. It can be retained by the bank, cancelled or torn up, the deeds being delivered to the customer. No statutory receipt is required, but should the mortgagor seek a receipt it can be given separately, or it may be endorsed on the equitable charge. It is unusual in practice for the bank to be asked for a receipt, the redelivery of the deeds free being sufficient for the customer's purpose.

WITH EQUITABLE MORTGAGE UNDER SEAL

The fact that the equitable mortgage is under seal does not alter the method of release. As it is an equitable mortgage only and does not create any legal estate, it can be discharged under hand as indicated above. Nevertheless, solicitors acting for customers occasionally call for a statutory receipt as though they were dealing with a legal mortgage and the bank, as a matter of courtesy or to avoid delay, follows the procedure outlined below.

WITH LEGAL MORTGAGE

A legal mortgage is an essential link in the chain of title to the land and has to be preserved with the deeds. Formal evidence is, therefore, necessary to prove that the bank's interest as mortgagee has been discharged. This is usually provided by means of a receipt for the mortgage moneys endorsed on the mortgage, which has the legal effect of extinguishing the mortgage term. A specimen form of receipt is given in the Law of Property Act, 1925, Third Schedule, but this may be varied as required providing always that it is expressed to be for all moneys secured by the mortgage and it states the name of the party paying the money. The same wording can be employed for all types of legal mortgage, regardless of whether the land is freehold or leasehold. The form of receipt is normally printed on the back of the bank's mortgage form and can easily be completed when required.

A statutory receipt on these lines need not be executed under seal and it could be signed by an authorised branch official. To maintain control of security and avoid the risk, however remote it may be, of wrongful releases of security, it is customary to have the receipt sealed by the bank or at least executed under hand by a director or Head Office official. This precautionary practice inevitably gives rise to delay whilst the mortgage is in course of post to and from the Head Office of the bank and, where the property is being sold by the mortgagor, it is often prudent to execute the receipt in advance so that the discharged mortgage can be delivered against the proceeds of sale at the completion. The solicitors acting in the matter will usually co-operate with the bank in this respect. Alternatively, an undertaking can always be given to the solicitor acting for the purchaser to deliver the discharged document as soon as it is available.

This mortgage, together with any others held to secure the account, must be denoted if dated prior to 1 August 1971: see *Stamp Duty*, Chapter I. As a matter of courtesy, the customer should be reminded that the mortgage has to be preserved intact with the deeds, being part of the title. Some people look upon the mortgage as a blot on the family escutcheon and think in terms of its discreet destruction.

The statutory receipt executed by the bank is normally in favour of the customer or the third party mortgagor entitled to redeem the mortgage, and it effects a surrender of the term created by the mortgage and merges it in the reversion held by the mortgagor. Occasionally, however, the bank debt may be repaid by a third party. For example, a guarantor might liquidate the entire indebtedness and take over all other securities held for the account of the principal. In such circumstances, the name of the third party will be inserted in the receipt, which will then operate as a transfer of the mortgage instead of a discharge of it. Section 115 (4) of the Law of Property Act, 1925, expressly states that where a receipt acknowledges that the money has been paid by someone other than the party entitled to redeem the mortgage, it operates as if the benefit of the mortgage had by deed been transferred to him.

OTHER METHODS OF DISCHARGING THE MORTGAGE

A plain receipt given under hand for the mortgage moneys is in itself quite sufficient to extinguish the mortgage. Section 116 of the Law of Property Act, 1925, provides that when a mortgage has been created by demise and the amount secured thereby is repaid, the term of years automatically ceases. As a receipt given for the entire mortgage debt is evidence of repayment, it operates as a discharge of the mortgage. This simple arrangement may not, however, appeal to customers or their legal advisers and is rarely adopted by the practical banker.

Before 1926, a legal mortgage had to be reconveyed or surrendered upon repayment because the legal estate was conveyed by the mortgage to the lender and he had in effect to return it to the borrower. A reconveyance can still be endorsed upon a mortgage evidencing that the bank as mortgagees surrenders and conveys to the mortgagor all the property vested by the mortgage. Some bank mortgages still have a form of reconveyance printed on the back of the form and it is used instead of a statutory receipt.

PARTIAL RELEASES

It sometimes happens that the bank has to release only a part of the land covered by a legal mortgage. A customer might, for example, charge ten houses by means of one deed and later sell one of them. A statutory receipt obviously cannot be given, unless the proceeds of the house are sufficient to repay the whole debt, and an express release has to be executed to free the particular house for conveyance to the purchaser. Such a document will recite the mortgage and proceed to surrender and release unto the mortgagor all the property specified in the annexed schedule. Alternatively, the bank may join in the conveyance of the house as mortgagee expressly releasing the interest of the bank. This latter course is normal where builder customers sell off plots which they have developed on an estate charged to the bank by way of legal mortgage. Incidentally, when the mortgagor is a limited company, the purchaser's solicitors, in such cases of partial release, may require release of the particular property from the company register. This can now be accomplished without difficulty by filing with the Registrar Form 49A duly completed under the seal of the company, and an entry will then be made specifying that the given property has been released from the charge to the bank (Section 100, Companies Act, 1948).

Partial releases are not, of course, required where the bank merely holds an equitable charge because no legal estate or interest vests in the bank. But the solicitors acting for a purchaser of land which is part of a larger plot included in a memorandum of deposit to secure borrowing from a bank may call for evidence that the bank has no further interest in the part in question. This can easily be provided by an appropriately worded letter signed by the branch manager.

NO NEED TO SEARCH ON REPAYMENT

Upon receiving repayment of an advance and the request of the mortgagor for the discharge of the mortgage, it is the duty of the bank to deliver the title deeds to the person who has the best right to them. In the normal way, this will be the mortgagor, but there may be another encumbrance, in which case the deeds have to be delivered to the second mortgagee. A bank cannot, however, incur liability to a subsequent mortgagee for delivering the deeds to the mortgagor, *unless it had actual notice of the later mortgage.* In this context mere registration of a mortgage as a land charge does not constitute notice to the bank and upon repayment there is no obligation to search before returning the deeds to the mortgagor.

In practice, *a second mortgagee* inevitably gives the bank, as first mortgagee, prompt notice of the creation of the fresh incumbrance and the account is stopped to avoid the operation of the Rule in *Clayton's Case* (1816) 1 Mer. 572. All security records are immediately marked warning officers not to release the deeds to the mortgagor without due reference to the second mortgagee. It follows that, when the customer repays his overdraft, the bank is well aware of the second mortgage and can deliver the deeds to the second mortgagee, who has the best right to them.

In theory a second mortgagee could omit to advise the bank of his charge and rest content with its registration as a puisne mortgage at the Land Charges Registry. If the bank debt is later repaid, the bank will be unaware of this second charge unless it makes a search before releasing the deeds. In the opinion of some, it is still prudent to search, but in practice the banker relies on the more general view that there is no obligation upon a satisfied mortgagee to search for subsequent charges of which he has no direct notice. This system relies on Section 96 (2) of the Law of Property Act, 1925, as amended by the Law of Property (Amendment) Act, 1926, whereby 'a mortgagee, whose mortgage is surrendered or otherwise extinguished, shall not be liable on account of delivering documents of title in his possession to the person not having the best right thereto, unless he has notice of the right or claim of a person having a better right' and 'in this sub-section notice does not include notice implied by reason of registration under the Land Charges Act, 1925, or in a local deeds register'. This despite the fact that according to Section 198 (1) of the Law of Property Act, 1925, anything registered under the Land Charges Act, 1925, is deemed to be actual notice to all concerned.

The same rule can be applied where the advance is repaid out of the proceeds of sale of the property *by the borrower*. Any surplus proceeds can be applied without searching to see whether any one is entitled to the surplus. The bank is delivering the deeds to the purchaser at the request of the mortgagor unaware of any second charge and there appears to be no risk in allowing the customer to draw the surplus proceeds as required. On the other hand, if the bank has direct notice of a second mortgage, it has to retain all surplus proceeds in trust for the second mortgagee. In practice, a second mortgagee will be alive to what is happening and will not hesitate to take all steps necessary to protect his position.

It is well to emphasise at this juncture that, *when a bank exercises its power of sale, it has to search* to ensure that there are no subsequent mortgages before releasing any surplus proceeds to the customer. The need to search is only excused where the customer sells or the deeds are released upon repayment from other sources.

REMOVAL OF OUTSTANDING ENTRIES ON REGISTERS

Whenever the bank charge has been registered anywhere, courtesy demands that, upon repayment and release of the security, all outstanding entries should be removed. Whilst there is no legal obligation upon the bank to register satisfaction, it is helpful at least to remind the customer of the need to clear the entries if the bank cannot arrange to remove the entries itself. For example, a second mortgage will be discharged by the bank in exactly the same way as a first mortgage, there will be no title deeds to deliver to the mortgagor, but the puisne mortgage will presumably be registered at the Land Charges Registry. To remove the entry, Form L.C.8 should be completed under the seal of the bank and forwarded to the Registrar. If internal regulations permit, it is possible instead to use Form L.C. 17, which can be signed by the branch manager, but it has to be sent to the

Registry with the discharge of the mortgage which may be inconvenient to the parties concerned.

Where the mortgagor is a limited company and the charge has been registered at Companies' House, steps should be taken to have the entry removed by the company completing Memorandum of Satisfaction Form 49. The procedure is a little complicated and, perhaps for this reason, many entries are left outstanding long after the relative mortgages have been repaid and discharged. In later years, when the company wishes to sell or mortgage the property, there is a frantic rush to correct the position. It is far better to clear the entry at the proper time to avoid misleading those who search thereafter against the company at Companies' House. The memorandum amounts not only to formal notice under the seal of the company of satisfaction of the charge but also requires a statutory declaration made by one of the directors or the secretary confirming the particulars contained in the memorandum. This has to be made before a Justice of the Peace or Notary Public, or a Commissioner of Oaths, and when all is completed, the form is filed with the Registrar and satisfaction registered.

To protect mortgagors, the Registrar sends a notice to the person in whose favour the charge is registered, affording opportunity to object to registration of the satisfaction. Partial satisfaction can be registered by completing Form 49A, as indicated above. Admittedly, it is the responsibility of the company customer, as satisfied mortgagor, to clear entries affecting its property, but the bank should not omit to remind the secretary or directors of the need to do so.

Apart from the question of clearing any entries recording the bank's interest as mortgagee, little difficulty is usually experienced in discharging the mortgage and releasing the deeds following repayment of the advance in the normal course of business. The real trouble arises when the bank has to exercise its remedies as mortgagee in order to recover its money.

RECOVERY OF THE DEBT

The statutory remedies available to equitable and legal mortgagees were outlined in Chapter XIX and the way in which they are normally utilised in practice can now be discussed. A banker is a patient lender and every latitude is granted to the average borrower before resort to legal rights, which only arise when the borrower is in default. In other words, all informal attempts in the ordinary course of business to recover the debt having failed, formal demand for repayment is served upon the customer. If he still fails to face up to his obligations, the services of a solicitor may be enlisted to impress upon the borrower the extent and effect of his default. By this stage the banker will have cleared the decks for action and can decide how best to recover from the security and/or the borrower.

The bank can, of course, sue the mortgagor on the personal covenant to repay whether the mortgage be legal or equitable, but any action will usually be for the amount owing on the account, regardless of the mortgage. Such a course is pointless where adequate security is held, but may be adopted in cases where the debt is largely unsecured or the security is difficult to realise and the borrower is believed to possess adequate means or has friends or relatives who may help him under such pressure to avoid the stigma of bankruptcy. The writ is the first step on the way to bankruptcy in such cases. If judgment is obtained and remains unsatisfied, a bankruptcy notice can be served and the obstinate debtor thus forced into bankruptcy. This last resort remedy can be ignored for our immediate purpose.

LEGAL MORTGAGE
Power of Sale
The best available remedy and the one most frequently used is to sell the security, which power can be exercised, except where the mortgage is an equitable one under hand, without application to the Court. As soon as the mortgage debt becomes due, the mortgage has a statutory power, which may be varied or extended by the parties, to sell the mortgaged property or any part thereof, either by public auction or by private contract, provided that the mortgage has been made by deed (Section 101, Law of Property Act, 1925).

Although the power of sale arises as soon as the mortgage debt is due, *it does not become exercisable until:—*

1. Notice requiring payment of the mortgage money has been served on the mortgagor, and default has been made in payment, or part thereof, for three months, after such service. This statutory period of three months can be expressly reduced by the terms of the mortgage and a bank mortgage provides for payment on demand or within one month of demand.

or

2. Some interest is in arrear and remains unpaid for two months after becoming due.

or

3. There has been a breach of some provision (other than the covenant to repay the advance and interest) which is embodied in the mortgage or in the Law of Property Act, 1925, and which imposes an obligation upon the mortgagor. This may include the breach of the covenant to keep the premises in repair. Such a breach enables the bank to exercise its powers of sale immediately, without first demanding repayment, but advantage is rarely taken in practice of this means of rapid action.

Before starting to sell any mortgaged property, it is clearly essential to verify that the power of sale has actually arisen. The appropriate terms of the relative mortgage will be known and in the usual course the branch will send a letter to the borrower by registered post formally demanding repayment of the quoted amount and stating that, in the event of default, the bank will exercise its legal remedies. If this letter has no effect, the power of sale will be exercisable automatically at the expiration of the period of notice set out in the mortgage, and further reference need not be made to the mortgagor, providing the property is vacant.

The bank may then sell to whosoever it may wish at whatever price it can obtain. There is no obligation to have regard to the morgagor's views, because a mortgagee sells for his own benefit and is not a trustee for the mortgagor. On the other hand, any mortgagee, particularly a bank, is expected to act prudently and to obtain the best price possible in conditions obtaining at the date of the sale. According to Sir George Jessel, M. R., in *Nash* v. *Eads* (1880) 25 Sol. J. 95, a mortgagee should 'conduct the sale properly and must sell at a fair value'. See also

185

Cuckmere Brick Co. Ltd. v. *Mutual Finance Ltd.* (1971) 2 All E.R. 633. Another guide (but not a legal direction) can be obtained from Section 10 of The Building Societies Act, 1939, which expects a building society when selling as mortgagee to exercise reasonable care to sell at the best price which can reasonably be obtained. The practical rule for the banker is to raise the highest possible price in the most expeditious manner. Where the bank has to sell as mortgagee there is rarely any margin between the amount of the debt and the current market value of the property if, in fact, it is saleable, so that the banker will always be anxious to attract the highest bidder.

The property will be entrusted to a local estate agent of proved worth who can explore the market in the hope of finding a buyer by private treaty. There is no need to sell it by auction. Throughout the bank's name as seller should not be disclosed in case it depresses the market or creates the erroneous impression that the bank is dealing harshly with a borrower. It is, of course, hardly prudent for the bank to sell in private (assuming it can find a buyer) unless it holds an independent professional valuation of the property indicating that the sale price is reasonable. In practice, however, the sale has usually to be by auction in the hope that it will attract a few buyers who will bid up to the reserve price. Selling land as a mortgagee is rarely a happy event.

Investment properties let to tenants have usually to be sold as such, subject to the tenancies. Leases granted after the creation of the mortgage to a bank are by the terms of the mortgage subject to the bank's consent and they will not be valid against the bank unless this consent was obtained. Such leases can, therefore, be upset, but the tenant will probably have to be evicted.

The frequent difficulty for the bank when forced to exercise the power of sale is to obtain vacant possession of the property. The borrower is in occupation and cannot be prevailed upon to vacate usually because he cannot afford to go elsewhere. Unless legal action is taken to force him to quit or a buyer can be found to take the property subject to the occupant, there is a stalemate. Such actions are undesirable because the borrower and his family are often thrown out on to the street. Where the borrower in the bank mortgage attorns tenant to the bank at a nominal rental, with the proviso that such tenancy does not constitute the bank a mortgagee in possession whilst the mortgagor is in occupation, the bank can apply for a summary judgment on a specially endorsed writ for possession by way of County Court Summons. In this way vacant possession can be obtained without undue delay unless the borrower has a sound defence, i.e. an ability to repay within a reasonable period (see Chapter XX, MORTGAGEE'S POWER OF SALE: Section 36 Administration of Justice Act 1970).

Having contracted to sell, the title can be conveyed by the bank as mortgagee without reference to the mortgagor (who sometimes cannot be found) and the purchaser will obtain a valid title free from any subsequent mortgage which may remain unpaid. The conveyance serves to extinguish the mortgage term vested in the bank and in any later mortgagee. According to Section 104 of the Law of Property Act, 1925, a mortgagee exercising the power of sale is empowered by deed to convey the property sold freed from all estates, interests and rights to which the mortgage has priority, but subject to all estates, interests and rights which have priority to the mortgage. The branch solicitor will usually attend to all these matters, calling upon the bank to seal the conveyance when completion is about to take place. Incidentally, when the bank as mortgagee has contracted to sell property, the mortgagor cannot suddenly emerge in an attempt to stop the sale by tendering cash to liquidate the mortgage debt (*Waring* v. *London & Manchester Assurance Co. Ltd.* [1935] 1 Ch. 310).

Search for Subsequent Mortgages

Where the bank is fortunate enough to realise from the security more than is required to repay the total lent, with interest and costs to date, the surplus cannot be credited to the customer's account or otherwise paid over to him unless and until the bank can be satisfied that there are no second or subsequent mortgages outstanding. Normally the bank will have received direct notice of any such mortgages and vivid warnings will appear in all the security records, but *a search* nevertheless *always has to be made in the Land Charges Register* (and at Companies' House in the case of a limited company mortgagor) *in case later mortgages have been registered but not advised direct to the bank.* Registration here is equivalent to notice to the bank and it dare not release any surplus proceeds of sale until the position has been verified. Any surplus has always to be paid to the second mortgagee, for whom it is held in trust by the bank.

Appointment of a Receiver

The next remedy of practical value to a bank as mortgagee is the power to appoint a receiver of the income of the mortgaged property. This course is helpful where the building is let and it is impracticable to sell it in current conditions, but some attempt has to be made to fund the interest accruing on the account and to force some reductions. Occasionally, it is a useful temporary expedient to collect the income pending vacant possession or an improvement in the value of properties. Where the income from tenants is appreciable in relation to the debt, this course is well worthwhile, but it rarely presents a satisfactory means of recovering the entire debt because of the time required to accumulate sufficient from income to achieve this purpose.

The statutory power to appoint a receiver is available to every legal mortgagee under Section 101 (1) of the Law of Property Act, 1925, but special provisions are normally introduced into the standard mortgage forms of banks. The power arises as soon as the mortgage debt becomes due, but it cannot be exercised until one of the three events which enable a mortgagee to exercise his power of sale has happened. It follows that when a bank wishes to appoint a receiver it has to demand repayment and await the period stated in the mortgage in much the same way as it would start to exercise its power of sale. Meantime, the receiver has to be selected from the professional agents available in the area convenient to the property. This could be the branch manager of the bank, but it is more usual to employ an estate agent or qualified accountant expert in such matters.

The appointment of the receiver is effected by a simple document reciting the details of the mortgage and stating that, consequent upon the default of the mortgagor, the named party has been authorised to act as receiver. The advantage from the bank standpoint is that the receiver is deemed to be the agent of the mortgagor who is solely responsible for his acts. The appointment can be under hand (Section 109 (1) Law of Property Act, 1925) but it is usually executed by a bank under seal. In either event, the document is stamped fifty pence.

Armed with his appointment, the receiver will contact the tenants and arrange with them in future to pay all rents direct to him. Although not empowered to grant leases without the sanction of the court (unless expressly authorised by the mortgagee) he has power to recover the income of the property by action or distress or otherwise, and to give effectual receipts.

By virtue of Section 109 (8) of the Law of Property Act, 1925, a receiver is bound to apply any money received by him in the following order:—

1. In discharge of rents, taxes, rates and outgoings.

2. In keeping down any payments which rank before the mortgage. For example, interest on prior charges.

3. In paying his own commission, fire and other insurances, and the cost of repairs.

   According to Section 109 (6) of the Law of Property Act, 1925, a receiver is entitled to retain for his remuneration and in satisfaction of all costs, charges and expenses a commission at such rate, not exceeding five per cent. on the gross amount of all money received, as is specified in his appointment. If no rate is set down the receiver can charge five per cent. on the gross amount collected or apply to the court to settle the rate. In many cases when the costs of collection of the rents is high this standard rate is insufficient to cover the actual expenses of the receiver and the work is unattractive to the expert who does not expect to operate at a loss. It is possible to overcome this difficulty by fixing in the appointment a commission of five per cent. per annum, *plus* all costs and expenses properly incurred. It is a point which has to be considered, particularly where there are a large number of small rentals from properties which require close management.

   So far nothing has been applied to the bank, and before appointing any receiver it is clearly essential to estimate all the above outgoings and to compare them with the gross rent roll to decide what surplus is likely to be available for the debt. If it is negligible, it may not be worthwhile troubling to appoint a receiver.

4. In payment of the mortgage interest. It is helpful if this can be covered out of the net income and is often the main purpose of appointing a receiver.

5. In reduction or discharge of the principal sum owing if so directed by the mortgagee. Needless to say, the bank will ensure that the appropriate direction is given, usually in the appointment.

Foreclosure

An equitable mortgagee, as well as a legal mortgagee, may apply to the court for an order for foreclosure, whereby the mortgagee acquires the land freed from the mortgagor's equity of redemption. The property is taken subject to any prior charges but free from any subsequent charges. A mortgagee who obtains such an order can then sell the property and retain all the proceeds which may be realised regardless of any surplus over the mortgage debt. As this remedy is seldom, if ever, used by the practical banker there is no point in outlining the legal procedure here.

Entering into Possession

Technically, the bank has a lease for the mortgage term and may take possession at any time, even if the mortgagor has not made default. However, it is inconceivable that the remedy would ever be pursued in these circumstances, or if pursued, that the bank would be successful. The situation where the bank as mortgagee wishes to enter into possession of a dwelling-house in order to sell with vacant possession has already been discussed, also the provisions of Section 36 of the Administration of Justice Act, 1970. It is possible that a banker may wish to enter into possession to receive income, but in practice he would not wish to become a mortgagee in possession himself because as such he is liable to account to the mortgagor not only for the actual income derived from the property, but also for what might have been obtained with greater care (*White* v. *City of London Brewery Co.* (1889) 42 Ch. D. 237). Hence a receiver will normally be appointed to collect rents and any other items of income and he does so as agent of the mortgagor.

There is one further case which is of passing interest, namely, *Alliance Building Society* v. *Yap* (1962) 1 W.L.R. 557. The Society was legal mortgagee of a property charged by the defendants and another, but when possession was sought only the former could be found. It was held that in such circumstances it was sufficient to effect service only upon the person in possession.

Death of Mortgagor

A complication arising from the death of a mortgagor was the background to *Barclays Bank Ltd.*, v. *Kiley* [1961] 1 W.L.R. 1050, and the decision is worth noting. The facts were these. In 1948, Mr. Lewis, a customer of Barclays Bank, mortgaged certain real property to that Bank as a lender to him under a form of charge which included these clauses:

'I agree as follows: (1) A demand for payment or any other demand under this security may be made by any manager or officer of the bank by letter sent by post addressed to me at my address as given in this security or at my last known place of business or abode and every demand so made shall be deemed to have been made on the day such letter was posted.

(2) . . . the power of leasing or agreeing to let . . . conferred by s. 99 and s. 100 of the Law of Property Act, 1925 shall not be exercised without the previous consent in writing of the bank.

(3) Section 103 of the said Act shall not apply to this security but the statutory power of sale shall as between the bank and a purchaser from the bank be exercisable at any time after the execution of this security provided that the bank shall not exercise the said power of sale until payment of the money hereby secured has been demanded and I have made default for one month in paying the same but this proviso is for my protection only and shall not affect a purchaser or put him upon inquiry whether such default has been made.

(4) The statutory power to appoint a receiver may be exercised at any time after payment of the moneys hereby secured has been demanded and I have made default in paying the same. . . .

(12) In this charge where the context so requires or admits references to me shall include my executors or administrators and assigns and successors in title and references to the bank shall include their assigns'.

In 1951 Mr. Lewis purported to grant a sub-tenancy of part of the property—without the Bank's consent—and in 1959 he died. There was no knowledge of a will and no one applied for letters of administration.

The Bank naturally wished to enforce its rights over the security and the problem arose as to how to demand repayment of the borrowing in order to cover the requirements of the charge. To this end a letter was addressed to 'Maurice Lewis Esq., 70 Colvestone Crescent, E.8' some six months after his death in these terms:

'Dear Sir,

We now make demand upon you for payment forthwith of the full amount of your liability to the bank as shown below: (The indebtedness was set out). Failing your immediate compliance the bank will be free to pursue its remedies against the property 70 Colvestone Crescent, E.8, charged as security'.

Not unnaturally there was no reply and a few weeks later the bank appointed a receiver of the rents of the property.

In July 1960 an originating summons was taken out under which the Bank asked for delivery of possession of the property.

Pennycuick, J., held:

(a) that the letter was a good demand in that there was nothing in clause (1) of the charge form which restricted its operation to the life time of Mr. Lewis;

(b) that the word 'include' in the first part of clause (12) was clearly a term of extension, but nothing in this clause could limit the operation of clause (1) so that a demand made under the latter was valid;

(c) that in consequence, possession of the property should be given in furtherance of the Bank's rightful powers.

EQUITABLE MORTGAGE

As already explained in Chapter XIX, a bank with an equitable mortgage under hand cannot exercise any remedies without resort to the courts, assuming that the mortgagor cannot be prevailed upon to implement his undertaking to execute a legal mortgage. An application has, therefore, to be made to the Court for an order to sell, or for an order for foreclosure and sale or for the appointment of a receiver. It is a matter for the branch solicitor and calls for patience on the part of the bank which has to pay for its failure at the outset to obtain a legal mortgage.

On the other hand, an equitable mortgage under seal being a deed within Section 101 of the Law of Property Act, 1925, enables a banker to appoint a receiver or to exercise its power of sale in the same way as a legal mortgagee. The difficulty is that a legal estate cannot be conveyed to a purchaser because the bank merely has an equitable interest. This weakness is usually overcome by inserting an irrevocable power of attorney in the mortgage, whereby the bank sells as the attorney of the mortgagor. This irrevocable power will prevail despite the death or bankruptcy of the mortgagor (Section 126 (1) Law of Property Act, 1925), but the banker in practice may prefer not to rely upon it in such events. An alternative method to the power of attorney clause is to insert a declaration of trust in the mortgage whereby the mortgagor acknowledges that he holds the property in trust for the bank which is empowered to remove him from the office of trustee and to appoint someone else in his stead. A deed can then be executed appointing the bank manager or a Head Office official as the new trustee which will enable him to convey the legal estate to a purchaser. These legal circumlocutions overcome the failure of the equitable mortgagee to co-operate with the bank when trouble arises, but a legal mortgage provides a much cleaner way to the required remedies.

Part Five: Land (continued)

Chapter XXIV Registered Land

INTRODUCTORY—SCOPE OF LAND REGISTRY

For some centuries past the traditional way in which an owner transferred his land to some one else was by delivering to the new owner a bundle of deeds together with a document, usually described as a conveyance, by which the land was stated as passing from the old owner to the new owner. This document, like others in the bundle, was under the seal of the person transferring his property; that is to say, it indicated not only that he had signed it, but that he had sealed it and delivered it as his deed. The other documents recounted the earlier transactions by which the property had changed ownership. These were usually the result of a sale but sometimes the effect of an inheritance, gift or some other arrangement for changing the ownership of the land. Where part of the land had been transferred and the documents passed to the new owner, the purchaser of the remainder of the land was told where the earlier documents could be examined. *This very broad description outlines the basis upon which most of the land in this country is still transferred;* with the transfer of the land there also passes, of course, the buildings that may be standing on it.

THE BENEFITS OF REGISTERED LAND

It requires little thought to appreciate the benefit to all concerned of being able to deal with a certificate of title rather than a collection of documents needing expert investigation and often numerous enquiries to avoid the possibility of unknown persons later establishing an interest in the land. A system is being set up under which the whole country will consist of land of which the title is registered with a central authority. Such a title is then virtually state guaranteed, eliminating the risk, which occasionally is not discovered by the most careful examination, of loss through deeds having been forged. The central authority, the Land Registry, which is a Government Department, keeps a record of the ownership of the land and issues a certificate of title to the freeholder or leaseholder as the case may be. It is to be emphasised that the registration of title to land is quite a different matter from the registration of certain dealings that are essential to the enforceability of the rights of those involved. For example, some dealings in land in Yorkshire have to be recorded at the Registry in the East Riding and, as is well known, a mortgage by a company of land must be registered at the Register of Joint Stock Companies if it is to withstand the challenge of a liquidator or of a creditor. It is true that once the title to land has become registered any dealings with that land have to be recorded at the Land Registry (in addition in the case of company mortgages to registration at the Register of Joint Stock Companies), but nevertheless there is the basic distinction that in the one case the *title* to the land is registered whereas in the other case only particular types of *transactions* have to be registered.

HISTORY

Registration of title to land in various forms was known in continental countries generations before it was introduced into English law and, as might be expected, was adopted in the dominions and other areas of comparatively recent development. The first two enactments, the Land Transfer Acts of 1862 and 1875, left the option of registration with the land owners, but the opportunity was taken infrequently, partly through the initial costs and partly through the conservatism of those involved or of their legal advisers. In 1897 the Land Transfer Act of that year enabled County authorities to seek an Order in Council making registration of title within their boundaries compulsory. In 1925 the Land Registration Act went further and provided that Registration areas could be designated by an Order in Council despite the objection of the County authority, but the Land Registration Act 1966 entrusted the future extension of compulsory registration to the central Government. Under the Act of 1897 the County of London, established in 1889, was selected as the first area of compulsory registration and by 1903 the whole of the area had been put on that basis.

In recent years many other areas have been added and district land registry offices are now maintained at Harrow, Tunbridge Wells, Lytham St. Annes, Nottingham, Gloucester, Stevenage, Durham, Croydon and Plymouth in addition to H. M. Land Registry at Lincoln's Inn Fields, London.

COMPULSORY AREAS OF REGISTRATION

That land is in a compulsory area does not mean that it will be on the register. To attempt suddenly to change all land in a particular locality from having evidence of title deduced from a bundle of deeds to having it provided by a simple certificate was an obviously impossible task. Not only does the first registration of a title necessitate an investigation into the existing title of a more exhaustive nature than most purchasers' solicitors would be under a duty to do, but the boundaries have to be inspected and mapped. In some cases there may be no existing boundaries and in other instances ownership may be divided or about to be divided in which event the Registry has found it necessary to insist upon the erection of substantial posts about four to five feet high at reasonable distances apart; of course a hedge or a ditch is quite sufficient. Whilst it has been open to owners during almost the past hundred years to have the title to their land registered, in most instances they have done so only under compulsion. This is brought about by providing that in compulsory areas *all land sold* or out of which a lease of forty years or more is granted *shall be registered;* registration must also be effected when a lease with more than forty years outstanding is sold or if the freehold title is already registered and any lease of over 21 years is created. In this way the greater part of the land in a compulsory area will gradually have its title registered. This is enforced by Section 123 of the Land Registration Act, 1925,

193

N

which states that every such transfer of land in a compulsory area which is *not* the subject of an application for registration within two months of the transaction shall be void. The harshness of this provision is relieved in several ways: if the court is satisfied that there was sufficient cause or excuse for the omission, a later application for registration may be made; the failure to register probably means that the former owner who retains the legal title cannot use the land for his own benefit. Yet, understandably, the law is effective. No purchaser in a compulsory area will accept a title that he cannot force a third party to take when the land is sold again. If, as is so often the case, property is being bought with the assistance of a mortgagee, that mortgagee will insist upon registration of title.

VOLUNTARY REGISTRATION

Since 13 January 1967, by virtue of the Land Registration Act 1966, there has been a temporary suspension of first registration in non-compulsory areas except for such classes of application as are specified from time to time by H.M. Land Registry. At present, the only voluntary applications that will be entertained by the District Land Registries are those which relate to:

(1) Grants of new leases or rent charges out of existing registered titles in non-compulsory areas where the legal estate is to vest in the lessee or rent charge owner.

(2) Properties in respect of which the title deeds were damaged or destroyed by enemy action during the Second World War or through some national calamity such as extensive flooding.

(3) Properties in respect of which the entire set of title deeds has been lost by the owner's solicitors, or destroyed whilst in their custody.

(4) Certain building estates. In this instance voluntary registration is allowed on applications which fulfil certain conditions which are laid down.

(5) Land for housing which local authorities and development corporations intend to sell as freehold to individual purchasers, or to lease for 90 years or more to individual lessees. Land which local authorities intend to sell to developers for the building of dwellings for sale or lease is also included. Although this may at first sight appear to be a retrograde step the provisions of the Act are so designed to allow the Land Registry to speed up the compulsory registration of land in built-up areas.

ADOPTION OF REGISTRATION IN PRACTICE

Long before registration became compulsory in an area it became customary for certain types of landowners to take advantage of the opportunity to register voluntarily. In particular, an estate developer is likely to be attracted to registration. Once he has had his title registered all house purchasers can be given a certificate based upon the title established for the main plot, with a consequent saving of time and expense. Many estate developers in 'voluntary' areas at present pursue such a course. From the areas in which compulsory registration has been introduced it may be seen that urban neighbourhoods are regarded as lending themselves to the adoption of the system more easily than rural districts. The problem of defining boundaries is obviously much less troublesome in a town where land is dear and jealously guarded than in the countryside where its value is agricultural only. The occupation and ownership of fields is sometimes even 'understood' by description in a community to whom the technicalities of business are an anathema, rather than 'defined' as for a calculating entrepreneur.

The introduction of the system and its compulsory extension has in the past encountered opposition from local solicitors. Sometimes this reaction has found support among their clients who have been discouraged by the prospect of paying fees on first registration and adding to the costs that would in any event be incurred on the sale of property. It cannot be denied that conveyancing was and still is an art. To define exactly and elegantly what rights are to pass from one person to another is as much a task demanding experience and skill as designing a building. This ability among lawyers is still a basic necessity but it would not seem to justify the retention of a system involving the examination every time property changes hands of the history of earlier transactions, which is eliminated where a title is once registered. The conservatism sometimes associated with the law was manifest at the time of the introduction of the Birkenhead reforming legislation in 1925. There were protests regarding the seemingly ruthless discarding of old forms and methods, and local protests against the prospect of an area becoming subject to compulsory registration were not uncommon until a few years ago. For better or for worse—it is suggested for better—the change is now fairly generally accepted.

INSPECTION OF REGISTERS

Not unexpectedly the right to search the Register, apart from provisions in favour of Government Departments and Local Authorities, needs the permission of the owner of the land. An owner may either give a specific authorisation to a third party to inspect the Register so that the owner's interest in property may be seen at a glance or may request an official search. This document emanating from the Registry affords also confirmation to the third party that the owner is interested in the particular land. The forward-looking attitude of the legislators can be seen by the provision in the Rules for searches to be obtained by telephone or telegram. As we shall see, there is a Register giving particulars of the land and another giving an indication of the proprietor. Provision is made for persons having an incidental interest in land to inspect the 'Property' Register, as distinct from the 'Proprietorship' Register, without the permission of the owner if he is given three days notice and the Registrar considers the circumstances appropriate, but if the owner objects or the Registrar thinks the circumstances inappropriate an applicant can seek the decision of the Court.

TYPES OF REGISTER AND OF TITLE

There are three Registers that will be seen upon inspection and which are reflected on the Land Certificate which is a copy of the entries on the Registers.

(i) *The Property Register.*—This describes the land giving an indication of the Map reference and the title number.

(ii) *The Proprietorship Register.*—This shows the kind of title (outlined below) with the name and address of the owner and the price paid when purchased. Sometimes special entries appear regarding the rights of more than one owner.

(iii) *The Charges Register.*—Here are found particulars of the rights of mortgagees and of persons in whose favour covenants in respect of the land have been granted.

TYPES OF TITLE IN REGISTERED LAND

There are four types of title that may be registered—

(i) *Absolute Title.*—This is where the owner has established that he is entitled to an estate in fee simple in freehold property. It is where he owns freehold land subject only to any interests shown in the Charges Register and to overriding and minor interests. Overriding interests are a miscellaneous collection of rights which are discoverable elsewhere or by inspection of the site. They include easements, such as rights of way, interest and rights protected by registration in the Local Land Charges Registry. Minor interests include trust interests.

(ii) *Good Leasehold Title.*—This is the equivalent for a leasehold of the absolute title for a freehold and is subject, as are most leases, to there being a right of the lessor to grant the lease. Only where the freehold is registered with absolute title is it possible for lessee to obtain an absolute title.

(iii) *Possessory Title.*—This title is subject to the rights of anyone interested in the property at the time of its registration. The practical risk is obvious, but there is the advantage that after ten years in the case of leasehold and fifteen years in the case of a freehold an owner still in possession will be able to obtain a good leasehold or absolute freehold title, as the case may be, unless the Registrar exercises, as he rarely does, his right to postpone such a conversion of title.

(iv) *Qualified Title.*—This is unusual in practice and is granted where a property is an absolute freehold or a good leasehold subject only to the particular qualifications mentioned.

RIGHTS OF REGISTERED TITLE HOLDER

'Land Registration and State Guaranteed Title' is the name given to an official publication describing the system. In practice, if there is an error by the Land Registry and the registered title holder is found to have no rights or less rights than shown on the Register, there is a Fund out of which persons who suffer are entitled to be compensated. This may arise not only when there has to be a rectification of the Register, but where there is an error in an official search or where a document is lost at the Registry.

The registration of land is officially compared with the registration of shares in a company. In both instances, as the publication indicates, the owner is entitled to be entered in the Register with a distinctive number and that entry rather than the certificate is the determining factor. Incorrect issue of a certificate may in both instances give rise to compensation. In neither register will a notice of trust be recorded and in each case a change in ownership is effected by submission of documents of transfer. One might comment, however, that a register of shareholders is notoriously open to inspection by all and sundry, whereas the Land Registry searches must usually be authorised, as noted above, by the proprietor.

HOW A BANK IS AFFECTED BY THE REGISTRATION OF LAND

It is well to pause and consider the manner in which a bank is affected by the introduction of this system which is evidently likely eventually to encompass the whole of the country. The chief practical change is that instead of receiving the customer's deeds a bank is handed a certificate of title. Whether or not he intends advancing against the property, much less trouble is involved in dealing with a certificate than a packet of deeds which can sometimes be very large. Less strong-room space is occupied and there is less chance of a document being mislaid. The number of documents accompanying a land certificate will be small but where title to a property is by deed the frequently numerous documents have to be scheduled naming dates and parties.

While some banks have occasionally relied upon their own examination of the title where deeds were taken as security and still do so, most send them to solicitors for a report on title. This may take some time, since solicitors' offices are always busy and the examination of title is regarded very often as one of the least urgent matters; it also involves the customer in expense, although the charge is only a modest one. With a land certificate no examination by solicitors is required. It may be that the entries, especially those showing the interest of joint owners or showing charges, need legal advice before their import is fully appreciated, but this will be infrequent. Again, where there is a land certificate the boundaries of the property will be defined with much greater certainty than where the description is to be discovered in a conveyance. With a conveyance there will sometimes be a map, but very often the boundaries will have to be elucidated from measurements described in a conveyance; and, if there is a map, it will be of less clarity and certainty than the copy of the Land Registry map to be found with the land certificate. In particular, where parts of a property have been sold off slowly over a number of years, as happens so often when taxation or death duties lead to the destruction of a country estate for building, the tracing of the relative area where title is by deed will sometimes even necessitate the assistance of a surveyor, whereas with a land certificate such a problem is eliminated formally. There is virtually no possibility of forgery of a land certificate but the forgery of deeds, although rare, is by no means unprecedented. For all these reasons, registered title is the more attractive for a lending bank. As will be seen later, this ease of handling and speed of unprofessional examination is not in any way discounted by the manner in which the bank may become a mortgagee, the mere possession of the land certificate being at least as strong a weapon as the possession of deeds.

SUMMARY

It may be convenient to note briefly the conclusions drawn:
   (i) Registration of title is being gradually applied to the whole country, a land certificate replacing deeds.
   (ii) In all areas an owner may have his title registered if he wishes, subject to the limitations imposed by the Land Registration Act, 1966.
   (iii) In areas where registration is compulsory this has to be effected usually only when the property is next sold.
   (iv) Registration is of *title;* although further dealings of many kinds have to be registered, the land is still subject to all the normal types of transaction such as leasing and mortgaging.
   (v) Inspection of the Register needs the owner's consent.
   (vi) There are four types of title; absolute; good leasehold; possessory; and qualified.
   (vii) The title is state guaranteed.

Chapter XXV Registered Land—*continued*

THE CONTENTS OF THE LAND CERTIFICATE— METHODS OF OBTAINING MORTGAGE

The fact that the title to land is registered makes no difference to the normal opening phases when land is offered to a banker as security. It has to be valued and the extent and adequacy of the current fire insurance has to be ascertained, but thereafter the ways part and the banker is involved in features which apply only to registered land. Instead of the usual parcel of deeds, the potential mortgagor produces a land certificate to the bank and a start can conveniently be made from this stage.

THE LAND CERTIFICATE

The certificate of title issued by H.M. Land Registry to the registered proprietor is called a land certificate and comprises an official certificate of title with a copy of the register inserted inside, including a copy of the official plan identifying the land. It has to be studied closely by the banker, and as it may not have been written up from the register for sometime it may be prudent to send it to the registry to be brought up to date, a service which is provided free from cost. Each land certificate bears the date on which it was last examined at the registry and written up to date to include all the entries recorded in the register. The position can thus be seen at a glance.

In the normal way no deeds will accompany the land certificate. At the time when the title is registered, all the deeds relating thereto are suitably marked with the registry stamp and returned to the proprietor for his safe keeping. Exceptions to this general rule will be explained below. The deeds should nevertheless be preserved by the proprietor (often by depositing them in safe custody in a sealed envelope with a bank) in case they contain records of matters known as 'overruling interests' which do not appear on the register of title and cannot, therefore, be found in the land certificate.

Where a land certificate has been destroyed or lost, application can be made to the Registrar for a new one. In the meantime, no dealing in the land can be undertaken which requires the production of the land certificate, but application for an office copy of the register and of the plan can be made on Form A44. Such copies are admissible in evidence in place of the land certificate. To obtain a new land certificate, application has to be made in writing supported by a statutory declaration by a responsible person who is in a position to speak for the facts describing in detail all the facts about the loss and the efforts made to find the certificate and confirming that it has not been deposited or dealt with in any way except as disclosed in the register. At the discretion of the Registrar, he may call upon the applicant to execute an indemnity to cover the Land Registrar and the trustees of the Land Registry Insurance Fund against any loss which they may sustain by reason of issuing a fresh certificate. Prudence demands that the greatest care should always be exercised in the custody of any land certificate and the wise owner deposits it in safe custody with his or her bankers.

The contents of a land certificate are relatively simple to read and understand and there is no need to seek the assistance of a solicitor in the straightforward cases. Being a facsimile of the entries in the register, it is divided into three parts:—

(*a*) The *Property Register,*
(*b*) the *Proprietorship Register,* and
(*c*) the *Charges Register,*
each of which will now repay close study.

(*a*) *The Property Register*

The Property Register gives a brief description of the land and estate comprised in the title, referring to the general map or to the filed plan of the land. It will disclose the date of first registration and suffice to enable the banker to determine the land for valuation purposes. Where appropriate, notes may appear relating to the ownership of mines and minerals or to easements, rights, privileges, etc., for the benefit of the land. If the property is leasehold, short details of the lease will appear, including the term, rent and premium (if any) and a reference to the lessor's title, if it is registered. In short, there is a complete picture to guide the lending banker.

(*b*) *The Proprietorship Register*

This part opens with a statement of the class of title registered and it is most important to note this information. Usually it is an *absolute title* which vests in the registered owner of the full legal estate denoting that the land registry is sufficiently satisfied with the title to guarantee its ownership. Such titles are largely restricted to freehold land, an absolute title to leasehold land being granted only where both the leasehold and the freehold titles have been examined by the registry and it is satisfied that the lessor or freeholder was entitled to grant the lease. An absolute title is subject only to any incumbrances or other entries recorded in the register and to any overriding interests of minor importance wihch are not registrable.

A *good leasehold title* applies only to leaseholds and is the nearest equivalent to an absolute title which a lessee of leasehold land can obtain where the registry is unable to guarantee that the lessor had any right to grant the lease. As Section 44 of the Law of Property Act, 1925, lays down that a purchaser of leasehold land must assume, unless the contrary appears, that the lessor had the legal right to grant the lease, it can be contended that a good leasehold title is for all practical purposes equivalent to an absolute title of leasehold property. It need not, therefore, cause any concern to the lending banker, but the original lease should be deposited with the land certificate.

Where the certificate shows a *possessory title*, the position is a little more complicated because it may be necessary to investigate the title prior to the date of first registration (shown in the certificate, see above) by examining all the relative title deeds. A possessory title does not guarantee that the first proprietor who originally applied for registration is the person fully entitled to the ownership of the property. It does, however, guarantee all subsequent ownership after the first registration, as if it were an absolute title. The length of time of registration is of importance because, with the passage of time, a possessory title becomes legally as good as an absolute title. By the provisions of the Land Registration Act, 1925, possessory titles can automatically be converted into absolute or good leasehold titles after they have been registered fifteen years in the case of freeholds and ten years in the case of leaseholds. Only a relatively small number of possessory titles outstand today, but when confronted with this class of limited title the bank will require, in addition to the land certificate, all the deeds prior to registration so that the title can be investigated by the bank's solicitor in the standard fashion obtaining for unregistered land. In other words, the deeds accompany the certificate until with the passage of time the title can be converted to absolute or good leasehold, as the case may be.

Lastly, there might be a *qualified* title which theoretically can be granted to applicants for an absolute title or good leasehold title where reservations have to be made. Any flaws are then specified in the Register and appear in the land certificate. In effect, there is an absolute title subject to the specified reservations and in practice very few qualified titles are granted. If faced with such a title, the banker would require complete evidence of title just as though the land was not registered.

Next the Proprietorship Register will quote the name, address and description of the registered proprietor which should be the same as that of the customer or third party who has undertaken to charge the land to the bank as security. Any differences call for enquiry and the charge form can be prepared from the stated details. There will follow particulars of the date when the proprietor was registered and the price paid for the land. Particulars of any restrictions or inhibitions affecting the power of the proprietor to deal with the land will then be set forth, followed by any cautions registered against the title which may entail notice to third parties of any dealing by the bank with the land. Any doubts concerning entries under the last two mentioned headings can always be raised with the branch solicitor.

(c) The Charges Register

Lastly, the banker studies the Charges Register which gives particulars of the mortgages, charges, restrictive covenants and other incumbrances on the title. The importance of this section to the banker needs no emphasis, but it must not be forgotten that the information may not be up to date. There may be charges on the register which were recorded after the date when the certificate was last written up. The next step, therefore, is to ensure that there are no charges registered which affect the bank's position.

SEARCHES

The Land Registry in its six sections is maintained on a card-index system with the three divisons of the register for each particular property normally listed on one card. The sections are not open to the public and cannot, therefore, be inspected by a bank representative without the express consent of the owner of the registered land under consideration. In the ordinary course, the register may be examined only by the registered proprietors of the land or of a charge thereon and their duly authorised agents.

Three alternative courses are available to a banker anxious to know the current position of the register in relation to any parcel of land. The land certificate can be sent to the Registry to be written up to date. It will then be examined, without charge, and if there are any items in the register which do not appear in the certificate the necessary entries will be made to bring the certificate up to date. When it is returned to the banker, the certificate will be a facsimile of the register and the date of examination endorsed thereon. This is a simple and cheap method but suffers from the danger that, after the return of the certificate, a charge might be registered unbeknown to the bank before its own charge had been completed. As priority depends upon the date of entry on the register (see later), it is clearly imperative to remove this risk. There is always a delay whilst the mortgagor signs the bank's charge and another charge can be registered in the interim. It is pointless to accept this risk when a much safer method is available. A personal search can be made with the written consent of the proprietor of the land offered as security, but it costs twenty five pence and any errors are the responsibility of the searcher. Prior to 1930 it was the usual practice to make personal searches, but they are now unnecessary and it is usual to obtain an official search certificate.

The Land Registration Rules, 1930, and 1936, introduced an official search form which saves the time and expense of attending at the Registry to make a personal search. The bank solicitor completes Form 94, applying for a search against the land described therein and sends it to the registry with the written authority of the mortgagor. A search certificate is then issued free of charge to the bank as an intending chargee. If any adverse entries appear, an office copy of them will be issued. Apart from the obvious advantage that any errors are the responsibility of the Registry, the bank has fourteen days in which to complete and register its charge and it will not be affected by any adverse entries made during these days of grace, unless they arise from a mortgage caution or a priority notice, both of which will be explained later. This period of grace is long enough to enable the bank, having found the register clear for its purpose, to obtain the charge from the mortgagor and to complete all other preliminaries to ensure priority. Unlike the confusion with unregistered land (see Chapter XXI) there is no doubt that this period of grace fully protects the banker lending by way of fluctuating overdraft.

Official search certificates are usually posted within two days if the application filed on Form 94 is in order. Urgent searches can, however, be made by telegram enquiring whether any entry has been made in the register since the stated date when the land certificate was last made to correspond with the register. The reply to any telegraphic application naturally has to be prepaid. A telephonic application may also be made by the proprietor or solicitor, but written confirmation has to follow on the same day. In this case the answer 'Yes' or 'No' will be given over the telephone and confirmed in writing. Urgent searches (which are rarely necessary) are subject to a fee of not less than £2 charged by the registry.

201

Anyone proposing to obtain a charge over registered land can file a *priority notice* with the Registry on Form 18, which should be accompanied by the land certificate. If the charge is then delivered for registration within fourteen days of the notice, it will have priority over any charge delivered for registration in the interim. In other words, the priority notice remains in force for fourteen days. The fee payable is one pound and at the end of the fortnight the priority notice is void unless it is renewed. As the same period of priority can now be obtained by means of an official search on Form 94, priority notices against dealings are very seldom used nowadays.

Searches outside the Land Registry are necessary only where either the registered land is to be charged by a limited company, when a search has also to be made at Companies House, or, in those cases where a search is prudent, in the local charges registers. Any land in Yorkshire with a registered title is quite beyond the Yorkshire deeds registers and no searches need be made in them. Few problems accordingly arise about searching when taking registered land as security. An official search certificate is obtained through the branch solicitor and the bank then has fourteen days in which to perfect its charge.

METHODS OF CHARGING REGISTERED LAND

The banker may take a legal mortgage or an equitable mortgage of registered land and in very much the same way as such charges are taken over unregistered land. Generally speaking, the law of mortgages of registered land is basically the same as that relating to unregistered land, subject to the formalities required by the Registrar. No special forms of mortgage are, therefore, required and the same printed charge can be used for both registered and unregistered land. It is, however, essential to identify the registered land by reference to the title number, thereby obviating any need to refer to other documents in order to determine the land in question. The standard charge supplied by the Land Registry (Forms 45 and 47) is of little use to a bank because it does not contain all the clauses essential to make it a continuing security and does not embrace all the other covenants by the borrower which are standard in bank mortgages. Some banks use a special mortgage form for registered land, but the provisions are virtually the same as those already discussed fully under unregistered land. Section 25 (2) of the Land Registration Act, 1925, permits any mortgage by deed to be in any form, providing that it describes the registered land by reference to the register or in any other manner sufficient to enable the Registrar to identify the land without reference to any other document. Two or more titles may be charged in the same mortgage.

In practice, three methods of charge can be distinguished:—
1. A *complete legal mortgage*, duly registered at the Land Registry.
2. An *equitable charge*, but *with notice given of the deposit of the land certificate.*
3. An *equitable charge* by mere deposit of the land certificate.

1. *Legal Mortgage—Registered*

To obtain full protection the bank must proceed to full registration of its title. When the legal mortgage has been sealed by the mortgagor, it has to be registered within fourteen days of the date of the official search certificate in order to ensure priority. Registration is the final step in the chain discussed so far and is effected by lodging with the Registry the charge, together with a copy thereof, the land certificate and the search certificate. All these documents are usually lodged by post by the solicitor acting for the bank, if it does not elect to do the work itself. The duplicate charge, the land certificate, and the search certificate are impounded by the Registry, which issues a charge certificate to the bank containing stitched within it the original legal mortgage executed by the depositor of the security. The charge certificate then represents the bank security and it is held in the same way as any other mortgage. It is perhaps a little disconcerting to some bankers to have to part with so much evidence in order to perfect the security.

Where mortgages are to be registered in H.M. Land Registry, Land Registry fees are to be calculated by reference to the amount certified by the branch to the appropriate Land Registrar as secured by the mortgage at the date of application for registration. The certificate can be couched in terms such as these:—

'The Chief Land Registrar,

—   Registry.   Date

Dear Sir,

Title No.

We hereby certify that at today's date there is owing upon the security of the mortgage in our favour, enclosed herewith for registration, the principal sum of £x. The appropriate Land Registry fee of £   has therefore been paid/or is enclosed.

Yours faithfully,

The prescribed fees for registration of a charge can be scheduled as follows:

Amount of Charge or Mortgage	Fee
Not exceeding £5,000	£1·30 for every £500 or part of £500.
Exceeding £5,000 but not exceeding £100,000	£13 for the first £5,000 and £1·10 for every £500 or part of £500 over £5,000.
Exceeding £100,000	£222 for the first £100,000 and £0·50 for every £1,000 or part of £1,000 over £100,000 with a maximum fee of £422.

The appropriate fee must accompany all the documents when they are filed by post for registration. A customer borrowing quite temporarily from the bank may well quibble at the costs of registration, but it is for the bank to decide whether this complete charge is essential. The following points regarding payment of land registry fees should be noted:

(i) once the proper fee has been paid to cover an advance, no additional fee is payable in respect of further advances made against the same security.

(ii) no registration fee is payable where the mortgage is sent to the registry with an application for the first registration of the land charged as security.

(iii) the normal negotiation fee is halved when the charge accompanies a transfer for value. This concession may help when a bank is lending to a customer to finance the completion of his purchase of a new house with registered title.

(iv) where no funds have actually been advanced to the customer at the time the bank proceeds to full registration, the minimum scale fee of £1.30 must be paid to the Land Registry.

(v) where the amount advanced is substantially more than the value of the security, or in the case of a second mortgage substantially more than the equity available, the Land Registry may agree to base the fee payable upon the bank's valuation of its security.

According to Section 29 of the Land Registration Act, 1925, registered charges on the same land rank as between themselves according to the order in which they are entered on the register, and not according to the order in which they are created. Thus priority depends, as we have previously seen, primarily upon registration. In addition, Section 30 (1) provides that 'when a registered charge is made for securing further advances, the registrar shall, before making any entry on the register which would prejudicially affect the priority of any further advances thereunder, give to the proprietor of the charge at his registered address notice by registered post of the intended entry, and the proprietor of the charge shall not, in respect of any further advance, be affected by such entry, unless the advance is made after the date when notice ought to have been received in course of post'. This means that the bank obtains prompt notice of any second mortgage and can stop the account to prevent the operation of the Rule in *Clayton's Case* and take other immediate steps to protect its interests. If a bank sustains loss through any failure on the part of the Registry to give such notice, it can recover from the Registry out of a special insurance fund established for the purpose. Where any overdrawn account is transferred from one branch to another, it is clearly desirable to advise the registry to avoid delay in the receipt of such notices. The Registry cannot be held responsible for losses arising through failure to notify changes of address.

The clear cut operation of this system is self-explanatory and a banker can rest back content in the knowledge that, in the absence of notice from the Registry of a second mortgage, it has continued priority of security. Prompt action can always be taken if and when any notice is received. Incidentally, although it is unlikely to concern the bank, where the proprietor of a charge is under an obligation, noted in the register, to make a further advance, a subsequent registered charge takes effect subject to any further advance made pursuant to the obligation (Section 5, Law of Property (Amendment) Act, 1926). This rule is similar to that applying to unregistered land.

It is well to reflect upon the great difference the effect of the registration of a second charge on registered land and the effect of the registration of a second charge at the Land Charges Registry. In the former case, prompt notice is served by the registrar upon the bank, but with unregistered land the bank may continue completely unaware of the second charge, in the absence of direct notice from the second mortgagee or otherwise, and, providing no search is made, advances made after the registration of the second charge, but without notice of it, have priority from the security aspect. They are not subject to the second charge.

To complete the picture, brief reference has to be made to another method of obtaining a legal mortgage over registered land prescribed by Section 106 of the

Land Registration Act, 1925. It is, however, a method which is rarely encountered and it is unlikely to appeal to the practical banker. An ordinary legal mortgage is taken over the registered land and protected by a special form of *caution*, which is filed at the Registry together with the land certificate, the mortgage concerned and a copy thereof. This mortgage caution is then entered in the Proprietorship Register and notice given by the registrar to the proprietor of the land. The copy of the mortgage and the land certificate are retained by the registrar and the original mortgage is returned marked with a suitable note of registration. Precisely the same fees are payable for a mortgage caution as those for registration of a charge and, as no expenses are saved, there is little point in recourse to the method. Nevertheless, it must be remembered that a mortgagee in whose favour a caution has been entered may later call for registration of his mortgage as a charge with priority from the date of the caution.

2. *Equitable charge with notice given of deposit of land certificate*
This half-way house method has long been popular with bankers; whilst avoiding all the expense of a registered charge, it has been regarded as placing them in a position to obtain a registered charge without further reference to the mortgagor. In essence, the mortgagor is called upon to execute a legal mortgage, but it is held unregistered as an equitable charge until circumstances demand, if ever, that it should be converted into a registered charge. Instead of registration, notice of deposit of the land certificate is filed in duplicate, on Form 85A in the same way as an equitable mortgage by simple deposit of the land certificate (see below). The registrar enters this notice on the charges register and returns the duplicate to the bank in the form of an acknowledgement. The entry on the register gives notice of the bank's interest to all who care to look and if any attempt is made to deal with the land which is the subject of the notice the registrar will advise the bank. The registrar is fixed with notice of the deposit of the land certificate, but is in no way concerned with the type of charge held by the bank.

The method of searching can also be simplified. Instead of obtaining an official search certificate by application on Form 94, the land certificate can be sent to the Registry to be written up to date, together with the notice of deposit of the land certificate (Form 85A). It will then be returned, bearing the entry relating to the notice of deposit and a glance will suffice to show whether there are any other entries on the register which affect the bank's position. No advances should, of course, be granted until the land certificate has been returned and the bank can be satisfied that its charge has the desired priority. Inevitably, there are awkward customers who raise objection to the appearance on the certificate of any entry concerning its deposit. If they need the money they should be prepared to meet the bank's reasonable requirements, but in exceptional cases the difficulty can be overcome by sending the certificate to be brought up to date, and immediately upon its return disclosing no detrimental entries, notice of deposit can be lodged without the certificate. It is also possible to make a personal search (accepting the risks of error) and to file notice of deposit afterwards if all is clear, retaining the land certificate throughout at the bank.

Until the case of *Barclays Bank Ltd.* v. *Taylor and another,* The Times, 24 February, 1972, it was considered that there was no need for the bank to take any further steps to perfect its legal mortgage; that although the mortgage was an equitable one, it was in effect a 'quasi legal' mortgage. If the borrower proved to be unsatisfactory, the bank's charge could easily be registered and the bank would then be endowed with all the powers and rights of a legal mortgagee without need for any assistance from the customer. On the other hand, if the borrower created a second charge on the property, prompt notice would be given to the bank by the registrar as soon as the second mortgagee attempted to register his charge, whereupon the bank had fourteen days in which to act. If the bank took no action, the notice of deposit was removed from the register, but in practice the charge would quickly be registered at the borrower's expense to protect the bank's position. In other words, banks have regarded filing notice of deposit of the land certificate as completely protecting their interest as from the date of filing in the same way as if it had been protected by a caution, and have quoted in support of this view the Appeal Court decision in *re White Rose Cottage* (1965) Ch. 940 (1965) 1 All E.R. 11; 108 Sol. Jo. 917. It was maintained that once notice of deposit was placed on the register it was a complete protection against subsequent encumbrancers as they could not claim to act without notice of the bank's mortgage. Further support is to be found in the standard work of reference on Registered Land by Curtis & Ruoff (page 721) and in Rule 239 of the Land Registration Rules, 1935 which states that notice of deposit shall operate as a caution.

In spite of this, a very different view was taken in *Barclays Bank Ltd. v. Taylor*, referred to above. In 1961 Martins Bank (who were subsequently merged with Barclays Bank) granted an advance to their customers Mr. & Mrs. Duxbury, taking as security an equitable mortgage of their house and registering a notice of deposit of the land certificate with themselves under Rule 239 of the Land Registration Rules, 1935. Subsequently Mr. & Mrs. Duxbury executed a legal mortgage in favour of the bank. In 1968 the defendants Mr. & Mrs. Taylor contracted to buy the property and although a transfer was not obtained they entered a caution in respect of the contract. When the bank tried to register its charge Mr. & Mrs. Taylor as cautioners objected and the Chief Land Registrar referred the dispute to the Court. Goulding, J., maintained that a mortgage of registered land could be protected either by registering it as a charge under sections 25 or 26 of the Land Registration Act, 1925, or alternatively by lodging a mortgage caution under section 106. Section 106 (2) of the Land Registration Act, 1925, provided that a mortgage of registered land 'may, if by deed be protected by a caution in a specially prescribed form and in no other way, and if not by a deed, by a caution'. The Judge held that the words 'in no other way' overruled Rule 239 and he considered that the protection that was supposed to be gained by lodging notice of deposit was 'illusory'.

The case is going to appeal and it is to be hoped that the decision will be reversed and the validity of Rule 239 speedily restored. Meanwhile, the banker is always at liberty to proceed to full registration if he considers circumstances warrant it.†

3. *Equitable Mortgage*
A mere equitable mortgage of registered land can be obtained by the simple deposit of the land certificate. Section 66 of the Land Registration Act, 1925, enables the proprietor to create a lien on the registered land by deposit of the land

† Decision reversed on appeal, 24 January 1973: The Times, 31 January 1973.

certificate, which lien is subject to any interest registered at the date of the deposit, but otherwise equivalent to a lien created in the case of unregistered land by the deposit of the documents of title.

Where a bank is content to rely upon an equitable mortgage by the deposit of the certificate with or without a memorandum of deposit, notice of the deposit of the land certificate should be given to the Registrar on Form 85A in duplicate so that the notice may be entered in the charges register. The bank's position is protected subject to the recognised drawbacks of an equitable mortgage with no power of sale without recourse to the court. Searches to ensure that there are no adverse entries are made in the same way as when a legal mortgage form is executed and held without registration, notice being given of the deposit of the land certificate. The certificate is sent to the Registry with the notice on Form 85A to be entered up to date.

There is little point in relying upon this simple method of equitable charge and it is more prudent to prevail upon the depositor to execute a legal mortgage at the outset.

NOTICE OF INTENDED DEPOSIT

Sometimes a customer requires accommodation to finance a purchase of registered land, but he is not in a position to deposit the land certificate because the transfer of the title to him is in course. To overcome this problem, the Land Registration Rules, 1925, provide that the purchaser may notify the registrar of his intention to deposit the land certificate, when issued, with the bank as security for an advance. Such a notice is given on Form 85C, signed by the borrower, and the land certificate will then be issued direct to the bank named as lender. When it is received, there is no need for the bank to give notice of deposit because the original notice of intended deposit remains effective. This method is helpful to bridge the gap when the title to the land is being registered for the first time.

SECOND MORTGAGES

Where it is deemed advisable to grant facilities against a second mortgage of registered land, no land certificate will be available to the bank. The certificate will be held either by the first mortgagee or deposited at the Registry. A search has to be made to ascertain the nature of the outstanding entries and an office copy is obtained upon payment of the fee of 20p. If the first mortgagee is under an obligation to make further advances, it will be disclosed in the register.

The second mortgage can be obtained on the bank's standard legal mortgage form with or without reference to the first mortgage and the charge can then be lodged, in duplicate, at the Registry which will issue a certificate of second charge. Registration should be completed within fourteen days from the date of the search, made on Form 94 in the way described above for first mortgages. Should the bank for some sound reason decide not to register its charge, its position may be protected by lodging a caution at the registry in the manner previously outlined. In any event, notice of the charge should be served upon the first mortgagee asking him to confirm in his acknowledgement the amount outstanding. The procedure follows the basic principles and presents no particular difficulty other than the defects applicable to any second mortgage.

SUB-MORTGAGES

When a customer has already lent money against the security of a registered charge and seeks to borrow from the bank upon the security of such a charge, the same steps have to be taken as those applicable to a sub-mortgage of unregistered land. The property has to be valued and the amount outstanding under the mortgage has to be confirmed. When the sub-charge has been completed, notice has to be given to the original mortgagor requesting him to make all reductions or repayment direct to the bank.

Two types of sub-mortgage can be taken over registered land. Section 36 of the Land Registration Act, 1925, and the Rules allow for sub-charges without prescribing any particular form of charge. A bank can use its standard mortgage detailing the title, number and charge number and describing the property. The charge certificate, plus the bank's sub-charge, are then produced to the Registry and exchanged for a certificate of sub-charge. The fees payable for the registration of a sub-charge are the same as those set out on page 203 for the registration of a mortgage. In this way the bank obtains a *legal sub-mortgage*. By virtue of Section 66 of the Land Registration **Act,** the proprietor of a registered charge can create a lien on the **charge by** depositing the charge certificate, in which event the lien is equivalent to a lien created in the case of unregistered land by the deposit of the original mortgage. Thus an *equitable sub-mortgage* of a registered charge can be taken by giving notice of deposit of the charge certificate to the Registry, in duplicate, on Form 85A. The registrar thereupon enters the **notice** in the charges register and returns the duplicate to the bank by way of acknowledgment. The bank's security then comprises the charge certificate and the registrar's acknowment of the notice of deposits. A legal mortgage will usually be executed by the borrowing customer and held unregistered in case it should ever prove necessary to convert the equitable mortgage into a legal sub-mortgage with its full powers.

Part Five: Land (continued)

Chapter XXVI Registered Land—*continued*

RELEASE OR REALISATION OF THE SECURITY— CHARGES BY LIMITED COMPANIES

RELEASE OF SECURITY

When the customer repays the advance, it is prudent in practice to retain the security undisturbed so that it is available without further expense should overdraft facilities ever be required in the future. Where the borrower, nevertheless, insists upon the release of the security, the procedure depends upon the type of charge held by the bank.

In the case of a *Registered Charge*, Form 53 (Discharge of Registered Charge) has to be completed by the bank as mortgagee and forwarded with the charge certificate to the Land Registry. Provided there is no other charge registered, the land certificate which was held by the Registry will be returned to the owner of the land upon appropriate request. No fee is payable to the Registry for the discharge of a registered charge. Sometimes the customer has sold the property charged to the bank and Form 55 can then be used combining a discharge by the bank with a form of transfer by the mortgagor to the purchaser. In this way the buyer obtains a title freed from the charge.

Where the security comprises the deposit of the land certificate with due notice of its deposit to the Registry, it is merely necessary to withdraw the notice. This is usually accomplished by using the form on the reverse side of the registrar's acknowledgment of the notice of deposit. The withdrawal can be signed by the branch manager and again no fee is payable to the Registry. The land certificate has to be sent forward with the application and it will be returned in due course with the notice of deposit deleted from the charges section.

Partial releases of security occasionally occur, particularly where a builder customer is developing an estate which is charged to the bank as security for the building finance. As each house is completed and sold off, the purchaser expects to receive a registered title with a land certificate free from any charge. When a registered charge is held, a partial release can be obtained by using Form 53 and introducing words which restrict the portion to be released to that edged in red on the attached plan. In other words, the area to be released out of the entire charge is clearly described. With an equitable charge, upon the sale of a part of the land,

209

O

it is sufficient to write to the Registry withdrawing the bank's charge over the plot or area described, enclosing the land certificate for amendment and return. Where there are likely to be frequent releases as an estate is developed, the registrar can be asked to retain the land certificate so that subsequent releases can be marked off as advices are sent by the bank.

In practice, a legal mortgage is often taken from the customer when the land certificate is deposited, but held unregistered, the bank relying on notice of deposit of the certificate (see page 205). Upon withdrawal of the notice of deposit, the bank is left with a mortgage which is no longer required and is quite redundant as far as the proprietor's title is concerned. It can be cancelled or destroyed with impunity, but occasionally a solicitor acting for the customer will call for a release to be executed on the mortgage, and this can be done as a matter of courtesy.

To complete the picture, in the unlikely event of the bank protecting its unregistered legal mortgage with a mortgage caution, it can be withdrawn by making application on Form 71, which has to be made by the bank's solicitor or sealed by the bank.

REALISATION OF SECURITY

When the bank has no alternative but to sell the land in order to recover the debt, it is endowed with the same rights and remedies as those which accrue to a mortgagee of unregistered land by the Law of Property Act. With a registered charge, the bank as legal mortgagee may sell, foreclose, appoint a receiver or enter into possession as circumstances may demand. In short, it can exercise all the powers conferred by law on the owner of a legal mortgage. These statutory powers and those of an equitable mortgagee were discussed fully in Chapter XIX, with suitable guidance on the practical aspects of realisation in Chapter XXIII, and there is no need to review them here because all the same features apply equally to registered land. The actual method of completing the sale is all that need be discussed.

It is nevertheless of interest to mention that, by virtue of Section 28 of the Land Registration Act, 1925, the holder of a registered charge has the benefit of the following three implied covenants by the morgtagor:—

1. To pay the principal and interest at the agreed time and rate.
2. In the event of non-payment of the principal amount or any part thereof at the agreed time, to pay interest half-yearly at the agreed rate on the principal sum outstanding.
3. With leasehold titles, to pay the rent and perform the covenants of the lease, keeping the lender indemnified for failure to pay or to perform.

In practice, all the necessary covenants required from the mortgagor are embodied in the mortgages and no reliance is placed upon these implied covenants, which do not apply to unregistered land. The difference at law is that, whereas the legal mortgagee of unregistered land sues the borrower on his express covenant to repay, the holder of a registered charge may sue on an implied covenant to repay.

When the bank with a registered charge succeeds in selling the property, the title is transferred by completing Form 31, the standard form of transfer on sale issued by the Registry amended to apply to a sale by the holder of a registered charge. When this transfer is registered the charge is cancelled, but by special application in writing to the Registry it is possible to keep the charge alive where the sale proceeds are insufficient to liquidate the debt and the bank deems it worthwhile to retain the benefit of the implied covenant of the mortgagor to repay. This remote refuge is rarely adopted in practice.

When the bank holds a legal mortgage executed by the mortgagor, but it is held unregistered relying on notice of deposit of the land certificate, the charge has to be registered before a sale can be made. It is, however, a simple matter to forward the land certificate, and the charge, in duplicate, to the Land Registry to obtain a charge certificate, and the value of securing a legal mortgage from the depositor at the outset is patent. In like manner, if the security comprises a legal mortgage protected by a mortgage caution, the charge has to be registered before a sale can be effected. In all these cases registration is essential before proceeding to sell.

It is needless to add that, when the bank is relying entirely upon an equitable mortgage by deposit of the land certificate, with or without a memorandum of deposit, it is in the same position as an equitable mortgagee of unregistered land and has to apply to the Court for an order for sale.

It will be recalled that when selling unregistered land as mortgagee the bank has to search where there are any surplus proceeds to ensure that there are no second or later mortgagees entitled to the balance. With registered land, subsequent mortgagees are equally entitled to any surplus proceeds, but it is not usually necessary to search at the Registry because the registrar will have given direct notice to the bank of the registration of any further charge if the bank's charge is drawn (as it is) to cover further advances.

CHARGES BY LIMITED COMPANIES

Finally, it is well to emphasise the additional steps which are necessary when taking as security registered land belonging to a limited company customer. In whichever way the charge is taken, by registered charge or mere notice of deposit of the land certificate, it has *also* to be registered at Companies' House, in keeping with Section 95 of the Companies Act, 1948. This registration at Companies' House has to be completed first (and within twenty-one days of the creation of the charge) because the certificate of registration has to be produced to the Land Registry. If the certificate is not produced, a note will be made in the register that the charge is subject to the Companies Act. Searches have also be to be made at Companies' House in the standard fashion.

It may happen that a limited company mortgagor sells land held by a bank which has registered its charge at Companies' House, but merely filed notice of the deposit of the land certificate at the Land Registry. The bank can then make application for the withdrawal of the notice of deposit, which will be accepted by the Land Registry, but the solicitor acting for the purchaser may cavil about the existence of the written charge disclosed in the files at Companies' House. In such event, the bank can join in the transfer and discharge on Land Registry Form 55.

Where a debenture to the bank includes as security a fixed charge on registered land, it has to be registered as a charge. The land certificate is sent to the Registry with the debenture and a certified copy thereof, and exchanged for a charge certificate which will have the original debenture sewn-up in it.

A floating charge can be protected by a notice under Section 49 of the Land Registration Act, 1925, but it cannot be registered on the land register. When the land certificate is not held with the floating charge, a caution can be lodged as a form of insurance. These steps are not usually taken because the bank relies on the floating charge itself.

Chapter XXVII Ownership, Valuation and Insurance

The sea is our heritage and, as an island, we depend upon ships to carry our imports and deliver our exports. Over the centuries we have been proud of our shipping industry and from time to time the banker may be called upon to assist customers engaged in the essential business of sea transport. To lend relying largely upon the security of a ship entails the acceptance of many unusual risks, which have to be recognised by the practical banker, and although such business may be limited to coastal branches, it is prudent here to review the main essentials to furnish a general picture of the pitfalls which await the unwary.

Whilst it is a relatively simple and inexpensive matter to obtain a good title to a ship as mortgagee, the following disadvantages are inherent in such security from the banking standpoint:—

(1) A ship is difficult to value and subject to heavy depreciation.
(2) It is exposed to peculiar risks from the perils of the sea which cannot always be completely covered by insurance.
(3) A ship may become subject to maritime, statutory and possessory liens ranking prior to the bank as mortgagee.

All these drawbacks will be apparent as the picture unfolds, but first it is necessary to define a ship for our purpose and to consider in outline the law relating to the ownership of a registered British ship.

The entire law relating to the registration and ownership of British ships is codified in the Merchant Shipping Act, 1894 (hereinafter referred to as 'the Act') with subsequent minor amendments. It is a lengthy Act covering merchant shipping generally, but much of it does not directly concern the banker.

REGISTRATION OF BRITISH SHIPS

With certain exceptions relating to small craft, all British ships have to be registered. If not so registered, they are not accepted as British ships. A ship is defined as 'including every description of vessel now in navigation, not propelled with oars' and, to all intents and purposes, it means a vessel capable of navigation and used for the carriage of cargo or passengers. The dividing line between what is or is not a ship in some cases may be very thin, but such problems are unlikely to harass the practical banker. For example, a motor boat which plied for hire on a tidal river between two points a few miles apart was held to be a ship, but an electric launch operating for pleasure on an artificial lake was held not to be a ship. Again, a barge used for dredging purposes without means of propulsion was found to be a ship, whereas a vessel previously registered as a ship but used as a coal hulk for four years was considered to be outside the definition and did not require to be registered.

The following British ships are exempt from liability to register:—

1. Ships not exceeding fifteen tons burden employed solely in navigation on the rivers or coasts of the United Kingdom, or on the rivers or coasts of some British possession within which the managing owners of the ships reside.
2. Ships not exceeding thirty tons burden not having a whole or fixed deck, and employed solely in fishing or trading coastwise on the shores of Newfoundland or in or around the Gulf of St. Lawrence.
3. Ships belonging to the Crown.

Occasionally, the banker has to decide whether a particular craft offered as security by mortgage is a ship within the Act, with title registered in one of the port registers. If so registered, the mortgage has to be taken in the prescribed form and duly registered at the port of registry, as will be seen later. The definition of a ship and the system of registration is, therefore, of more than passing interest.

The following conditions have to be carried out before a vessel can be registered:—

1. The name of the ship has to be painted on each side of her bows and the name of her port of registry on the stern.
2. The official number and the number showing her registered tonnage has to be cut on her main beam.
3. The draught of the ship has to be marked on each side of her stern and of her sternpost in Roman capital letters or in figures.

These essentials can be seen at a glance on any ship in a port or dock. They are not merely decorative or descriptive features, but legal requirements.

4. A certificate of survey has to be furnished to the Registrar quoting the tonnage, and build of the ship with descriptive details of her identity.
5. When first registered, the builders have to give a certificate quoting the build and tonnage of the ship and the time and place of her construction. Where she has been sold details of the bill of sale vesting the ship in the owner are required.
6. Finally, a declaration of qualification has to be filed, including *inter alia* the name of the master.

It is thus clear that registration of a ship cannot be effected until its construction has been finished. Registers are maintained at most of the United Kingdom ports and at certain ports in British possessions overseas and, when the particulars have been entered in the Register, a copy of the register described as a Certificate of Registry is furnished to the applicant for registration. The certificate is one of the essential ship's papers and any change of ownership or of description has to be recorded by endorsement thereon as quickly as possible. If a ship is sunk or constructively lost or where it ceases to be a British ship by sale to foreign owners, prompt notice of the event has to be given to the registrar at the port of registry.

OWNERSHIP OF A BRITISH SHIP

The property in a British ship is divided into sixty-four shares and it is illegal for more than sixty-four persons to be registered as owners of any one ship. The title of each owner of a share is distinct and indivisible, but the whole sixty-four shares may be (and usually are) held by a single owner.

The legal or equitable interest in a British ship, or a share therein, can be held only by natural born and naturalised British subjects and corporations and companies established within and whose principal place of business is within the British dominions.

Nobody is entitled to registration as the owner of a fractional part of a share, but any number of persons not exceeding five may be registered as joint owners of any share or shares in a British ship. A corporation may be registered as owner by its corporate name and in many cases a limited company is the owner of a ship or a fleet of ships.

Ownership is transferred by means of a bill of sale in the special form described in the Act, but no transferee can be registered as owner unless he makes a declaration of transfer certifying that he or the limited company for whom he acts is qualified to own a British ship. Again, when death, or bankruptcy, intervene, ownership is transmitted to the personal representative or to the trustee in bankruptcy, as the case may be, but the person to whom the ownership is thus transmitted must be capable of owning a British ship. He has also to make a declaration of transmission quoting details similar to those contained in a declaration of transfer and producing evidence of his rights to transmission. Where anyone to whom ownership is transmitted is not qualified to own a British ship, it may have to be sold and the proceeds paid over to the parties entitled to them.

Mere possession of a ship, whether it is registered or not, does not prove title to it. There is no market overt for the sale of ships and title does not pass by delivery. Written documents are necessary to evidence title and British ships which do not require to be registered are transferred by any document purporting to pass the ownership. It need not be a bill of sale and does not require registration under the Act or within the Bills of Sale Act, 1878.

Armed with this elementary introduction to the law relating to the ownership and registration of British ships, it is now possible to examine the steps taken by the practical banker to obtain security by way of the mortgage of a ship.

VALUATION OF A SHIP AS SECURITY

At the outset an estimate has to be made of the value of the ship to the bank as security and, in view of the high rate of depreciation due to normal wear and tear and the difficulties of realisation which inevitably arise, particularly in times when the supply of ships vastly exceeds demand, a most pessimistic attitude has necessarily to be adopted. A professional valuation can be obtained to give a reliable indication of the current worth of the ship, which can then be heavily discounted for the bank's purpose, but more often the banker is content to estimate the value of such security, calling for a large margin where circumstances demand. If the basic principles of lending are applied to the proposal, greater reliance will be placed upon the capacity of the borrower to repay from trading or other satisfactory sources within a reasonable period, and the real value of the security is not so very material if there is ample margin between the maximum amount to be taken and the bank's estimate of the forced sale value of the ship.

To form an opinion of the worth of the ship, based usually on its age, size, and type in relation to the available market, various details have to be collated. The certificate of registry, which gives the particulars of the ship entered in the registry, is for use on the ship for its lawful navigation and cannot be deposited with the bank, but a search can be made personally in the register, to verify any points. Most ships are, however, also registered at Lloyd's Register of Shipping and this register quotes details of tonnage, builders, age, survey, classification, owners and port of registry. Normally, all the required information can be obtained from the customer, but these sources of verification may be helpful.

The registered tonnage of a ship, quoted in units of 100 cubic feet of space, gives its internal capacity. The net register tonnage is calculated in the manner set out in the Act, deducting from the gross tonnage certain allowances for all engineering and crew spaces. Dock dues and kindred fees are based upon the net register tonnage of the vessel. The deadweight tonnage of a ship is the equivalent of the weight of water it displaces and the deadweight carrying capacity is the difference between the displacement when fully loaded and when empty of cargo. Where the ship is authorised to carry passengers, her maximum capacity can be ascertained. The age, type of propulsion, and any other specialist features will be known and an inspection of the ship can usually be made to get some idea of her state of repair and attractiveness or otherwise. The date and number of the last survey, which a ship has to undergo every four years to satisfy Lloyd's Registry, is also material. When the vessel is old, a large outlay may be necessary to satisfy the surveyors. These technical features alone suffice to show that a bank manager cannot expect to walk round a ship and thereby value it as a floating security. The original cost and age of the vessel in relation to current costs for building new vessels of a similar size and type provides a rough guide from which to start deducting a prudent margin to lead to a very rough estimate of the value of the ship as bank security. It is obviously a matter for an expert marine surveyor, but rarely in practice does the banker resort to such a professional valuation. The vessels most frequently taken as security are fishing trawlers, tugs, barges and pleasure boats when local knowledge and standardised types enable the banker to reach an estimated value which is reasonably satisfactory taking the other features of the lending into account.

Like any other form of security, a ship has to be revalued by the bank at reasonable intervals with due regard to the wear and tear from advancing years and suitable check by reference to the survey certificate issued by Lloyd's surveyors. This four-yearly survey does ensure that the ship is maintained in satisfactory condition and its value in this limited respect is not materially reduced. The survey certificate can always be exhibited to the bank for record purposes. Changing market conditions for ageing vessels, depending upon the inter-play of supply and demand for the particular type of ship, have always to be brought into consideration. A fair warning of deterioration in value is given, regardless of current market conditions, when the surveyors require that extensive repairs and renovations shall be carried out before they will renew the classification of the ship and pass the survey. As always, the banker has to keep an ear close to the ground to know promptly of developments likely to jeopardise the security position.

INSURANCE OF THE SHIP

The next convenient step is to verify that the ship is fully insured against all known risks and that the bank as mortgagee is fully protected against loss.

Here again, it is strictly a matter for an expert in this specialised subject and, unless the bank seeks special advice, it has to rely largely upon the character and integrity of the borrower. A few general principles can, however, be stated as an elementary guide.

Three main forms of ship insurance can be distinguished: marine, war risks and club or mutual insurance.

The *marine policy* covers marine perils accidental in character and consequent upon or incidental to the navigation of the sea, all of which are specified in the policy under standardised clauses. Two of these clauses demand special mention.

The *Inchmaree Clause* introduced and named after the vessel *Inchmaree* in *Thames & Mersey Marine Insurance Co. Ltd. v. Hamilton Fraser & Co.* (1887) 12 App. Cas. 484, covers 'loss of, or damage to, hull or machinery through the negligence of master, mariners, engineers or pilots, or through explosions, bursting of boilers, breakage of shafts, or through any latent defect in the machinery or hull, provided such loss or damage has not resulted from want of due diligence by the owners of the ship or any of them or by the managers'. Accidents in loading, unloading or bunkering and other contingencies are thus covered. In the case of the *Inchmaree*, the donkey engine pump was damaged either accidentally or negligently due to a valve being closed and it was decided that the loss did not fall within 'perils of the seas'. This loophole has now been closed by the special clause.

The *Running Down Clause* covers three-quarters of the liability for damage done to another ship in collision. This clause was introduced following *De Vaux* v. *Salvador* (1836) 4 Ad. & E. 420, when it was held that payments made to a third party by the insured for damages caused by collision, which was wholly or partly the responsibility of the insured ship, were irrecoverable under the standard policy. The remaining quarter of the risk is usually covered by club insurance, which also provides cover against other third party injuries, including loss of life and damage to harbours, wharves and piers.

The club or mutual insurance is cover obtained from an association or club formed by shipowners operating in a given area who, on a mutual protection basis, insure themselves against various risks which cannot be covered at a reasonable cost elsewhere. Liability of the shipowners to cargo-owners for damage to cargo is often covered in this manner.

Insurance against war risks has often to be arranged in addition to ordinary marine insurance. This may be effected under a mutual insurance scheme or under open market policies, which are often issued for a limited period of cover.

There is little point in studying a long policy replete with complicated clauses couched in ancient language if care is not also taken to ensure that the proceeds of any claim will be paid to the bank. According to marine insurance usage, a 'constructive total loss' is the loss which is suffered when a ship is reasonably abandoned, either because its total loss appears to be unavoidable or because it could not be preserved without an outlay exceeding the value of the ship when repaired. From the practical banking angle, a constructive total loss is failure to obtain a watertight assignment of the policy.

As a counsel of perfection, the ship should be insured to cover the separate interests of both the owner mortgagor and the bank as mortgagee. The policy can be effected directly on behalf of the bank instead of being assigned by the owner. In the latter event, the insurance is subject to any defences available against the owner, and the policy may be useless if the ship is wilfully lost or scuttled by the mortgagor or his agents. If the bank, as mortgagee, is an original party to the insurance, misconduct on the part of the owner will not damage the cover unless there is a breach of warranty.

On the other hand, if a banker is content to lend against the security of a ship, the borrower will not be of the type likely to scuttle the ship in the hope of recovering insurance monies. In practice, the mortgagor is usually left unfettered to insure his own ship and the underwriters and indemnity associations are duly advised of the bank's interest in the relative policies. The bank then holds the policies usually assigned to it by the endorsement of the assured, and an undertaking is obtained from the insurance company, or brokers, that the proceeds of any claim under the policies will be held to the order of the bank. A mortgage of the ship does not alone give the bank any legal interest in the insurance moneys and, in the absence of due notice to the brokers the proceeds of any claim may be paid direct to the customer and be available for the benefit of his creditors generally. In other words, parallel steps have to be taken as those when the fire insurance policy is obtained covering a house which is mortgaged to the bank. Finally, a diary system has to be introduced to ensure that all premiums are paid promptly when they fall due. The brokers may undertake to advise the bank in the event of premiums remaining unpaid, but an independent check is always a prudent measure. As will be seen later, the mortgagor usually covenants in the mortgage of the ship to keep it fully insured and in good state of repair.

The practical points to watch to cover the problem of the satisfactory insurance of the ship to protect the bank's position throughout may, therefore, be listed as follows:—

1. Obtain the policy or policies and study all the clauses to prove that the insurance of the mortgaged vessel is adequate and every risk is covered. In any case of doubt, refer to an expert broker for verification.
2. Have the policies assigned to the bank by the mortgagor, give notice to the insurance house or brokers and obtain their undertaking to hold the policies and the proceeds of any claims thereunder on behalf of the bank.
3. Verify the due payment of all premiums. In the event of delay, pay the premiums to the debit of the borrower's account.

The bank clearly has to be fully covered at all times against all insurable risks.

Chapter XXVIII Taking the Security-Release—Remedies of the Mortgagee—Sub-Mortgages

THE LEGAL MORTGAGE

Before 1854 a mortgage of a ship was effected by means of a transfer, as in the case of a sale, which had to be endorsed on the certificate of registry and entered in the register. A mortgage of a ship was created by the Merchant Shipping Act, 1854, when the need for endorsement on the certificate of registry was abolished. The whole question of mortgages of ships is now clearly set out in the Act, Section 31 of which requires that a legal mortgage must be in the form prescribed in the First Schedule to the Act or as near thereto as circumstances permit. All mortgages take priority according to the times when they are entered in the register.

For the purpose of the banker, there are two forms which can be obtained from H.M. Stationery Office, or through booksellers:—

1. Mortgage to secure a current account by individuals or joint owners (Form 12).
2. Mortgage to secure a current account by a body corporate (Form 12a).

There are also forms to cover:—

3. A mortgage to secure a principal sum and interest by individuals or joint owners (Form 11), and
4. A mortgage to secure a principal sum and interest by a body corporate (Form 11a),

but these last two are not normally used by a banker because advances are generally taken on current account.

The reader is recommended to study a print of Form 12a, which is most frequently used. At the outset, it calls for details of the ship, including its official number, name, port of registry, whether it is a sailing, steam or motorship and the horse power of its engines, if any, together with its principal dimensions and tonnage. In other words, the ship is described in standard fashion. There then follows a space in which the transactions between the parties to the mortgage can be recited. This can be filled in to explain that there is an account current between the named limited company owner and the lending bank, and in consideration of that bank making or continuing advances, or otherwise affording banking facilities for as long as the bank may deem fit, the company executes the mortgage as security for all moneys, etc., which may at any time be owing to the bank on any account of the company, etc. The security is usually described as a continuing security, not satisfied by any intermediate payment, and the bank is stated to be at liberty at any time to grant time and indulge, exchange, release and renew any securities, etc., as it may think fit without affecting its rights under the mortgage. The form then proceeds to state in print that the company mortgages the ship to the bank, that it has power so to mortgage it and that the ship is free from encumbrances or that, if there are incumbrances, they are only 'save as appears by the Registry of the said ship'. The main portion of the form is supplied printed and the inset reciting the transaction between the mortgagor and the bank can be overprinted by the bank's printers ready for practical use.

Altogether it is a relatively simple form of mortgage (far shorter and easier to follow than a typical mortgage of land) and it is completed by the seal of the company affixed and attested in conformity with its articles of association. Immediately following execution it has to be registered as described later.

Some banks may prefer to have the mortgage supported by a separate memorandum embodying many of the clauses found in standard bank mortgage forms. The mortgagor usually undertakes therein to keep the ship fully insured at all times and to maintain it in a good state of repair to maintain the Lloyd's classification. The advances are stated to be repayable upon demand and the security becomes enforceable if repayment is not made within seven days or one month of the date of demand, or in the event of a breach of covenant, liquidation, or the arrest or seizure of the ship. All the usual precautionary measures can be introduced into such a memorandum, but this accompanying document may be dispensed with in approved cases, the bank relying on the standard form of mortgage prescribed by the Act.

SHIP AS COLLATERAL SECURITY

It may happen that a ship is taken as collateral security, in which event a collateral deed of agreement has to be prepared to overcome the deficiencies in the statutory form. Such a deed sets out in detail the terms on which the advance is made and the conditions on which the mortgagor is to retain the control and management of the mortgaged ship, including all the points outlined above in a memorandum for direct security relating to the enforceability of the mortgage and otherwise.

In case there may be two or more mortgages of ships by the same mortgagor to secure the principal debt, Section 93 of the Law of Property Act, 1925, will be expressly excluded by words to the effect that the borrower is not entitled to repay the amount outstanding in respect of one mortgage, thereby redeeming it without also repaying anything due in respect of the other mortgage.

Finally, it is well to emphasise that a ship in course of construction cannot be mortgaged. It cannot be registered until it is finished and registration is a prerequisite to the creation of a legal mortgage. An equitable mortgage only can be obtained, but more usually it is caught by a floating charge created by the owner company in favour of the bank. Everything naturally depends upon when the property in the unfinished ship passes to the shipping company. It may be that nothing is paid until completion and the property vests in the builder until the ship is delivered. On the other hand, the buyer may pay by stage advances or instalments on the understanding that the property in the ship in its current state of construction passes to him. It is the old story of transferring the ship from being a floating asset under work-in-progress in the balance sheet of the shipbuilder to a fixed asset in the balance sheet of the shipowner, which usually occurs when the ship is afloat and duly registered.

REGISTRATION OF THE MORTGAGE

Upon the completion of the mortgage by the borrower or collateral depositor, it has to be registered at the ship's port of registry and, where the mortgagor is a limited company, the mortgage has also to be registered with the Registrar of Companies at Companies' House, in accord with Section 95 of the Companies Act, 1948.

Omission to register at the port of registry does not affect the validity of the mortgage in itself, but it will be seen later that priority depends upon the date of registration and a registered mortgage always takes precedence over an unregistered mortgage. Whilst there is nothing to compel the bank to register the mortgage, it would be foolish to delay registration because later charges may obtain priority by their prompt registration. On the other hand, it will be recalled that failure to register at Companies' House a charge created by a limited company within twenty-one days after the date of its creation renders it void against a liquidator and any creditor of the company.

It is a simple matter to register a ship's mortgage at the port of registry. Section 31 of the Act provides that mortgages shall be recorded by the registrar in the order in time in which they are produced to him for that purpose, and the registrar shall by memorandum under his hand notify on each mortgage that it has been recorded by him, stating the day and hour of that record. No fee is charged for registration. If the mortgage is the first entry made on the register after the Bill of Sale initially registering the ship, the memorandum will be designated 'Mortgage A' and all subsequent mortgages will be described by successive letters alphabetically as and when they are registered. In point of fact the designation 'Mortgage A' suffices to prove to the bank that no prior charges have been registered, but in the normal course a search will be made in the register before accepting the ship as security.

SEARCHES AT THE PORT REGISTRY

A personal search can be made in the port registry at a cost of sixty five pence, but it is more usual and safer to obtain, upon written request, a copy of all entries in the register, concerning the ship. This transcript is issued upon payment of a fee of £2.60p, or £3.25p for a dated and closed copy, i.e. a certified copy. The extra cost is a prudent investment because the details are extracted by experts and the transcript is certified by the Registrar to be correct. It is akin to an official search certificate issued by the Land Charges Registry and admissible as evidence in any court (Section 695 of the Act).

PRIORITIES BETWEEN MORTGAGES

As already indicated, priority depends upon the time of registration of the mortgage over the ship. The precise rule is set out in Section 33 of the Act, which states that 'if there are more mortgages than one registered in respect of the same ship or share, the mortgagees shall, notwithstanding any express, implied or constructive notice, be entitled in priority, one over the other, according to the date at which each mortgage is recorded in the register book, and not according to the date of each mortgage itself. Any mortgage which has not been registered is postponed to all registered mortgages and this rule applies notwithstanding the fact that the registered mortgagees were fully aware of the unregistered charge created prior to their own charges. This view was upheld in *Black* v. *Williams* [1895] 1 Ch. 408, where the holders of debentures giving an equitable charge on certain steamships were postponed to persons having a subsequent registered legal mortgage on the same ships, though the latter had notice of the debentures when they obtained their mortgages.

There are thus *three clear steps* necessary to perfect the bank's security when a ship has been accepted as satisfactory security:—

1. To search the port registry by obtaining a certified copy of the entries relating to the ship. If the transcript reveals an existing charge, the security will usually be unacceptable unless there is a large equity available to the bank as second mortgagee.
2. To take the mortgage on the appropriate statutory mortgage form.
3. To register the mortgage promptly at the port of registry, obtaining a memorandum bearing the description 'Mortgage A'.

All will then be well unless and until a second mortgage is created over the ship. As ever, when the bank receives notice of a second mortgage, the account has to be stopped promptly to avoid the operation of the Rule in *Clayton's Case* (1816) 1 Mer. 572, otherwise all fresh advances would rank for security after the second mortgagee, whilst all credits received would reduce the amount secured by the bank's first charge. In practice, a subsequent mortgagee with evidence of the bank's prior charge in the register will give direct notice of his second charge to the bank and, provided it then stops the account, no difficulty arises. The customer can open a fresh account for his purposes providing it is kept in credit.

In the absence of direct notice of the second charge, however, the bank might suffer loss because it would continue the current account in complete ignorance of the second charge. Nevertheless, it is probable that the Rule in *Clayton's Case* would be applied against the bank. As every mortgagee is deemed to have notice of the entries in the port register the bank may be held to have notice of the mortgage when it is registered and future advances will then rank for security after the second mortgage. The Merchant Shipping Act embodies no protections similar to those available to a bank when advancing against the security of land. It will be remembered that Section 94 of the Law of Property Act, 1925, as amended by the Law of Property Amendment Act, 1926, provides that where a mortgage is made expressly for securing a current account, the mortgagee shall not be deemed to have notice of a mortgage merely by reason that it was registered as a land charge or in a local deeds registry, if it was not so registered at the time when the original mortgage was created or when the last search, if any, by or on behalf of the mortgagee was made, *whichever last happened*. Moreover, when lending against registered land, Section 30 of the Land Registration Act, 1925, demands that where a registered charge is created for securing further advances the registrar has to notify the lender before making any entry in the register which would prejudice the priority of any further advances. These provisions do not apply to ships' mortgages.

If a bank wishes to ensure maximum safety, the best course is always to advance against ships on fixed loan account and not to extend a loan without a fresh search in the register to ensure that no charge has been entered subsequent to the bank's charge. In some cases prudence may demand this safety measure, but, generally speaking, the bank relies upon the integrity of the borrower not to create fresh charges without reference, and the customary caution of a second mortgagee in giving direct notice of his interest.

OTHER PRIORITIES—MARITIME LIENS

The complete priority of a bank's mortgage on a ship can be upset by a maritime lien, which may be defined as a privileged claim upon a ship in respect of a service done to it or injury caused by it which is capable of being carried into effect by legal process and arrest, with the sale of the vessel, where necessary. This privileged claim travels with the property in the ship, no matter into whose possession it may come. As between a lien holder and a mortgagee, the rights of the mortgagee in the ship are subject to all existing maritime or possessory liens upon it. A distinction can be drawn between liens arising for money due under a contract (bottomry and respondentia) and liens for damage done by the ship in collision or otherwise. Most of these risks can now be covered by insurance and the extent of the cover can be verified by the bank lender, whilst with rapid communication system the need for extreme measures to finance the movement of the ship rarely arises. A brief outline may nevertheless be of interest to the reader.

During the voyage the master of the ship is an agent of necessity and may hypothecate or even sell the ship or cargo or pledge the owner's credit for necessaries for the ship. Where money is required urgently for the purposes of the ship, or cargo, and there is no other means of raising it, the master may borrow against the security of the ship or cargo by means of bonds.

A *bottomry bond* is a contract in writing by which the master pledges the ship or the ship and cargo as security for a loan of money to enable the voyage to be completed. A *respondentia bond* is a hypothecation of the cargo only for the same purpose. Both are very rare nowadays with the rapid means of communication available to the master. The name of bottomry arises because the ship's bottom or keel is said to be pledged by the bond. The lender accepts the maritime risk that the money is repayable only in the event of the safe arrival of the ship. The bonds can be given only at a foreign port from which it is impossible to communicate with the owners of the ship. Such contracts entered into by the master for the preservation of the ship or the continuance of the voyage obtain priority to mortgagees because the master himself has a lien in respect of such disbursements and the creditor can avail himself of the *master's lien*. It would certainly be difficult for the master to collect essential supplies if contracts entered into by him were postponed to mortgages. In modern conditions these risks are too remote to worry the bank.

RELEASE OF SECURITY

When the advance is repaid or the security otherwise no longer required, the mortgage of the ship can quickly be discharged. A form of receipt is printed on the statutory mortgage forms issued by the Stationery Office, which merely acknowledges receipt of the stated amount in discharge of the 'within written security'. Section 32 of the Act provides that, when the mortgage deed, with a receipt for the mortgage money endorsed thereon, duly signed and attested, is produced to the registrar, he must make an entry in the register, recording the discharge of the mortgage. No fee is payable to the registry and no stamp is required on the receipt (Section 721). In addition, appropriate notice has to be given to the insurance brokers and any others who have been advised of the bank's interest in the insurance of the vessel.

REMEDIES OF MORTGAGE

Power of Sale

According to Section 35 of the Act, a registered mortgagee has full power to sell the ship or share in respect of which he is registered and to give a valid receipt for the purchase money. In other words, the power of sale of a legal mortgage is available and, in the absence of any express provision in the mortgage or collateral deed, this right arises whenever the mortgagor is in default under the mortgage or has acted in a way which will jeopardise the security. The precise statutory power is that:—'Every registered mortgagee shall have power absolutely to dispose of the ship or share in respect of which he is registered, and to give effectual receipts for the purchase money; but, where there are more persons than one registered as mortgagee of the same ship or share a subsequent mortgagee shall not, except under the order of a court of competent jurisdiction, sell the ship or share without the concurrence of every prior mortgagee.' (Section 35.)

If no express provision for repayment appears in the mortgage, difficulty may be experienced in deciding whether the mortgagor has defaulted. In such circumstances the ruling from *Deverges* v. *Sandeman Clark & Co.* [1902] 1 Ch. 579 may be helpful. In that case it was decided that where no day for repayment was fixed by the terms of the mortgage, the power of sale arose on the mortgagee giving reasonable notice to the mortgagor requiring repayment and stating that in default thereof the mortgagee would sell. In practice, a bank will always afford the mortgagor ample time in which to repay. Needless to add that, where a bank does not hold a mortgage on all the shares in a ship, it will be beset with problems in attempting to sell and may have to bring a foreclosure action to arrange the sale of the ship by order of the court.

The steps to be taken in practice before exercising the power of sale follow the usual procedure. Notice will first be served by registered post upon the mortgagor demanding repayment of the amount owing, including interest to date, and stating clearly that if payment is not made within the given period (being the time embodied in the mortgage or a reasonable time, whichever applies), the bank will exercise its power of sale. If the customer fails to meet this demand, the vessel can be sold at the best price obtainable in the market. If an attempt is made to sell at an improper price, the court may grant an injunction at the application of the mortgagor to restrain the bank from completing the sale. The best course is to sell by public auction, but sale by private treaty through an expert agent cannot be upset where there is no doubt that the contract price is the equivalent of the market value of the ship on the date of the sale. A second or later mortgagee cannot, of course, sell without the approval of all prior mortgagees or the blessing of the court.

The standard rules apply if and when the vessel realises more than sufficient to liquidate the bank debt. The surplus has to be held to the order of any second or subsequent mortgagees and a search at the registry is, therefore, necessary before the balance can be paid over to the mortgagor.

Incidentally, a ship is normally sold subject to any contracts for her employment arranged by the owner. A mortgagee is bound by such contracts, always providing that they are normal and do not prejudice the security. For example, if a third party has chartered the ship from the mortgagor, the bank cannot prevent the ship from performing the chartered voyage.

Taking Possession

An alternative right available to the bank as mortgagee of a ship is to take possession. This right arises upon default or even before the mortgage debt falls due, but it rarely appeals to the bank because it assumes liability for all expenses incurred in the future operation of the ship and is bound to perform the contracted obligations incurred by the mortgagor as owner. Thus, upon possession, claims for wages or disbursements may have to be met, but the outlay can be recovered from the mortgagor if there is sufficient equity in the security. Where a bank, upon expert advice, elects to take possession, it is accomplished by physically putting a man on board the ship. When in possession, a registered mortgagee obtains a legal right to the freight accruing due (but cannot recover freight already received by the mortgagor) and can employ the ship subject to any outstanding commitments entered into by the mortgagor before possession. Generally speaking, a bank will avoid taking possession, with all the attendant responsibilities, unless satisfied beyond doubt that the indebtedness can be recovered from the profits of running the ship.

The case of *The Prince Bernhard* (1963) *The Times*, October 11, is a somewhat picturesque commentary on procedure in this regard. It has, over the years, always been the practice to serve proceedings involving a ship by nailing the relevant writ to the mast, as the judgment is against the vessel and not against the parties involved. It could reasonably be thought that in these days it would be appropriate nevertheless to hand the writ to the master of the ship, but in this case it was held that this was bad service and the mast remains the proper place.

SUB-MORTGAGES

Reference has already been made to the defects of an equitable mortgage of a ship. Perhaps it is well to mention in conclusion that sub-mortgages cannot be registered. They are not recognised by the port registry and can be effected only by obtaining the standard statutory form of transfer of the existing mortgage.

Chapter XXIX An Outline Survey

The finance of the movement of goods against the security of the goods themselves is one of the most fascinating types of bank lending and it is, moreover, an extremely important service to the trading community. Furthermore, it is usually a highly remunerative type of business and, provided the goods are not held for an undue length of time, rapidity of turnover ensures compliance with the basic principles of sound lending. There are many opportunities for this type of business to-day, and in consequence occasions often arise where the banker is called upon to finance an import or perhaps afford an internal bridge-over facility when the only security available comprises the goods concerned. Such work necessarily requires specialised legal and practical knowledge. It is a wide subject but an outline survey of the basic principles involved may be helpful.

THE GOODS ARE ALWAYS THE SECURITY

In whichever manner a bank may be called upon to afford facilities against goods by way of a direct advance against documents of title or produce stored in a warehouse; the acceptance of bills of exchange with documents of title attached; the grant of confirmed credit facilities opened in favour of a foreign seller; or a mere loan to enable the customer to collect the goods himself, it is essential to realise throughout that the bank security comprises the actual goods which, in due course, are to be sold by the customer to liquidate the indebtedness. It follows that a close watch must always be maintained on the market price of the produce or goods concerned and an adequate margin ensured to meet the possible depreciation in value on a falling market. Normally the security should be saleable in a wide market subject to little short-term variation in price, thereby enabling the banker to value his security from the daily press or trade papers. Wool or raw cotton are within this category. Frequency of valuation will naturally depend upon the type of produce and margin available, which may be provided in cash; by the deposit of other approved security; or by the surplus value of the goods held as security. However watertight the bank's position may be at law, it will afford little compensation if the goods upon sale yield much less than the amount lent. In like manner, it is essential to ensure that the security is fully insured against all known risks until such time as it becomes the property of a buyer.

THE BORROWER

In this type of business probably more than any other form of lending, it is incumbent upon the banker to satisfy himself concerning the ability, experience, and integrity of the customer. Unless the borrower buys in the right market and sells at a profit, losses will accumulate, leaving the bank with goods of inadequate value to cover the debt. An experienced trader with established connections is normally expert at his work and enjoys the confidence of his banker, but the dabbler or casual speculator cannot expect support in the absence of alternative approved security. Undoubted integrity is equally essential because it will be readily realised later that much more opportunity for fraud arises, particularly when goods are released to the customer on trust for sale or warehousing, and substantial losses have unfortunately been incurred by banks through breaches of trust by customers.

The dealings of a fictitious provision merchant customer may serve as an example for our purpose. With long experience, and of undoubted integrity, he seeks assistance in the finance of his proposed purchase of a consignment of tea from Ceylon. At the initial interview, when the tea import is still subject to negotiation with the foreign seller, this customer will, in response to the manager's enquiry, explain whether he is entering into a *c.i.f. contract* or an *f.o.b. contract*. Under the latter terms it is merely the duty of the seller to deliver the tea to a stated ship upon which cargo space has been engaged by the buyer. The importer pays the freight and insures his cargo for the voyage, and after shipment, the contractual liability of the seller, as such, ceases.

C.I.F. CONTRACT

In a c.i.f. (cost, insurance, freight) contract, which is more usual, the seller provides the goods, obtains cargo space, loads on ship, effects all the insurance and then tenders the required documents to the buyer, who, provided they are in order, is bound to pay for them. If the buyer discovers after payment for the documents that the goods upon arrival are not in accordance with the contract, he has the right to reject them or claim damages for breach of contract, but the buyer under a c.i.f. contract is always bound to pay against the proper documents.

To quote McCardie, J., in *Manbre Saccharine Co. Ltd.* v. *Corn Products Co. Ltd.* (1919) 1 K.B. 198: 'All that the buyer can call for is the delivery of the customary documents; this represents the measure of the buyer's right and extent of the vendor's duty. The buyer cannot refuse the documents and ask for the actual goods, nor can the vendor withhold the documents and tender the goods which they represent.' It is apparent, therefore, that under such a contract the seller can obtain payment before arrival of the goods at their destination, whilst the buyer, in turn, may re-sell the goods on c.i.f. terms before they reach him.

The inherent advantages of a c.i.f. contract are quite apparent. The seller can obtain payment long before the goods reach their destination, whilst the importer may dispose of them before arrival. It is possible for goods to be bought and sold on c.i.f. terms several times by delivery of the documents, whilst the cargo concerned is on the high seas.

Let us assume that the customer is entering into a c.i.f. contract and his seller in Ceylon requires payment immediately the tea is shipped. The bank is asked to open a confirmed credit. In the form of request will be set out in standard fashion the quantity, exact trade description, etc., of the commodity purchased, detailing the amount to be paid by the foreign agents of the bank to a stated seller against the delivery of the scheduled documents evidencing shipment of the goods by a specified ship or route before a given date. Payment may be authorised against documents with or without a draft drawn on the bank. It must not be forgotten that once opened such confirmed credit is a definite obligation to pay the amount required and the initial contingent liability, in the absence of other cash cover, will become an actual advance when payment is affected in accordance with the instructions received. Against this liability of the customer the bank will hold the documents (received direct from its agents after payment) relating to the shipment of the tea, the value of which can be readily ascertained and suitable margin maintained pending realisation.

It is convenient now to consider the documents usually required under a c.i.f. contract, examining them both from the legal and practical aspect for the purposes of banking security.

The law under such a contract requires the seller to tender an invoice, a marine insurance policy, and a bill(s) of lading. These are the minimum documents, but the seller and the buyer may agree upon additional documents, such as a certificate of origin, but they are beyond the scope of this outline.

Invoice
This is the document which details the description and value of the goods despatched. It is not a document of title and has no security value, but it provides the banker with a ready means of describing the security and its cost price in the security records. As will be appreciated later, it is essential to preserve a complete chain of identification of the goods throughout and the first entry will be made direct from the invoice. Naturally, it is necessary to ensure that the description of the goods tallies with the description in the bill(s) of lading and insurance policy.

Marine Insurance Policy
This document, which proves that the merchandise is adequately covered against stated risks, is essential to the c.i.f. contract and for obvious reasons invaluable to the lending banker. It should be issued by a reputable company and cover precisely the goods specified in the invoice and bill(s) of lading for the voyage shown therein, usually for cost price, plus a margin of ten per cent. It should extend cover from the earliest date of shipment into warehouse in the importing country or for a specified period at the port of discharge. The beneficiary named in the policy (usually the exporter) should endorse it in blank, and the cover should include war risks in addition to the perils in the normal Lloyd's policy. Unless it contains the words 'and/or other steamer or steamers', it is prudent to ensure that the ship detailed in the policy is the same as that described in the bill of lading. In short, it is essential that the banker should be satisfied that all the goods are adequately insured against every known risk until such time as they are safely stored in a warehouse or sold ex quay. The closest examination of every policy is clearly vital to ensure that, in the event of loss or serious damage to the

goods, the lending banker can expect repayment from the proceeds of the insurance claim. Many clauses may appear in small print on the back of the policy but they are usually expressly excluded unless special endorsements, generally made by a rubber stamp, appear on the face of the document.

Bill of Lading

The bill of lading is the only document of title in the set required by the c.i.f. contract. It is a document signed by the master or shipowner, or his agent, which is given to the shipper. It constitutes firstly a receipt for the goods referred to therein, and as such by mercantile custom is regarded as a symbol of the right of the property in the goods. Secondly, it evidences the contract of carriage between the shipowner and the consignee, and lastly it is a document of title to the goods. Normally upon shipment a mate's receipt is issued and the bills of lading are issued later.

Under the Bills of Lading Act, 1855, every consignee of goods, and every endorsee to whom the property in the goods named in a bill of lading shall pass, has transferred to him all rights of action and is subject to all liabilities in respect of such goods as if the contract had been made with himself, and the bill of lading is conclusive evidence of the shipment as against the master. It is thus by mercantile custom a document of title which the shipper may endorse and deliver to a third party.

A bill of lading is not, however, a negotiable instrument. It will be recalled that the three essential attributes of negotiability are:—

(1) that the property therein, and not mere possession, is transferred by delivery (with or without endorsement as the case may be);

(2) that the transferee obtains a title free from equities; and

(3) that the holder can sue on the instrument in his own name.

The second essential is missing with a bill of lading. It merely represents the goods, and transfer of the symbol operates only as a transfer of what is represented. A valid title cannot be obtained from a thief as is possible in the case of a negotiable instrument. A transferee takes a bill of lading subject to any defects in the title of the transferor and prior parties. Except for the purposes of the Factors Act and of defeating the right of stoppage *in transitu*, no better title can be obtained to the goods than that possessed by the transferor. This limitation must always be borne in mind and indicates the need for dealing only with persons of integrity.

The sole exceptional feature of a bill of lading which is akin to negotiability is that, upon endorsement and delivery to a *bona fide* transferee for value, it defeats the unpaid vendor's right of stoppage *in transitu*. Where goods are at sea and the consignee, who has not paid for them, becomes insolvent, the unpaid vendor has the right to stop the goods before delivery and retake possession. By Section 47 of the Sale of Goods Act, 1893, where a document of title to goods has been lawfully transferred by the buyer or owner of the goods to a person who takes the document in good faith and for value, the seller's right of lien, retention, or stoppage *in transitu* is defeated.

The effect of endorsement of a bill of lading was explained at length by Lord Justice Bowen in *Sanders* v. *Maclean* (1883) 11 Q.B.D. 327 as follows:—

'A cargo at sea while in the hands of the carrier is necessarily incapable of

229

physical delivery. During this period of transit and voyage the bill of lading by the law merchant is universally recognised as its symbol, and the endorsement and delivery of the bill of lading operates as a symbolic delivery of the cargo. Property in the goods passes by such endorsement and delivery of the bill of lading whenever it is the intention of the parties that the property should pass; just as under similar circumstances the property would pass by an actual delivery of the goods. And for the purpose of passing such property in the goods and completing the title of the endorsee to full possession thereof the bill of lading, until complete delivery of the cargo has been made on shore to someone rightfully claiming under it, remains in force as a symbol, and carries with it not only the full ownership of the goods, but also all rights created by the contract of carriage between the shipper and the shipowner. It is a key which, in the hands of the rightful owner, is intended to unlock the door of the warehouse, floating or fixed, in which the goods may chance to be. The above effect and power belong to any one of the set of original bills of lading which is first dealt with by the shipper. Except in furtherance of the title so created of the endorsee the other originals of the set are, as against it, perfectly ineffectual and have no efficacy whatever, unless they are fraudulently used for the purpose of deceit.'

Although by the Bills of Lading Act the transferee of a bill of lading is subject to the same liabilities in respect of the goods as if the contract had been made with himself, this does not apply when the bill is endorsed and delivered as security by way of pledge. The banker, as pledgee, only obtains a special right to the goods, they are not his absolute property, and he, therefore, avoids any liability for unpaid freight (*Sewell* v. *Burdick* (1884) 10 App. Cas. 74). On the other hand, should the banker wish to collect the goods from the ship, freight will have to be paid. Under a c.i.f. contract, of course, freight is paid at the time of shipment.

The type of bill of lading acceptable to the banker is the next consideration. It must be drawn 'to order' or 'to order of assigns' and endorsed in blank by the shipper. The goods described therein should agree with the invoice and policy, and the voyage covered by the policy should be the same as that described in the bills of lading. Under a c.i.f. contract it will normally be a '*port*' or '*Shipped-on-board*' bill indicating that the merchandise has actually been received on board a stated steamer in good condition (*a clean bill*). A '*received for shipment*' bill of lading merely indicates that the goods are held awaiting a suitable vessel. They may wait some time, deteriorating on the quay in bad weather and, unless circumstances leave no alternative, such a bill is not acceptable. It naturally depends somewhat on the situation of, and the conditions prevailing at, the port of shipment. For example, one can hardly expect a shipped bill of lading when liners call irregularly for only a few hours and cargo has to be ready on the quay for rapid loading. On the other hand, beware of the seller who is so impatient to negotiate the documents that he cannot await the actual delivery of the goods on board a steamer. A '*through*' bill of lading is one which covers the carriage of goods from one place to another by several shipowners or railway companies, *e.g.* cotton from the hinterland of U.S.A. to a British port. A '*dirty*' bill is one which evidences that the goods were received in a defective state, packages being broken, or bales damp, and the banker can be guided accordingly.

Bills of lading are usually drawn in sets of three. One bill may be retained by the shipper as evidence, if required, whilst the other two are forwarded to the consignee (or negotiated through a bank) by different mails to reduce the risk of loss in course of delivery. The question arises as to whether a bank may pay against one bill out of the set, or should it insist upon the production of the complete set? Under a credit opened the instructions of the customer will be followed, but when the goods are required as security it is prudent, in the absence of a complete set, to account for those which may be missing. At law, the first party to whom a bill of lading is transferred for value undoubtedly acquires the property, but the ship-owner is entitled to deliver the goods to the first person who presents a valid bill (assuming that the shipowner has no notice of the earlier dealing with the other bill). Thus a bill may be negotiated for value to a bank on a Monday and another valid copy for the same shipment negotiated for value to another party on Wednesday of the same week. If this other party reaches the quay first when the vessel docks and the goods are delivered to him, the shipowner will be discharged, but the property in the goods must still remain in the bank (*Barber* v. *Meyerstein* (1870) L.R. 4 H.L. 317). Naturally, the banker will wish to avoid such a risk, with the subsequent trouble and the cost of recovery, by obtaining, wherever possible, a complete set and the terms of the credit should be drawn accordingly.

In *Sze Hai Tong Bank Ltd.* v. *Rambler Cycle Co. Ltd.* (1959) 3 W.L.R. 214; 2 All E.R. 182, a case heard by the Judicial Committee of the Privy Council, emphasis was laid on the imperative need of the shipowner to have regard to the importance of the bill of lading as a document of title. As Lord Denning said in the judgment:—

'It is perfectly clear law that a shipowner who delivers without production of a bill of lading does so at his peril. The contract is to deliver, on production of the bill of lading, to the person entitled under the bill of lading. In this case it was "unto order or his or their assigns", that is to say, to the order of the Rambler Cycle Company, if they had not assigned the bill of lading, or to their assigns, if they had. The shipping company did not deliver the goods to any such person. They are therefore liable for breach of contract unless there is some term in the bill of lading protecting them. And they delivered the goods, without production of the bill of lading, to a person who was not entitled to receive them. They are therefor liable in conversion unless likewise so protected'.

It has been argued that the shipping company was protected by clause 2 of the bill of lading which provided, *inter alia*, that '(c) . . . the responsibility of the carrier . . . shall be deemed . . . to cease absolutely after the goods are discharged' from the vessel. Lord Denning observed that this exemption could hardly have been more comprehensive and the question was whether it absolved the shipping company from responsibility for its act of delivering the goods to a person who, to its knowledge, was not entitled to receive them. 'If the exemption clause upon its true construction absolved the shipping company from an act such as that', continued Lord Denning, 'it seems that by parity of reasoning they would have been absolved if they had given the goods away to some passer-by or had burnt them or thrown them into the sea'. As a matter of construction, the Judicial Committee declined to attribute to it the unreasonable effect contended for.

Furthermore, it was pointed out in the judgment that if such considerable breadth were read into the exemption clause, it would run against the main object of the contract, which was the proper delivery of the goods by the shipping company 'unto order or his or their assigns', against the production of the bill of lading. It would be manifestly wrong if the shipping company was at liberty to deliver the goods to someone who was not entitled, without being liable for the consequences. The clause had thus to be limited to the extent necessary to ensure that effect was given to the principal purpose of the contract.

The main question therefore was to decide to what extent it was necessary to limit the clause to attain this object and the Judicial Committee held that it must at least ensure that the shipping company could not deliberately disregard its obligations as to delivery. 'No court', said Lord Denning, 'can allow so fundamental a breach to pass unnoticed under the cloak of a general exemption clause.'

THE CONTRACT OF PLEDGE

Having reviewed the three essential documents required under a c.i.f. contract from the banking standpoint, the stage is reached where these documents come into the possession of the bank, acting on behalf of the importer customer, after making payment to the exporter in accord with the instructions in the credit. The goods are then at sea but the banker has advanced part or the whole of the purchase price. Where is the security?

The answer is that the bank obtains a pledge of the goods. A contract of pledge has been defined as one 'where the owner of a chattel agrees with another person that it shall be held by the latter (the pledgee) as security for the payment of a debt or performance of an obligation. This entitles the pledgeee to hold the chattel until payment or performance at the proper time, to sell it, but until he does so, the pledgor may redeem it by payment or performance'. The essence of pledge is possession, actual or constructive, but there is no original need for any written evidence of the contract. If a man borrows £10 from his brother and hands to the brother his watch as security, the transaction is a simple example of a contract of pledge. The chests of tea consigned to the customer do not, however, have to be passed across the bank counter and stored in the safes. The bank obtains constructive possession either by endorsement in blank of the bills of lading by way of security, which amounts to the symbolic delivery of the tea represented therein, or by endorsement to the bank of negotiable warehouse keepers' warrants (which will be explained later), or by warehousing the tea in an independent warehouse in the bank's name. These various methods demand examination.

Possession is the essence of the contract, but without suitable written evidence the pledgee will be entitled only to hold the goods until the pledgor defaults. For the sake of liquidity the banker normally reserves the right of sale, with or without reasonable notice, and the contract is evidenced by the execution of a document setting out the facts and embodying, amongst other things, a power of sale. Care is, however, necessary to avoid the need for registration of such a document as a declaration of trust without transfer within Section 4 of the Bills of Sale Act, 1878. It is prudent to ensure wherever possible that the pledge is completed before any document is signed, thereby avoiding any suggestion of a contract of hypothecation amounting to an agreement to create a pledge, and, as such, a validity requiring registration as a bill of sale. For example, in *Rex* v. *Townshend* (1884) 15 Cox c.c. 466 a fruit broker applied to his bankers for an advance against certain goods which had been consigned to him and were then at sea. Before making the advance the banker obtained a letter of hypothecation from the customer by which he undertook to hold the goods in trust for the bank and to hand over to it the proceeds of the goods as and when received. There was no prior pledge, and it was decided that such an hypothecation letter was a bill of sale within the Acts of 1878 and 1882. In this case, however, the goods had not arrived at the date of execution of the letter of hypothecation and they were, therefore, within the exception as to 'goods at sea' contained in the 1878 Act. Prior to this case it had been common practice to leave the goods in the possession of the customer and to rely upon a letter of hypothecation as security, but thereafter it was realised that such course would be dangerous unless the document was registered as a bill of sale. Get your goods first is, therefore, the prudent banking maxim. When they are at sea or in transit from quay to warehouse, the Bills of Sale Acts do not apply and the banker can rely upon a letter of hypothecation without a prior pledge, but where the goods are in a warehouse any agreement to create a pledge or any contract of hypothecation without delivery or possession, will be invalid unless registered as a bill of sale. As far as the tea imported by our fictitious customer is concerned, the pledge is, of course, obtained upon the receipt of the bills of lading, but suppose instead the customer approached the bank for an advance against tea already stored in a London warehouse. Prudence would then dictate the transfer of the goods into the name of the bank in an independent warehouse before drawing up any document recording the conditions of such a pledge. The Bills of Sale Acts strike only at documents and not at the transactions themselves, and when a transaction is one of pledge, and nothing more, the document which describes it is not a bill of sale. In re *Hardwick Ex parte Hubbard* (1886) 17 Q.B.D. 690, a borrower deposited with the lender, by way of security for a loan of £20, two tricycles which were retained by the lender until the borrower's bankruptcy. On the same day that the loan was granted, an agreement was signed by the borrower reciting the facts and affording a power of sale upon his default. There were similar transactions, all of which were challenged by the trustee in bankruptcy, but it was decided on appeal that the Bills of Sale Act did not apply to a pledge of goods and the document, which merely evidenced a prior pledge, was not a bill of sale. Again, in re *Cunningham & Co. Ltd.*, *Attenborough's Case* (1885) 28 Ch.D. 682, the secretary of a company, acting under proper authority, deposited with Attenborough a pawnbroker, a wharfinger's warrant for 400 cases of tin plates. At the same time, the secretary signed a memorandum of charge on behalf of his company which stated that the goods were to be held as security for £200 plus interest, and contained a power of sale. It was held that the memorandum was not a bill of sale as the Act did not apply where possession of the goods was given to the lender at the time of the borrowing. For these reasons it is the practice of most bankers, where possible, to ensure that the letter recording the pledge is dated subsequent to the pledge itself. If it should be impossible first to obtain a pledge of the merchandise there is an alternative method of obtaining the security which is discussed in Chapter XXX.

In connection with the validity of a pledge the case of *Barclays Bank* v. *Commissioners of Customs & Excise* (1936) 1 Lloyd's Rep. 81 is of interest.

The Customs and Excise were judgment creditors of Bruitrix Electrical Company Ltd. and sought to bring execution against goods of the company which had been warehoused on behalf of the shipper. Barclays Bank were pledgees of the bill of lading, the pledge being after the goods were landed. The Sheriff on behalf of the

Customs had taken possession of the goods which were claimed by the Bank. The goods had in fact been sold by the Sheriff and the proceeds held pending the decision, but this aspect was not material. The point at issue was whether there was a valid pledge by the Bank's possession of the bill of lading, notwithstanding that the goods were warehoused at the time. For the Customs and Excise it was contended that the bill of lading was exhausted and no longer operative at the time of the pledge. However, the decision was given in favour of the Bank, Diplock, J., saying that the point was one of great importance to bankers and merchants. To hold that because the goods were warehoused by the shipping company, who were not prepared to part with them without delivery of the bill of lading, the pledgee of the bill of lading had no right to the goods, would be to turn the clock back to 1794. From that time the courts accepted the custom of merchants that possession of the bill of lading gave a right to the possession of the goods and the decision had been the foundation of overseas trade.

Part Seven: Advances Against Produce (continued)

Chapter XXX Trust Letters—Warehousekeepers' Receipts and Warrants—Factors Act—Imperfect Pledge

THE TRUST LETTER

After the brief examination of the general principles of pledge in Chapter XXIX, we can again return to the case of the fictitious provision-merchant customer importing tea from Ceylon. At this stage the bank will hold the bills of lading relating to the tea which is on the high seas. In due course, the ship arrives and the tea is unloaded on the quay from where it must, with due speed, be removed to a warehouse or delivered to a purchaser. The shipowner will only deliver the tea against the production of the bill of lading, a complete set of which by this time will be in the possession of the bank. How then is the produce to be removed without impairing the security position, and how can constructive possession be converted into actual possession by obtaining a warehouse receipt in the bank's name? If the bank so wishes, and the customer raises no serious objection, the goods can be collected and warehoused by an approved carrier employed by the bank, but it is probably more usual to let the customer attend to the movement of the goods himself by appointing him as trustee of the bank for a limited purpose, and thereby maintaining the original contract of pledge. If the bills of lading were released to the borrower without any restriction, the pledge would be extinguished and dealings in the goods by the customer with third parties could take place outside the control of the bank. When, therefore, the documents of title are needed for warehousing or for the sale of the goods, the customer executes a *trust letter* whereby he contracts as trustee for the bank to warehouse the goods in a stated independent warehouse in the name of the bank, or to deliver them to a named seller and apply the proceeds in due course in reduction or liquidation of his indebtedness. The contract of pledge thus continues, but it will be appreciated that the banker must have confidence in his customer, who has ample opportunity to defraud by dealing with the goods in breach of trust. Unhappily, it is not unknown for a pledgor to obtain delivery of goods on a trust letter from one bank and then to pledge the same goods as security for an advance obtained from another bank. In such circumstances, the prosecution of the customer as a fraudulent trustee does not always result in the recovery of the unsecured loans. If the customer fails whilst the goods are in his possession, they are, by virtue of the trust letter evidencing the pledge, outside the grasp of the trustee in bankruptcy.

In like manner, where the goods have been delivered to the buyer, the proceeds can be collected by the banker direct without the intervention of any trustee in bankruptcy.

The well-known case of *North Western Bank Ltd.* v. *Poynter Son and Macdonalds* [1895] A.C. 56 provides evidence of the value of a trust letter in maintaining the contract of pledge. These Liverpool bankers granted an advance of £5,000 to their customers, Page & Company, againt the security *inter alia* of 1,629 tons of phosphate rock, pledged to the bank, which held the bills of lading. To facilitate the sale of the goods, the bill of lading was delivered against a trust letter to the pledgors, who had sold the cargo to Alexander Cross & Sons of Glasgow and had advised the bank suitably of the sale contract. Part proceeds were duly received by the bank, but the outstanding balance, amounting to £1,039 was attached by John Poynter Son and Macdonald, Chemists of Glasgow (who were the Scottish agents of Page & Company), to meet sums due to them by the pledgors. It was contended that the bank by the delivery of the bill of lading to Page & Company had lost its rights as pledgee of the cargo and that the proceeds were arrestable by the creditors of Page & Company in preference to the bank. This view was ultimately overridden. It was decided that the bank's security was not affected and it was entitled to the proceeds of the cargo as against the claims of the creditors of the borrowers. It was said, 'there can be no doubt that the pledgee might hand back to the pledgor as his agent for the purpose of sale, as was done in this case, the goods he had pledged, without in the slightest degree diminishing the full force and effect of his security'.

A later case where the pledgor was a limited company serves to confirm the position. In *re David Allester Ltd.* [1922] 2 Ch. 211 the company, being wholesale seed merchants, constantly borrowed from Barclays Bank, amongst others, by way of overdraft secured by the deposit of bills of lading and other documents of title to seed bought for re-sale. When they had agreed to sell, they obtained the documents from the bank against a trust letter in the normal manner. The company went into liquidation owing £1,200 to the bank with goods outstanding unsold, released against such trust letters. The liquidator wished to determine whether the bank was entitled to priority in respect of the proceeds of the sale of goods so released by the bank prior to liquidation, and contended that the trust letters required registration either under the Bills of Sale Acts as a declaration of trust, or as a charge upon book debts under the Companies Acts. It was held that, as the trust letter merely recorded the terms on which the company was authorised to realise the goods on behalf of the bank and did not really create any charge at all, it did not require registration. The bank's previous rights as pledgee remained unaffected by this mode of realisation and its charge had been created quite independently of and prior to the trust letter—'the bank as pledgee created a trust agency in the company for the purpose of realisation of the bank's security. That trust agency was acknowledged and recorded in the letters of trust. That is the whole of the transaction.'

Provided, therefore, that the bank has a pre-existing valid pledge the validity of the trust letter can be accepted and the proceeds of goods sold can be followed. It is advisable, of course, to keep in close touch with the position throughout and, when the bill of lading is released for warehousing, to press for a warehouse-keeper's receipt in the bank's name within a reasonable period, or to watch for the proceeds when the goods are sold. Different types of letter are generally used for warehousing and for sale. In the former the customer usually undertakes to keep the goods fully insured at his expense.

WAREHOUSEKEEPER'S RECEIPTS

Returning again to the tea which was imported from Ceylon, the stage had been reached where the bills of lading were taken away from the bank against a trust letter, whereby the customer undertook to hold the tea in trust for the bank and to warehouse it in an approved independent warehouse, instructing the warehousekeeper to issue a receipt direct to the bank evidencing that the goods are held to the order of the bank. The normal period which must elapse before completion of this movement of the merchandise will be known locally and failure to receive the required receipt within such reasonable time will occasion enquiry to verify the position. As soon as the receipt is held the pledge is again complete, and the tea cannot be removed from the constructive possession of the bank without its express consent by the issue of a delivery order signed by duly authorised officers.

A warehousekeeper's receipt may be defined as a document issued by a warehousekeeper evidencing that the goods described therein are held in his warehouse at the disposal of the party named. It is not a document of title as it does not purport to represent the goods themselves, and title can only be passed by the issue of a *transfer order or delivery order* executed by authorised officials of the bank, whose specimen signatures will be filed with the warehousekeeper. If possible, steps should be taken to limit the usual lien of the warehousekeeper for unpaid charges to those in respect of the goods described in the receipt issued to the bank, otherwise the goods may be held pending the payment of charges relating to other merchandise stored by the customer in the same warehouse. Some warehousekeepers will not, however, waive their general lien. It is always advisable to verify that warehouse charges are paid regularly by the customer. If they are allowed to fall into arrears, additional security margin may be required to meet the costs paid by the bank before the goods are released.

Where goods are already warehoused before an approach is made to the bank for an advance, it is not sufficient to rely upon the deposit of a receipt in the name of the pledgor, plus his transfer order directing the warehousekeeper to hold the goods in the name of the bank. The pledge is by no means complete. Both the receipt and the transfer order should be lodged with the warehousekeeper and a fresh receipt obtained in the name of the bank before the advance is granted. The receipt in the customer's name may refer to goods which have already been released against delivery orders.

WAREHOUSEKEEPER'S WARRANTS

A few warehousekeepers in England have authority under special Acts of Parliament to issue warrants which are transferable instruments. For example, the Liverpool Warehousing Co. Ltd. Delivery Warrants Act, 1896, empowers that company to issue warrants transferable by endorsement. As such they are documents of title and the lending banker has a valid pledge of the goods when he holds the relative warrants. It does not follow that every warrant is transferable and they should not, therefore, be accepted unless the private Act under which they are said to be transferable is known or has been examined. Unless the advance is quite temporary, it is preferable to lodge the warrant with the warehousekeeper in exchange for a receipt so that releases can be made only against delivery orders signed by the bank.

According to the Stamp Act, 1891, a warrant for goods means any document in writing being evidence of the title of any person therein named to the property in any goods lying in any warehouse or dock, or upon any wharf, signed or certified by or on behalf of the person having custody of the goods.

It is prudent to record for reference those warehousekeepers who have power to issue warrants under special Acts and to distinguish those who issue warrants which are not transferable. Any of the latter warrants should immediately be lodged with the warehousekeeper and a receipt obtained in the bank's name. Pledge is not then complete until a fresh warrant or receipt is issued in favour of the bank. Unless the bank is dealing with a factor under the Factors Act the endorsement of such a warrant does not pass the ownership of the goods, even though the warrant itself purports to represent the goods.

The above review of warehouse warrants and warehousekeeper's receipts shows that only a bill of lading and a warehousekeeper's warrant issued under a special Act of Parliament are documents of title. To avoid confusion, it is convenient now to refer to the definition of a document of title contained in the Factors Act of 1889, where it is stated the expression shall include any bill of lading, dock warrant, warehousekeeper's certificate and warrant or order for the delivery of goods, and any other document used in the ordinary course of business, as proof of the possession or control of goods, or authorising or purporting to authorise, either by endorsement or by delivery, the possessor of the document to transfer or receive *the goods thereby represented*. It cannot, however, be accepted from this definition that a warehousekeeper's receipt or a delivery order or warrant is automatically a document of title. Firstly, the Act covers only dealings with a mercantile agent, and a bank may frequently be dealing with the absolute owner of the goods. Secondly, the definition is qualified by the final three words 'goods thereby represented'. The usual type of warehousekeeper's receipt or order does not purport to represent the goods. It is merely 'a token of an authority to receive possession', which is quite different from one which purports to represent the goods in such manner that the goods cannot be passed without its endorsement. The safest course remains to take the goods out of the control of the customer by warehousing in the bank's name and not to rely on any documents other than the bill of lading and transferable warrants as documents of title.

SALE OF PLEDGED GOODS BY BORROWER

In due course, the merchandise pledged by the borrower will be sold, probably in different lots, to several purchasers. The customer will advise his banker of each sale and obtain delivery of the goods against a trust letter disclosing the name of the buyer, and stating that the proceeds of sale are due on or before the given date. To avoid extinguishing the pledge, all delivery orders should be drawn by the bank in favour of the pledgor, who acts as a trustee to apply the proceeds to the account. If the delivery order authorised delivery to the buyer, it would destroy the link and end the pledge. Where deemed advisable, enquiries can be made through normal channels to verify the financial standing of the buyer and a careful record is always maintained to ensure that the proceeds are received within the period accepted as usual in the particular trade.

Throughout the whole procedure which has now been outlined, it is essential to maintain in the bank's books a complete record of each transaction in such manner that at any time it is possible to show precisely which goods (in whatever form) are pledged to the bank. Unlike the normal security entries, records of goods pledged are constantly changing with movements from quay to warehouse and out for sale. Nevertheless strict accuracy of detail is necessary to maintain a complete chain of identification and to be in a position to prove, in case of need, that the goods in question are pledged to the bank. It may be necessary to follow the proceeds of goods taken out against a trust letter by a customer subsequently adjudged bankrupt, and to prove to the trustee in bankruptcy that the bank is entitled to such proceeds, or it may be necessary to prove that merchandise in the possession of a bankrupt customer is outside the doctrine of reputed ownership exercisable by his trustee. Starting from the original record made from the invoice, the marks, weight and full description of the goods should be scheduled in all documents, including the delivery order authorising the customer to obtain possession, and the stock records of the bank should enable them to schedule the goods pledged for each customer whenever required for purposes of security valuation. If, for example, any discrepancy arises between the description of the produce originally pledged and the description in the trust letter and the delivery order, difficulty might arise because the chain of identification had been broken. Admittedly, marks can be altered on merchandise withdrawn from warehouse, thereby complicating the problem of identification, but usually such alterations will be recorded in the books of the pledgor.

FACTORS ACT, 1889

Up to this stage it has been assumed that the pledgor had full power to pledge the produce as security to the bank. There is the common law rule— *nemo dat quod non habet*—that a person cannot give a better title to property than that which he himself possesses. If, therefore, the banker obtains a pledge of goods which the pledgor has stolen, the pledge is worthless. Pledge of a bill of lading is equally useless where the pledgor has no title to the bill, which, it will be recalled, is not a fully negotiable instrument. According to the provisions of the special Act under which it is issued, a transferable warrant may be fully negotiable and a valid pledge obtained from a thief in the absence of any prior forgery. Apart from negotiable instruments and sales in market overt, any defect in the title of the pledgor is passed to the pledgee unless protection can be obtained under the Factors Acts codified in the Act of 1889.

Space does not permit of an exhaustive analysis of the scope of this Act and indeed it is doubtful whether the practical banker will wish to rely to any great extent upon its provisions. Excluding dispositions by sellers and buyers, the protections apply only when dealing with a mercantile agent, being one who in the customary course of his business has authority either to sell goods, or to consign goods for the purposes of sale, or to buy goods, or to raise money on the security of goods. Frequently the banker will be dealing with the absolute owner of the goods, and not merely one who is acting as an agent for the true owner. In the ordinary course of business it may be difficult to distinguish between customers who are dealing on their own account or as mercantile agents, but the defence may be available in case of need.

Section 2 of this Act provides that where a mercantile agent is, with the consent of the owner, in possession of goods or the documents of title to goods, any pledge made by him when acting in the ordinary course of his business shall be as valid as if he were expressly authorised by the owner to make the pledge, provided, of course, that the pledgee acts in good faith and has no notice that the agent had not authority to make the pledge. The limitations which have already been discussed on the interpretation of a document of title within this Act must be borne in mind. There is the further restriction in Section 4 that a pledge of goods by a mercantile agent to secure an antecedent debt is void except, of course, when the agent has a valid title to the goods, or makes the pledge with the consent of the owner. A banker cannot therefore expect to rely upon a pledge of goods as security for any overdraft incurred before the pledge, although it is possible that where the advance is granted to enable the customer to lift documents pledged thereafter to the bank, this will form part of the same transaction and will not be construed as pledge for an antecedent debt. The principle in general is merely a strict application of the rule that a past consideration is normally void and insufficient to support a contract.

By way of illustration of this protection it is interesting to recall the case of *Lloyds Bank* v. *Bank of America National Trust and Savings Association* [1938] 2 K.B. 147 when the English banker suffered loss following the pledge to another bank by a mercantile agent of goods released against a trust letter. Messrs. Strauss & Co. pledged to Lloyds Bank merchandise which they owned and then obtained possession of the documents of title by giving a trust letter to the bank. In fraud, they later pledged the same goods to the American bank who acted in good faith and in complete ignorance of the previous pledge. The question to be decided was which banker was entitled to the security. The Master of the Rolls held that Strauss & Company were mercantile agents within the Factors Act and the pledge to the Bank of America was consequently valid. They were in possession of the goods as mercantile agents with the permission of Lloyds Bank, who were deemed to be the owners of the goods within Section 2 of the Factors Act. This appears to be a somewhat liberal interpretation of the Act, but serves here as an example of the protection available to the pledgee bank.

DISPOSITIONS OF GOODS BY SELLERS AND BUYERS

Sections 8 and 9 of the Factors Act, 1889, and Section 25 of the Sale of Goods Act, 1893, provide some protection where goods are pledged by a customer who has not paid for them or has previously sold them to a third party. Where a person, having sold goods, continues in possession of them, any delivery by that person, or by a mercantile agent acting for him, of the goods under any sale or pledge, to any person receiving them in good faith and without notice of this previous sale, shall have the same effect as if the person making the delivery were expressly authorised by the owner of the goods so to do . In the absence of this provision, a banker receiving goods, already sold, as security from a seller would have no title to them against the owner. Moreover, this protection is not limited to a pledge by a mercantile agent and it obtains when the goods are pledged for an antecedent debt. Under Section 9 of the Act where a buyer, with the consent of the seller, obtains possession of goods, the delivery by that person, or by a mercantile agent acting for him, of the goods under any sale or pledge, to any person receiving them in good faith and without notice of any lien or other right of the original owner, shall have the same effect as if the person making the delivery were a mercantile agent in possession of the goods with the consent of the owner. Here protection is limited by the powers of a mercantile agent and a valid pledge cannot necessarily be obtained to cover an antecedent debt.

A banker is naturally pleased to hear that goods pledged as security have been sold because the source of repayment is then in sight, but doubt may arise where the customer seeks to pledge as security goods which according to him have already been sold. When does the property pass? A valid pledge cannot be obtained when, to the express knowledge of the pledgee, the title has passed to the buyer. If a customer seeks to pledge goods and does not inform the banker that they have been sold, protection is clearly given by Section 8 of the Factors Act, and it may not always be prudent, therefore, to enquire whether the goods have been sold at the time of the pledge. When the customer informs the banker that they have been sold, he will wish to know whether the actual goods have been allocated to the particular contract. Where there is a contract for the sale of unascertained goods, no property in the goods is transferred to the buyer unless and until the goods are ascertained (Section 16 of the Sale of Goods Act, 1893). The sale of an unascertainable portion of a larger ascertained quantity of goods passes no property to the buyer until that portion is identified and appropriated to the contract. If a seller agrees to deliver a certain quantity of tea described as '5 out of 25 cases', no one can say which part of the whole quantity he has agreed to deliver until an allocation is made. This necessarily means that if 5 cases were pledged to the bank they must be ascertained by being separated from the bulk (or bear distinguishing marks) before any property in the tea can pass to the bank. *Wait & James* v. *Midland Bank* (1926) 31 *Com. Cas.* 172 is worthy of study in this respect.

Assuming that the customer gives notice of a prior sale, it will depend upon whether he has sold the specific goods about to be pledged or merely contracted to sell a quantity of goods of the same description. In the former event the banker cannot obtain a valid title against the buyer, but in the latter case the contract is merely an agreement to sell unascertained goods and there is nothing to prevent the banker obtaining a valid security. Again, it may be that the customer has reserved his right of disposal of the goods which he wishes to pledge to the bank. Section 19 of the Sale of Goods Act provides that where there is a contract for the sale of specific goods, or where goods are subsequently appropriated to the contract, the seller may, by the terms of the contract or appropriation, reserve the right of disposal of the goods until certain conditions are fulfilled. In such a case the property in the goods does not pass to the buyer until the conditions imposed by the seller are fulfilled. It is probable, therefore, that frequently when a customer announces that the goods have been sold, the property will not have passed to the buyer and a pledge can be obtained. Everything depends upon the detailed circumstances, and whilst hesitating to suggest an ostrich-like attitude, deep enquiry fixing the bank with notice should be avoided. A banker relies upon the commercial integrity of the customer and a real risk will rarely arise. At worst it will be appreciated that where the bank has notice of a sale of specific

Q

goods before they are pledged to the bank, and the pledgor disappears with the proceeds of sale, the buyer can rightly claim the goods from the bank.

IMPERFECT PLEDGE

Frequently a customer readily agrees to execute a charge over goods but insists upon retaining them upon his own premises. A timber merchant may be prepared to stack timber in a particular corner of his yard, but decline to move it to an independent store to be held in the name of the bank. In such event, there is no delivery of the goods into the possession of the pledgee and, if the bank is dealing with a limited company, such a charge would require registration at Companies' House. Likewise any document issued by a partnership or private trader seeking to give the banker a charge over produce would require registration as a bill of sale.

The only means of avoiding such complications would be for the bank to rent a portion of the customer's premises, access to which could be obtained solely by the banker or his authorised agents, and to store the pledged goods therein. Thus, part of a warehouse might be sealed off, rented nominally to the bank, and all keys to the doors held by the bank. To avoid the need for attendance of a bank representative when goods were to be withdrawn, an official of the pledgor might be appointed trustee and agent for the bank, to hold the keys and to control the contents of the building. The weaknesses of this system are obvious, but circumstances may occasionally dictate acceptance to obtain some degree of security, and to remove the goods from the reputed ownership powers of a trustee in bankruptcy.

WHERE PLEDGE IS IMPOSSIBLE—USE OF LETTER OF HYPOTHECATION

Lastly, brief reference can be made to the method whereby, despite the dangers of failure to register under the Bills of Sale Acts, a pledge is not taken and the banker relies for his security upon a letter of hypothecation over the goods. Obviously a pledge cannot always be obtained. Accommodation may have to be granted to enable the customer to take up documents, or delays may occur before the goods can be warehoused in the bank's name. Resort may then be had to a letter of hypothecation, relying upon the decision in *re Hamilton Young & Co.*, [1905] 2 K.B.772.

This case concerned advances made to traders who were exporting goods which had to be bleached and packed prior to shipment. They were sent to bleachers and thereafter returned to the customers or sent direct to packers for shipment. When each advance was granted the banker took a letter of lien in the following terms, together with the bleacher's receipt for the goods:—

'We beg to advise having drawn a cheque on you for £ . . . which amount please place to the debit of our loan account No. 2 as a loan on the security of goods in course of preparation for shipment to the East. As security for this advance we hold on your account and under lien to you the under-mentioned goods in the hands of (here followed a list of goods and names of bleachers) as per their receipt enclosed. These goods, when ready, will be shipped to Calcutta, and the bills of lading, duly endorsed, will be handed to you, and we then undertake to repay the above advance either in cash or from the proceeds of our drafts on Messrs. Ewing & Co., Calcutta, to be negotiated by you and secured by the shipping documents representing the above-mentioned goods. But in no case is the advance to extend beyond two months from date hereof, unless by special arrangement, at the expiry of which we undertake to repay the same or any portion thereof then outstanding. Interest on this advance to be at the rate of 6 per cent. per annum. We undertake that the goods, while in course of preparation for shipment, shall be covered against fire risk under a general policy of assurance, which we shall desposit with you.'

It was decided by the Court of Appeal that these letters of lien were not void as being bills of sale in the prescribed form and unregistered under the Bills of Sale Acts but were 'documents used in the ordinary course of business as proof of the possession or control of goods' within the exceptions of Section 4 of the Bills of Sale Act, 1878. From this ruling it would appear that an owner by agreement in the shape of a mercantile trust letter and a letter of hypothecation can charge goods retained in his possession as bailee for the lender, and the instrument recording the arrangement will not be void as a bill of sale and will also take the goods out of the lending 'order and disposition' within the bankruptcy rules. To ensure that any document executed by the customer will be regarded as one used in the ordinary course of business as proof of the possession or control of goods, it is customary to adopt a form very similar to that used in the *Hamilton Young* Case. Any departure from that form might result in the document being looked upon as one which required registration as a bill of sale. It has, however, to be amended suitably to avoid the creation of an equitable mortgage which would require registration in the case of a limited company at Companies' House.

Doubt is expressed in some quarters upon the validity of this practice and some suggest that reliance cannot be placed upon the *Hamilton Young* Case. Nevertheless, the decision has not been reversed in the past half-century and the acknowledged practice of many bankers would greatly strengthen the defence against any action suggesting the documents were invalid for want of registration. For obvious reasons, it is prefereable to take the goods out of the possession of the borrower and to obtain a valid pledge with subsequent control over the goods, but where this course is impracticable resort can be had to a letter of hypothecation as a document used in the ordinary course of business as proof of the possession or control of the goods within the *Hamilton Young* decision.

Chapter XXXI Assignment of Contract Moneys

It sometimes happens that a customer in whom the bank has every confidence can offer no tangible security for borrowing apart from a charge over the amounts due from contracts which are being financed partly by the bank advances. In practice, these cases are usually confined to builder and contractor customers. The assignment of an ordinary book debt due to a private or trading customer is a security which is rarely taken and then only as a last resort. Nevertheless, the law and practice relating to the assignment of debts is worthy of consideration.

An assignment of this kind has obvious limitations as security. In the case of a builder or contractor customer assigning to the bank all moneys at any time due under a contract, its value depends upon the due execution of the work in a satisfactory manner by the contractor and is subject to the terms of the contract and any rights of set-off enjoyed by the employer. Moreover, if the borrower uses the advances for purposes other than work on the contract, there will be no security created for the bank. Everything depends, therefore, upon the integrity and ability of the borrower, and the ability of the employer or other third party to pay the debt so assigned. In the case of a limited company contractor, a floating charge will usually be obtained to cover the entire assets, but it must not be forgotten that, if the bank has to appoint a receiver, the claims of all preferential creditors have to be settled out of the proceeds of the assets before anything can be applied in reduction of the bank debt. It may, therefore, be helpful to obtain a specific charge over certain contract moneys in addition to the floating charge. To be valid, any assignment of contract moneys by a limited company has to be registered at Companies' House within twenty-one days of its creation. This requirement will be emphasised later.

From the legal standpoint, the assignment of an existing debt may be legal or equitable.

LEGAL ASSIGNMENT

Section 136 of the Law of Property Act, 1925, requires a legal assignment to be made in writing, signed by the assignor customer, and express notice of the assignment has to be given in writing to the debtor. The legal assignment is incomplete without this written notice to the party liable to pay the amount to the customer. It is essential to enable the bank, in case of need, to sue in its own name to recover the debt. If the bank omitted to give notice and the debtor duly paid the assignor, he would be discharged, but when notice is served, any payment made thereafter direct to the assignor customer will not prevent the bank from recovering the amount from the debtor. Failure to serve notice also entails the risk that a subsequent assignee for value of the same debt, who obtained it without knowledge of the assignment to the bank and duly gave notice in writing to the debtor, can obtain priority for his security (*Marchant* v. *Martin Down & Co.* [1901] 2 K.B. 829). All assignments are subject to equities arising prior to the date of notice, but when notice is not served on the debtor, they will continue to be subject to equities arising after the date of the assignment. Notice is clearly essential to determine the position and to remove the debt from the order or disposition of the debtor within the meaning of Section 38 of the Bankruptcy Act, 1914 (*Rutter* v. *Everett* [1895] 2 Ch. 872).

In practice, the bank serves prompt notice in writing upon the debtor asking for his acknowledgement of it and for confirmation of the amount owing. It is also prudent to ask the debtor to state whether he has any right of set-off against the assignor and whether he has received notice of any previous assignments. These last precautions relate to the assignment of a specific debt.

EQUITABLE ASSIGNMENT

Any assignment which does not fulfil the above requirements set out in Section 36 of the Law of Property Act, 1925, is an equitable assignment which does not enable the assignee to sue in his own name. An assignment is often only equitable because notice is not given to the debtor, in which event all the risks described above are accepted. A borrowing customer may object to the bank sending notice of the assignment to a particular debtor and the bank may be disposed to rely on an equitable assignment for what it may be worth.

A general assignment of book debts cannot be obtained as a valid security unless it is registered as a bill of sale, a course which a bank is unlikely ever to adopt. According to Section 43 (1) of the Bankruptcy Act, 1914, where a person engaged in any trade or business makes an assignment to any other person of his existing book debts, or any class thereof, and is subsequently adjudicated bankrupt, the *assignment is void against the trustee* as regards any book debts which have not been paid at the commencement of the bankruptcy, *unless the assignment has been registered as if it were a bill of sale* given otherwise than by way of security for the payment of a sum of money. Nothing in this Section invalidates any assignment of book debts due at the date of the assignment from specified debtors, or of debts growing due under specified contracts. This Section is quoted merely to emphasise how imperative it is always to take an assignment of specific debts or over specified contracts, giving due notice in writing to the third party who is liable to the customer or collateral assignor to the bank. For example, a farmer customer is sometimes called upon to assign to the bank all sums due or to become due to him under his milk contract with the Milk Marketing Board, notice of which is duly served upon the Board.

EFFECTING THE SECURITY

Ignoring for our purpose the isolated cases where in exceptional circumstances the bank might take as security an assignment of an existing debt in a forlorn attempt to strengthen the bank's position, it remains to consider the practical means of obtaining a charge on the contract moneys of a builder or contractor customer. The legal rules outlined above apply throughout. Whilst a legal assignment strictly cannot be obtained over a future debt, an assignment taken by a bank over contract moneys due in the future after carrying out the contract work will be treated in equity as a contract to assign which protects the bank, always providing that notice is served upon the employer who will be liable for the future debts.

A *legal assignment* is usually taken from the customer declaring that, in consideration of the bank making or continuing advances or otherwise affording banking facilities, the mortgagor assigns unto the bank all moneys now, or to become due, to the assignor from the debtor under or by virtue of the stated contract. Other standard provisions will be introduced to protect the bank (*e.g.*, Section 93 of the Law of Property Act, 1925, will usually be expressly excluded). Notice is given, in duplicate, to the employer calling for his acknowledgment by way of receipt on the carbon copy and confirmation that no notice of any prior assignment or charge in respect of the contract has been received.

In approved cases the bank may be content with a much more informal document creating an *equitable charge* over the contract moneys. This may be reduced in its simplest form to a letter addressed by the borrower to the employer instructing the latter to pay all moneys when due direct to the bank. After reference to the contract, the customer calls upon or authorises the employer to remit all moneys due, or to become due, thereunder direct to the bank for the credit of his account, stating that the receipt of the bank can be regarded as an adequate discharge. In all these cases, notice is given to the employer or other party liable, or to become liable, to the customer. The real worth of the security depends upon the capacity of the customer to complete the contract in accord with its requirements, the ability of the employee or debtor to meet the payment, with the ever present risk of set-off rights, and the validity of the assignment in case trouble arises.

NEED FOR LIMITED COMPANY TO REGISTER CHARGE

Where the assignment is given by a limited company it has to be registered at Companies' House within twenty-one days of its creation. The dangers of omission so to register such an assignment and the general effect of these informal letters were discussed at length in *Re Kent & Sussex Sawmills Limited* [1947] Ch. 177, which can now be considered in order to complete this review of assignments as banking security.

In June, 1944, Kent & Sussex Sawmills Ltd. obtained a contract with the Ministry of Fuel and Power for the supply of 30,000 tons of cut logs and Westminster Bank agreed to finance this contract. As security, the company wrote a letter to the Ministry of Fuel and Power which, after reference to the contract, stated: '*With reference to the above mentioned contract, we hereby authorise you to remit all moneys due thereunder direct to this company's account at Westminster Bank Ltd., Crowborough, whose receipt shall be your sufficient discharge. These instructions are to be regarded as irrevocable unless the said bank should consent to their cancellation in writing, and are intended to cover any extension of the contract in excess of 30,000 tons if such should occur.*'

This letter was sent by the bank to the Ministry, who acknowledged it by letter agreeing to follow the directions for payment of all moneys direct to the bank. A year later the company entered into a further contract for the supply of 70,000 tons of logs to the Ministry of Fuel and Power and the bank agreed to lend up to a maximum of £70,000, on the understanding that the company wrote another letter to the Ministry authorising it to pay all moneys due under this contract also direct to the bank. This letter was in similar terms to the previous letter quoted above and was sent by the bank to the Ministry, who acknowledged it stating that payments would be made to the bank with the authority of the company. Early in 1946, the company went into a creditors' voluntary liquidation, at which time £30,000 remained outstanding due to the company under the two contracts with the Ministry of Fuel and Power, and the indebtedness on the account of the company with Westminster Bank totalled £83,674. The liquidator claimed that, as the two letters of authority had not been registered at Companies' House within the requirements of Section 79 of the Companies Act, 1929 (now Section 95 of the Companies Act, 1948) they were void, and the bank had therefore no security from them. It rested with the Court to interpret the legal effect of the letters of assignment and to decide whether in fact they constituted a charge on the book debts of the company and had to be registered to be effective. The Court decided that the letters were equitable assignments, there being by way of implication an equity of redemption in that it was stated that they were to be regarded as irrevocable unless the bank consented to their cancellation in writing. They were thus an assignment by way of security or a charge on book debts and, as they had not been registered, the charge was void.

To appreciate the way in which the Court interpreted the letters, with reference to previous examples, it is of interest to follow the judgment of Wynn-Parry, J., which is set out fully below:—

'This summons comes before me, in which the liquidator asks for a declaration that the two letters of authority constitute charges on the book debts of the company under Section 79 (2)(e) of the Companies Act, 1929, and that, not having been registered under that section—as is admitted—they are void as against the applicant, the liquidator. It is admitted on behalf of the bank that the subject-matter of the application is properly to be regarded as coming under the heading of book debts within the section, and the first point was therefore not taken. That leaves the second point for consideration, namely, whether the transaction evidenced by the two letters of September 18, 1944, and June 4, 1945, respectively, amounted to an out-and-out assignment in each case of the whole of the company's beneficial interest in the proceeds of the respective contracts or whether in each case nothing more was effected than the hypothecation of the respective book debts by the company to the bank by way of security.

'It is clear from the authorities that it is the duty of the court to come to a conclusion on what is the substance of the matter, and for the sake of convenience I shall test this matter by reference solely to the language of the letter of September, 18, 1944. On behalf of the liquidator, Mr. Strangman, as his first point, submitted that the proper conclusion is that in this letter there can be found no assignment at all, in which case *cadit quaestio*. In support of that argument he referred to the case of *Bell* v. *The London & North-Western Ry Co.* ([1852]. 15 Beav. 548, 552, 553.) In that case, a railway contractor gave his bankers a letter directing the railway company to pass the cheques which might become due to him to his account with the bank and it was held that that was not an equitable assignment, but that it would have been if it had directed the cheques to be passed to the banker. In his judgment Lord Romilly, M.R. said: "The words of this letter are these: 'You will oblige by passing the cheques that may become due on my contract No. 1, of the Rugby and Stamford Railway, into the National Provincial Bank of England . . .' I should have thought that an effectual assignment of all that might become due to Thomas Burton under that contract has been made to the bank; but his order directs it to be paid to the account of Thomas Burton, not therefore, as it appears to me, doing more than constituting the bank to be Thomas Burton's agents for the receipt of the money." If the letter of September 18, 1944, had stopped at the end of the first paragraph, then, in my view, it would have followed that this case was completely covered by what was said by Lord Romilly in *Bell* v. *London and North-Western Ry. Co.* I have to consider the effect on this aspect of the matter of the second paragraph, which opens with these words: "These instructions are to be regarded as irrevocable unless the said bank should consent to their cancellation in writing". I think that the effect of those words on the matter is really as submitted by Mr. Buckley for the bank, because, as he points out, it appears from the paragraph in *Bell* v. *London and North-Western Ry. Co.* that the Master of the Rolls arrived at the conclusion at which he did in view of the circumstance that, as he said, "an order of that description would always be revocable by the person giving it, but not so an order to pay to the third person absolutely".

'Effect must be given to those words, and in my judgment the proper way of construing this letter, looking at it as a whole, is to bear in mind and never to lose sight of the circumstances that the relationship of the two parties in question, the company and the bank, was that of borrower and lender, and that this letter was brought into existence in connection with a proposed transaction of borrowing by the company and lending by the bank. So regarded, I think the opening words of the second paragraph fall naturally into the picture and that they must be regarded as having been introduced for the protection of the bank. But once that is admitted, it throws light upon the whole of the letter and serves to underline what is obviously equally the intention of the first paragraph, namely, to provide protection for the bank. It therefore appears to me that the result of that is to take this case out of *Bell* v. *London and North-Western Ry. Co.* and to lead to the conclusion that I must treat this letter as amounting to an equitable assignment.

'That, however, does not conclude the matter, because I have then to investigate the question whether that assignment on its true construction is an out-and-out assignment of the whole of the benefit accruing or to accrue to the company under the contract or whether it is no more than an assignment by way of security. Here, again, I think the truth is to be found by bearing in mind the relationship between the parties. *Prima facie*, at any rate, when one has to look at a document brought into existence between a borrower and a lender in connection with a transaction of borrowing and lending, one must approach the consideration of that document with the expectation of discovering that the document is intended to be given by the borrower to the lender in order to secure repayment of a proposed indebtedness of the borrower to the lender.

'Mr. Buckley for the bank, however, has submitted, in a very attractive argument, that the true view of this matter, particularly when one regards the effect of payments made to a bank on behalf of a customer, is that this letter amounts to a sale by the company to the bank of the whole of the company's interest in the moneys due or to become due under a contract. He points out that the ultimate test of whether this can be said to amount to a security is that one must be able to discover on the face of the letter, either in express words or by necessary implication, an equity of redemption in the company and that, properly read, this letter discloses neither expressly nor by implication any such equity of redemption. As I say, I approach this matter more in the expectation of finding that the parties have brought into existence a document consistent with their relations of borrower and lender rather than finding that notwithstanding those relations they brought into existence a document in which their relationship changed to that of vendor and purchaser. In my judgment, by implication an equity of redemption is to be discovered in the language of the second paragraph. I can see no commercial business reason for the introduction of those words: "These instructions are to be regarded as irrevocable unless the said bank should consent to their cancellation", except upon the basis that the parties did deliberately contemplate that circumstances might arise in which it might become desirable that a cancellation of the instructions should be given by the bank; but the existence of that previous paragraph appears to me to operate strongly to lead to the conclusion that there was nothing in the nature of a sale. One is entitled to test the matter by looking at the situation in September, 1944, unembarrassed by what has happened since, and to consider what possibilities were open. Suppose that in fact through one source or another the company's account had become in credit with the bank, is it to be supposed that the parties ever contemplated that notwithstanding that circumstance it should remain entirely a matter for the bank to determine whether it should give its consent to the cancellation of these instructions so that if it did not give that consent, then for the rest of the period over which the contract had to be worked out, the payments still have to be paid into the company's account at the bank; so that whatever might have been the change in the friendly relations between the company and its bankers, it would have been compelled to maintain that account with the bank until the contract had been worked out? I recoil from coming to such a conclusion. In my view, if the company's account had come into credit the company would then have been entitled, in the true view of this letter, to require the bank to give the necessary instructions to the Ministry. The Ministry is in no way concerned with the position as between the bank and the company, and as between those two parties I can see no ground either at law or in equity on which the bank could have resisted a request or a requirement by the company to cancel the instructions. That at once shows that there is discoverable in this latter paragraph a true equity of redemption. I think the matter is if anything underlined by the other half of the sentence, which is to the effect that the instructions are intended to cover any extension of that contract in excess of 30,000 tons if that should occur.

'The authorities, except to the limited extent to which I have referred to them on the first point, really do not help in this matter, which is primarily one of construction, but I should mention that, as is made clear in *Saunderson & Co.* v. *Clark* ([1913], 29 T.L.R. 579), the requirements of this section, to use the words of Buckley on *The Companies Act* in the 11th edition at page 173, "cannot be evaded by making what is in fact a mortgage or charge in form of an absolute assignment, or otherwise adopting a form which does not accord with the real transaction between the parties". Mr. Buckley very properly pressed on me that the court should not be astute so to construe the letter as to bring it within the terms of the section. On the other hand, looking at the matter as best I can, and giving to it such reality as I can, I think if I were to hold that this was an out-and-out sale I should be guilty of being astute: to extract from what appears to me the reasonable plain language of this section a result which in my view upon its language can never have been intended by the parties.

'For these reasons I propose to declare in answer to question 1 of the summons that the two letters of authority which I have read constitute charges on the book debts of the company under Section 79 (2) (e) of the Companies Act, 1929, and not having been registered under that section are void as against the appellant'.

More recently came the case of *Independent Automatic Sales Ltd. and Another* v. *Knowles & Foster* [1962] 1 W.L.R. 974, where the circumstances were somewhat similar. In April 1960 the plaintiff company opened an account with the defendants with a view to borrowing and executed a document—referred to in the report as a letter of hypothecation—whereby bills of exchange and other documents 'then or thereafter' deposited should be and remain pledged as continuing security. In furtherance of the arrangement the company deposited with Knowles & Foster fifty-three hire purchase agreements and advances equivalent to 80 per cent. of the remaining instalments were made against these. Neither the letter of hypothecation nor the hire purchase agreements deposited were the subject of a registration under Section 95.

In July 1960 the company went into a creditors' voluntary liquidation and it was later held that the charges created by the deposit of the hire purchase agreements were registrable and, not having been registered, were void as against the liquidator.

PRACTICAL CONCLUSIONS

The assignment of a book debt or an assignment of contract moneys due or to become due may not be one of the best types of banking security, but, in the case of a limited company borrower, it has obvious advantages over a floating charge, always providing that it is duly registered, and in many instances it is the only tangible security available to finance contract work. If the bank has confidence in the integrity and ability of the customer to complete the contract within the agreed amount to be lent by the bank, the assignment will usually suffice to cover the position. In many cases it is, of course, taken to support existing fixed security. The risk of set-off rights intervening to reduce the amount ultimately owing to the customer has to be accepted and there is always the possibility that the borrower may fail before completing the contract, when any amounts remaining outstanding will be swallowed up in penalties payable within the terms of the contract.

Subject to these ever present risks, the practical steps to be taken when obtaining this class of security can be scheduled as follows:—

1. To obtain details of the contract and to consider its terms and requirements from both the technical and financial standpoint. The arrangements, if any, for progress payments and retentions will be material in the case of a building or kindred type of contract. From this review and its knowledge of the customers' experience and resources, the bank can decide whether it is a reasonable contract to undertake and if the finance available, comprising the agreed bank facilities, the customer's own cash resources and trade credit, is sufficient to cover the cost of all work to be done pending the receipt of progress payments.

2. To take a legal assignment of the contract moneys in the most comprehensive form possible. The bank may, however, be content to rely upon a simple letter on the lines of that used by Westminster Bank in *Re Kent & Sussex Sawmills Ltd.*, above.

3. To give notice promptly to the employer or other person who is, or will be liable to the customer. This notice is essential in all cases and should call for a written acknowledgment confirming, where applicable, the amount due, and stating that no other notices of assignment have been received.

4. If the assignor is a limited company, to register the assignment at Companies' House as a charge upon book debts, within twenty-one days of its execution.

5. Thereafter, it may be desirable to keep in close touch with the progress of the contract work to ensure, as far as possible, that drawings by the customer are used on the contract, and not diverted to other work, and that reductions are duly received from progress payments in accord with the terms of the contract.

By and large, the whole arrangement and its control, leading to a satisfactory conclusion, when the advances are repaid from the contract moneys, is a real test of banking skill and judgment.

Chapter XXXII Cash as Security—A Banker's Right of Set-off

For obvious reasons, cash is the finest type of banking security available. There are no problems of valuation, depreciation or realisation when cash is held to cover a banking facility and, providing the charge over it is complete, no difficulty can arise when it is needed to liquidate the indebtedness.

Cash may be held as security in two distinct ways:—

1. When cash is deposited by a third party expressly to secure the indebtedness of the borrower.
2. When the banker relies on credit balances of a customer as security by way of set-off to cover the overdraft of the same customer.

CASH DEPOSITED AS COLLATERAL SECURITY

It is not often in practice that a borrowing customer has a friend or relative who is prepared to deposit cash as security, but occasions do arise where the special set-off rate usually allowable on the credit balance is an attraction to the depositor. For example, the director of a private company may be willing to deposit cash in an account in his own name to support the borrowing of the limited company and part of the arrangement will be that interest is allowed exceptionally on such moneys up to the extent of the indebtedness of the company at a rate which is slightly lower than that charged on the company's account. In such cases, care is necessary to make it clear that it is a set-off arrangement and the depositor cannot expect to obtain the special credit interest rate on any part of his balance which exceeds the total indebtedness of the borrower. The danger of quoting a rate for the credit moneys without explaining these set-off restrictions is obvious, but mistakes do occur in practice and it is well to emphasise the point.

Any express arrangement for collateral cash security has to be evidenced in writing and a special agreement or letter of set-off will normally be executed by the depositor detailing the transaction. The cash will be held as security for all sums due from the borrower, either solely or jointly with any other person on any account, and the bank will usually be empowered to use the credit moneys in reduction or repayment of the customer's indebtedness at any time without notice to the depositor. In practice, a bank would not seize the collateral moneys without discussing the position with the depositor, but it is advisable always to obtain full rights to act without reference to meet extreme cases where the depositor declines to co-operate when the security has to be applied in reduction or repayment of the principal debt.

In some cases, a guarantee is taken instead from the depositor and the bank relies on the lien clause included therein to catch the cash deposited in the name of the guarantor as collateral security. In effect, the bank has a guarantee supported by cash. But some people may be unwilling to sign a guarantee with its innumerable clauses. The problem can easily be solved by the preparation of a special agreement or letter of set-off which may be relatively short and simple in its terms.

DIRECT SET-OFF

Between debtor and creditor there is an undoubted right to set off amounts due to and from each other in the ordinary course of business. When X buys wool from Y at a cost of £500 and later supplies Y with machinery worth £300, he is perfectly entitled to set off the cost of the machinery against his liability for the wool and to pay only £200 to Y in settlement of the net indebtedness. The implied right of a banker to set off at any time the balances on the accounts of the same customer in order to ascertain the net amount then due to or from the customer is, however, subject to several restrictions and it does not always follow automatically that credit moneys are valid security for the indebtedness of the same customer on other accounts. In daily practice it is essential to appreciate when credit balances may, or may not, be regarded as security by way of set-off for debit balances, and the position can be explained conveniently under three main headings:—

1. *On the face of it all the moneys must belong to the customer in his own right.*
There can be no question of any right of set-off where, to the knowledge of the banker, credit balances on any of the accounts are held by the customer in a fiduciary capacity as trustee or agent. Notice of such trust may be actual or constructive. Clearly, an overdraft on a private current account cannot be set off against a balance on deposit in the name of the same customer but marked 'Swimming Club A/c.' Where X has two accounts designated 'No. A 1/c.' and 'No. 2 A/c.' the balances are apparently entirely his own assets and/or liabilities. Without such an essential basis the possibility of any right of set-off can never arise.

Many examples can be drawn from practice of accounts in the same name but clearly not available for set-off. There is perhaps the sole executor or administrator who has an account for the relative estate as well as an overdraft on private account. Funds in the estate account obviously cannot be set off against the private debt of the personal representative. The solicitor customer who, in compliance with the rules contained in the Solicitors Act, 1933, conducts a separate account marked 'Clients A/c.' for his clients' moneys cannot expect the banker to set off such credit balances against any overdraft on his business or private account. Where an accountant opens separate accounts designated in such manner as to suggest trusts in the background, the bank cannot accept any instruction that it is to have regard only to the net balance on all accounts. There cannot be any power of set-off unless the moneys on all the accounts actually belong to the same trust.

253

In re Gross, ex parte Kingston (1871) 6 Ch. App. 632 a county treasurer conducted two accounts at a bank in his own name, but one was described as 'Police Account'. When he absconded leaving his private account overdrawn against a credit balance on the account headed 'Police Account', it was decided that the bank had no right to set-off the two balances. It was then said 'if an account is in plain terms headed in such a way that a banker cannot fail to know it to be a trust account, the balance standing to the credit of that account will . . . belong to the trust'.

Another example of an implied trust defeating the bank's right of set-off occurred in *Barclays Bank Ltd.* v. *Quistclose Investments Ltd.* (1968), 3 All E.R. 651. Rolls Razor Ltd. declared a dividend of 120 per cent, but had insufficient liquid resources with which to pay it, their account at Barclays Bank being overdrawn £485,000 against a limit of £250,000. A loan of £209,719 8s. 6d. was obtained from Quistclose Investments Ltd. with which to pay the dividend and a cheque for this amount, drawn by Quistclose Investments Ltd., was sent to Barclays Bank with a covering letter in the following terms: 'Confirming our telephone conversation of today's date, will you please open a No. 4 Ordinary Dividend Share Account. I enclose herewith a cheque valued at £209,719 8s. 6d. being the total amount of dividend due on the 24th July 1964. Will you please credit this to the above-mentioned account. We would like to confirm the agreement reached with you this morning that this amount will only be used to meet the dividend due on the 24th July 1964'.

Rolls Razor went into liquidation before the dividend could be paid and Barclays Bank attempted to set-off the No. 4 account against the outstanding overdraft. It was decided that the essence of the bargain was that the sum advanced should not become part of the assets of Rolls Razor Ltd., but should be used exclusively for the payment of a dividend. Failing this, there existed an implied secondary trust whereby the money should be returned to Quistclose Investments Ltd., and it was held that the letter to Barclays Bank was sufficient notice of this.

Unless a partner has contracted to be severally liable for the indebtedness of his firm, the banker cannot set off credit moneys on the private account of the partner against the overdraft of the partnership, and even then there must be some precise authority from the partner in the absence of any happening to determine the position (see later). Likewise in the absence of express agreement there is no right of set-off between joint and separate debts. The overdraft on the joint account of X and Y cannot be set off against the substantial credit balance on the current account of Y unless, of course, Y expressly agrees or X and Y have contracted for joint and several responsibility for their joint account overdraft.

Not only must the accounts be in the same right but the liability must be accruing due. For example, a credit balance due on current account or deposit cannot be held against a contingent liability on bills discounted (*Bower* v. *Foreign & Colonial Gas Co.* [1874] 22 W.R. 740).

'You cannot retain a sum of money which is actually due against a sum of money which is only to become due at a future time' (*Jeffryes* v. *Agra & Masterman's Bank Ltd.* [1866] 35 L.J. Ch. 686). This position is changed, however, by the bankruptcy of the customer, which in effect determines the position and gives the banker the right of set-off (*Baker* v. *Lloyds Bank* [1920] 2 K.B. 322).

2. The right of immediate set-off is undoubted where anything happens to determine the position and the net amount due to or from the bank has to be ascertained.

In the event of the death, bankruptcy, or mental incapacity of a customer, all balances due to or from him in the same right have to be combined to decide how much is due net to or from the estate. The same procedure applies upon the failure of a firm or the liquidation of a limited company. The position is also determined when a garnishee order is served upon the bank. In all such cases the immediate need to combine the balances is obvious and the power to set-off without notice is undoubted. The right of set-off in the event of bankruptcy is clearly laid down in Section 31 of the Bankruptcy Act, 1914, and the case of *National Westminster Bank Ltd. v. Halesowen Pressworks & Assemblies Ltd.*, The Times, January 27, 1972, confirms this. The facts were as follows. In 1968 the defendant Halesowen Company had a single loan account with the Westminster Bank and a credit trading account with Lloyds Bank. The Westminster Bank was concerned about the company's financial position and objected to this double banking. It was, therefore, agreed that the company should transfer its trading account to the Westminster Bank; that it would be styled No. 2 account and that the existing loan account would become No. 1 account, and frozen. It was further agreed that there would be no set-off for four months, but within this period there was a voluntary winding-up. On the day of the creditor's meeting a cheque for £8,611 was credited to the No. 2 account and the liquidator asked the bank to pay over the credit balance. The bank refused, claiming that the agreement not to off-set came to an end on the commencement of liquidation.

At the trial, Roskill, J., found for the bank, but in the Court of Appeal the liquidator won, by a majority. It was held that the bank had no right to combine the accounts, because they had agreed to keep them separate for a fixed period and the agreement did not show a sufficient degree of mutuality to bring it within the set-off provisions of Section 31 of the Bankruptcy Act, 1914, which is applied to the winding-up of an insolvent company by Section 317 of the Companies Act, 1948. Section 31 provides that 'where there have been mutual credits, mutual debts or other mutual dealings, between a debtor against whom a receiving order shall be made under this Act and any other person proving or claiming to prove a debt under the receiving order, an account shall be taken of what is due from the one party to the other in respect of such mutual dealings, and the sum due from the one party shall be set off against any sum due from the other party, and the balance of the account, and no more, shall be claimed or paid by either side respectively . . . '.

The House of Lords reversed the decision of the Court of Appeal and decided in favour of the bank. Certain previous decisions were examined at length and the majority took the view that it was not possible for the parties involved to contract out of Section 31. The word used in Section 31 was 'shall', not 'may', and its effect was held to make the Section mandatory. Moreover, with regard to the agreement reached between banker and customer, it was unanimously held that it was operative while the contractual relationship existed between the parties, i.e., while the company was a going concern. Immediately something happened to determine the relationship, that is, the moment the winding-up resolution was passed, the agreement came to an end.

Again, the undoubted right of set-off without notice arises where the banker as a first mortgagee receives notice that a second charge has been created over the security. In such event the accounts have to be stopped to determine the amount which can be looked upon as secured first out of the given security. Any advances made subsequent to such notice will rank after the second mortgagee and circumstances may demand the immediate set-off of all accounts to determine the position.

Finally, the position can always be determined by a demand for repayment of any indebtedness, but reasonable notice has normally to be given to enable the customer to make the necessary arrangements. Although the debt may be repayable upon demand, it is doubtful whether, in the absence of an express agreement, a credit balance could be combined with an overdraft and cheques drawn on the credit account dishonoured all on the same day as demand is served for repayment. There is, however, no need to become involved in such a delicate position if steps are taken to obtain a letter of set-off from the customer.

3. *Any implied right of set-off with which the banker may be legally endowed is subject to the ever present obligation to honour cheques properly drawn by the customer.*
The problem of set-off in relation to continuing accounts can perhaps best be introduced by means of a simple practical illustration. Suppose customer Z conducts for his convenience two current accounts described as No. 1 A/c. and No. 2 A/c. respectively. There is no question of trust moneys and nothing happens to determine the position. On March 1, when the No. 1 A/c. was credit £36 and the No. 2 A/c. credit £150, a cheque for £90 drawn on the No. 1 A/c. was paid without reference to Z, relying entirely on the credit moneys in No. 2 A/c. At the close of business the No. 1 A/c. was debit £54 and the net balance credit £96. On the following day, however, a cheque drawn on the No. 2 A/c. for £136 is presented for payment. Assuming inability to contact Z, no security, and disinclination to grant unsecured accommodation, can the banker dishonour this second cheque which, if paid, would cause a net overdraft of £40? There are still adequate funds on the No. 2 A/c. to meet his cheque for £136 and dishonour can be upheld only if in fact the banker has an implied right to set off the balances without notice to the customer. The legal position first demands consideration.

In *Garnett* v. *McKewan* (1872) L.R. 8 Ex. 10 a bank was considered to be justified in setting off without notice a credit account at one branch against a debit balance at another branch and dishonouring cheques drawn on the credit account. More recent cases, however, distinguished between the position of a banker and that of a debtor in regard to set-off. A debtor is under no obligation to honour cheques. In *Buckingham* v. *The London & Midland Bank Ltd.* (1895) 12 T.L.R. 70 a customer of twelve year's standing who had a loan of £600 against the security of house property, was suddenly informed that his account was closed and £160 in a separate current account had been transferred in reduction of the loan account. Certain outstanding cheques were subsequently dishonoured and the customer brought an action for damages. On behalf of the bank, it was contended that it could terminate its 'agency' for the customer at any time. As the customer had the right to close his account at any moment, the bank was entitled to do the same. Mr. Justice Mathew in summing up said that the case for the plaintiff was that the course for the bank was to honour his cheques without reference to the loan account and that to transfer the loan account to the current account, without giving him notice, was not the course of business agreed upon between them. It was decided that as the customer had been entitled to draw upon his current account without reference to his loan account and reasonable notice had not been given of the termination of this arrangement, the bank was liable and damages were assessed at £500. The facts in this latter case were, however, blatantly against the bank and quite remote from the practical problem which was posed at the beginning of this enquiry.

The words of Swift, J., in *Greenhalgh* v. *Union Bank of Manchester* (1924) 2 K.B. 153 have sometimes been quoted in support of the view taken in the *Buckingham* case of 1895. The actual words in the written judgment were 'with regard to the question whether a banker, having two accounts open for a customer and having appropriated bills to one, is entitled to transfer their proceeds to the other without the customer's permission, I hold that a banker has no right, without the assent of the customer, to move either assets or liabilities from one account to the other. The very basis of his agreement with the customer is that the accounts shall be separate'. These words have been quoted out of context inasmuch as this case concerned the appropriation of bills and had no connection with the duty of a banker to pay cheques. The circumstances of the case were such that the bank were on notice that the proceeds had been earmarked to meet other bills drawn by W. P. Greenhalgh & Sons and accepted by the customers. Nonetheless, Swift's words have been an embarrassment to many bankers, because in some quarters they have been interpreted as meaning that bankers have no basic right of set-off. However, at last this issue seems to have been placed beyond all reasonable doubt. In the House of Lords, Lord Kilbrandon expressed his agreement with Lord Denning's views to the effect that in the absence of agreement, express or implied, the banker's right of set-off is undoubted (*National Westminster Bank Ltd.* v. *Halesowen Pressworks & Assemblies Ltd.*, The Times, January 27, 1972).

Each set of circumstances must be examined to ensure that no express or implied agreement exists which is likely to defeat the right of set-off. *The Buckingham case,* already discussed, illustrates this, where there was an implied agreement that the customer could draw on his current account without reference to his loan account, unless, of course, something happened to determine the position. From past experience it would seem dangerous to dishonour cheques drawn on an adequate credit account merely because the balance has been set off by the banker against a debit account without *reasonable notice* to the customer. What constitutes *reasonable notice* must be decided by the Courts in the light of the facts of each case. On the other hand, the banker would presumably be justified in ignoring credit moneys in another account, dishonouring cheques drawn without arrangement on an account which itself has a balance insufficient to meet the cheques. It is surely not unreasonable to expect the customer to know the extent of his balances on all his accounts and, if he draws like friend Z in excess of No. 1 account hoping that the banker will rely upon the surplus available in the other account, he can hardly complain if cheques drawn by him on the other account are later returned for lack of funds. After all, had the cheques been presented in the reverse order, thereby first exhausting the larger credit amount, there could be no question of paying those drawn against the account with an insufficient balance. Current business practice demands that the banker should be entitled always to have regard to the net balance on all accounts, except where there is by express arrangement a separate fixed loan account.

THE PRACTICAL SOLUTION REGARDING SET-OFF

All the theoretical complications referred to above can easily be avoided in practice if steps are taken to obtain evidence of an agreement with the customer that all his accounts may be set off without notice. In other words, it is made plain that the bank will at all times have regard to the net balance on all accounts. The credit moneys can then be held unquestionably as security for any indebtedness arising on other accounts of the same customer. Evidence of a set-off arrangement may be formal or informal.

The enthusiastic manager may perhaps require every customer with more than one account to execute a formal letter of set-off empowering the banker at any time without notice to combine all accounts and have regard only to the net figure. When the customer concerned is a limited company, the letter of set-off may have to be drawn in such terms that it cannot be construed as a charge upon the credit balances of the company, thereby requiring registration at Companies' House under Section 95 of the Companies Act, 1948. Admission of the right of set-off without notice should not require registration, but some authorities are of the opinion that words suggesting a charge on credit balances might render the letter invalid unless registered as a charge on book debts. Assuming the words to be satisfactory (or the letter is to be registered within twenty-one days of execution), such a document should be signed by officers of the company duly authorised by board resolution. Such procedure puts the matter beyond doubt, but letters of set-off cannot always be obtained.

Some bankers have introduced into appropriate forms of charge words empowering the bank to set off all the accounts of the borrower without notice and even a guarantee may contain a clause whereby credit balances on the account(s) of the guarantor can be set off against his liability (when determined) under the guarantee. But such clear formal proof of the power to set off is not essential. It may be proved from correspondence or even interview notes.

Where the banker agrees to afford accommodation to a customer, the limit of any such borrowing will be (or should be) agreed at the outset and it should then be made clear that the maximum is the net balance at any time on all accounts. The arrangement may be evidenced in writing—'we confirm that we shall be pleased to place at your disposal accommodation up to a maximum of £1,000 net on all accounts available at any one time subject to normal banking conditions . . . etc.'—or verbal arrangement may suffice if it can later be proved by witnesses. Correspondence can always be worded suitably to advise the customer of the intention to set off and, if such reasonable notice is given, no objection can be raised if cheques subsequently have to be dishonoured. Obviously, it is a question of watching the account and, where necessary, taking suitable steps to establish the right of set-off without further notice. To delay may be fatal with the unsatisfactory type of customer, but advantage is not otherwise likely to be taken of the banker's delicate position in this respect. Adverting to the original practical example, it is clear that immediately after paying the cheque for £90 drawn on the No. 1 A/c. written advice of the position should be sent to the customer, emphasising that the banker has paid against the net balance on both accounts. Whilst such advice may not be in time to cover the return the next day of the cheques drawn on the No. 2 A/c. it will certainly insure for the future.

It follows that, in order to rely confidently upon cash as security by way of set-off, the banker must arm himself with reasonable evidence of the arrangement made with his customer, whereby the net balance on all the accounts maintained by the customer, both current and deposit, is at all times the material point at issue.

LETTER OF HYPOTHECATION

This review can be concluded on a warning note. A letter of set-off is sometimes described erroneously as a letter of hypothecation. The two terms are quite different and they should not be confused. A letter of hypothecation was discussed in Chapter XXX. It is a charge over the proceeds of goods which are not in the possession of the lender. 'Where property is charged with the amount of a debt but neither the ownership nor possession is passed to the creditor, it is said to be hypothecated' (Hart). Where cash is held as security, it is certainly in the possession of the lender and there can be no question of any hypothecation. The correct designation of the document evidencing the arrangement is a letter of set-off.

Part Eight: Other forms of Security (continued)

Chapter XXXIII Debentures in a Limited Company

The limited company borrower frequently issues a debenture to a bank as security. This may take the form of a legal mortgage and floating charge, or an equitable fixed charge and floating charge, or it may be merely a floating charge. All three types are here considered, although the debenture most suitable as bank security follows a standard pattern.

At the outset, it is of interest to attempt a definition of the instrument. According to Section 455 (1) of the Companies Act, 1948, the term debenture includes debenture stock, bonds and any other securities of a company, whether constituting a charge on the assets of the company or not, and in *Lemon* v. *Austin Friars Investment Trust* [1926] Ch. 1, it was decided that any document which contains an acknowledgement of indebtedness on the part of a company is a debenture within the Act. A typical bank form of debenture leaves no doubt concerning the nature of the document, and the essential conditions which are normally embodied therein can now be examined.

AMOUNT OF THE DEBENTURE

The debenture may be drawn in the same way as most forms of charge to the bank, whereby it is expressed to cover the maximum amount which may at any time be owing by the company to the bank (an 'all money' debenture), or it may be for a fixed sum, in which case a series of debentures, usually for the same round amount, may be taken, their total nominal value being equivalent to the maximum the banker has agreed to advance at the time when they are issued.

The fixed sum debenture has many disadvantages from the banking standpoint and is rarely used today. The issuing company covenants in such debentures to pay, usually on demand, a fixed sum to the payee named therein. Where they are taken as security for a fluctuating indebtedness, these debentures have to be deposited under a memorandum of deposit evidencing *inter alia* that the company intends the debentures to be a continuing security for all sums due to the bank and giving the bank power to sell the debentures in the events stated. In other words, the fixed sum debenture has to be linked by the memorandum of deposit to the banking account of the company. The bank's rights are not limited to those contained in the debenture and, if need be, it can sue the company on the overdraft regardless of the debenture. The memorandum contains all the usual provisions to safeguard the bank. It is often called in legal circles the 'Buckley Agreement' from the fact that Mr. H. B. Buckley, Q.C. (who later became Lord Wrenbury) expressed the opinion that, in the absence of the memorandum, the rights of the bank might be restricted to those of an ordinary debenture holder.

The advantages of a fixed sum debenture compared with an all money debenture are more theoretical than real. In theory, it is easier to dispose of a fixed sum debenture and a buyer might be found instead of exercising the rights under the debenture itself. Few people are likely, however, to buy a debenture when the bank is unhappy about the advance, unless, of course, the price is much lower than the nominal value of the debenture. Another possible advantage lies in the fact that upon liquidation of the company the bank can prove for the full nominal amount of the debentures, less the estimated value of any property charged thereby, but the entire assets of the company are normally caught by the debenture so that the advantage is of little value in practice.

The disadvantages of a fixed sum debenture, on the other hand, are much more practical. The amount of the debenture has to be disclosed when the security is registered at Companies' House and the extent of the indebtedness of the company to the bank is thus revealed to all interested parties, including the trade creditors of the company. No amount is disclosed upon the registration of an all money debenture. Moreover, when the company customer wishes to increase its borrowing against fixed sum debentures, additional debentures have to be issued, sealed by the company and registered at Companies' House to cover the increased indebtedness. All this trouble can be avoided if an all money debenture is taken instead. Apart from the fact that it is a straightforward security in favour of the bank without any need for an accompanying memorandum, the all money debenture thus has the advantages of simplicity, providing full security at all times, without undue disclosure of the position to outside parties. A fixed sum debenture may be drawn payable to the bank, but is more often issued in favour of the bank's nominees.

REPAYMENT OF AMOUNT SECURED BY DEBENTURE

Despite the fact that the bank advance will be repayable upon demand, provisions will be inserted in the debenture to cover the repayment of the amount secured by the debenture. The events which make the principal moneys immediately repayable are always set out clearly and they normally include most, if not all, of the following:—

(a) demand in writing by the bank;
(b) default in the payment of interest for a stated period—usually two or three months;
(c) the cessation of business by the company;
(d) the institution of winding-up proceedings;
(e) the appointment of a receiver;
(f) any breach of covenant or attempt to prejudice the bank's security by amending the Memorandum or Articles of Association of the company.

Express power will be given to enable the bank to appoint a receiver when the principal sum falls due upon the happening of any of the above events. This receiver will be described as the agent of the company, which will thus be responsible for his remuneration, acts and defaults. His rights and powers will be examined later.

SUNDRY PROVISIONS IN THE DEBENTURE

The company may undertake to carry on the business to the best of its ability and adequately to insure all property and assets, producing the premium receipts to the bank as required. It may also undertake to produce audited accounts each year and agree to allow the bank to inspect the books of the company if it should so wish. Special provisions on these lines can always be inserted to meet particular requirements.

Before taking any debenture or lending to the company customer, the banker will first ensure that the company and its directors have the requisite power to borrow the amount required for the particular purpose and that they are authorised to issue the debentures to the bank as security. Nevertheless, reference to the clauses in the memorandum and articles empowering the issue may be inserted in the debenture itself, together with reference to the resolution of the directors authorising the creation of the debenture.

SECURITY EMBRACED BY DEBENTURE

The security obviously has to be described clearly and, from the banker's standpoint, it should comprise a charge on all the available assets of the company. There can be several variations, from a mere floating charge, with its many defects, to a legal mortgage on the properties listed in the schedule *and* a floating charge on the whole of the undertaking of the company present and future. In between and probably most common is a fixed charge on the assets listed in the schedule and on any fixed plant, goodwill and uncalled capital, plus a floating charge over the remainder of the assets. The fixed charge is an equitable charge unless it is expressed to be by way of legal mortgage. The security clause will usually conclude with an undertaking by the company not to create any further mortgages or charges ranking prior to, or *pari passu* with, the debenture to the bank, the terms of which should be set out in the registration of the debentures at Companies' House to constitute effective notice to all who may later seek to obtain a charge over the assets of the company.

The effect of a legal mortgage of properties specified in the debenture is precisely the same as any other legal mortgage by the company. A fixed charge which is not expressed to be by way of legal mortgage is an equitable charge whereby the company remains in possession of the property, but its beneficial interest is limited to the right to redeem the property upon repayment of the bank debt. The company cannot sell or otherwise dispose of any property subject to the fixed charge without accounting to the bank for the proceeds. A floating charge is quite different from a fixed charge. It is an original type of security peculiar to limited companies.

FLOATING CHARGES

The fixed charge created by a limited company in the bank debenture will normally be supported by a floating charge on all the remaining assets of the company, present and future. Before quoting legal definitions of a floating charge, it may be described simply as a charge which floats or hovers like a hawk over all the assets of the company as they change in the ordinary course of business. No property in the assets subject to the floating charge passes to the debenture holder and the company remains entirely free to deal with the assets as it pleases until crystallisation occurs, when, in effect, the hawk descends and the floating charge becomes a fixed charge on the assets which remain. It is thus a charge on assets which are ever changing in the ordinary course of the business of the company and, until some legal step is taken by the debenture holder to determine the position, the company is entirely free to deal with the assets, selling them and reinvesting the proceeds in fresh assets as it wishes. The most important assets caught by a floating charge in the average trading company are the trade debtors, the stock and work-in-progress, all of which change from day to day. The company may deal freely with these assets without seeking the permission of, or accounting to, the debenture holder, who cannot intervene until anything happens within the terms of the debenture to crystallise the charge, when a receiver will be appointed to take over the assets as they are at the date he appears on the scene. To illustrate the freedom so granted to the company, it is worthy of note that in *Foster* v. *Borax Co.* [1901] 1 Ch. 326, it was decided that the sale by a company of its entire assets to another company was valid despite the fact that the assets were subject to a floating charge, the sale being authorised by the memorandum of association of the vendor company.

A farmer can create a floating charge over his farming stock and other agricultural assets within Part II of the Agricultural Credits Act, 1928. Also, Industrial and Provident Societies can create fixed or floating charges over any of their assets under the Industrial and Provident Societies Act, 1967. These societies pool the buying requirements of members and co-ordinate the marketing of produce. These two exceptions apart, no individual or firm can create a valid floating charge over their personal chattels. To obtain a charge on the book debts of such personal customers, an assignment has to be taken, whilst their stock can be charged only by way of a bill of sale. A floating charge is, therefore, almost exclusively peculiar to a limited company and is a popular and convenient form of banking security in England.

Until 1961 it was, however, a form of security unknown to Scots Law. For example in *Carse* v. *Coppen* (1951) S.L.T. 145 a company registered in Scotland which had assets and a place of business in England, executed debentures which purported to create a floating charge over all its assets and the attempted encumbrance was registered at the Companies Registry in London. It was held that the debentures did not create a valid charge over either the Scottish assets or the English assets. In 1961 came the Companies (Floating Charges) (Scotland) Act which provided that a company in Scotland could henceforth create a floating charge over any or all of its property (Section 1 (1)) and laid down (in Section 5) rules concerning priorities which in the interests of completeness are here recorded and may be summarised thus:

1. A fixed charge has priority over a floating charge unless—
   (i) the fixed charge was created after the commencement of the new Act and
   (ii) the floating charge was registered before the right of the creditor under the fixed charge was constituted as a real right, and
   (iii) the instrument creating the floating charge prohibited the company from subsequently creating any fixed charge having priority over, or

ranking equally with, the floating charge.

2. Where a company's property is subject to two or more floating charges, those charges rank with one another according to the time of their registration, unless the instruments creating them provide that they are to rank equally.

3. The registration of any two or more floating charges which are received by the Registrar of Companies for registration by the same post shall be deemed to be simultaneous; such charges are to rank with one another equally.

It is important to note that this security differs in a material way from the English equivalent in that the holder cannot seek the appointment of a receiver without having the company wound up.

The moment of action for the holder is when he considers the underlying security is in jeopardy, and for the purpose of this Act the security is so imperilled if—as defined in Section 4 (2)—"events have occurred or are about to occur which render it unreasonable in the interests of the [holder of the charge] that the company should retain power to dispose of the property which is subject to the floating charge". At such a point the holder of the charge may petition for the company to be wound up and if and when the liquidation begins the security crystallises.

Another part of the Act amends the Companies Act, 1948, to provide that fixed and floating charges created by companies registered in Scotland are to be registered with the Registrar of Companies in Edinburgh in the same way as similar encumbrances on the assets of English companies are registered at Companies' House.

May it finally be noted that a floating charge created by an English company with assets in Scotland as well as in England is apparently a valid charge over all its assets (In re Anchor Line (Henderson Brothers) Ltd. [1937] 1 Ch. 483). Such complications are, however, unlikely to worry the practical banker.

LEGAL DEFINITIONS OF A FLOATING CHARGE

Having attempted a simple description of a floating charge, it will now be useful to record the following definitions laid down in the Courts.

According to Lord Macnaghten in *Governments Stock and Other Securities Investment Co. Ltd.* v. *Manilla Railway Co. Ltd.* [1897] A.C. 81, 'A floating security is an equitable charge on the assets for the time being of a going concern. It attaches to the subject charged in the varying condition in which it happens to be from time to time. It is of the essence of such a charge that it remains dormant until the undertaking charged ceases to be a going concern, or until the person in whose favour the charge is created intervenes. His right to intervene, may, of course, be suspended by agreement. But if there is no agreement for suspension, he may exercise his right wherever he pleases after default.'

In *re Yorkshire Woolcombers' Association* [1903] 2 Ch. 284, Romer, L.J., said: 'I think that if a charge has the three characteristics that I am about to mention, it is a floating charge:

1. if it is a charge on a class of assets of a company present and future;
2. if that class is one which, in the ordinary course of the business of the company, would be changing from time to time;

3. if you find that by the charge it is contemplated that, until some future step is taken by, or on behalf of, those interested in the charge, the company may carry on its business in the ordinary way as far as concerns the particular class of assets I am dealing with.'

Here is Lord Macnaghten again from *Illingworth* v. *Houldsworth* [1904] A.C. 355: 'A floating charge . . . is ambulatory and shifting in its nature, hovering over and so to speak floating with the property which it is intended to affect until some event occurs or some act is done which causes it to settle and fasten on the subject of the charge within its reach and grasp.'

Finally, guidance can be obtained in full measure from Buckley, L.J., in *Evans* v. *Rival Granite Quarries Ltd.* [1910] 2 K.B. 979, who stated 'A floating security is not a future security; it is a present security, which presently affects all the assets of the company expressed to be included in it. On the other hand, it is not a specific security; the holder cannot affirm that the assets are specifically mortgaged to him. The assets are mortgaged in such a way that the mortgagor can deal with them without the concurrence of the mortgagee. A floating security is not a specific mortgage of the assets plus a licence to the mortgagor to dispose of them in the course of his business, but is a floating mortgage applying to every item comprised in the security, but not specifically affecting any item until some event occurs or some act on the part of the mortgagee is done which causes it to crystallise into a fixed security.'

CRYSTALLISATION OF A FLOATING CHARGE

The floating charge crystallises into a fixed charge when any of the conditions set out in the debenture come into operation. These were described briefly above in connection with the circumstances which bring about the liability to repay, but it is well to emphasise that in all cases, other than the liquidation of the company, the debenture holder has to take positive action to crystallise the charge. The mere fact that the company fails to meet the written demand of the bank for repayment does not itself convert the floating charge into a fixed charge. A receiver has to be appointed to intervene so that the charge ceases to float and becomes fixed or fastens on to all the assets which the receiver can then sell by exercising the remedies available to the bank under the specific charge thereby created. It is a breach of contract for the bank to interfere in the conduct of the business of the company whilst the floating charge floats, but upon the appointment of a receiver the licence to the company to deal with the assets as it pleases in the ordinary course of business is determined and the charge is fixed. According to Fletcher Moulton, L.J., in *Evans* v. *Rival Granite Quarries Ltd.* (*supra*) 'That which changes the character of a floating security to that of a fixed charge is either the cessation of the carrying on of business by the company or the actual intervention of the debenture holder, *but not his mere right to intervene.*' In practice, the bank serves demand for repayment upon the company and promptly appoints a receiver, unless it has to await the expiry of a term of notice defined in the debenture. Alternatively, arrangements are sometimes made whereby a receiver is appointed by the bank at the express invitation of the Company when the directors realise that nothing can be done to save the business. In the unlikely event of the debenture containing no express power to the bank to appoint a receiver, an application has to be made to the Court to make the appointment.

S

Where a company goes into liquidation, the floating charge automatically crystallises at the date of the commencement of the winding-up. The company has thus ceased to carry on its business and it has lost its right to deal with the assets in the ordinary course of business. The floating charge becomes fixed and, unless the bank appoints a receiver to protect its interests, the liquidator has to have regard to the fixed charge of the bank over all the assets concerned. Where there is no liquidation but the company ceases to carry on business, the floating charge is also automatically converted into a fixed charge, whether the indebtedness secured by the debenture becomes repayable or not, but this rarely happens in practice.

WEAKNESSES OF A FLOATING CHARGE

A mere floating charge alone, without any specific charge on the fixed assets of a company borrower, is not sound banking security because there are many legal and practical weaknesses which may jeopardise the bank's position. These may be summarised and explained as follows:—

1. *Depreciation in value of assets covered by the charge*

As the company borrower remains at liberty to deal with its assets in the ordinary course of business, the realisation of stocks and the collection of moneys from trade debtors to meet pressing unsecured creditors may be unknown to the bank, so that when the bank appoints a receiver the value of the assets remaining may be a mere fraction of the value of the assets originally maintained by the company in the ordinary course of its business. There is nothing to prevent this forced realisation of assets and the bank can be left high and dry with a fixed charge on a relatively few remains. In any event, when failure occurs the assets will always be at their lowest ebb because shortage of cash prevents replacements and repairs. The method of valuation of a floating charge will be discussed later after explaining other features which may affect its worth, but this primary weakness is plain and it often happens in practice that, when a receiver is appointed, the assets produce barely sufficient at auction to satisfy the preferential creditors who have to be paid out of the proceeds before the bank.

2. *A fixed charge has priority*

In the absence of any express agreement by the company customer in the debenture *not* to create any subsequent mortgage or charge ranking prior to the floating charge, the company may create fixed charges, legal or equitable, over assets comprised in the floating charge and the fixed charges will have priority over the floating charge (*Wheatley* v. *Silkstone, etc., Coal Co.* (1885) 29 Ch. D.715). The power of the company to deal with the assets subject to the floating charge in the ordinary course of business is well established and, if it proves necessary to raise cash, it can create a specific charge on given assets to secure the fresh borrowing. Any later fixed charges, legal or equitable, so created under implied licence, will rank prior to the floating charge even where the specific mortgagees were aware of the floating charge.

To limit this risk, the bank form of debenture expressly removes the power of the company to create fixed charges on assets subject to the floating charge in favour of the bank. A condition is inserted stating that the company is not at liberty to create any mortgage and charge on any of its property and assets in priority to, or *pari passu* with, the said debentures. These restrictions will not, however, protect the bank unless they are brought to the notice of any subsequent mortgagee, and the registration of the floating charge at Companies' House is not sufficient for this purpose. It was decided in *English, etc., Investment Co.* v. *Brunton* (1892) 2 Q.B. 700 and in *Re Valletort Sanitary Steam Laundry Co. Ltd.* [1903] 2 Ch. 654 that a subsequently created fixed charge ranked in priority to a floating charge where the person in whose favour the fixed charge was created had no notice, actual or constructive, when he obtained his charge, that the company was precluded from creating any subsequent charges with priority over the debentures.

The problem, therefore, is to ensure that any subsequent mortgagee is fixed with notice of the restriction contained in the bank's debenture. The easiest solution is to recite the restrictive clause in Form 47 when registering the debenture at Companies' House. The words can be embodied in the description of the instrument evidencing the charge. It is then notice to the world. Alternatively, the company customer may be prevailed upon to authorise the creation of the debenture to the bank by special resolution setting out the restriction in the description of the document. As every special resolution has to be filed at Companies' House, the notice duly appears to warn any lenders who may later seek to obtain security on the assets of the company. It frequently happens in practice that a hire-purchase finance house, being aware of the restriction in an existing debenture to the bank, seeks express confirmation from the bank that a specific asset (usually new plant or machinery) is not caught by the floating charge. This weakness of a floating charge can, therefore, be safely overcome if care is exercised in the wording and registration of the debenture.

3. *Execution creditors may intervene and obtain priority*

When a bank is relying on a floating charge as security and the borrowing company is in a weak financial position, execution creditors may obtain priority on certain assets before the bank can intervene. For example, a landlord might levy a distress for rent before winding-up occurs and before the bank appoints a receiver under its floating charge. In such an event, the distress is valid against the bank as debenture holder (*In re Roundwood Colliery Co., Ltd.* [1897] 1 Ch. 373). Furthermore, any creditor of the company may obtain judgement against the company and, if he then obtains payment by execution before the bank can appoint a receiver, the execution creditor is entitled to retain the proceeds of his collection (*Evans* v. *Rival Granite Quarries Ltd.* [1910] 2 K.B. 979).

Under this heading, execution is completed when the assets of the company are seized and sold by the sheriff or where the company, in order to avoid a sale of the assets after seizure, liquidates the debt by payment to the sheriff to recover the assets. The execution in such circumstances is completed notwithstanding the fact that the sheriff may not have paid the cash over to the creditor (*Heaton & Dugard Ltd.* v. *Cutting Bros. Ltd.* (1925) W.N. 45). Whenever the bank hears that creditors of the company are taking legal action to recover the amounts due to them, steps should be taken promptly to appoint a receiver in order to avoid the further depletion of assets. Where the bank thus crystallises the floating charge before the assets have been sold by the sheriff, it will obtain priority (*In re Opera Ltd.* [1891] 3 Ch. 260). Again, where an execution creditor obtains a garnishee order absolute attaching moneys of the company held by a third party, it will be valid against the bank's floating charge, always providing the order absolute is made before the charge crystallises.

These dangers only arise when the company customer is in grave financial difficulties, but they are weaknesses of a floating charge and clearly show how essential it is to keep in close touch with the position of the borrower and to act quickly when the news that creditors are suing reaches the bank.

4. *Section 322 (1) of the Companies Act,* 1948, *may apply*

This Section provides that when a company is being wound up, a floating charge on the undertaking or property of the company created *within twelve months* of the commencement of the winding-up shall, unless it is proved that the company immediately after the creation of the charge was solvent, be invalid, except to the amount of any cash paid to the company at the time of, or subsequently to the creation of, and in consideration for, the charge, together with interest on that amount at the rate of five per cent. per annum or such other rate as may for the time being be prescribed by order of the Treasury. This period for the validity of a floating charge was extended from six months to twelve months by the 1948 Act to afford greater protection to creditors. Whether or not a company is solvent when it creates a floating charge is a question of fact depending upon whether it can pay its debts as they fall due. The fact that the assets exceed the liabilities is not of itself sufficient to prove solvency (*re Patrick & Lyon Ltd.* [1933] Ch. 786).

It follows that when a bank takes a floating charge as security and the company goes into liquidation within twelve months of the date of the charge, the security will be available only to cover amounts advanced by the bank in consideration for, or subsequent to, the creation of the floating charge, unless, of course, it can be shown that the company was solvent when the floating charge was given. In other words, a floating charge may prove to be useless as security to cover a dormant debt incurred before the charge was created. But the Rule in *Clayton's Case* (1816) 1 Mer. 572 will operate in favour of the bank where the account is active and all withdrawals made after the date of the charge will be secured thereby. The security will, therefore, be of some value and better than remaining unsecured.

The position can be illustrated by reference to *In re Thomas Mortimer Ltd.* (1925), *Journal of the Institute of Bankers,* Vol. XLVI, p. 259 which concerned the validity of a floating charge within Section 212 of the Companies (Consolidation) Act, 1908, whereby the period was three months instead of twelve months. On January 11, 1924, when Thomas Mortimer Ltd. owed about £58,000 to the National Provincial Bank on overdraft, it issued a £50,000 debenture to the bank's nominees comprising a floating charge on the undertaking or property of the company. It was a continuing security to cover all moneys then and thereafter owing by the company to the bank. The company went into liquidation on March 20, 1924, within the three months set out in the 1908 Act, but between January 11 and March 11 £41,311 was credited to its account and £51,248 was withdrawn by cheque. The liquidators of the company applied by summons for the determination of whether the floating charge was valid and, if so, to what extent.

It was held by Romer, J., that all cash paid to the company by the bank was secured by the floating charge. The bank made payments in cash to the company when it paid the cheques issued by the company after the issue of the debenture and these payments were 'in consideration for the charge' within the Act. The £51,248 so paid by the bank to the company had not been repaid to the extent of the £41,311 credited to the account because the bank was entitled to appropriate the credits to the earlier debt before the creation of the debenture. The floating charge was thus held to be valid to the full extent of £50,000.

The effect of the Mortimer case was challenged in *In Re Yeovil Glove Co. Ltd.* [1964] 2 All E.R. 849 in which the National Provincial Bank were concerned. Despite the arguments of the liquidator it was successfully submitted by the Bank that the Rule in *Clayton's Case* should be applied in the circumstances in question —which involved several accounts being open at the same time—and the Court of Appeal, quoting the Mortimer judgment with approval, held that payments made by the Bank after the execution of the floating charge were in consideration of the existence of that charge.

Apart from the extent to which *Clayton's Case* may operate in favour of the bank, depending upon the rapidity of turnover on the account, the vital period is now twelve months from the creation of the floating charge. A previous agreement or undertaking to give the bank a floating charge as security will not usually serve to lengthen the life of the charge. It was decided in *Gregory Love and Company; Francis v. The Company* [1916] 1 Ch. 203 that a floating charge created within three (now twelve) months before the actual commencement of the winding-up, but in pursuance of an agreement made previously that in certain events the charge should be created, was invalid, and the agreement could not be relied upon to correct the position. On the other hand, the bank might succeed where it could prove that advances granted prior to the date of the floating charge were made 'in the anticipation of, and in reliance on, a promise of the debenture' and the bank was in no way responsible or acquiesced in the delay in the issue of the debenture (*In re F. and E. Stanton Ltd.* [1929] 1 Ch. 180). These are, however, finer points available in case of need. The practical aspect is that little reliance can usually be placed upon the security of a floating charge taken as a last resort to cover the existing unsecured indebtedness of a company which is in financial difficulty.

5. *There may be prior claims of preferential creditors*

By virtue of Section 319 (5) of the Companies Act, 1948, in the case of the winding-up of a company registered in England, where the available assets are insufficient to meet the creditors, the preferential creditors have priority over the claims of holders of debentures under any floating charge created by the company, and have to be paid accordingly out of any property comprised in, or subject to, that charge. This priority is not, however, limited to cases of liquidation because Section 94 provides that where either a receiver is appointed on behalf of the holders of any debentures of the company secured by a floating charge, or possession is taken by, or on behalf of, those debenture holders of any property comprised in, or subject to, the charge, then, if the company is not at the time in course of being wound up, all preferential creditors have to be paid out of any assets coming into the hands of the receiver or other person taking possession in priority to any claim for principal or interest in respect of the debentures. All the preferential creditors are set out in Section 319 (see below) and the periods of time mentioned therein are, for our present purpose, reckoned from the date of the appointment of the receiver, or taking of possession, as appropriate, instead of from the date of the commencement of the winding-up which is the 'relevant date' in the case of liquidation.

In other words, whenever or however the floating charge crystallises, the receiver or liquidator has to discharge all the claims of the statutory preferential creditors before applying the proceeds of the security to the bank debt. This applies only to a floating charge. The preferential creditors are not so entitled to payment out of the proceeds of any fixed charge in the debenture created in addition to the floating charge.

In current conditions with unduly heavy taxation it often happens that a very large slice of the proceeds of the assets realised under the floating charge has to be used by the receiver to satisfy the preferential creditors and insufficient remains to repay the bank debt. This weakness is, therefore, the greatest disadvantage of a mere floating charge as bank security.

To appreciate the likely extent of these prior claims, it is prudent to list the more important preferential creditors described in Section 319 of the Act. They are as follows:—

   (a) All local rates due from the company and having become due and payable within twelve months next before the relevant date.

   (b) All land tax, income tax or other taxes assessed on the company up to the fifth day of April next before the relevant date, and not exceeding in the whole one year's assessment. The Inland Revenue are not restricted here to any particular year and may select any one year's tax.

   (c) The amount of any purchase tax due from the company at the relevant date, and having become due within twelve months next before that date.

   (d) All wages or salary of any clerk or servant or workman in respect of services rendered to the company during four months next before the relevant date, not exceeding £200 for any one claimant.

   (e) All accrued holiday remuneration becoming payable to any clerk, servant, workman or labourer on the termination of his employment before or by the effect of the winding-up order or resolution.

All these and a few other preferential creditors rank equally among themselves and the relevant date in the case of a company ordered to be wound up compulsorily is the date of the appointment of a provisional liquidator, or, if no such appointment was made, the date of the winding-up voluntarily before that date. In any other case, the relevant date is the date of the passing of the resolution for the winding-up of the company.

   6. *Problems and expense of the realisation of assets under a floating charge.*

To realise a floating charge when it crystallises, the receiver appointed by the bank has to dispose of the available assets in the best market available and this may often be a difficult, prolonged and costly process. The assets will inevitably be found in a poor condition and most of the readily saleable items may have been realised by the company before the appointment of the receiver to meet pressing creditors, in an attempt to avoid the failure of the business.

Apart from a few fixed assets, such as motors and machinery not subject to fixed charges, the receiver will normally have to collect what he can from the floating assets. The trade debtors may include a number of doubtful or slow payers with the possibility of instituting proceedings or employing a debt collector to recover amounts owing. The total may be further reduced where debtors have a right to set-off their liability against amounts due by the company to them. The stock has to be sold by auction and may include many unsaleable items. Any work-in-progress may be unsaleable except as scrap unless it is completed, and the receiver may not deem it worthwhile to incur the expense of labour and materials to convert the work-in-progress into the finished goods. The problem of realisation may, therefore, be considerable and a large proportion of the proceeds may be expended in the costs and fees of the agents employed by the receiver. And out of the net proceeds after the receiver's expenses all the preferential creditors have to be satisfied, so that the ultimate surplus available to the bank may be far less than the amount required.

All these disadvantages seriously limit the value of a floating charge as bank security, but nevertheless it is better than no security whatsoever on the assets of the company and in some cases it represents the only security available to the lending banker.

VALUATION OF THE DEBENTURE

Having regard to all these weaknesses of a floating charge, it will be appreciated that any attempt to estimate the value of a debenture as bank security calls for a detailed analysis of all the assets caught by the debenture and of the creditors who may have prior rights to the proceeds of realisation. Any estimate must necessarily err on the side of excess caution and be based on the gone concern approach to the latest available balance sheet of the borrowing company. For a detailed review of the principles involved, the reader is referred to *The Lending Banker*, as it is appropriate here to limit the treatment to a brief outline of the method adopted.

Armed with a complete picture of the business of the company, details of the security in the debenture, and the knowledge of how the bank advance is to be spent, the audited balance sheet is analysed in the following manner:

1. The forced sale value of each asset is estimated according to the market likely to be available if and when liquidation occurs. The estimated forced sale value of the assets, if any, bought with the proceeds of the bank advance is then added to give in total the minimum amount which, in the opinion of the banker would be realised from the sale of all the assets in the worst possible conditions.

2. The liabilities are then analysed to extract all creditors who have a fixed charge on certain assets and those who are entitled to payment before the bank out of the proceeds of the floating charge. Where the amount owing to a secured creditor exceeds the estimated forced sale value of the asset charged to him, he will rank *pari passu* with the other unsecured creditors of the company for the excess, and the value of the security only need be deducted from the estimated total proceeds of all the assets. There may be hire purchase creditors who for simplicity can be regarded as fully secure on appropriate assets. All tax liability will, of course, be preferential and an arbitrary allowance may be made on the assumption that a proportion of the trade creditors obtain payment by pressure before the bank appoints a receiver or liquidation occurs.

3. From the total estimated forced sale proceeds of the assets there will then be deducted all outside secured creditors (the amount due to them or the value of their security, whichever may be the smaller), all preferential creditors and any allowance deemed necessary for creditors paid before

271

the crash. The net result, ignoring any question of costs, is the estimated value of the bank's debenture.

This method of valuation obviously has many weaknesses. It is purely an estimate based on balance-sheet figures which may quickly be out of date. The floating assets change rapidly in the trade cycle and unbeknown to the bank many things can happen to the assets, particularly when the business is experiencing financial difficulty. Nevertheless the valuation is based on experience and is revised whenever fresh audited or draft figures are available. At worst, it is a general guide and there is no alternative means of valuing a floating charge.

The value of the debenture will, of course, be seriously jeopardised if all the assets charged thereby are not fully insured against all known risks for their peak value. The fire policy for any properties will no doubt be held by the bank and its interest as mortgagee endorsed thereon, but with a floating charge it is also essential to ensure that all stock and work-in-progress is likewise fully covered against fire and theft. Is the amount of this policy sufficient always to cover the value of the stock, etc., held and are the premiums regularly paid?

When the case of *N. W. Robbie Co. Ltd.* v. *Witney Warehouse Co. Ltd.* [1963] was decided in the court of first instance (2 All E.R. 199) it seemed that a new problem had arisen for receivers. The facts were these. In the early part of 1961 N. W. Robbie Co. Ltd. sold goods on credit worth £95 to the defendant company and then on July 6, 1961, the former business came under the control of a receiver and manager appointed by a bank. Further goods valued at £1,251 were sold by the receiver to Witney Warehouse Co. Ltd. on dates up to September 12, 1961.

It is also relevant that between November 1960 and January 1961 N. W. Robbie Co. Ltd. had *bought* goods from English Spinners Ltd., a company associated with Witney Warehouse Co. Ltd. and £852 was owing in this regard. After the commencement of the receivership—namely on October 6, 1961—Witney Warehouse Co. Ltd. then took an assignment of the £852 due by N. W. Robbie Co. Ltd.

The plaintiffs then sued the defendants for the £95 and £1,251 due to the receiver and the defendants sought to set off the debt of £852, admitting that remainder was still owing.

It was decided in the Assize Court:

(a) that the £95 would not be the subject of set-off as it was attached as a debt due at the time the receiver was appointed.

(b) that the floating charge—by then crystallised—though seizing the goods of the plaintiff did not attach equally to the indebtedness created on their sale by the receiver and thus Witney Warehouse Co. Ltd. as assignees of the debt for £852 *could exercise a set off for this sum against the amount due by them.*

It seemed at this point as if receivers could only avoid this danger by selling for cash, but the Court of Appeal (3 All E.R. 613) reversed this decision and the legal position is that a floating charge attaches all assets as they come into existence *including debts owed to the receiver as a result of his trading.*

What could have been a serious practical problem has thus been eliminated.

TAKING THE DEBENTURE AS SECURITY

Being satisfied that the debenture is drawn to give the bank the maximum security available and its value is sufficient for the requirement, the formalities necessary to complete the security are similar to those adopted when taking any other security from a limited company customer.

A search will first be made at Companies' House to ensure that there are no charges registered which affect the security and care exercised to see that there are no uncancelled redeemed debentures outstanding. Section 90 of the Companies Act, 1948, provide that where a company has redeemed any debentures previously issued it has power to reissue the debentures, either by reissuing the same debentures or by issuing other debentures in their place, unless there is any provision to the contrary, express or implied, in the articles or in any contract entered into by the company, or unless the company has, by passing a resolution to that effect or by some other act, manifested its intention that the debentures shall be cancelled. The danger is that when redeemed debentures are reissued the person to whom they are issued has the same priorities as the original holders just as though they had never been redeemed. The initial warning will always be found in the balance sheet of the company because particulars of any redeemed debentures which are capable of reissue have to be disclosed therein. Where redeemed debentures are found to be outstanding, they should be cancelled or, where suitable, reissued to the bank. The next step is to have the debenture sealed by the company, and it has then to be registered at Companies' House within twenty-one days of its execution and a copy of the certificate of registration will be endorsed on the debenture. If the debenture creates a charge on land, it will not need to be registered separately because Section 95 (7) states that the holding of debentures entitling the holder to a charge on land shall not for the purposes of this Section be deemed to be an interest in land. But, where there is a specific charge in the debenture on registered land or land in the East Riding of Yorkshire, registration also has to be effected at the appropriate registry. It is always prudent to obtain possession of all title deeds, etc., relating to fixed assets comprised in the security created by the debenture. If they are deposited with the bank, the company cannot deal with them without the knowledge of the bank.

When registration is accomplished, the security is complete and, subject to the possible risk of the creation of second charges without notice to the bank demanding a diligent study of *Stubbs' Gazette*, for reasons well known, the bank can rest content until the next opportunity arises to revalue the debenture. Incidentally, when a debenture is taken to secure advances on current account, it is not deemed to have been redeemed by reason only that the account of the company ceases to be in debit whilst the debenture is still held by the bank (Section 90 (3), Companies Act, 1948).

INDEX

INDEX (continued)

INDEX (continued)

INDEX (continued)